46th EDITION

Warman's®
Antiques&
Collectibles
2013

ZAC BISSONNETTE

Copyright ©2012 F+W Media, Inc.

Published by

Krause Publications, a division of F+W Media, Inc.
700 East State Street • Iola, WI 54990-0001
715-445-2214 • 888-457-2873
www.krausebooks.com

To order books or other products call toll-free 1-800-258-0929
or visit us online at www.krausebooks.com.

ISBN-13: 978-1-4402-2943-5
ISBN-10: 1-4402-2943-0

Cover Design by Jana Tappa
Designed by Sharon Bartsch, Donna Mummery & Jana Tappa
Edited by Mary Sieber

Printed in CHINA

On the Cover, clockwise from upper left:
Chinese gilt bronze figure of Vajrasattva, **$1,530,000;** *Eero Saarinen/Knoll, womb settee upholstered in
green fabric on black metal frame,* **$3,250;** *Forbidden Planet (MGM, 1956), half sheet, 22" x 28",* **$2,151;**
Full-bodied gilt and paint decorated copper rooster weathervane, circa 1870, **$2,700**

On the back cover
American hand-carved cigar store Indian, **$203,150**

Contents

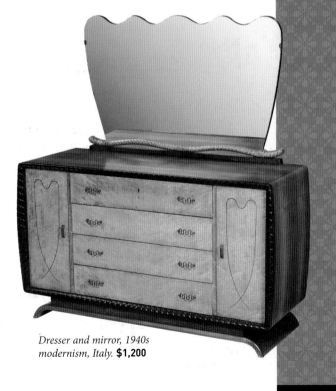

Dresser and mirror, 1940s modernism, Italy. **$1,200**

Introduction

Looking Back to See Forward

— By Zac Bissonnette

To understand the antiques market of today it's helpful to look back to the last time America was emerging from a once-in-a-generation economic crisis. By 1937, the United States was well on its way to digging out of the Great Depression that had begun with the stock market crash of October 29, 1929. Gross Domestic Product had been rising steadily for a few years, and the unemployment rate had fallen below 15% for the first time that decade.

That recovery had a profound effect on American tastes in home décor. In June of 1937,

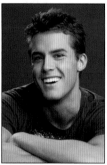

Zac Bissonnette

Better Homes & Gardens reported, "With sales charts and curves erasing frowns from the faces of businessmen, it's intensely interesting to watch the effect of this improved state of mind on the color trend in our homes. The forced laughter of bright, sharp colors we used, perhaps unconsciously, to relieve the gray mood of depression days is now giving way to the warm, friendly smile of soft, pastel shades of cheerful colors in decorating walls."

Fast forward to today where America is once again embarking on a tepid economic recovery. Jean Vidos, founder and president of New Orleans Auction Galleries, said that one of the defining trends of the post-bubble antiques market is a heightened focus on décor—and less interest in aesthetics.

"There's not as much conspicuous consumption as there was," Vidos said. "People want to buy something that has a really good look but is not necessarily great quality. We saw a lot more connoisseurship before the recession."

Guy Regal of New York City-based Guy Regal/Newel, sees that trend too, but frames it differently. Where once collectors specialized in particular periods and furnished entire rooms or even homes in one style, the trend today is in favor of eclecticism—with lighter neoclassical furniture mixed in with contemporary art and sometimes even mid-century modern furniture.

"People don't collect by period as much anymore," Regal said. "Italian 18th century carved baroque is very desirable because contemporary art looks really good around that furniture. People are far more interested in putting art on their walls than mirrors or anything else, and they're looking for things that complement that. People are really enjoying the juxtaposition of period furniture with contemporary art."

The antiques and collectibles market of the first decade of this millennium has been dominated by a few demographic and technological developments:

• **The rise of eBay.** In seemingly a wink of an eye, eBay exposed items once thought to be rare to be not rare at all. The good news is that this market shift is already reflected in today's prices. The bad news is that the prices of the more common flea market staples—vintage *Life* magazines, post-1970 sports cards, limited edition collectibles—have basically cratered, with only the most rare examples still holding any value at all. The emergence of eBay and similar Internet sites makes it easy for anyone to instantly find out what something is actually selling for, replacing price guides of dubious reliability that collectors once relied upon.

• **The decline of tchotchkes.** Look at a modern decorating magazine and compare it to a similar magazine from 20 years ago. You'll notice homes cluttered with knickknacks aren't as prevalent. Julie Hall, an estate liquidator and the author of *The Boomer Burden: Dealing with Your Parents' Lifetime Accumulation of Stuff* said, "People appear to want something clean, simple, fresh and very different these days. The trend is already in motion. What was once the rage, traditional possessions, aren't selling for much at all. The trend is clearly going in the direction of contemporary or vintage modern." This won't impact the finest and rarest examples of traditional antiques, but it has been and will likely continue to be bad news for the middle- and lower-end. As dealers often lament, sturdy, well-made furniture from the late 19th and early 20th centuries often sells for less than its Ikea equivalents. The shift away from traditional furniture has blindsided many longtime dealers. "Retail shops are struggling and they're sitting on a lot of traditional inventory that they've had for years and can't get rid of," said Vidos. "Brown furniture is not what people are finding appealing right now. People are just being more creative with that whole process. The key is creativity versus traditional."

And what about the future? What will be the object of our collecting desires?

Matthew C. Quinn of Virginia-based Quinn's Auction Galleries gave me this advice on the future of collecting: "Look for things we used for purposes of utility. Nostalgia and rarity are the two biggest factors that will determine what people are paying for in 20 or 40 years."

What's more, there's a new kid on the block in the antiques market: diversification. The global financial meltdown of a few years ago exposed investors to a fundamental truth: The interconnectedness of the global economy means that owning stocks and bonds from a wide variety of countries no longer provides adequate diversification. More people are looking to put their money in tangible assets.

With the volatility of the stock market scaring off some, many investors are taking comfort in the fact that art and antiques don't evaporate overnight. To paraphrase what personal finance expert David Bach once told me about real estate, you don't have to worry about waking up one day to find out that your Chippendale chair is gone because some CEO lied about earnings. "The degree to which the art market lost value during the recent economic downturn was a fraction of the downturn in the securities markets," Jim Hedges, president of Montage Finance, an investment advisory firm specializing in fine art, said. "The recovery in the art market was quite quick because there are a large number of global investors who are putting more to work in art as an investment class."

"I believe that you're going to see more people utilizing art as an investment tool for diversification and superior, equity-like returns," Hedges added. "It is a global currency and people will use it as a substitute for liquidity in their own currency."

Leslie Hindman, founder and CEO of Chicago-

Sun Valley / Chicago and North Western Line, poster, 1940. **$4,800**

based Leslie Hindman Auctioneers, is seeing that trend in her own business as well. "Rich Americans are investing in tangible assets. They're calling and saying, 'We've got a lot of cash that we don't want to put in the market. We're thinking of buying some contemporary art.' People who aren't even serious collectors are looking to buy tangible assets."

While these experts were referring to high-end art collectors rather than casual antique buyers, it's a dynamic that applies to some degree at all levels of the market. Art, antiques and collectibles can be a valuable part of a diversified portfolio.

Outside of asset-seeking investors, there are a number of other trends that dealers should be aware of:

• **Echo boomers furnishing their homes.** Nearly 80 million Americans were born between 1982 and 1995—and the oldest members of this generation are closing in on the age when they'll be marrying, having kids—and furnishing long-term residences for the first-time. Their tastes in home décor often differ from their parents and grandparents. "It's been so long with the wood tables," said Trish LeTemp of Eddyville, Ky.-based The Red Door Antiques. "Younger people don't want things to be matchy-matchy. Look at the way people dress; it's the same thing." With many older collectors heading into the "simplify and downsize" stage of life, dealers hoping to be successful in the years to come will need to shift their attention toward the tastes of the people who will drive demand for the foreseeable future: Echo Boomers.

• **The story of many categories has become a tale of two markets:** great strength at the high-end and stagnant or worse at the middle-tier and bottom. A great example of this comes from the world of car collecting. In August 2011, California auctioneer Goodings & Co. sold a 1957 Ferrari Testa Rossa for $16.4 million, the highest price ever paid for a car at auction. Many in the media took that to mean that the classic car market was strong, but that's not what it means. The sales price simply means that at least two really rich people wanted the car. As the Cleveland Plain Dealer reported back in 2009, "One restorer estimated that sale prices for 1960s muscle cars are down by as much as 40 percent in the past two years. Yet at the other end of the market, the rarified air of multimillion-dollar luxury cars from the 1930s, sales are just fine." That's a dynamic in many categories.

• **Entrepreneurs from the developing world repurchasing their heritage.** When Leslie Hindman Auctioneers held its Asian arts sale in May 2011, they expected sales of somewhere around a million dollars. The sale racked up $4.2 million—with 80% of the buyers coming from China. Hindman said, "Jade that we thought would bring $6,000 to $8,000 was bringing $50,000." It's a trend that's been in motion for some time: As the economies of the developing world boom, people who have disposable income for the first time are looking to repurchase their cultural history. One risk? The boom and bust nature of economic growth in these countries could make them especially volatile. For instance, the Japanese art market absolutely collapsed in the early 1990s when that country's economy hit a rough patch. But American collectors who were savvy (or lucky) enough to start collecting Asian art early are often sitting on goldmines. In July 2011, a Tulsa,

A rare and early Delaware River pintail drake dating to the last quarter of the 19th century to early 20th century. **$27,500** Guyette & Schmidt, Inc.

Okla. man brought his collection of five late-17th or early 18th-century Chinese carved rhinoceros horn cups to the Antiques Roadshow. He'd begun collecting them in the 1970s for very little money. The collection was valued between $1 million and $1.5 million— a new record for the show.

• **Baby boomers getting nostalgic.** According to the United States Census Bureau, a Baby Boomer is someone born between the years 1946 and 1964—which puts the oldest boomers in their mid-60s and the youngest in their late forties. Many of these soon to be empty nesters are devoting some of their spare time (and money, once the college bills have stopped coming) to collecting, often with an emphasis on nostalgia. When my brother and I moved out, my mother embarked on a new project: scouring flea markets, yard sales and eBay for the finds that would transform her kitchen back to the 1950s summer cottage that she loved. 1950s kitchenware is still very affordable—in many cases, cheaper than what you'd pay for glasses at Wal-Mart—but it generally sells at a fairly brisk pace.

• **Everybody's a collector.** Hits TV shows like *American Pickers*, *Storage Wars*, and *Pawn Stars* have helped increase interests in antiques—and especially interest in the fantasy of striking it rich. Whether these shows will have staying power is an open question, but for now they are certainly a significant driver of traffic to flea markets and antiques shows.

• **Everybody's a decorator.** Just as the antiques shows have increased interest in antiquing for resale, networks like HGTV and shows like *The Nate Berkus Show* have increased interest in decorating—and people are willing to take more chances. In a blog post on Realtor.com, North Carolina

What's Hot and What's Not

with Jean Vidos, founder and president of New Orleans Auction Galleries

HOT:

• **Silver, said Vidos,** noting that precious metals of all types have been on the rise. **But be careful:** We may be in a bubble and, as a general rule, precious metals have not been particularly good stores of value over the long-term. Buying silver or gold at record high prices has historically been a strategy that's led to miserable long-term results.

• **Mid-century modern furniture and artwork.** Vidos said this stuff has tremendous appeal to younger collectors, and continues to sell very swiftly. Combined with some industrial, I would look for this to be the dominant style of retro-savvy Gen-Yers (Echo-Boomers).

• **Asian art.** As Hindman noted, Chinese buyers are driving prices through the roof in an effort to reclaim their cultural heritage. But Vidos suspects a bubble. "We give this advice to our clients who have Asian stuff: Take it out of the closet, dust it off, and send it over because you're never going to make more money than you're going to make right now. Everything that goes to that extreme goes to some sort of bubble, and bubbles end badly." Historically, developing world economies have been volatile and even if the long-term outlook for Chinese art is good, there will likely be a downturn in the near future that provides an opportunity to get in at better prices.

NOT:

• **Traditional brown wood furniture.** "One of the bread and butter things used to be the Georgian chest of drawers. And you'd estimate them at $1,200-$1,800; now you can't give them away," Vidos said.

• **French Provincial.** While the shabby chic look brought the French Provincial look back for a while, it's gotten hard to sell – along with the rest of the country look that boomed during the 1990s. It still has its core following, though, and Vidos thinks it will come back eventually.

• **American Victorian.** Vidos said that this look appeals "less and less to the younger audience, and most of the people who like it are past the stage where they're actively adding to their collections."

real estate agent Sarah Gray Lamm declared the death of "Realtor beige" as the preferred color by homebuyers, citing HGTV as a driver of increased creativity in home décor. "They have gotten people excited about what fun it can be to live in a beautiful home," she wrote. "Your large furniture is olive drab or brown or, gulp, beige. But your walls are eggplant or aqua, terra cotta or chocolate, and you can find pillows and throws and rugs and wall art and knickknacks and candles to match and in any color palate that makes you happy." The increased willingness of middle Americans to go eclectic with their home decorating gives savvy dealers who know how to merchandise a new market.

For dealers, professional and casual, there's another development: Inventory is no longer enough. With the Internet, every single collector has access to a far greater selection of merchandise than any dealer can provide – and high fees and competition have led to a race to the bottom – making selling on the Internet a challenging way to earn a living. For dealers looking to shows and flea markets for revenue, salesmanship and marketing are more important than ever.

"The people who go to shows [or stores] want an experience," said Sally Schwartz, the promoter behind Chicago's Randolph Street Market. "Anybody who walks into a store wants the fun of actually walking into a store. No one wants a bland cookie cutter experience; they can get that online. They want that stepped up, more extreme."

The bottom line for the antiques and collectibles market of the next few years is this: very probably continued weakness in most traditional antiques, except for those of the highest quality. Connoisseurship is in decline, and most buyers are more interested in creating an eclectic look than furnishing an entire room with a certain period.

In the Beginning

Edwin G. Warman was an entrepreneur in Uniontown, Pa. He dabbled in several ventures, including ownership of a radio station. He was also an avid antiques collector who published his price listings in response to requests from friends and fellow collectors. The first modest price guide was published in 1948 as *Warman's Antiques and Their Current Prices*. It was a bold move. Until then, antiques were sold primarily through dealers, antiques shops and at auctions. The sellers and buyers negotiated prices and were forced to do their own research to determine fair prices. Under Warman's care, the price guide changed all that forever. Warman also published some specialized price guides for pattern glass and milk glass, as well as his "Oddities and Curiosities" editions, under the banner of the E.G. Warman Publishing Co.

Although the name varied slightly over the years, *Warman's Antiques and Their Current Prices* covered such collectible areas as mechanical banks, furniture and silver, just like the Warman's of today. His pages consisted of a brief statement about the topic, either relating to the history or perhaps the "collectibility" of the category. A listing of current prices was included, often containing a black and white photograph.

E.G. Warman died in 1979. His widow, Pat Warman, continued the tradition and completed work on the 15th edition after his death. The estate sold the E.G. Warman Publishing Co. to Stanley and Katherine Greene of Elkins Park, Pa., in 1981. Chilton Books bought the Warman Publishing Co. in the fall of 1989. With the 24th edition, Warman's was published under the Wallace-Homestead imprint. Krause Publications purchased both the Warman's and Wallace-Homestead imprints in 1997.

We are proud to continue the rich tradition started some 65 years ago by Mr. Warman, a man driven by his love of antiques and collectibles and by a thirst for sharing his knowledge.

Photograph, gelatin silver, Birmingham Special, Rural Retreat, Virginia, 1957, O. Winston Link. **$13,145**

The Warman's Advantage

The Warman's Advantage manifests itself in several important ways in the 2013 edition. As we reviewed past volumes, we wanted to make this book as easy to use as possible. To that end, we've consolidated and reorganized how we present several key categories. Our new mantra is, "What is it first?"

For instance, an antique clock may also have an advertising component, an ethnic element (like black memorabilia), reflect a specific design theme (like Art Deco) and be made of cast iron. But first and foremost, it's a clock, and that's where you'll find it listed, even though there are other collecting areas involved.

There are a few categories that remain iconic in the collecting world. Coca-Cola collectibles cross many interests, as do folk art, Asian antiques and Tiffany designs, to name just a few. These still have their own broad sections.

In addition to space memorabilia and John Wayne collectibles, newly expanded sections include ceramics, jewelry, toys, illustration art, books, and glass.

Prices

The prices in this book have been established using the results of auction sales across the country, and by tapping the resources of knowledgeable dealers and collectors. These values reflect not only current collector trends, but also the wider economy. The adage that "an antique (or collectible) is worth what someone will pay for it" still holds. A price guide measures value, but it also captures a moment in time, and sometimes that moment can pass very quickly.

Beginners should follow the same advice that all seasoned collectors will share: Make mistakes and learn from them; talk with other collectors and dealers; find reputable resources (including books and websites), and learn to invest wisely, buying the best examples you can afford.

Words of Thanks

This 46th edition of the Warman's guide would not be possible without the help of countless others. Dozens of auction houses have generously shared their resources, but a few deserve special recognition: Heritage Auctions, Dallas; Backstage Auctions, Houston; Woody Auction, Douglass, Kan.; Greg Belhorn, Belhorn Auction Services LLC, Columbus, Ohio; Andrew Truman, James D. Julia Auctioneers, Fairfield, Maine; Anthony Barnes at Rago Arts and Auction Center, Lambertville, N.J.; Karen Skinner at Skinner Inc., Boston; Morphy Auctions, Denver, Pa.; Susan Pinnell at Jeffrey S. Evans & Associates, Mount Crawford, Va.; Rebecca Weiss at Swann Auction Galleries, New York; and Leslie Hindman Auctioneers, Chicago. And, as always, special thanks to Catherine Saunders-Watson for her many contributions and continued support.

Read All About It

There are many fine publications that collectors and dealers may consult about antiques and collectibles in general. Space does not permit listing all of the national and regional publications in the antiques and collectibles field; this is a sampling:

- *Antique Trader*, published by Krause Publications, 700 E. State St., Iola, WI, 54990 – *www.antiquetrader.com*
- *Antique & The Arts Weekly,* 5 Church Hill Road, Newton, CT 06470 – *www.antiquesandthearts.com*
- *AntiqueWeek*, P.O. Box 90, Knightstown, IN 46148 – *www.antiqueweek.com*
- *Maine Antique Digest*, P.O. Box 358, Waldoboro, ME 04572 – *www.maineantiquedigest.com*
- *New England Antiques Journal,* 24 Water St., Palmer, MA 01069 – *www.antiquesjournal.com*
- *The Journal of Antiques and Collectibles,* P.O. Box 950, Sturbridge, MA 01566 – *www.journalofantiques.com*
- *Southeastern Antiquing & Collecting* magazine, P.O. Box 510, Acworth, GA 30101 – *www.go-star.com/antiquing*

Let Us Know What You Think

We're always eager to hear what you think about this book and how we can improve it. Contact:

Paul Kennedy
Editorial Director,
Antiques & Collectibles Books
Krause Publications
700 E. State St.
Iola, WI 54990-0001
715-445-2214, Ext. 13470
Paul.Kennedy@fwmedia.com

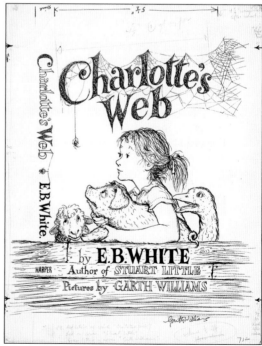

Charlotte's Web, book cover, 1952 by Garth Montgomery Williams, graphite and ink on paper. **$155,350**

Visit an Antiques Show

One of the best ways to enjoy the world of antiques and collectibles is to take the time to really explore an antiques show. Some areas, like Brimfield, Mass., and Manchester, N.H., turn into antiques meccas for a few days each summer when dealers and collectors come for both specialized and general antiques shows, plus auctions.

Here are a few of our favorites:

Brimfield, Mass., shows, held three times a year in May, July and September, *www.brimfield.com.*

Round Top, Texas, antique shows, held spring and fall, *www.roundtop.com/antique1.htm*

Antiques Week in and around Manchester, N.H., held every August

Palmer/Wirfs Antique & Collectible Shows, including the Portland, Ore., Expos, *www.palmerwirfs.com*

The Original Miami Beach Antique Show, *www.dmgantiqueshows.com*

Merchandise Mart International Antiques Fair, Chicago, *www.merchandisemart.com/chicagoantiques*

High Noon Western Americana Show & Auction, Phoenix, *www.highnoon.com*

Ask an Expert

Many contributors have proved invaluable in sharing their expertise during the compilation of the 46th edition of the Warman's guide. For more information on their specialties, call or visit their websites.

Caroline Ashleigh
Caroline Ashleigh Associates LLC
1000 S. Old Woodward, Suite 105
Birmingham, MI 48009-6734
248-792-2929
www.auctionyourart.com
Vintage Clothing, Couture and Accessories, Textiles, western wear

Tim Chambers
Missouri Plain Folk
501 Hunter Ave.
Sikeston, MO 63801-2115
573-471-6949
E-mail: plainfolk@charter.net
Folk art

Noah Fleisher
E-mail: noah.fleisher@yahoo.com
Modernism

Reyne Haines
Reyne Gallery
4747 Research Forest Dr. #180-274
The Woodlands, TX 77381
513-504-8159
www.reyne.com
E-mail: reyne@reyne.com
20th century decorative arts, lighting, fine jewelry, wristwatches

Ted Hake
Hake's Americana & Collectibles Auctions
P.O. Box 1444
York, PA 17405
717-848-1333
E-mail: auction@hakes.com
Pop culture, Disneyana, political

Leslie Holms
Antique Purse Club of California
55 Ellenwood Ave.
Los Gatos, CA 95030
408-354-1626
E-mail: cree56@comcast.net
Antique handbags of all kinds

Mary P. Manion
Landmarks Gallery & Restoration Studio
231 N. 76th St.
Milwaukee, WI 53213
800-352-8892
www.landmarksgallery.com
Fine art and restoration

Suzanne Perrault
Perrault Rago Gallery
333 N. Main St.
Lambertville, NJ 08530
609-397-1802
www.ragoarts.com
E-mail: suzanne@ragoarts.com
Ceramics

David Rago
Rago Arts and Auction Center
333 N. Main St.
Lambertville, NJ 08530
609-397-9374
www.ragoarts.com
Art pottery, Arts & Crafts

Dennis Raleigh Antiques & Folk Art
P.O. Box 745
Wiscasset, ME 04578
207-882-7821
3327 Cones Ct.
Midland, MI 48640
989-631-2603
www.dennisraleighantiques.com
E-mail: dgraleigh@verizon.net
Decoys, silhouettes, portrait miniatures

Henry A. Taron
Tradewinds Antiques
P.O. Box 249
Manchester-By-The-Sea, MA 01944-0249
(978) 526-4085
www.tradewindsantiques.com
Canes

Morphy Auctions

Watling 25-Cent Cherry Rol-a-Top slot machine.
$5,500

Andrew Truman
James D. Julia, Inc.
P.O. Box 830
Fairfield, ME 04937
207-453-7125
www.juliaauctions.net
E-mail: atruman@jamesdjulia.com
Toys, dolls, advertising

Auction Houses

Sanford Alderfer Auction & Appraisal
501 Fairgrounds Rd.
Hatfield, PA 19440
215-393-3000
www.alderferauction.com
Full service

American Bottle Auctions
2523 J St., Suite 203
Sacramento, CA 95816
800-806-7722
www.americanbottle.com
Antique bottles, jars

American Pottery Auction
Waasdorp Inc.
P.O. Box 434
Clarence, NY 14031
716-759-2361
www.antiques-stoneware.com
Stoneware, redware

American Sampler
P.O. 371
Barnesville, MD 20838
301-972-6250
www.castirononline
Cast-iron bookends, doorstops

Antiques and Estate Auctioneers
44777 St. Route 18 E.
Wellington, OH 44090
440-647-4007
Fax: 440-647-4006
www.estateauctioneers.com
Full service

Auctions Neapolitan
1100 First Ave. S.
Naples, FL 34102
239-262-7333
www.auctionsneapolitan.com
Full service

Belhorn Auction Services LLC
P.O. Box 20211
Columbus, Ohio 43220
614-921-9441
www.belhorn.com
Full service, American art pottery

Backstage Auctions
448 West 19th St., Suite 163
Houston, TX 77008
713-862-1200
www.backstageauctions.com
Rock 'n' roll collectibles and memorabilia

Bertoia Auctions
2141 DeMarco Dr.
Vineland, NJ 08360
856-692-1881
www.bertoiaauctions.com
Toys, banks, holiday, doorstops

Brunk Auctions
P.O. Box 2135
Asheville, NC 28802
828-254-6846
www.brunkauctions.com
Full service

Caroline Ashleigh Associates LLC
1000 S. Old Woodward, Suite 105
Birmingham, MI 48009-6734
248-792-2929
www.auctionyourart.com
Full service, vintage clothing, couture and accessories, textiles, western wear

Clars Auction Gallery
5644 Telegraph Ave.
Oakland, CA 94609
888-339-7600
www.clars.com
Full service

Cowan's
6270 Este Ave.
Cincinnati, OH 45232
513-871-1670
www.cowanauctions.com
Full service, historic Americana, Native American objects

Mason-Kay, Inc., image Zalephoto.com

Ring with intense, fine lavender 3/5" cabochon, 18k white gold, .53ct pavé-set diamonds. **$15,500**

Cyr Auction Co.
P.O. Box 1238
Gray, ME 04039
207-657-5253
www.cyrauction.com
Full service

Early Auction Co. LLC.
123 Main St.
Milford, OH 45150
513-831-4833
www.earlyauctionco.com
Art glass

Elder's Antiques
901 Tamiami Trail (US 41) S.
Nokomis, FL 34275
941-488-1005
www.eldersantiques.com
Full service

Greg Martin Auctions
660 Third St., Suite 100
San Francisco, CA 94107
800-509-1988
www.gregmartinauctions.com
Firearms, edged weapons, armor, Native American objects

Grey Flannel
8 Moniebogue Ln.
Westhampton Beach, NY 11978
631-288-7800
www.greyflannel.com
Sports jerseys, memorabilia

Guyette & Schmidt Inc.
P.O. Box 1170
24718 Beverly Road
St. Michaels, MD 21663
410-745-0485
www.guyetteandschmidt.com
Antique decoys

Hake's Americana & Collectibles Auctions
P.O. Box 1444
York, PA 17405
717-848-1333
www.hakes.com
Character collectibles, pop culture

Heritage Auctions Inc.
3500 Maple Ave., 17th Floor
Dallas, TX 75219-3941
800-872-6467
www.ha.com
Full service, coins, pop culture

iGavel Inc.
229 E. 120th St.
New York, NY 10035
866-iGavel6 or 212-289-5588
auction.igavel.com
Online auction, arts, antiques and collectibles

Ivey-Selkirk
7447 Forsyth Blvd.
Saint Louis, MO 63105
314-726-5515
www.iveyselkirk.com
Full service

**Jackson's International Auctioneers
and Appraisers**
2229 Lincoln St.
Cedar Falls, IA 50613
319-277-2256
www.jacksonsauction.com
*Full service, religious and Russian objects,
postcards*

James D. Julia Inc.
P.O. Box 830
Fairfield, ME 04937
207-453-7125
www.juliaauctions.net
Full service, toys, glass, lighting, firearms

*Russian Soyuz flown Sokol KV-2 pressurized
spacesuit, 1980s.* **$31,070**

Jeffrey S. Evans & Associates
2177 Green Valley Ln.
Mount Crawford, VA 22841
540-434-3939
www.jeffreysevans.com
Full service, glass, lighting, Americana

John Moran Auctioneers Inc.
735 W. Woodbury Rd.
Altadena, CA 91001
626-793-1833
www.johnmoran.com
Full service, California art

Keno Auctions
127 E. 69th St.
New York, NY 10021
212-734-2381
www.kenoauctions.com
Fine antiques, decorative arts

Lang's Sporting Collectibles
663 Pleasant Valley Rd.
Waterville, NY 13480
315-841-4623
www.langsauction.com
Antique fishing tackle and memorabilia

Leslie Hindman Auctioneers
1338 W. Lake St.
Chicago, Il 60607
312-280-1212
www.lesliehindman.com
Full service

McMasters Harris Auction Co.
5855 John Glenn Hwy
P.O. Box 1755
Cambridge, OH 43725
740-432-7400
www.mcmastersharris.com
Dolls and accessories

Michael Ivankovich Auction Co.
P.O. Box 1536
Doylestown, PA 18901
215-345-6094
www.wnutting.com
Wallace Nutting objects

Leland Little Auctions & Estate Sales Ltd.
246 S. Nash St.
Hillsborough, NC 27278
919-644-1243
www.llauctions.com
Full service

Litchfield County Auctions Inc.
425 Bantam Road (Route 202)
Litchfield, CT 06759
860-567-4661
212-724-0156
www.litchfieldcountyauctions.com
Full service

Morphy Auctions
2000 N. Reading Rd.
Denver, PA 17517
717-335-3435
www.morphyauctions.com
Toys, banks, advertising, pop culture

Mosby & Co. Auctions
905 West 7th St., #228
Frederick, MD 21701
301-304-0352
www.mosbyauctions.com
Mail, phone, Internet sales

New Orleans Auction Galleries Inc.
801 Magazine St.
New Orleans, LA 70130
800-501-0277
www.neworleansauction.com
Full service, Victorian

Noel Barrett Vintage Toys @ Auction
P.O. Box 300
Carversville, PA 18913
215-297 5109
www.noelbarrett.com
Toys, banks, holiday, advertising

Old Town Auctions
P.O. Box 91
Boonsboro, MD 21713
240-291-0114
301-416-2854
www.oldtownauctions.com
Toys, advertising, Americana; no Internet sales

Tiffany Studios Pomegranate table lamp. **$16,100**

Old Toy Soldier Auctions USA
P.O. Box 13324
Pittsburgh, PA 15243
Ray Haradin
412-343-8733
800-349-8009
www.oldtoysoldierauctions.com
Toy soldiers

Old World Auctions
2155 W. Hwy 89A, Suite 206
Sedona, AZ 86336
800-664-7757
www.oldworldauctions.com
Maps, documents

Past Tyme Pleasures
39 California Ave., Suite 105
Pleasanton, CA 94566
925-484-6442
www.pasttyme1.com
Internet catalog auctions

Philip Weiss Auctions
1 Neil Ct.
Oceanside, NY 11572
516-594-0731
www.prwauctions.com
Full service, comic art

Pook & Pook Inc.
463 East Lancaster Ave.
Downingtown, PA 19335
610-629-0695
www.pookandpook.com
Full service, Americana

Professional Appraisers & Liquidators LLC
16 Lemington Ct.
Homosassa, FL 34446
800-542-3877
www.charliefudge.com
Full service

**Quinn's Auction Galleries
& Waverly Rare Books**
431 N. Maple Ave.
Falls Church, VA 22046
703-532-5632
www.quinnsauction.com
www.waverlyauctions.com
Full service, rare books and prints

Rago Arts and Auction Center
333 N. Main St.
Lambertville, NJ 08530
609-397-9374
www.ragoarts.com
Arts & Crafts, modernism, fine art

Red Baron's Antiques Inc.
6450 Roswell Rd.
Atlanta, GA 30328
404-252-3770
www.redbaronsantiques.com
Full service, Victorian, architectural objects

Rich Penn Auctions
P.O. Box 1355
Waterloo, IA 50704
319-291-6688
www.richpennauctions.com
Advertising and country-store objects

Richard D. Hatch & Associates
913 Upward Rd.
Flat Rock, NC 28731
828-696-3440
www.richardhatchauctions.com
Full service

Robert Edward Auctions LLC
P.O. Box 7256
Watchung, NJ 07069
908-226-9900
www.robertedwardauctions.com
Baseball, sports memorabilia

Rock Island Auction Co.
4507 49th Ave.
Moline, IL 61265-7578
800-238-8022
www.rockislandauction.com
Firearms, edged weapons and accessories

St. Charles Gallery Inc.
1330 St. Charles Ave.
New Orleans, LA 70130
504-586-8733
www.stcharlesgallery.com
Full service, Victorian

Samuel T. Freeman & Co.
1808 Chestnut St.
Philadelphia, PA 19103
215-563-9275
www.freemansauction.com
Full service, Americana

Seeck Auctions
P.O. Box 377
Mason City, IA 50402
641-424-1116
www.seeckauction.com
Full service, carnival glass

Skinner Inc.
357 Main St.
Bolton, MA 01740
978-779-6241
www.skinnerinc.com
Full service, Americana

Sloans and Kenyon
7034 Wisconsin Ave.
Chevy Chase, MD 20815
301-634-2344
www.sloansandkenyon.com
Full service

Slotin Folk Art
Folk Fest Inc.
5619 Ridgetop Dr.
Gainesville, GA 30504
770-532-1115
www.slotinfolkart.com
Naïve and outsider art

Strawser Auctions
P.O. Box 332, 200 N. Main
Wolcottville, IN 46795
260-854-2859
www.strawserauctions.com
Full service, majolica, Fiestaware

Swann Galleries Inc.
104 E. 25th St.
New York, NY 10010
212-254-4710
www.swanngalleries.com
Rare books, prints, photographs, posters

Theriault's
P.O. Box 151
Annapolis, MD 21404
800-638-0422
www.theriaults.com
Dolls and accessories

Tom Harris Auction Center
203 S. 18th Ave.
Marshalltown, IA 50158
641-754-4890
www.tomharrisauctions.com
Full service, clocks, watches

Chinese gilt bronze figure of Vajrasattva. **$1,530,000**

Tradewinds Antiques
P.O. Box 249
Manchester-By-The-Sea, MA 01944-0249
978-526-4085
www.tradewindsantiques.com
Canes

Treadway Gallery
2029 Madison Rd.
Cincinnati, OH 45208
513-321-6742

John Toomey Gallery
818 North Blvd.
Oak Park, IL 60301
708-383-5234
www.treadwaygallery.com
Arts & Crafts, modernism, fine art

Woody Auction
P.O. Box 618
317 S. Forrest
Douglass, KS 67039
316 747-2694
www.woodyauction.com
Glass

Advertising

Commercial messages and displays have been found in the ruins of ancient Arabia. Egyptians used papyrus to create sales messages and wall posters, while lost-and-found advertising was common in ancient Greece and Rome. As printing developed in the 15th and 16th centuries, advertising expanded to include handbills. In the 17th century, advertisements started to appear in weekly newspapers in England.

Illustration, gouache on board, 21" x 15.5", Pepsi-Cola, reads: "So sociable, so smart. Today's trim, sociable moderns are giving a new light look, a fresh elegance and grace to themselves and all their possessions. Join this happy new crowd. Look smart. Stay young and fair and debonair. Be sociable. Have a Pepsi — the lighter Pepsi of today, reduced in calories. Pepsi-Cola the Light refreshment." **$2,151**

Poster, Raleigh Bicycles (Causton and Sons, circa 1960s), 30" x 40", boy on bicycle with jet in sky. Just as the jet plane indicates a new age is dawning, so it was for Raleigh as this was one of the last all steel models. After the mid 60s, Raleigh finally relented and starting using other alloys in the construction of its bikes. **$460**

Poster, Schwinn Bicycles (circa 1938) poster (22" x 38"). Boy and girl with lighthouse. The Schwinn Lightweight was introduced in 1938. Using special construction techniques and lighter materials, this line of bicycles faded out in the late 1970s. This is one of the earliest known posters for the popular specialist line of bicycles. **$575**

Illustration, oil on canvas, for Cream of Wheat, 29" x 18", original art signed by artist Mabel M. Buckmaster. **$2,270**

Illustration, oil on canvas, 28" x 21" each, for The House of Kuppenheimer (Men's Clothing), fall/winter 1918-1919, by artist Joseph Christian Leyendecker, (American, 1874-1951), titled "Lovebird." Leyendecker was one of the most successful commercial illustrators of his time, best known for his advertisements for the "Arrow Collar Man." He created 321 covers for the Saturday Evening Post. The piece was exhibited at the Art Institute of Chicago in 1920. **$155,350**

Illustration, oil on canvas, 18" x 13.5", Karo Corn Syrup, by artist Joseph Christian Leyendecker, (American, 1874-1951). **$21,510**

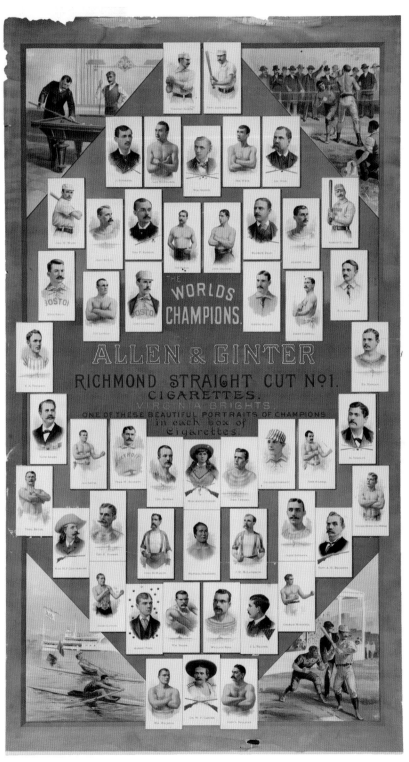

Poster, 1887 G20 Allen and Ginter "The World's Champions" Advertising Banner, 16" x 28", Victorian-era lithography and portraiture featuring an intriguing assortment of 19th century sporting legends, true masterpieces of the early trading card hobby. Among the baseball stars pictured are eventual Hall of Famers Cap Anson, John Clarkson, Charles Comiskey, Tim Keefe, Mike "King" Kelly and John Ward. John L. Sullivan anchors the roster of bare-knuckle pugilists, while "Buffalo Bill" Cody and Annie Oakley provide firepower for the gun enthusiast. Rowers, wrestlers and billiards players help to round out the cast of 50 names. **$15,535**

Perfection Leather Oil Baird advertising clock, original dial and manufacturer's paper on the inside. Complete with pendulum, the piece maintains a terrific country store ambiance, 18" x 31.5". **$2,031**

Vending, Smilin' Sam From Alabam Peanut Vendor, cast aluminum, ca. 1934. **$2,031**

James G. Blaine cigar lighter honoring the 1884 GOP presidential candidate, circa 1880s. Although dismissed by some collectors as a relatively unimportant presidential candidate, Blaine was a towering political figure of his day. The "Plumed Knight" of Maine not only ran for president, but also served as speaker of the house and secretary of state. Republican organizations named after him were common well into the 1900s, as were products and advertising images honoring him. This rare brass cigar lighter was issued by the makers of the James G. Blaine Cigar, "the greatest of them all". His name and slogan are colorfully emblazoned on the base, while all four sides of the protective metal shade around the wick are perforated, so when the wick was lighted "Jas. G. Blaine Cigar" shone forth. Minor surface wear, otherwise excellent condition. Without a doubt, one of the rarest and most appealing three-dimensional political display items of that era. Height 12.25". **$1,792**

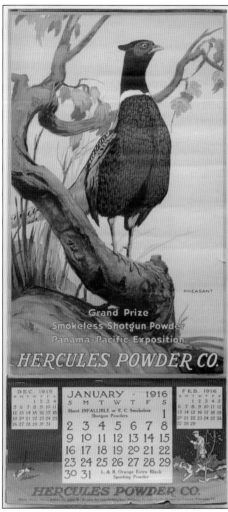

James D. Julia Auctioneers

Calendar, Hercules Powder Co., 1916, four-page calendar with cover illustration of ring-neck pheasant. Other images include farm scene, black-breasted plovers and a gold miner; 11 1/2" w x 27 1/2" h; retains original metal hanging strip, subtle edge tears. **$1,725**

James D. Julia Auctioneers

Calendar, Peters Cartridge Co., 1908, one of the rarest of the Peters calendars, showing duck hunters in a marsh by the Strowbridge Litho. Co., Cincinnati; 13 3/4" w x 27 1/4" h; some edge wear and fingernail-sized hole at bottom left corner. Retains both metal bands and what appears to be the balance of a June date pad. **$7,762**

Calendar, S.S. Patterson, 1904, stone lithographed image of reclining damsel with her beer from this Dillon, Mont., distributor of Val Blatz Brewing Co.'s Milwaukee Beer; 16" w x 24" h in frame; small circular surface cut at bottom margin, possibly a minor repair. One or two tiny edge tears. **$632**

James D. Julia Auctioneers

James D. Julia Auctioneers

Display, Whitman's Chocolate, scarce Lego-style messenger boy with original Whitman's Sampler candy box under arm. These were distributed in limited numbers during the 1920s to the sales force for selected accounts where Whitman's was sold. Base bears an aluminum tag which reads, "Designed and produced by W.L. Stensgaard & Associates, Inc., Chicago, Illinois"; 18 3/4" h. Some wear to corners of cardboard box but the balance of the display in very good to excellent condition. **$2,645**

My! how Baby hollers,
Riding Popper's knee,
Still, the shave's delightful
Pop's got a GEM you see.

GEM DAMASKEENE RAZOR $1.00

Old Town Auctions LLC

Display, Gem Damaskeene Razor, clockwork mechanical, depicting a man shaving as he rocks his baby, in original shipping crate, light edge wear to top of man's head, scattered light spotting to paper, sign at bottom as minor paper damage on right side, clockwork housing retains paper labels, has original key, works fine, 29 1/4" h, 20 3/4" w, wood crate still retains original shipping labels, lid has cracked board.
$3,850

James D. Julia Auctioneers

Lithograph, Bunker Hill Breweries, 1896 illustration by Leon Moran and lithographed by Louis Prang for A. G. Van Nostrand, Bunker Hill Breweries of Charlestown, Mass. Complete with original mat. Matted image measures 17 1/2" w x 23 1/2" h in frame. Some moisture stains around perimeter of mat board, and to the far right margin of the lithographed image, otherwise in good condition. **$240**

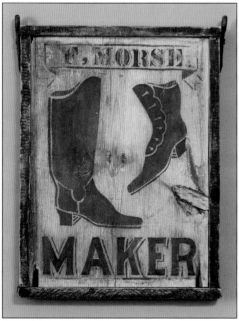

Skinner Inc.

Sign, boot maker, painted wood and iron, American, late 19th century, double-sided rectangular painted panel with applied molding, painted with a man's and woman's boot and lettering "F. MORSE MAKER," iron hardware, (weathered surface), about 2" x 1 1/2" loss to lower right corner of panel reverse side, 24" x 17 3/4". **$2,014**

Skinner Inc.

Sign, Albis Barber Shop, painted wood, American, late 19th/early 20th century, (weathered surface), old gilt surface shows through top and bottom bulbed areas, 35 1/2" h, 9 1/2" w. **$296**

James D. Julia Auctioneers

Sign, Job Cigarette papers, cardboard, Art Nouveau illustration of red-headed damsel by the artist Edgard Maxence, 1900; 14 3/4" w x 20" h. Good to very good condition; has some light surface foxing, a few paper ripples along top margin; and two small vertical punctures to lower right corner, which may have held a sample packet of rolling papers. **$345**

Skinner Inc.

Sign, L. Coe's House of Entertainment, tavern, painted wood, American, early 19th century, oval sign with brass hanging ring, with black lettering on a gray-blue ground over previous white-painted ground, (loss, lacks frame), 33 3/4" h, 20 1/4" w. **$2,014**

James D. Julia Auctioneers

Sign, Mentor Comfort Underwear, die-cut countertop advertisement with metal easel features an illustration of a mom with young daughter, both comfortably clad in their Mentor long johns; 19 1/2" w x 27 1/4" h. Generally good to very good condition with a few soft creases and light surface scuffs. **$3,335**

Old Town Auctions LLC

Sign, Standard Oil, 1940, painted tin, with Mickey Mouse, some discoloration to finish, minor bends, 24" d. **$2,090**

Skinner Inc.

Sign, polychrome painted oval country club drink, American, mid-20th century, oval wood panel with applied molding depicting a tennis ball canister topped with fruit and a straw with painted lettering "try our Overhead Smash," 16" x 23 1/4". **$296**

Skinner Inc.

Signs, pair of painted turned wooden barber poles, American, 19th century, including wall mounts, (old repaint, paint losses), each 30" l. **$1,541 pair**

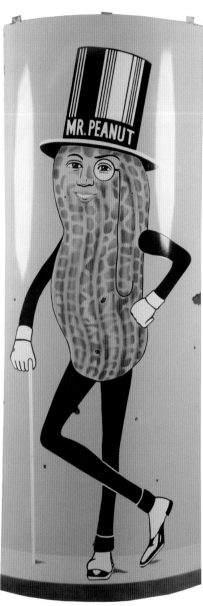

Morphy Auctions

Planters porcelain half-moon-shape Mr. Peanut advertising sign made in the 1930s-40s. **$16,100**

Skinner Inc.

*Sign, painted wood, "Fresh Eggs," American, early 20th century, double-sided rectangular panel, 7 3/4" x 24".
Normal wear with some paint losses, stains, surface grime.* **$830**

*Sign, relief carved and
painted gent's head,
American, late 19th/
early 20th century, 14"
x 9 3/4". Possible repair
to ear or else it is the
original attachment.*
$1,500+

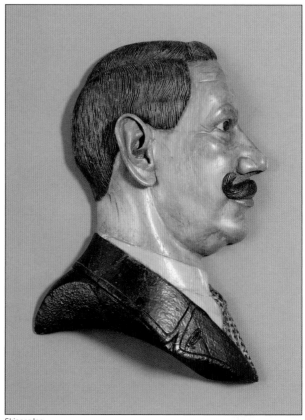

Skinner Inc.

American hand-carved cigar store Indian, 75.5" tall from headdress to toes, 16" wide, 20.5" deep, features colorful headdress, bear-claw necklace and central medallion. Piece is carved in the manner of classic cigar store Indian maker Samuel Robb. **$203,150**

Illustration, oil and tempera on canvas laid on board, 32" x 21.5", Lucky Strike cigarettes ("Be Happy…Go Lucky"), 1950, by artist Jack Wittrup (American, 1912-1987). **$5,078**

Art

Illustration Art

— By Brent Frankenhoff and Maggie Thompson, Comics Buyer's Guide

Collectors, whether looking for a distinctive decoration for a living room or seeking a rewarding long-term investment, will find something to fit their fancy — and their budget — when they turn to illustration art. Pieces of representational art — often, art that tells some sort of story — are produced in a variety of forms, each appealing in a different way. They are created as the source material for political cartoons, magazine covers, posters, story illustrations, comic books and strips, animated cartoons, calendars, and book jackets. They may be in color or in black and white. Collectible forms include:

Brent Frankenhoff and
Maggie Thompson

• **Mass-market printed reproductions.** These can range from art prints and movie posters to engravings, clipped advertising art, and bookplates. While this may be the least-expensive art to hang on your wall, a few rare items can bring record prices. Heritage Auction Galleries, for example, commanded a price of $334,600 for a Universal 1935 Bride of Frankenstein poster (artist unidentified).

• **Limited-run reproductions.** These range from signed, numbered lithographs to numbered prints.

• **Tangential items.** These are hard-to-define, oddball pieces. One example is printing plates (some in actual lead; some in plastic fused to lightweight metal) used by newspapers and comic-book printers to reproduce the art.

• **Unique original art.** These pieces have the widest range of all, from amateur sketches to finished paintings. The term "original art" includes color roughs produced by a painter as a preliminary test for a work to be produced, finished oil paintings, animation cels for commercials as well as feature films, and black-and-white inked pages of comic books and strips. They may be signed and identifiable or unsigned and generic. "Illustration art" is often differentiated from "fine art," but its very pop-culture nature may increase the pool of would-be purchasers. Alberto Vargas (1896-1982) and Gil Elvgren (1914-1980) bring high prices for pin-up art; Norman Rockwell (1894-1978), James Montgomery Flagg (1877-1960), and J.C. Leyendecker (1874-1951) were masters of mainstream illustration; and Margaret Brundage (1900-1976) and Virgil Finlay (1914-1971) are highly regarded pulp artists.

Taking a look at a specific genre, consider comic-book-related illustration art. Two of the top painters in the field were heroic-fantasy artist Frank Frazetta (1928-2010) and "Disney ducks" artist Carl Barks (1901-2000).

The original art for printed comic-book pages and covers also can command high prices, especially if they're from particularly rare or historic comics.

Other comics art forms include magazine cartoons and newspaper strips. Charles Addams (1912-1988) in the former category and Charles Schulz (1922-2000) in the latter have active collecting communities. Spending time with dealers at shows, browsing online auctions, and even following favorite creators on Twitter can turn up low-priced opportunities to get a collection started. Often, art that's returned to the original writers and artists is later sold by those same creators when they need space in their studios, providing excellent opportunities to get that one-of-a-kind collectible and even get it signed by the creator. Remember: Charles Schulz gave away originals of his Peanuts strips — originals that bring thousands of dollars to their owners today.

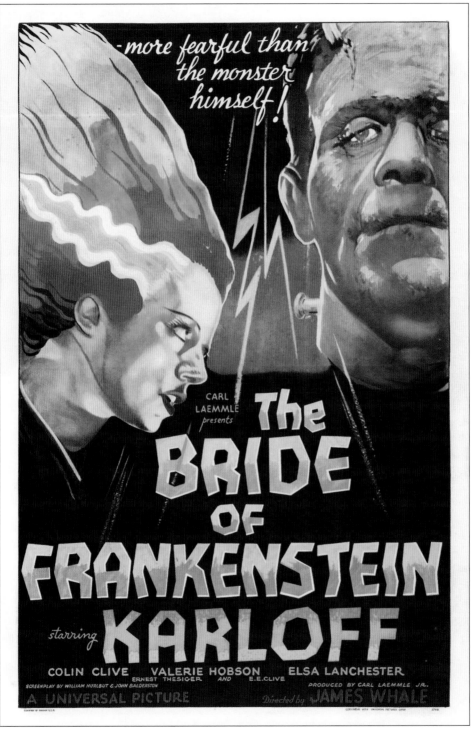

The Bride of Frankenstein movie poster (Universal, 1935). **$334,600**

Carl Barks "Business as Usual" oil painting (1976), featuring Uncle Scrooge and his nephews working deep in his Money Bin. **$179,250**

Carl Barks "Nobody's Spending Fool" oil painting (1974). **$101,575**

Carl Barks "Only a Poor Old Duck" oil painting (1974) featuring Donald rowing Scrooge across a lake of money.
$107,550

Carl Barks "Voodoo Hoodooed" oil painting (1974). **$101,575**

"Warrior with Ball and Chain," used as cover for Flashing Swords Vol. 1 paperback cover (1973). Oil on board by Frank Frazetta. **$150,000**

"The Ones," Marvel Science cover, May 1951. Oil on board. 18" x 11 1/2" by Norman Saunders. **$50,787**

"The Altar of Melek," Weird Tales cover, September 1932. Pastel on paper. 20" x 17 1/2" by Margaret Brundage.
$50,787

The Shadow cover, March 1932. Oil on canvas. 21 1/2" x 20 1/2" by George Rozen. **$33,460**

"*Apocalyptic New York." Wonder Stories cover, February 1933. Gouache on board. 22" x 17 1/2"*
by Frank R. Paul. **$20,315**

Galaxy Science Fiction Magazine October 1962 painted cover original art, 11" x12" by Virgil Finlay. **$17,925**

Wednesday Addams illustration, Interior Design magazine, Decorators Walk ad illustration, February 1983, ink and watercolor on paper, 11 1/4" diameter, by Charles Addams. **$3,585**

Walter Whitehead (American, 1874-1936), Encore, Cream of Wheat ad illustration, 1908, oil on canvas, 31 1/4" x 20", signed with a monogram lower right. Many of the Cream of Wheat paintings traveled across the U.S. in a series of landmark museum exhibitions presented by Nabisco's historian and archivist, David Stivers. **$3,585**

Heritage Auction Galleries

"*Naughty Santa,*" *oil on canvas, 27" x 21", Haddon Hubbard Sundblom, American artist (1899-1976), Playboy magazine cover, December 1972. Sundblom was considered a master of illustration art, training many of the best pin-up artists including Gil Elvgren, Al Buell and Joyce Ballantyne.* **$47,800**

"The Song of Bernadette," oil on canvas, 53" x 28", Norman Rockwell, American artist (1894-1978), originally used for the film by the same name starring Jennifer Jones, 1943. Rockwell claimed the painting was his most reproduced work, appearing in magazines, newspapers and on theater posters. **$478,000**

Journey into Mystery #83, Page 8, by Jack Kirby and Joe Sinnott (1st Appearance of Thor and his Enchanted Hammer Mjolnir, Marvel, 1962). **$65,725**

X-Men #116 cover by John Byrne and Terry Austin (Marvel, 1978). **$65,725**

Sketch, black ink sketch of Harvey rabbit signed in blue ink "Harvey James Stewart" by actor James Stewart, who made the invisible rabbit character famous in the classic 1952 film "Harvey," 12 1/2" by x14 5/8".
$632

Sketch, Snoopy accompanied by signature by artist Charles Schulz, on the title page of the third printed edition of the book "The Gospel According to Peanuts," sketch is in ballpoint pen and inscribed "Best Wishes, Charles M. Schulz," January 1965, 5 3/8" by 8".
$695

Zap Comics #1 two-page story "Kitchen Kut-Outs" by Robert Crumb (Apex Novelties, 1968). **$47,800**

Peanuts All-Snoopy Sunday comic strip dated May 19, 1963 (United Feature Syndicate, 1963) by Charles Schulz.
$35,850

Batman: The Dark Knight #3, Page 24, by Frank Miller and Klaus Janson (DC, 1986). **$38,837**

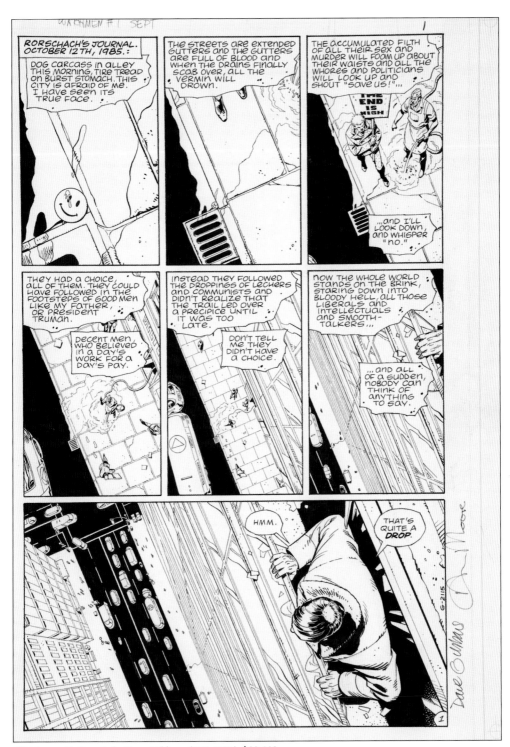

Watchmen #1, Page 1, by Dave Gibbons (DC, 1986). **$33,460**

Vault of Horror #22 "Fountains of Youth," Page 6, by Johnny Craig (E.C., 1952). **$836**

The Hawk and the Dove #3, Page 2, by Gil Kane (DC, 1968). **$507**

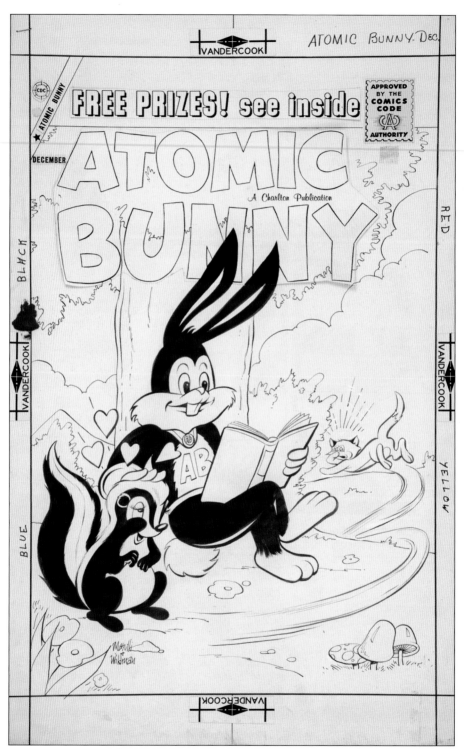

Atomic Bunny #19 cover by Pat Masulli and George Wildman (Charlton, 1959). **$250**

Speed Comics #32 Captain Freedom story, Page 2 (Harvey, 1944). **$101**

No Longer Child's Play

Children's Book Illustration Art Worth a Second Look

— By Zac Bissonnette

Richard Michelson, an up and coming western Massachusetts gallerist, reacted with skepticism when one of his artists, Barry Moser, told him that he had received a call from an editor at Harcourt asking him if he wanted to illustrate a children's book.

"A children's book?" Michelson remembers asking, concerned that the artist's credibility within the art world would be tainted by something so commercial. "Are you going to start painting cute little watercolor bunnies?" Michelson feared that the decision was "career suicide."

Today, Michelson's R. Michelson Galleries, a must-visit destination in Northampton, Mass., is among the largest sellers of children's book art in the country – and the first gallery to show fine art and illustration art in the same space.

"I was dragged into this field," Michelson remembers with a laugh. But on further examination, he realized that children's book art was among the most under-appreciated work in the art world. When Moser entered the world of illustration art, he began introducing his illustrator friends to Michelson – and over time Michelson's gallery became a hub for top illustrators.

"I began looking at the books written and illustrated by my new friends, and I was introduced to a whole world I knew nothing about," he wrote in an exhibition catalog. "The best of them were, I had to admit, the equal in both skill and vision to anything I had been reading or seeing in my favorite galleries and museums."

The art establishment is beginning to catch on, too: Where once Michelson couldn't get his phone calls returned, leading museums now regularly approach him to lend works for their exhibitions.

And while the market is booming and the prices of top artists in the field have been rising steadily, it's a field that is within the reach of collectors in a way that fine art often isn't. The prices required to acquire the work of recognizable illustrators are a tiny fraction of what you'd pay to acquire the work of recognizable fine artists.

The nostalgic appeal is also hard to beat. For example, Dallas-based Heritage Auction Galleries sold the original painting used for the cover of *Nancy Drew #25: The Ghost of Blackwood Hall*. The price was $3,883 – for a cover that has been reproduced more than a million times. In that same auction, an original ink and colored marker drawing of the Cat in the Hat, created by Dr. Seuss himself, sold for $1,434.

Michelson says that while the prices of a few top illustrators can stretch into the six figures – an illustration from Maurice Sendak's 1990 book *Where the Wild Things Are* carried a pre-sale estimate of $400,000-$700,000 at Bonham's – smaller works and sketches by the artist can still be had for less than $5,000.

And if you buy outside of the most prominent, best-established illustrators in the field, it is possible to collect original art used to illustrate children's books produced by major illustrators with almost any budget. Most artists' work can be had starting in the low three digits, and the cover illustration for one of my favorite books from childhood, *The Rookies*, recently sold for a paltry $59 at Heritage Auction Galleries.

As an investment, children's book illustrations have this going for them: Studies show that children who are read to frequently grow up to have, on average, greater financial success as adults. Those bedtime stories you read to your children and grandchildren will leave them with the desire to own this art – and the means to pay you high prices for it.

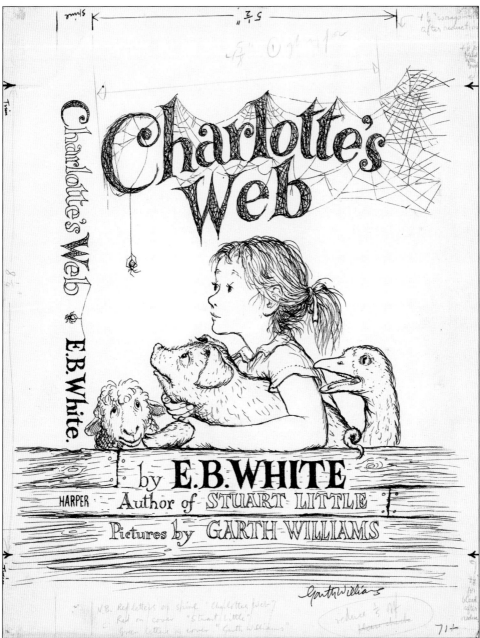

Charlotte's Web, book cover, 1952 by Garth Montgomery Williams, graphite and ink on paper, 14" by 11", signed lower right. **$155,350**

Rudy Nappi, gouache on board, Nancy Drew Mystery Stories: The Ghost of Blackwood Hall book cover, 14" x 9.75", signed lower left corner. **$3,883**

Cliff Miller, acrylic on canvas, Nancy Drew Files #101: The Picture of Guilt, paperback illustration, 31.5" x 19.5", signed lower right. **$508**

Maurice Sendak, ink and watercolor on paper, illustration, Where the Wild Things Are backdrop landscape, 15.5" x 35.5", signed lower right. **$74,687**

Maurice Sendak, watercolor on paper, illustration, The Nutcracker by E.T.A. Hoffman and Maurice Sendak, 1984, 13.25 x 24.25, **$14,937**

Theodor Seuss Geisel (Dr. Seuss), ink and colored marker on paper, Cat in the Hat, 10" x 8", signed lower right. **$1,434**

Ed Tadiello, acrylic on board, part of the Rookies series for young adult paperbacks, 30" x 20". **$59**

Artists, A to Z

Heritage Auction Galleries

William Herbert Dunton (American, 1878-1936), The Badger Hole (The Spill), 1906, oil on canvas 28" x 19", signed lower right: W. Herbert Dunton / '06. **$143,400**

James D. Julia Auctioneers

Johann Berthelsen (American, 1883-1972), Times Square, New York City, oil on board, winter street scene shows the intersection at Times Square. Several pedestrians cross in front of stopped cars. Signed lower right. Housed in a partial gilt French-style frame, 20" x 14". **$18,400**

Daniel Garber (American, 1880-1958), May Day, completed 1941, oil on canvas, 30" x 28", signed lower center, "Daniel Garber". In a Ben Badura frame. Exhibited: Woodmere, 1942. Included in the Daniel Garber catalog raisonne (2006), written by Lance Humphries, published by Hollis Taggart Galleries, Volume II, page 268, plate 765. **$207,000**

Sanford Alderfer Auction & Appraisal

Walter Emerson Baum (American, 1884-1956), winter scene of village with snow falling, oil on canvas, signed lower right, 25" x 30". **$31,625**

Sanford Alderfer Auction & Appraisal

Reynolds Beal (American, 1867-1951), Downey Bros. Circus, Elephants and Appaloosa, mixed media, scene shows a wide view of a circus with three large tents flying American flags, two large elephants with riders, a man on horse and other performers. Signed lower left, dated "1934" and inscribed "Downey Bros. Circus." Housed in a carved and gilt double frame with white matte, 14 1/4" x 17 3/4" (sight). **$2,640**

James D. Julia Auctioneers

Sanford Alderfer Auction & Appraisal

George W. Sotter (American, 1879-1953), Winter Hillside, oil on canvas, 22" x 26", signed lower right, "G.W. Sotter." **$172,500**

Quinn's Auction Galleries

Bert Geer Phillips (American, 1868-1956), Voices of the Woods, 35" x 48" (framed) oil on canvas by noted Taos school painter. Woolsey Brothers frame. Originally purchased from artist in 1911 by Iowa Senator James Henry Trewin. **$300,000+**

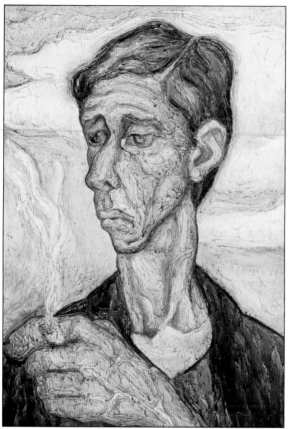

Rago Arts and Auction Center

Oswaldo Guayasamin (Ecuadorian, 1919-1999), Hombre Fumando, 1941; oil on board (framed); signed, dated and titled; 26 1/4" x 19" (sight). **$39,000**

James D. Julia Auctioneers

Abbott Fuller Graves (American, 1859-1936), Nature's Color Pallet, oil on canvas still life shows a variety of colorful flowers in a tiered arrangement against a mottled background. Flowers include red, pink and white zinnias, blue lupines, yellow and white wildflowers. All with different shades of green leaves. Signed lower right "Abbott Graves." Housed in its original gilt frame liner, 30" x 15", professionally cleaned, some light craquelure. **$31,625**

John Moran Auctioneers Inc.

Nicolai Fechin (Russian-American, 1881-1955), The Wood Engraver, this image won the 1924 Thomas R. Proctor Award for Portraiture at the National Academy of Design. **$1,092,500**

Rago Arts and Auction Center

John Stuart Gibson (American, b. 1958), Arrangement in Blue and White, 1990; oil on canvas (framed); Signed, dated and titled; 47" x 42". **$4,200**

James D. Julia Auctioneers

George Inness Jr. (American, 1854-1926), After the Storm, oil on canvas, panoramic scene shows a valley landscape with cultivated fields and a village nestled on the valley floor. Hills are seen in the background, partially obscured by dark rain clouds, and a rainbow is present. Two travelers follow a hay wagon in the foreground. Signed "G Inness 18_8." Housed in an antique gilt frame, 14" x 20". Relined, restored with in-painting. **$2,990**

John Moran Auctioneers Inc.

William Joseph McCloskey (American, 1859-1941), Florida Oranges, signed and dated oil on canvas of his best-known subject of oranges with paper wrappers. **$546,250**

Rago Arts and Auction Center

Walt Francis Kuhn (American, 1877-1949), Apples, 1933; oil on canvas (Newcomb-Macklin frame); signed and dated; 13" x 22", 22 1/4" x 31" (frame); Exhibition: Walt Kuhn Memorial Exhibition, Cincinnati Art Museum, Cincinnati, 1960 (label on verso). **$9,600**

Heritage Auction Galleries

American Artist (20th century), Cupid, oil on canvas, 20" x 16 1/2", unsigned. **$926**

Sanford Alderfer Auction & Appraisal

George W. Sotter (American, 1879-1953), The Valley of the Delaware, hillside view of the Delaware River, oil on canvas, 22" x 26", signed lower left, Sotter; complemented by a signed gilt floral-carved Ben Badura frame, minor loss to frame, height: 21 1/2" x 25 1/2", width: 2 1/2", painting titled verso. **$97,750**

William Matthew Prior (American, (1806-1873), portrait of a young boy, circa 1852, oil on canvas, the child seated wearing a red dress bordered in white, holding a white rose with a whip laid across his legs. Signed and inscribed on reverse, "Wm. M. Prior East Boston Trenton Street./Kingly Express," 26" x 20", unframed. Good condition, minor retouch. **$112,575**

Skinner Inc.

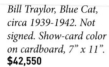

Bill Traylor, Blue Cat, circa 1939-1942. Not signed. Show-card color on cardboard, 7" x 11". **$42,550**

Slotin Auction, Buford, Ga.

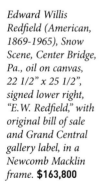

Edward Willis Redfield (American, 1869-1965), Snow Scene, Center Bridge, Pa., oil on canvas, 22 1/2" x 25 1/2", signed lower right, "E.W. Redfield," with original bill of sale and Grand Central gallery label, in a Newcomb Macklin frame. **$163,800**

Sanford Alderfer Auction & Appraisal

Morphy Auctions

Guy Carleton Wiggins (American, 1883-1962), The Public Library, oil on canvas, active scene of Manhattan in the snow, with the focal point being the New York Public Library, with its well-known lion statues. Depiction includes seven American flags, pedestrians with umbrellas, a bus and taxicabs. Snow is blowing at an angle, and awnings are visibly out. Signed lower right. 29 1/2" x 23 1/4" (framed). **$17,250**

Morphy Auctions

Guy Carleton Wiggins (American, 1883-1962), 5th Avenue and 2nd Street, oil on canvas, signed Guy Wiggins. N.A. Manhattan snow scene features pedestrians walking with umbrellas, city traffic, a row of apartment buildings and two American flags, 15 1/2" x 11 1/2" (framed). **$23,000**

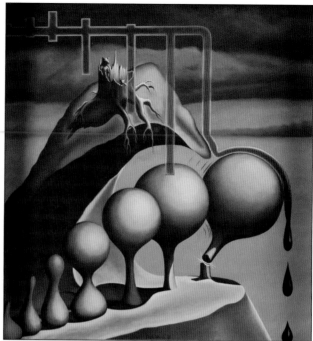

Franz Jozef Ponstingl (American, 1927-2004), Pollution, 1984, 1965; oil on board (framed); signed, dated and titled; 22" x 21". **$1,320**

Rago Arts and Auction Center

Rago Arts and Auction Center

Orrin Augustine White (American, 1883-1969), Untitled; oil on canvas (framed); signed; 20" x 24". **$7,200**

Asian

Art and antiques from China, Japan, Korea, the Pacific Rim, and Southeast Asia have fascinated collectors for centuries because they are linked with the rich culture and fascinating history of the Far East. Their beauty, artistry and fine craftsmanship have lured collectors through the ages.

The category is vast and includes objects ranging from jade carvings to cloisonné to porcelain, the best known of these being porcelain.

Large quantities of porcelain have been made in China for export to America from the 1780s. A major source of this porcelain was Ching-te-Chen in the Kiangsi province, but the wares were also made elsewhere. The largest quantities were blue and white.

Nippon is the term used to describe a wide range of porcelain wares produced in Japan from the late 19th century until about 1921. Many Japanese factories produced Nippon porcelain, much of it hand-painted with ornate floral or landscape decoration.

Prices for Asian antiques and art fluctuate considerably depending on age, condition, decoration, etc.

Chinese gilt bronze figure of Vajrasattva, with an incised six-character Xuande mark.
$1,530,000

Clars Auction Gallery

Iwata Sentaro (1901-1974), a half portrait of a Japanese beauty, signed "Sentaro-ga" (some toning, staining), 15 1/4" h x 10 1/2" w. **$110**

Clars Auction Gallery

Paul Jacoulet (1896-1960), titled "Le Mandarin Aux Lunettes, Mandchoukuo," pencil signed LR, with duck seal, right margin with printer and carver cartouches of Honda and Maeda, the reverse numbered 75/150 (glue residue to top margin, some toning, especially to the margins), 19" h x 14" w. **$750**

Clars Auction Gallery

Hiroshi Yoshida (1876-1950), titled "Naiyagara bakufu" (Niagara Falls), dated Taisho 14 (1925), from the United States Series, impressed signature LR (traces of tape residue to top reverse corners, otherwise very good condition), 10 3/4" h x 15 3/4" w. **$250**

Seeck Auctions

Noritake, plate, Lady In Garden, 9" sq, **$325.**

Sloans & Kenyon Auctioneers and Appraisers

Apple jade vase, Rouleau form, flowering lotus decoration, elephant head loose-ring handles, Chinese, 19th century. **$945.**

Clars Auction Gallery

Vessel, Chinese, fine spinach jade archaic-style, 19th century, well carved and incised as a jia (family), a tripod wine vessel with a wide trumpet mouth surmounted by a pair of tall cap-form knobs, a single animal-head handle attached to the body decorated with taotie masks centered on pierced flanges, all resting on three splayed leaf-form supports with further archaic motifs, the translucent muted green stone with occasional dark flecks, together with a conforming hardwood stand with silver wire inlay, 8" h excluding stand. **$2,250**

Clars Auction Gallery

Chinese gilt and cloisonné enamel-decorated tripod censer, early 20th century, the globular body decorated with stylized lotus and scrolling tendrils on a turquoise ground and applied with a pair of gilt animal-mask and loose ring handles, further animal masks fronting the splayed supports, a gilt repoussé band of jeweled lappets encircling the waisted neck below the high reticulated domical lid with a fu-lion finial and decorated en suite (some repairs), 7 1/4". **$1,000**

Clars Auction Gallery

Sino-Tibetan gilt and copper-alloy figure of Vasudhara (the Buddhist bodhisattva of wealth, prosperity and abundance), 18th/19th century, the six-armed female tantric deity seated lalitasana (royal pose) with her right foot supported on a kalasa (water pot or jug) issuing from the lotus pedestal, one hand in the gift-granting gesture (varada mudra), the other displaying various attributes, the finely cast gilt face with an elaborate diadem fronting a tall chignon surmounted by a half-vajra (a ritual object), with silver accents (wear, resealed), 7 1/4". **$500**

Jacket, Chinese, Han, woman's silk, finely embroidered with bird roundels surrounded by scattered butterflies and flowers on a purple satin ground, framed by a white satin ground neck band and border featuring shou medallions further by auspicious animals and florals, bracketing a blue ground trim woven with stylized white birds, all forming a large ruyi head pattern to the front and back, (some fading and staining to the exterior, further staining to the lining), 30 1/2" l. **$800**

Clars Auction Gallery

Robe, Chinese, Manchu-style embroidered red satin ground, child's, displaying eight dragons couched in metallic threads chasing sacred jewels amid scrolling clouds and auspicious emblems executed with Peking knots, all above a modified lishui (standing water) border, the collar and sleeve band decorated en suite with dragons meandering above waves on a black satin ground, (loose couching, wear, staining to exterior and lining), 30 1/2" l. **$1,700**

Clars Auction Gallery

Clars Auction Gallery

Japanese ivory and patinated bronze figure, Meiji period, featuring a Japanese farm girl seated next to her carrying basket with back straps, the ivory head well carved with demure features picked out with black and colored pigment and framed by a coiffure covered by a patterned scarf, further ivory employed for the hands and feet, the body and basket and base of dark patinated bronze, 5 3/4" x 7". **$250**

Clars Auction Gallery

Chinese gold and silver inlaid bronze animal-form censer from the 17th/18th century. **$81,000**

Chinese ivory vase, 20th century, of rouleau (small roll) form with a thick rolled rim above a cylindrical body carved with contorted dragons amid stylized clouds bounded by lappet bands, all supported on a foliate-accented pedestal base, 9 1/4". **$350**

Two Oriental scrolls, one featuring characters and the other with two panels of a galloping horse and characters. **$6,325**

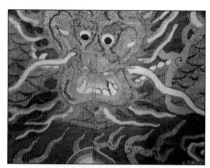

Embroidered blue silk dragon robe having nine five-claw dragons with couched gold-wrapped threads leaping amidst clouds, bats and other auspicious emblems, all above a hem of crusting waves with other auspicious objects and the lishui stripe. **$10,925**

Chinese Ming Dynasty landscape painting on silk, dated 1535, 66" long by 16 3/4" wide, formerly the property of the Honolulu Academy of Arts. **$14,760**

Chinese carved jade mortar, spinach-colored jade, motif features scrolling dragons, clouds, waves, 10 1/4" tall, late 19th/early 20th century. **$14,760**

Southeast Asian gilt-bronze covered bowl on stand with seated figure of Buddha, shaped in the form of a lotus, the bowl topped by a seated Buddha figure whose hand touches the earth – a gesture meant to represent a renunciation of worldly desires. **$22,000**

Chinese brass mounted Jichimu long table (Huazbo). **$41,125**

White jade vase with cover, ovoid with lion-form finial, 10" tall. **$22,320**

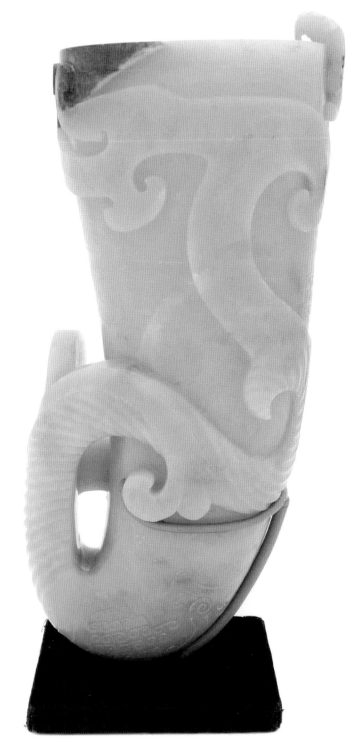

Chinese yellow jade rhyton, relief carved with spiraling design, 10" tall. **$17,360.**

Chinese silver export tray, Wang Hing & Co., pierce carved dragon design, 145.87 ozt. **$17,360**

Chinese translucent white jade carving of two crickets atop a cabbage, late 19th century (Qing/early Republic) 6 1/2" long, 3.25 pounds. **$1,800**

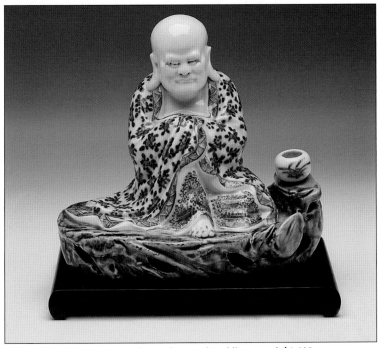

Chinese blue and white Imari figure of a seated Buddha, signed. **$1,100**

Rare intact set of 10 Canton porcelain nesting bowls with figural scenes on each. **$5,060**

Ovoid form Chinese vase with puce ground and turquoise, 19th century, 6 3/8". **$11,500**

Japanese Woodblock Prints

— By Zac Bissonnette

In a letter to his brother Theo in 1885, Vincent van Gogh wrote, "My studio is not too bad, especially as I have pinned up a number of Japanese prints on the walls, which amuse me very much. You know those little women's figures in gardens on the beach, horsemen, flowers, knotty thorn branches."

Today, an ever-increasing number of collectors are willing to pay handsomely to amuse themselves with Japanese prints on their walls. But it remains a field where, beginning with a very small budget, you can acquire reasonably rare, beautiful works on your own. Authentic Japanese woodblock prints from the 18th and 19th centuries can be found through reputable dealers starting at as little as $100.

In 1872, Jules Claretie coined the term Japonisme, which referred to the influence of Japanese art—especially woodblock printing—on the modern art in Europe. The lack of perspective and the use of bold, un-lifelike outlining, and the depiction of subjects off-center influenced the development of impressionism and later cubism. The list of European modernist painters whose style owes a significant debt to Japanese woodblock printing is extensive: van Gogh, Degas, Cassatt, Whistler, Monet, Gauguin, Klimt, and Renoir, just to name a few.

Woodblock in colors by Hasui Kawase (Jap., 1883-1957), titled Zojoji Temple. **$5,500**

Indeed, it is impossible to browse through late-18h and early 19th century Japanese prints without being stunned at how modern they seem. We see their reflection in European modernism right on through pop art and illustrators like Patrick Nagel – and, of course, in the Anime cartoons that have soared in popularity over the past decade.

But even without the context of their influence on western art, ukiyo-e is interesting.

The story of the rise and fall of Japanese woodblock printing is a sad one; it is also the story of the decline of artistic freedom and the rise of totalitarian government. In his 1954 book The Floating World, a history of Japanese woodblock printing, the novelist James Michener lays out why the story of this art form needs to be told.

"[T]his book tries to explain what happens to an art when a powerful and practical civil government begins to regulate all aspects of that art," he writes. "We shall watch such a government, benign and extraordinarily wise, as it begins to build its strait jacket for art: what colors may be used, what unpatriotic subject matter must excluded, what immoral material must be stopped. We shall see this government exhort its artists to produce only those subjects which glorify the history of the nation. And we shall clearly see that those laws hastened the death of the art."

By the 1830s, the Japanese government had stipulated that blue was the only color that could be used.

"The government was concerned with extravagance, and they were concerned with controlling the middle class," notes Bill Stein of Chicago's Floating World Gallery. "The government told the publishers you can only print in blue, which seems crazy to you and me but it was sending a message: You need to be austere, extravagance is bad, and prints with lots of color and action are bad for you."

But it's not all darkness. Michener writes that "the Japanese print is fun. It comprises one of the most totally delightful art forms ever devised. Its colors are varied, its subject matter witty, its allurement infinite."

That infinite allurement that attracted the great European modernists has also attracted collectors from all over the world – and that's given the Japanese woodblock print market a stability that Asian art at large hasn't had.

"If you're just looking at the domestic market coming from Japan, it's really stagnated over the past 20 years," notes Stein. "The market picture is much more complicated than that, particularly in the west. Japanese art appeals to people everywhere. So while their domestic market is important, a very substantial part of the demand comes from the United States and Asia."

While many artists still haven't climbed back to the prices they reached during Japan's bubble economy of the 1980s, demand has risen steadily since the bust, and did not abate during the recent economic crisis in the United States.

A few tips for getting started: If you're going to spend a significant amount of money on a Japanese Woodblock print – and by significant I mean you are not buying the work purely for decoration, and it is important to you that the piece have some enduring value – buy through either a major auction house or a member of the International Fine Print Dealers Association.

Stein notes that the world of Japanese prints is confusing because many prints had different "states," as the woodblocks were used over several decades, oftentimes with repairs made to the blocks in between printings. Works that look the same to the untrained eye can vary by a factor of 10 in terms of value.

"It gets easy after you look at the first 10,000," says Stein.

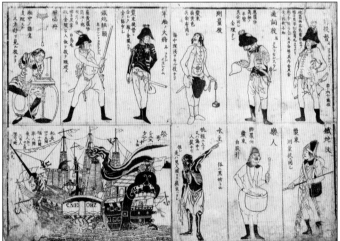

Heritage Auction Galleries

1800s Japanese woodblock print illustrating the Japanese stylized concept of the appearance of Western European people. A 19" x 13 1/2" print showing a steam-powered ship, several officers, sailors and a black man. These images are remarkably similar to drawings the Japanese made of Admiral Perry on his opening U.S. visit to Japan; this print possibly pre-dates that period. Generally very good condition with old file folds, some light soiling, and edge wear. **$1,015**

Heritage Auction Galleries

Ando Hiroshige (Japanese, 1797-1858), Canyon Scene, color woodblock on paper, minor foxing. Matted and framed, not examined out of frame, 20" x 6 1/2". **$143**

Autographs

— By Zac Bissonnette

In *The Meaning and Beauty of Autographs*, first published in 1935 and translated from the German by David H. Lowenherz of Lion Heart Autographs, Inc. in 1995, Stefan Zweig explained that to love a manuscript, we must first love the human being "whose characteristics are immortalized in them." When we do, then "a single page with a few lines can contain the highest expression of human happiness, and... the expression of deepest human sadness. To those who have eyes to look at such pages correctly, eyes not only in the head, but also in the soul, they will not receive less of an impression from these plain signs than from the obvious beauty of pictures and books."

John M. Reznikoff, founder and president of University Archives, has been a leading dealer and authority on historical letters and artifacts for 32 years. He described the current market for autographs as "very, very strong on many fronts. Possibly because of people being afraid to invest in the market and in real estate, we are seeing investment in autographs that seems to parallel gold and silver."

Reznikoff suspects that Civil War items peaked after Ken Burns' series but that Revolutionary War documents, included those by signers of the Declaration of Independence and the Constitution are still undervalued and can be purchased for under $500.

Currrently, space is in high demand, especially Apollo 11. Pop culture, previously looked at as secondary by people who dealt in Washingtons and Lincolns, has come into its own. Reznikoff anticipates continued growth in memorabilia that includes music, television, movies and sports. Babe Ruth, Lou Gehrig, Ty Cobb and Tiger Woods are still good investments but Reznikoff warns that authentication is much more of a concern in sports than in any other field.

The Internet allows for a lot of disinformation and this is a significant issue with autographs. There are two widely accepted authentication services: Professional Sports Authenticator (PSA/DNA) and James Spence Authentication (JSA). A dealer's reliability can be evaluated by seeing whether he is a member of one or more of the major organizations in the field: the Antique Booksellers Association of America, UACC Registered Dealers Program and the National Professional Autograph Dealers Association (NPADA), which Reznikoff founded.

There is an additional caveat to remember and it is true for all collectibles: rarity. The value of an autograph is often determined less by the prominence of the signer than by the number of autographs he signed.

Swann Auction Galleries

Kurt Vonnegut (1922-2007), ink drawing, signed twice, self-portrait on a card with a note: "Why should it make me so happy every time I see it? That's crazy." **$480**

Swann Auction Galleries

George Armstrong Custer, 1868, letter to Captain W.J. Lough, concerning the alleged poor treatment of Custer's horses, Phil and Mack, under Lough's care. Custer writes in part: "I do not want him kept from his regular full account of work merely because he shys . . . I certainly do not intend to pay for any time not even a day that my horse does not receive the work and care on the track which I intended he should . . . I distinctly told you that I did not want my horses taken outside the track enclosure and I still desire that except for shoeing." Four pages, written on a single folded sheet; soiling on terminal page, vertical fold through signature, small stain through text on terminal page. With Captain Lough's letter in response to Custer, defending his work. **$7,200**

Heritage Auction Galleries

Alex Rodriguez, 8" x10" photo depicts the day he signed with the Yankees. **$179**

Heritage Auction Galleries

Roger Maris, 1976 diamond jubilee card. **$358**

Heritage Auction Galleries

Tiger Woods, Masters flag, 2002. Framed against green velvet background to final measurement of 20" x 25". **$844**

Frank Sinatra, 2 1/2" x 2" autograph, cut, framed along with a color 8" x 10" photo. **$143**

Heritage Auction Galleries

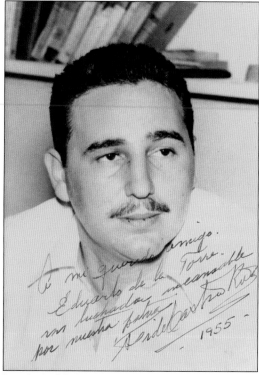

Swann Auction Galleries

Fidel Castro, photograph signed, "Fidel Castro Ruz," and inscribed: "To my dear friend / Eduardo de la Torre, / a tireless fighter / for our country / 1955," in Spanish, bust portrait showing the young revolutionary clean-shaven except for a mustache. Signed in the image at bottom. Approximately 7" x 5"; slight silvering along top edge; owner's ink stamp on back: "Propiedad de Gaston Bernal." Castro was arrested in 1953 and sentenced to 15 years in prison for his part in an ill-fated attack on the Batista regime. He was released in 1955 and almost immediately went to Mexico and the United States to revive his movement, raise money and recruit supporters. This photo dates from that trip. **$3,000**

Swann Auction Galleries

George Herbert Walker Bush and Mikhail Sergeyevich Gorbachev, photo signed by both, showing each with one arm around the other and smiling at the 10-year-anniversary celebrations of the fall of the Berlin Wall. Approximately 11 1/2" x 8" overall. **$700**

Swann Auction Galleries

Color photograph signed by all seven members of the Columbia Space Shuttle mission STS-107, an official NASA lithograph showing each member of the crew in a space suit. Signed in the image, above the relevant portrait. Crew biographies printed on the back, approximately 8" x 10". **$8,500**
(All seven crewmembers died when Columbia was destroyed on re-entry on Feb. 1, 2003.)

Swann Auction Galleries

Leon Trotsky (1879-1940), typed document, signed in blue pencil in Russian, ordering authorities to drive away animals upon the approach of Mamontov gangs and to search anyone suspicious, especially plant managers. One page, two small holes punched in left margin, docketed at top in pencil in Russian, bottom margin trimmed (not affecting signature). **$2,280**

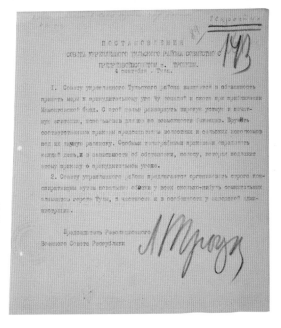

Hans Christian Andersen, signed, "H.C. Andersen," carte-de-visite portrait by Georg E. Hansen, showing the Danish fairytale author seated at a desk holding an open book. Signed on the mount at bottom. Approximately 3 1/2" x 2 1/4" (image), framed. **$2,600**

Swann Auction Galleries

Swann Auction Galleries

Custer's Own Portrait of Officers of the Seventh Cavalry, photograph inscribed and signed "G.A.C." twice, in ink and pencil. An albumen print group portrait (by Orlando S. Goff), showing Custer and the officers under his command and their wives. On the mount below the image, Custer has written, in ink, the name of each person in the group, adding, in pencil, "Names written in the order of the persons in the picture. G.A.C." On the back, in pencil, he notes, "Our house at Fort Lincoln, Dakota." Approximately 5" x 7 1/4" (image), 8" x 10" overall; minor toning at edges of mount, scattered minor foxing on verso. (Fort Lincoln, N.D., November 1873). **$20,000**

Christopher "Kit" Carson, carte-de-visite portrait by Brady, showing the soldier and frontiersman in civilian attire. Signed on the mount below the image. Photographer's full imprint on back. Approximately 3 1/4" x 2 1/4" (image), corners and top edge trimmed, minor scattered soiling. **$28,000**

Swann Auction Galleries

Ernest Hemingway signed letter, 1956, discussing bull fighting, hunting, Spain. **$2,868**

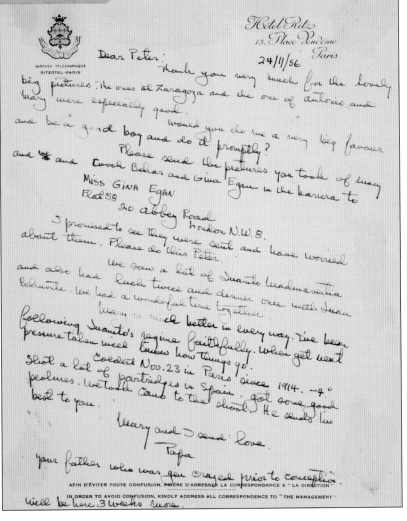

Mary Astor and Dolores Del Rio signed photos, black and white, 11" x 14" inscribed and signed portraits includes Del Rio in black ink and Astor in blue, with mild toning, curling, and corner wear, and tack holes to the corners of the Del Rio photo. **$334 pair**

Heritage Auction Galleries

Samuel Clemens, signed albumen print, "Mark Twain" and "S. L. Clemens," with quotation and sentiment dated Sept. 28, 1900. Rare twice-signed photograph, 3" x 5 3/4", is mounted to an overall size of 5" x 8 1/4". Above the image, Clemens has written, "Truth is the most valuable thing we have. Let us economise it. Truly yours, Mark Twain" - a quotation from a chapter epigraph in "Pudd'nhead Wilson's New Calendar" in Twain's "Following the Equator" (1897). Twain's signature begins on the photo and ends on the backing. Below the photo, Clemens has written, "To Mr. Pinkhorn, with the compliments of S L. Clemens." The photographer's stamp is in three places (each a version of "H. Walter Barnett/ Park Side Hyde Park Corner/ London S.W."): in the lower right corner of the photo, below the photo, and on the back. **$2,629**

Heritage Auction Galleries

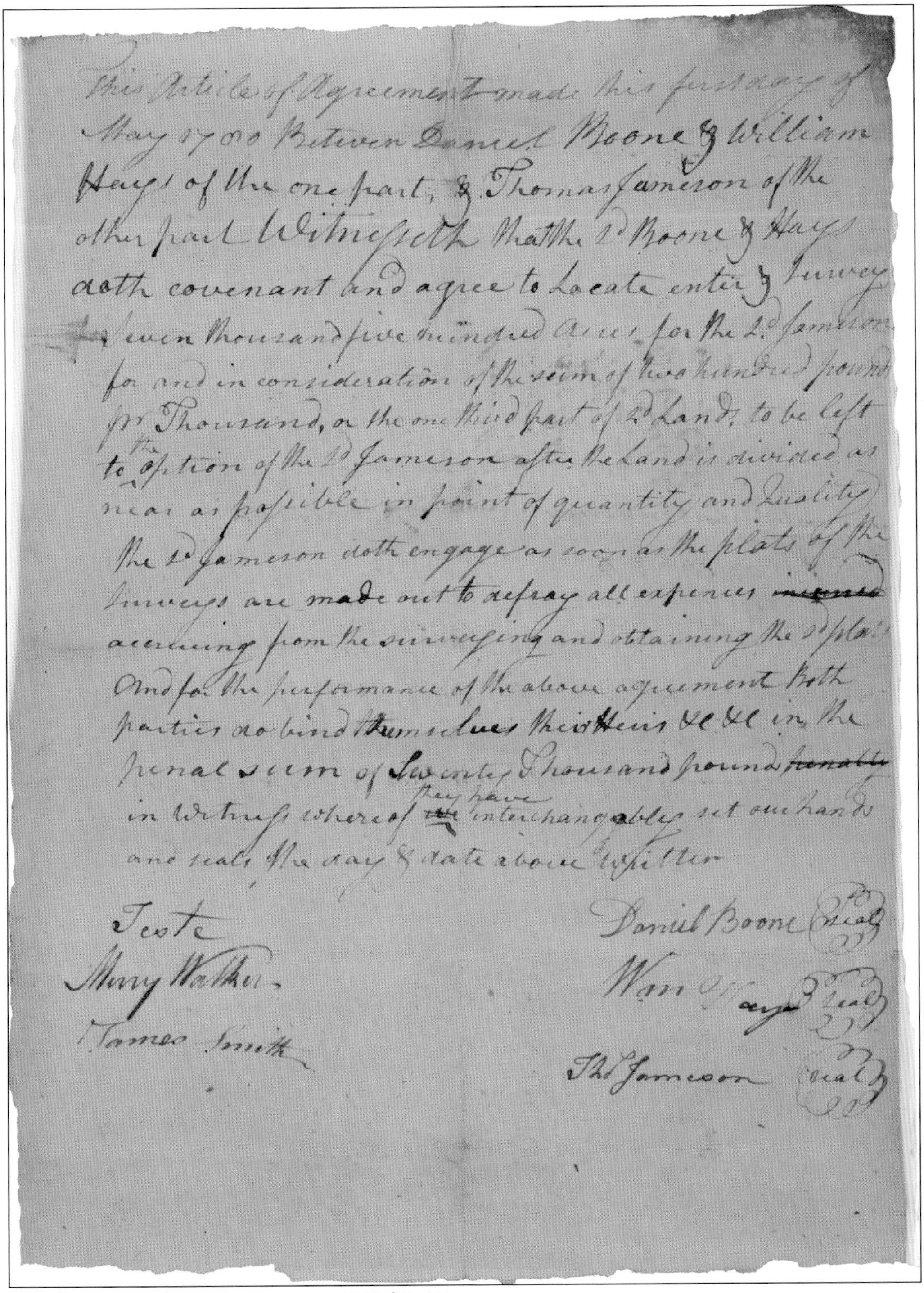
This Article of Agreement made this first day of
May 1780 Between Daniel Boone & William
Hays of the one part, & Thomas Jameson of the
other part Witnesseth that the sd Boone & Hays
doth covenant and agree to Locate enter & Survey
Seven thousand five hundred Acres for the sd Jameson
for and in consideration of the sum of two hundred pounds
pr Thousand, or the one third part of sd Land, to be left
to the option of the sd Jameson after the Land is divided as
near as possible in point of quantity and Quality
the sd Jameson doth engage as soon as the plats of the
Surveys are made out to defray all expences ~~incurred~~
accruing from the surveying and obtaining the sd plats
And for the performance of the above agreement both
parties do bind themselves their Heirs &c &c in the
penal sum of Seventy Thousand pounds ~~penalty~~
in Witness whereof ~~we~~ they have interchangably set our hands
and seals the day & date above written

Teste
Henry Walker
James Smith

Daniel Boone (Seal)
Wm Hays (Seal)
Thos Jameson (Seal)

Daniel Boone signed surveying agreement, 1780. **$13,146**

Heritage Auction Galleries

Chuck Berry, white Signature Series electric guitar with Chuck Berry logo and image on the body, signed on the pick guard. **$478**

John Hancock signed document, 1776. **$13,145**

Banks

Banks that display some form of action while accepting a coin are considered mechanical banks. Mechanical banks date back to ancient Greece and Rome, but the majority of collectors are interested in those made between 1867and 1928 in Germany, England, and the United States. More than 80 percent of all cast-iron mechanical banks produced between 1869 and 1928 were made by J. E. Stevens Co. of Cromwell, Connecticut. Tin banks are usually of German origin.

Banks with no mechanical action are known as still banks. The first still banks were made of wood or pottery or from gourds. Redware and stoneware banks, made by America's early potters, are prized possessions of today's collectors. Still banks reached a golden age with the arrival of the cast-iron bank. Almost every substance has been used to make a still bank. The banks were often ornately painted to enhance their appeal.

Morphy Auctions

J. & E. Stevens, circa 1901, the Magician bank performs a trick in which the coin placed on the table disappears beneath the top hat. This example was accompanied by its factory box. **$25,875**

Charles A. Bailey, Cobalt, Conn., Darky Fisherman, 1880s, when a coin is placed in the slot at the front of the bank and the lever is pressed, the boy raises his pole to discover he has caught a fish. His cap flips up and the fish nudges coin into bank slot, ex-Stephen and Marilyn Steckbeck collection. **$287,500**

Morphy Auctions

James D. Julia Auctioneers

Stevens Boy Scout Camp Bank, boy looks out from tepee while another boy cooks over a cauldron. When lever is pressed, a third boy raises flag announcing "Boy Scout Camp," 6" h x 9 3/4" l. Bank appears all original and is in very good to excellent condition. **$6,900**

James D. Julia Auctioneers

Stevens, Columbus World's Fair Bank, painted gold and silver with green vines and copper-colored log. This is the slightly more rare painted version, with the embossed lettering. Flip lever and Indian rises from under log. Columbus raises his hand greeting the Indian; 6 3/4" h x 8 1/2" l. Near excellent condition. **$4,600**

Morphy Auctions

Barrel-shaped man with outstretched arms. **$1,100**

Bertoia Auctions,

Smith & Egge, late 19th-century Boston State House, in the small version at 5 1/8". **$12,650**

Morphy Auctions

Kyser & Rex painted cast-iron still bank depicting an apple on a branch. **$3,200**

Morphy Auctions

Chronometer, cast-iron mechanical bank in original condition. **$20,700**

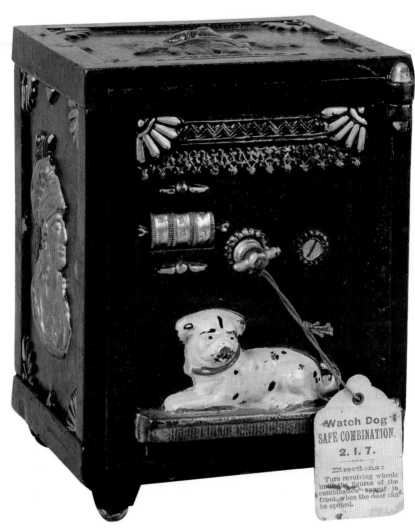

Morphy Auctions

Watch Dog Safe, cast iron, J. & E. Stevens and Co. Original, working condition. Original tag, bellows and drawer, 6". **$3,162**

Morphy Auctions

'Spise a Mule, cast iron, J. & E. Stevens and Co. bench variation. **$517**

Morphy Auctions

Tiger, tin mechanical, Saalheimer and Strauss, with advertisement for Lyons Toffee on back, 5 1/8". **$12,075**

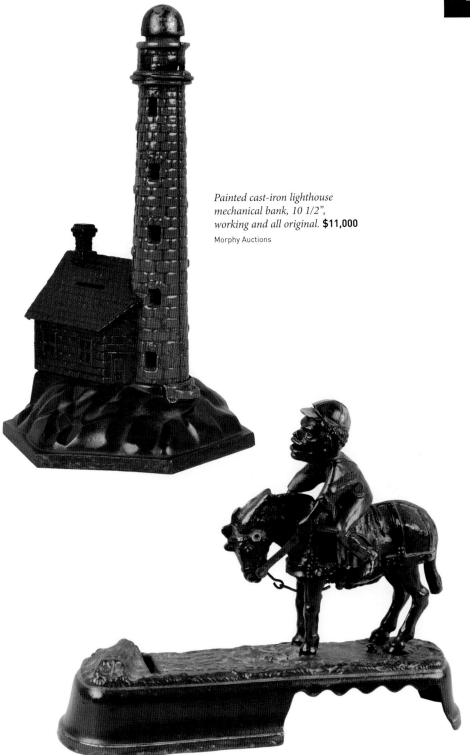

Painted cast-iron lighthouse mechanical bank, 10 1/2", working and all original. **$11,000**
Morphy Auctions

Morphy Auctions

'Spise a Mule, cast iron, J. & E. Stevens and Co., jockey-over variation with brown base. **$517**

J. & E. Stevens "Calamity" football cast-iron mechanical bank, circa 1905, with original wooden box. **$78,975**

RSL Auction Co.

Morphy Auctions

Armored Car still bank, cast iron, A.C. Williams, circa 1920s, rare. Original paint and solid gold-washed wheels, 4" x 6 1/2". **$1,955**

RSL Auction Co.

Turtle cast-iron mechanical bank, Kilgore Mfg. Co., Westerville, Ohio, circa 1930. **$72,900**

Painted-lead still bank depicting Mickey Mouse on a round of cheddar cheese, 5". **$4,600**

Morphy Auctions

*Kenton State Bank,
near mint, 6" h.* **$400**

Morphy Auctions

RSL Auction Co.

*Only known example of J. & E. Stevens' cast-iron mechanical "Novelty" bank in
a sea-foam green, cream, tan and red color motif.* **$29,160**

Books

Collecting early books is a popular segment of the antiques marketplace. Collectors of early books are rewarded with interesting titles and exquisite illustrations, as well as fascinating information and stories. The author, printer, and publisher, as well as the date of the printing, can increase the value of an early book.

Heritage Auction Galleries provided the following images.

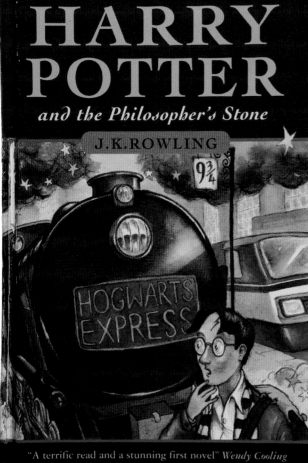

J. K. Rowling

23/1./04

Dear Adam,

firstly, I am *very* sorry about the huge delay in responding to your letter. I had a baby last year and took some time off, hence the vast backlog of mail. However, here is a signed picture for your auction. You have all my admiration for the great work you are doing.

With love from

JK Rowling

(Jo)

J. K. Rowling. Harry Potter and the Philosopher's Stone. [London]: Bloomsbury, [1997]. First edition, first printing, one of 500 copies of the first and rarest of the Harry Potter books, and likely one of approximately 300 copies sent to British libraries. Correct full number line ("10 9 8 7 6 5 4 3 2 1"), "Copyright © Text Joanne Rowling 1997" (rather than "J. K. Rowling"), and "Taylor1997" (rather than "Taylor 1997") on the copyright page, and with "1 wand" appearing twice (first and last) in the list of "Other Equipment" on page 53. Accompanying the book are two unique pieces of Rowlingiana. The first is a black-and-white photograph signed "J K Rowling" measuring 4 1/2" x 6 3/4". The second item is an autographed note signed "J K Rowling / (Jo)" on her personal cardstock stationery. **$11,950**

Joseph Smith, Junior. *The Book of Mormon: An Account Written by the Hand of Mormon, Upon Plates Taken From the Plates of Nephi. By Joseph Smith, Junior, Author and Proprietor.* Palmyra, [New York]: Printed by E. B. Grandin, for the Author, 1830. First edition. This copy belonged to John Wesley Brackenbury (1829-1902), the son of Joseph Blanchett Brackenbury (1788-1832), a very early follower of Joseph Smith, who was baptized as a Latter-Day Saint in 1831. Along with The Book of Mormon, this lot also includes 17 original photographs, mostly cabinet portraits (and one tintype), made circa 1900, of members of the Brackenbury, Smith, and Curtis families of Missouri, Kansas, and Iowa. **$47,800**

First Quorum Of Elders

APRIL 1900.

1. Samuel Ackerley
2. F. L. Sawley
3. Thomas Whiting
4. T. R. White
5. N. C. Enge
6. Thomas Hougas
7. E. H. Durand
8. A. W. Moffet
9. S. V. Bailey
10. E. A. Blakeslee
11. Alfred White
12. H. N. Snively
13. Wm. Newton
14. J. W. Brackenbury
15. D. S. Holmes
16. W. R. Pickering
17. H. J. Davison
18. Geo. Smith
19. E. Hayer
20. R. N. Burwell
21. W. W. Gaylord
22. E. Short
23. J. M. Stubbart
24. P. P. Starke
25. Lehi Ellison

JULIAN & BRACKENBURY, LAMONI, IOWA.

JULIAN & BRACKENBURY, LAMONI, IOWA.

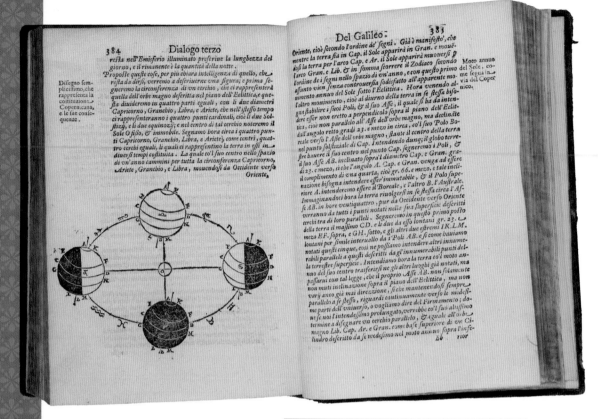

Galileo's 1632 "Masterly Polemic for the New Science"; Galileo Galilei. Dialogo...Doue ne I congressi di Quattro giornate si discorre sopra I due Massimi Sistemi del Mondo Tolemaico, e Copernicano... Florence: Giovanni Batista Landini, 1632. First edition. Quarto. [viii], 458, [32] pages, with Errata leaf (2F6) and final blank present. Page 92 with correction slip supplying side note pasted in the margin. Woodcut device on title page, with 31 woodcut diagrams and illustrations, woodcut decorations and woodcut initials. Contemporary mottled calf with double-ruled borders and floral blindstamped devices in the corners. Text edges sprinkled red. **$65,725**

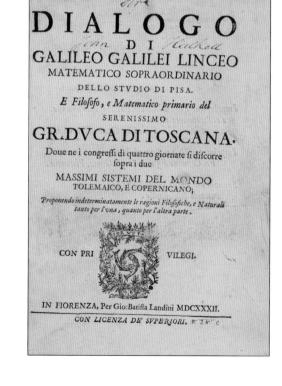

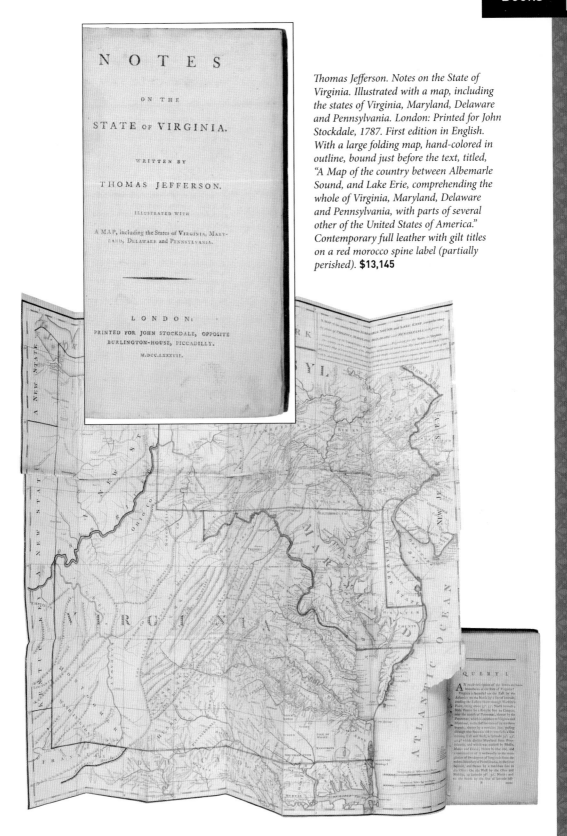

Thomas Jefferson. Notes on the State of Virginia. Illustrated with a map, including the states of Virginia, Maryland, Delaware and Pennsylvania. London: Printed for John Stockdale, 1787. First edition in English. With a large folding map, hand-colored in outline, bound just before the text, titled, "A Map of the country between Albemarle Sound, and Lake Erie, comprehending the whole of Virginia, Maryland, Delaware and Pennsylvania, with parts of several other of the United States of America." Contemporary full leather with gilt titles on a red morocco spine label (partially perished). **$13,145**

Ernest Hemingway. For Whom the Bell Tolls. New York: Charles Scribner's Sons, 1940. First edition. Presentation copy, inscribed by Hemingway on the front free endpaper: "For Popsie and Frankie / Steinhart [Hemingway's neighbors in Havana] from their friend / and neighbor this copy of the 15 / original edition copies of this book / Best always / Ernest Hemingway." **$25,095**

H. A. Rey. Curious George. Boston:
Houghton Mifflin, 1941. First
edition. Unpaginated. Illustrations
by the author. Publisher's brick
red cloth with Curious George
vignette in black on front board
and lettering in black on spine.
Illustrated endpapers. Original dust
jacket with $1.75 price.
A couple of faint scratches to cloth
on rear board. **$26,290**

ULYSSES

BY

JAMES JOYCE

James Joyce. Ulysses. Paris:
Shakespeare and Company,
1922. First edition. Number
540 of 750 numbered copies
on handmade paper, out
of a total edition of 1,000
copies. **$12,547**

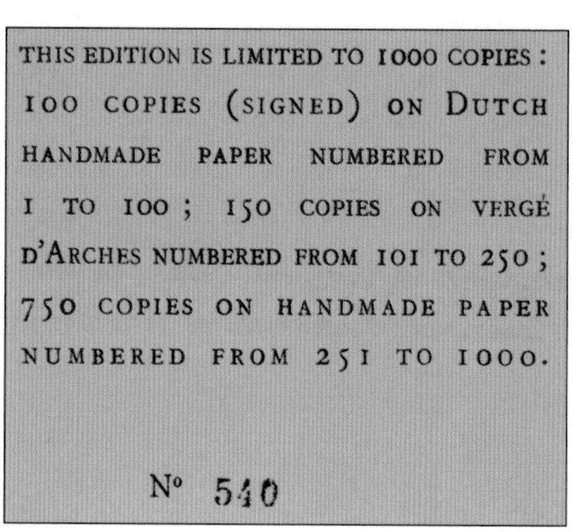

THIS EDITION IS LIMITED TO 1000 COPIES :
100 COPIES (SIGNED) ON DUTCH
HANDMADE PAPER NUMBERED FROM
1 TO 100 ; 150 COPIES ON VERGÉ
D'ARCHES NUMBERED FROM 101 TO 250 ;
750 COPIES ON HANDMADE PAPER
NUMBERED FROM 251 TO 1000.

Nº 540

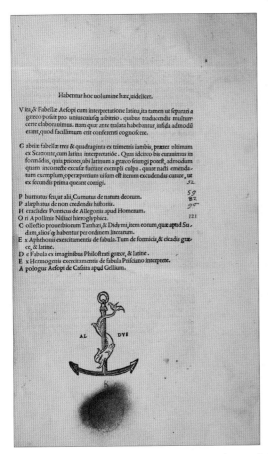

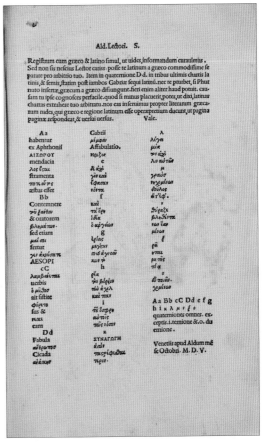

Aesop. Vita et Fabellae Aesopi...Gabriae Fabellae...Collectio Proverbiorum Tarrhaei &c.
[Venice]: Aldus Manutius, [1505]. First Aldine edition, in Greek only. An excellent copy of
the very rare Greek-only Aldine edition of Aesop. **$4,481**

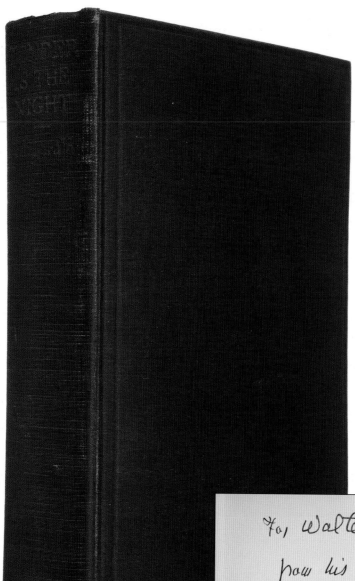

F. Scott Fitzgerald. Tender is the Night. A Romance. New York: Charles Scribner's Sons, 1934. First edition, third printing ("Devereux" on page 320, line 17). Inscribed by Fitzgerald on the front free endpaper: "For Walter Bruington / from his friend / F Scott Fitzgerald / This story of a Europe / that is no more. / Sept 1940." **$11,352**

Paperbacks

The first mass-market, pocket-sized, paperback book printed in the U.S. was an edition of Pearl Buck's *The Good Earth*, produced by Pocket Books in late 1938, sold in New York City.

At first, paperbacks consisted entirely of reprints, but publishers soon began publishing original works. Genre categories began to emerge, and mass-market book covers reflected those categories. Mass-market paperbacks had an impact on slick magazines (slicks) and pulp magazines. The market for cheap magazines diminished when buyers went to cheap books instead. Authors also turned from magazines and began writing for the paperback market. Many pulp magazine cover artists were hired by paperback publishers to entice readers with their alluring artwork. Several well-known authors were published in paperback, including Arthur Miller and John Steinbeck, and some, like Dashiell Hammett, were published as paperback originals.

For more information and details on condition grades (values here are in three grades: good, very good and fine), consult *Antique Trader Collectible Paperbacks Price Guide* by Gary Lovisi, or visit *www.gryphonbooks.com.*

Warped Women by Janet Pritchard, Uni Book #9, 1951, digest-size paperback. **$12-$100**

Girl-Crazy Professor by Florence Stonebraker, Croydon Book #46, 1953, digest-size paperback. **$9-$55.**

Dance-Hall Dyke by Toni Adler, Playtime Book #699-S, 1964. Cover art by Robert Bonfils. **$12-$55**

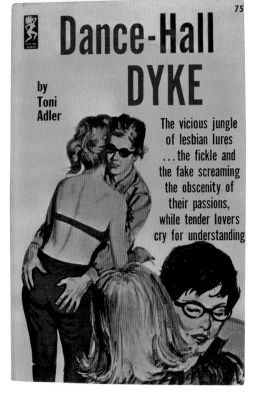

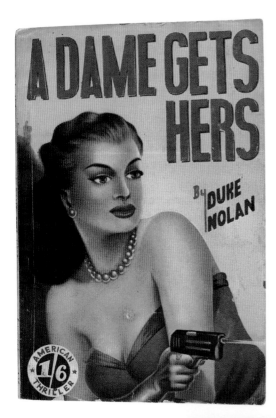

*A Dame Gets Hers by
Duke Nolan, Scion
Books, 1952, UK
digest-size paperback.*
$15-$125

*Office Hussy by John
Hunter, Star Novels
#767, 1957, digest-size
paperback.* **$12-$75**

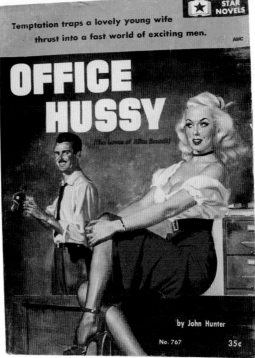

Rock 'N Roll Gal by Ernie Weatherall, Beacon Book #B379, 1957. Cover art by Owen Kampen. **$12-$65**

Knock On Any Head by Frank S. Miller, Vega Book #V-19, 1962. **$7-$40**

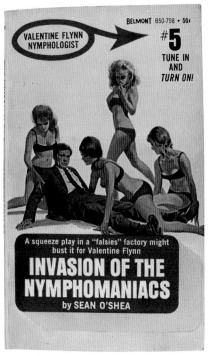

Lingerie Ltd. by Ralph Dean, Beacon Book #B300, 1960. Cover art by R. Gifford. **$9-$35**

Invasion of the Nymphomaniacs by Sean O'Shea, Belmont Book #B50-798, 1967. **$9-$35**

Sin Street by Dorine Manners, Pyramid Book #21, 1950. **$9-$50**

I Made My Bed by Celia Hye, Beacon Book #B188, 1958. **$7-$35**

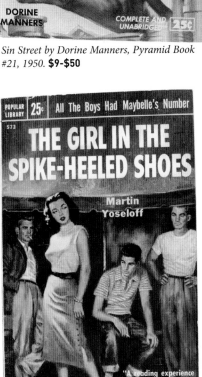

The Girl in the Spike-Heeled Shoes by Martin Yoseloff, Popular Library #573, 1954. **$5-$28**

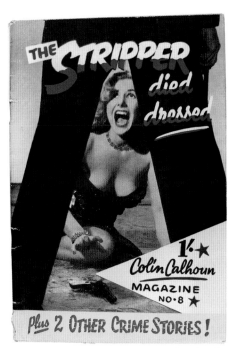

The Stripper Died Dressed by Conrad Paul, Colin Calhoun Magazine #8, circa 1952, Australian digest-size magazine. Photo cover. **$10-$65**

Run Tough, Run Hard by Carson Bingham, Monarch Book #487, 1964. Cover at by Ray Johnson. **$9-$45**

Gorrila's Moll by Ben Sarto, Modern Fiction, circa 1952, UK digest-size paperback. Cover art by Leonard Potts. **$15-$125**

Sex Racket by Mark Lucas, Tropic Book #928, 1966. **$9-$35**

This Way For Hell by Spike Morelli, Leisure Library #7, 1952. Cover art by Reginald Heade. **$12-$65**

Bottles

— By Michael Polak, author, Antique Trader Bottles Identification and Price Guide

Interest in bottle collecting is strong and continues to gain popularity, with new bottle clubs forming throughout the United States and Europe.

More collectors are spending their free time digging through old dumps, foraging through ghost towns, digging out old outhouses, exploring abandoned mine shafts, and searching out their favorite bottles at antiques shows, swap meets, flea markets, and garage sales. In addition, the Internet offers collectors opportunities and resources without ever leaving the house.

Most collectors still look beyond the type and value of a bottle to its origin and history. Researching the history of bottles can be as interesting as finding the bottle itself.

Baker's - Orange Grove - Bitters, square with rope twist corners, applied sloping collar mouth, smooth base, ca. 1865-75, medium pinkish puce, 9 1/2" h. **$2,464**

Bitter [over horseshoe design] Trade Mark (within horseshoe) Witch, flask shape, smooth base, applied double collar mouth, medium yellowish amber, ca. 1870-80, faint inside haze, 8 1/8" h. **$364**

St / Drakes / 1860 / Plantation / X / Bitters – Patented / 1862, yellow green (citron), 9 3/4", American, 1862-1875. **$1,500-$2,500**

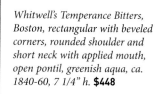

Russ' / Stomach / Bitters / New York, medium yellow amber, 10 1/8", American, 1860-1865. **$6,000-$8,000**

Whitwell's Temperance Bitters, Boston, rectangular with beveled corners, rounded shoulder and short neck with applied mouth, open pontil, greenish aqua, ca. 1840-60, 7 1/4" h. **$448**

Poison – cobalt blue, 4 1/4" long, American 1885-1900, **$1,500-$2,000**

Shoe, lace-up shoe with toe protruding from hole in front, ground lip with original screw-on cap at ankle, "PAT. APL. 00" on smooth base, black amethyst with original flesh-color paint on toe, ca. 1890-1910, 3 3/4" h. **$258**

GIX-45 -, Scroll, corset-waist style, elaborate scroll decoration forming acanthus leaves with four-petal flower at top and diamond at center obverse and reverse, vertical medial ribs, pontil scarred base, sheared and tooled lip, deep aqua, pt. **$840**

GVIII-14a -, Sunburst centered by ring with a dot in middle, horizontal corrugated edges, pontil scarred base, sheared and tooled lip, extremely rare color, emerald green, 1/2 pt. **$4,760**

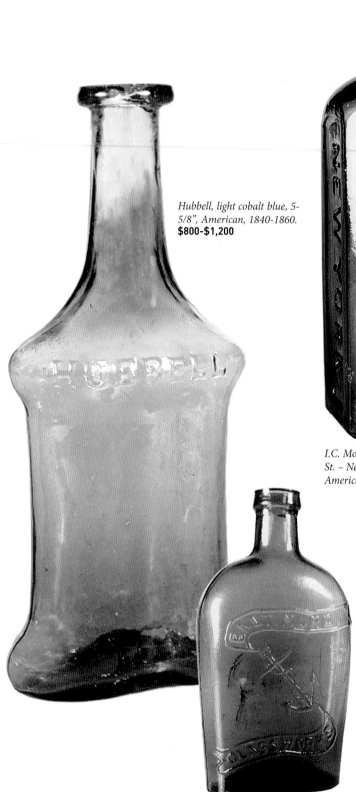

Hubbell, light cobalt blue, 5-5/8", American, 1840-1860.
$800-$1,200

I.C. Morrison's / Sarsaparilla – 188 Greenwich St. – New York, deep cobalt blue, 9 1/2", American, 1840-1860. **$4,000-$6,000**

GXIII-49 -, Anchor with fork-ended pennants inscribed "Baltimore" and "Glassworks," sheaf of grain with rake and pitchfork crossed behind sheaf, smooth edges, smooth base, applied mouth, yellow olive, 1/2 pt. **$3,080**

A. Livingston – Wholesale & Retail – Carson City, Nev, clear, pint, American, 1865-1875. **$1,000-$1,300**

Corn For The World / ear of corn / monument / Baltimore, deep pink puce, quart, American, 1865-1875. **$2,500-$4,000**

Stripe-pattern domed inkwell, clear glass with white and pink alternating stripe pattern swirled to right, 2 1/4", Sandwich Glass Works, Sandwich, Mass., American, 1830-1850. **$1,200-$1,800**

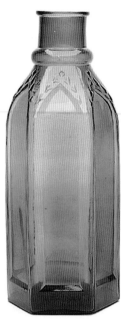

Honey amber, six-sided cathedral-type with simple Gothic windows, cylindrical ringed neck with outward rolled mouth, smooth base, ca. 1860-80, rare color, 13 1/8" h. **$960**

Igloo ink, medium cobalt blue, 2", American, 1865-1880. **$800-$1,400**

Teakettle ink, milk glass, 2 3/8", American, 1875-1885. **$375-$500**

Wishart's (L.Q.C.) - Pine Tree Tar Cordial, Phila. - Patent (design of pine tree) 1859, square with beveled corners, applied sloping collar mouth, smooth base, emerald green, 9 1/2" h. **$224**

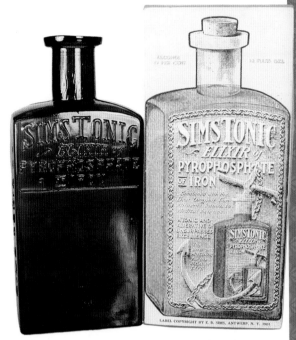

Sims Tonic / Elixir / Pyrophosphate / Of Iron Sims Tonic Co. – Antwerp N.Y., medium amber, 7 1/4", American, 1901-1905. **$140-$200**

Stockton's / Antiseptic – Stockton Medicine Co. / Nashville, Tenn, label reads: Stockton's Antiseptic For Internal Use, It Kills Microbes, Price One Dollar, Prepared by the Stockton Medicine Co., Nashville, Tenn, medium amber, 10", American, 1885-1895. **$200-$300**

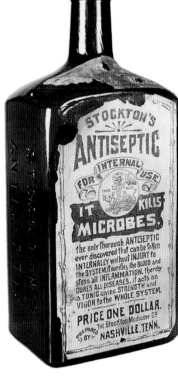

Friedgen, irregular hexagon poison, 12 oz., 6 7/8", extremely rare, at present, no other examples in the 12 oz. size exist are known to exist, American, 1890-1910. **$4,500-$5,500**

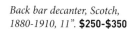

Back bar decanter, Scotch, 1880-1910, 11". **$250-$350**

Whiskey, "Booz's (E.G.) Old Cabin Whiskey - 120 Walnut St. Philadelphia" (on roof), "1840 - E.G. Booz's Old Cabin Whiskey" (on sides), cabin-shaped, applied sloping collar mouth, smooth base, medium amber, ca. 1860-65, 7 5/8" h. **$7,840**

Spirits, mold-blown, globular, 24 ribs swirled to the right, tall neck with outward rolled lip, pontil scar, Zanesville, Ohio, ca. 1825-35, medium amber, shallow surface bottle, 7 1/2" h. **$616**

Star Whiskey / New York / W.B. Crowell Jr., 8 1/2", American, 1860-1875. **$500-$800**

Ceramics

America
Batchelder and Brown

Ernest Allan Batchelder founded the Batchelder Tile Co. in Pasadena, Calif., in 1909. He took on Frederick L. Brown as his partner, renaming the pottery Batchelder and Brown in 1912. The firm closed in 1932.

Rago Arts and Auction Center

Batchelder and Brown early and large triptych of pumpkin field. (Featured in the exposition, "California Tile: The Golden Era 1910-1940," The California Heritage Museum, Santa Monica, 2001.) A few small edge chips. Stamped BATCHELDER PASADENA. 19 1/2" x 63". **$10,800**

Burley, and Burley Winter

Several generations of the Burley and Winter families operated potteries in and around the Ohio communities of Crooksville, Zanesville and Mt. Sterling from the early 19th to the early 20th centuries.

Burley Winter floor vase with Grecian women and green over brick red glazes. Marked "Burley Winter, Crooksville, O." Mint. 17" h x 10 1/2" w. **$575**

Belhorn Auction Services LLC

Belhorn Auction Services LLC

Burley Winter handled and lidded vessel in matte green over pumpkin. Unmarked, but there is a nearly perfect four-finger print to the bottom left by the pottery's glazer. Some very small nicks to the inner rim are hidden by the lid, 9" x 6 1/2". **$98**

Rose Cabat

Rose Cabat, born 1914, New York, is a Tucson, Ariz.-based potter known for her "feelies" — small, narrow-necked porcelain pots with soft glazes that feel feathery to the touch.

Rose Cabat "Feelie" with rare performance trial glaze. Marked 84T Cabat 28N. Mint. 2 1/2" h x 2 1/4" w. **$700**

Belhorn Auction Services LLC

Rose Cabat Feelie in cobalt blue with green streaks. Marked 841 Cabat 47. Mint. 2 1/2". $209

Camark

Camark Art Tile and Pottery Co. operated in Camden, Ark., from 1926 until the mid-1970s. Art director John Lessell created many of the firm's distinctive glazes.

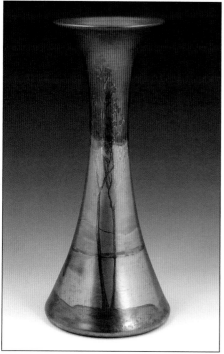

Belhorn Auction Services LLC

Camark Lessell tapered trumpet vase with scene of trees on a lake with deep red upper sky and golden iridescent tones. Marked Lessell. 10" h. $1,100

Belhorn Auction Services LLC

Camark vase with horizontal ribs in matte green over blue. Marked Camark. Mint. 5 3/4". $22

Clark House Pottery

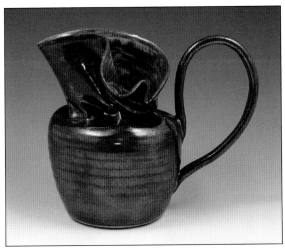

Clark House Pottery, Greenville, S.C., is operated by Bill and Pamela Clark and influenced by the Arts & Crafts movement of the early 1900s. In addition to original, hand-thrown and decorated art pottery, the Clarks produce wares in the style of George Ohr (1857-1918), the self-proclaimed "Mad Potter of Biloxi."

Belhorn Auction Services LLC

Clark House Pottery tornado pitcher in copper glaze made in the style of George Ohr's works. Signed Clark and marked "Clark House Pottery 09." Mint. 6 3/4". **$34**

Clark House Pottery "Uplifting" vase in green lichen glaze. Marked "Clark House Pottery LLC, CHP, 10" and signed Clark. Mint. 8 7/8". **$126**

Belhorn Auction Services LLC

Clifton Art Pottery

The Clifton Art Pottery, Newark, N.J., was established by William A. Long, once associated with Lonhuda Pottery, and Fred Tschirner, a chemist.

Production consisted of two major lines: Crystal Patina, which resembled true porcelain with a subdued crystal-like glaze, and Indian Ware or Western Influence, an adaptation of the Native Americans' unglazed and decorated pottery with a high-glazed black interior. Other lines included Robin's-Egg Blue and Tirrube. Robin's-Egg Blue is a variation of the Crystal Patina line, but in blue-green instead of straw-colored hues and with a less-prominent crushed-crystal effect in the glaze. Tirrube, which is often artist signed, features brightly colored, slip-decorated flowers on a terra-cotta ground.

Marks are incised or impressed. Early pieces may be dated and impressed with a shape number. Indian wares are identified by tribes.

Rago Arts and Auction Center

Clifton vases (two) in matte green glaze, one embossed with poppies. Both marked, poppy vase hand-incised Clifton First Fire October 1905. 5 1/2" and 6 1/2". **$1,200 pair**

Belhorn Auction Services LLC

Clifton Indian Ware lidded teapot. Marked "Clifton 275". Mint. 3 3/4" x 8 3/4". **$71**

Coors Pottery

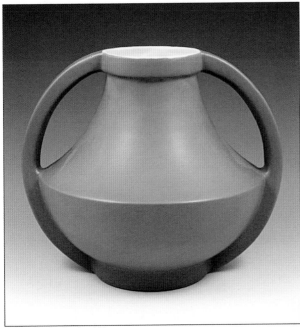

Coors Pottery was established by John J. Herold, formerly superintendent of the art pottery section at Roseville Pottery, in 1910 in Golden, Colo., financed by Adolph Coors Sr. The company was renamed Coors Porcelain in 1920, producing lines that included Rosebud, similar to Fiesta; Decalcomania, also resembling some of the Homer Laughlin patterns; MelloTone, similar to LuRay; plus a Golden Ivory. Pottery production ended after World War II.

Coors Pottery circle vase in matte blue. Marked with Coors stamp. Mint. 7 1/2". **$38**

Belhorn Auction Services LLC

Cowan Pottery

R. Guy Cowan was born in 1884 in East Liverpool, Ohio, and educated at the New York State School of Ceramics at Alfred. He founded the Cowan Pottery Studio in Lakewood, Ohio (a suburb of Cleveland) in 1912. The firm closed in 1931.

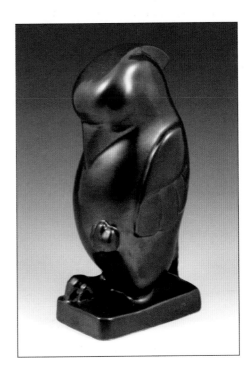

Cowan Art Deco figurine titled, "Introspection." Finish in black semi-matte glaze. Designed by A. Drexler Jacobson, the piece is marked with die-impressed circular Cowan mark and the artist's monogram on the plinth. Mint and uncrazed. 8 3/8" h. **$1,600**

Belhorn Auction Services LLC

Belhorn Auction Services LLC

Rare Cowan vase signed by Arthur E. Baggs from 1927. Hand thrown and simply glazed, this vase is a historical piece of Ohio's ceramic history. Having founded and built the highly successful Marblehead Pottery, Baggs moved to Ohio to work at Cowan and teach at the Cleveland School of Art. Soon after the production of this vase, Baggs went on to teach at The Ohio State University, which houses one of the oldest ceramics programs in the country. Marked with hand-incised RG Cowan mark and signed AEB in script with the date. There are a couple of insignificant scratches to the high-glaze finish on the body and a thin strip of roughness to the rim. 7 1/2". **$2,530**

Belhorn Auction Services LLC

Cowan V-99 handled vase in melon green designed by Viktor Schreckengost with drypoint decoration attributed to Whitney Atchley. Marked with die-impressed circular Cowan mark, COWAN in die-impressed letters and V99 in black crayon. Mint. 6". **$990**

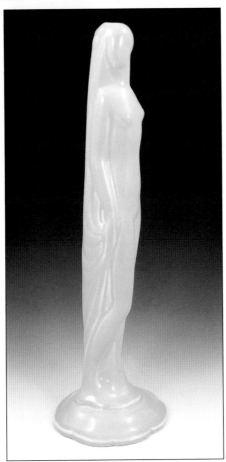

Cowan Lorelei lamp base in April green by Wayland Gregory. Marked COWAN in die-impressed letters. There is a tight 1" stress line to the base. 16 3/4" h. **$875**

Belhorn Auction Services LLC

Suzanne Crane

Suzanne Crane grew up in a family of botanists and bird-watchers in Wisconsin, but now lives in central Virginia, on the east side of the Blue Ridge Mountains. With her husband, Matthew, she opened Mud Dauber Pottery in Earlysville, Va., in 1997. She creates botanical-themed pottery and tiles.

Suzanne Crane tall lidded jar with fern motif, late 1990s, 10 1/2". **$600+**

Dedham Pottery

Alexander W. Robertson established a pottery in Chelsea, Mass., in about 1866. After his brother, Hugh Cornwall Robertson, joined him in 1868, the firm was called A. W. & H. C. Robertson. Their father, James Robertson, joined his sons in 1872, and the name Chelsea Keramic Art Works Robertson and Sons was used.

The pottery's initial products were simple flower and bean pots, but the firm quickly expanded its output to include a wide variety of artistic pottery. It produced a fine redware body used in classical forms, some with black backgrounds imitating ancient Greek and Apulian (an Iron and Bronze Age Greek colony) works. It experimented with under-glaze slip decoration on vases. The Chelsea Keramic Art Works also produced high-glazed vases, pitchers and plaques with a buff clay body, with either sculpted or molded applied decoration.

James Robertson died in 1880 and Alexander moved to California in 1884, leaving Hugh alone in Chelsea, where his experiments eventually yielded an imitation of the Chinese Ming-era blood-red glaze. Hugh's vases with that glaze were marked with an impressed "CKAW." Creating these red-glazed vases was expensive, and even though they received critical acclaim, the company declared bankruptcy in 1889.

Recapitalized by a circle of Boston art patrons in 1891, Hugh started the Chelsea Pottery U.S., which produced gray crackle-glazed dinnerware with cobalt-blue decorations, the rabbit pattern being the most popular.

The business moved to new facilities in Dedham, Mass., and began production in 1896 under the name Dedham Pottery. Hugh's son and grandson operated the business until it closed in 1943, by which time between 50 and 80 patterns had been produced.

The following marks help determine the approximate age of items:
- "Chelsea Keramic Art Works Robertson and Sons," impressed, 1874-1880.
- "CKAW," impressed, 1875-1889.
- "CPUS," impressed in a cloverleaf, 1891-1895.
- Foreshortened rabbit only, impressed, 1894-1896.
- Conventional rabbit with "Dedham Pottery" in square blue-stamped mark along with one impressed foreshortened rabbit, 1896-1928.
- Blue rabbit stamped mark, "reg. stamp" beneath, along with two impressed foreshortened rabbit marks, 1929-1943.

Dedham Pottery Tri-Color "Rabbit" pattern plate. Painted in medium to dark blue with a border of crouching rabbits alternating with rare raised green decorated foliage. Impressed with "CPUS" mark (Chelsea Pottery US, circa 1881-1895). 8 5/8" diameter. **$8,190**

James D. Julia Auctioneers

James D. Julia Auctioneers

Dedham Pottery pitcher, eggcup and creamer. Including a No. 14-size Rabbit pattern pitcher (6 1/2" h.) in the design of a No. 2 (with single blue line above rabbit band), a single eggcup in Elephant and Baby pattern (2 1/2" h.), and a Style of 1850 pattern pitcher with fluted shaped sides and leaf-tip handle (5" h.). Nominal glazing defects. **$1,404 all**

James D. Julia Auctioneers

Two Dedham Pottery "No. 2" sugar bowls. The first in Elephant and Baby pattern, the second in Elephant pattern. Each with lid and decorated with a dark blue border of striding elephants. Both with "DEDHAM POTTERY REGISTERED" rabbit mark in under-glaze blue. Each 3 1/2" overall h. x 4 1/4" diameter. **$1,380 both**

Six Dedham Pottery butter plates. Consisting of two Duck plates, one Horse Chestnut plate, one Iris plate, one Magnolia plate, and one Pond Lily plate. Four with impressed rabbit marks, and all with "DEDHAM POTTERY" rabbit marks in under-glaze blue. Average diameter 6". Iris plate with worn glazing and minor discoloration, the Pond Lily with rim chips, glazing loss, and wear. **$300 all**

Door Pottery

Door Pottery of Madison, Wis., was founded by Scott Draves in 2001, creating wares in the Arts & Crafts tradition.

Door Pottery vase with geese in the style of Paul Revere/SEG pottery in matte green from 2004. Retired motif. Marked "Door," Scott Draves' name and Meyer. Mint. 7 1/4" x 8 1/4". **$276**

Belhorn Auction Services LLC

Fiesta

The Homer Laughlin China Company originated with a two-kiln pottery on the banks of the Ohio River in East Liverpool, Ohio. Built in 1873-'74 by Homer Laughlin and his brother, Shakespeare, the firm was first known as the Ohio Valley Pottery, and later Laughlin Bros. Pottery. It was one of the first white-ware plants in the country.

After a tentative beginning, the company was awarded a prize for having the best white-ware at the 1876 Centennial Exposition in Philadelphia.

Three years later, Shakespeare sold his interest in the business to Homer, who continued on until 1897. At that time, Homer Laughlin sold his interest in the newly incorporated firm to a group of investors, including Charles, Louis, and Marcus Aaron and the company bookkeeper, William E. Wells.

Under new ownership in 1907, the headquarters and a new 30-kiln plant were built across the Ohio River in Newell, West Virginia, the present manufacturing and headquarters location.

In the 1920s, two additions to the Homer Laughlin staff set the stage for the company's greatest success: the Fiesta line.

Dr. Albert V. Bleininger was hired in 1920. A scientist, author, and educator, he oversaw the conversion from bottle kilns to the more efficient tunnel kilns.

In 1927, the company hired designer Frederick Hurten Rhead, a member of a distinguished family of English ceramists. Having previously worked at Weller Pottery and Roseville Pottery, Rhead began to develop the artistic quality of the company's wares, and to experiment with shapes and glazes. In 1935, this work culminated in his designs for the Fiesta line.

For more information on Fiesta, see *Warman's Fiesta Identification and Price Guide* by *Glen Victorey*.

Fiesta Colors

From 1936 to 1972, Fiesta was produced in 14 colors (other than special promotions). These colors are usually divided into the "original colors" of cobalt blue, light green, ivory, red, turquoise, and yellow (cobalt blue, light green, red, and yellow only on the Kitchen Kraft line, introduced in 1939); the "1950s colors" of chartreuse, forest green, gray, and rose (introduced in 1951); medium green (introduced in 1959); plus the later additions of Casuals, Amberstone, Fiesta Ironstone, and Casualstone ("Coventry") in antique gold, mango red, and turf green; and the striped, decal, and Lustre pieces. No Fiesta was produced from 1973 to 1985. The colors that make up the "original" and "1950s" groups are sometimes referred to as "the standard 11."

In many pieces, medium green is the hardest to find and the most expensive Fiesta color.

Fiesta Colors and Years of Production to 1972

Antique Gold—dark butterscotch...............(1969-1972)
Chartreuse—yellowish green...............(1951-1959)
Cobalt Blue—dark or "royal" blue...............(1936-1951)
Forest Green—dark "hunter" green...............(1951-1959)
Gray—light or ash gray...............(1951-1959)

Green—often called light green when comparing it to other green glazes; also called "Original" green..(1936-1951)
Ivory—creamy, slightly yellowed...(1936-1951)
Mango Red—same as original red ....(1970-1972)
Medium Green—bright rich green ....(1959-1969)
Red—reddish orange ....(1936-1944 and 1959-1972)
Rose—dusty, dark rose...(1951-1959)
Turf Green—olive...(1969-1972)
Turquoise—sky blue, like the stone...(1937-1969)
Yellow—golden yellow..(1936-1969)

Ashtray in red. **$65-$72**

Covered onion soup bowl in cobalt blue. **$680-$739**

Cream soup cup in gray. **$61-$72**

11 3/4" fruit bowl in yellow. **$280-$315**

Footed salad bowl in yellow. **$375-$395**

Individual salad bowl in turquoise. **$89-$95**

Dessert bowl in rose. **$45-$55**

#1 mixing bowl in red, **$249-$295**, with an ivory lid, **$875-$1,000**.

#5 mixing bowl in ivory. **$225-$265**

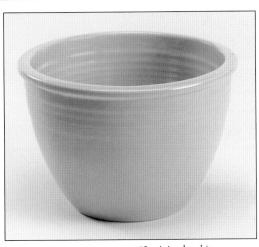

#2 mixing bowl in yellow. **$115-$140**

#3 mixing bowl, **$138-$165**, and lid in cobalt blue, **$900-$1,100**.

#4 mixing bowl in turquoise. **$130-$157**

#7 mixing bowl in light green. **$449-/$589**

#6 mixing bowl in red. **$282-$327**

Very rare bowl lids in red, **$900-$1,100**, *light green,* **$800-$900**, *and yellow,* **$800-$900**.

9 1/2" nappy in ivory. **$69-$71**

Bulb candleholder in cobalt blue. **$115-$125/pair**

Tripod candleholders in cobalt blue, **$575-$630/pair,** *and red,* **$635-$699/pair.**

Carafe in light green. **$275-$295**

Coffeepot in cobalt blue. **$238-$270**

Demitasse coffeepot in light green. **$475-$525**

Sweets comport in cobalt blue. **$85-$95**

Comport in red. **$190-$200**

Ring-handle creamer and covered sugar bowl in medium green. **$120-$135** *for the creamer and* **$195-$215** *for the sugar bowl.*

Stick-handle creamer in red. **$65-$72.**

Demitasse cup and saucer in yellow. **$60-$79/set**

Teacup and saucer in rose. **$42-$51/set**

Eggcup in ivory. **$66-$72**

Covered sugar in turquoise. **$49-$58**

Tom & Jerry mug in medium green. **$125-$140**

Marmalade jar in ivory. **$350-$370**

Three mustards in yellow, **$270-$295**, *light green,* **$260-$280**, *and turquoise,* **$295-$320**.

Ice pitcher in yellow. **$135-$145**

10" plate in medium green. **$140-$165**

Disk water pitcher in medium green. **$1,500-$1,600**

Two-pint jug in chartreuse. **$130-$140**

6" plate in gray. **$10-$11**

13" chop plate in rose. **$85-$90**

9" plate in red.
$18-$20

*Top and side views of
a cake plate in yellow.*
$1,200-$1,300

10 1/2" compartment plate in red, **$65-$75**, *and 12" compartment plate in light green,* **$58-$65**.

*Medium teapot
in medium green.*
$1,475-$1,595

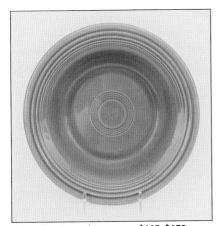

Deep plate in medium green. **$135-$150**

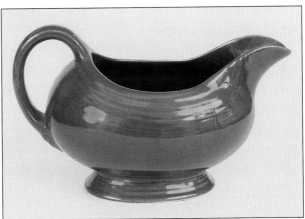

Sauceboat in forest green. **$72-$84**

Oval platter in chartreuse. **$50-$60**

Water tumbler in yellow. **$67-$70**

Shakers in gray. **$48-$52/pair**

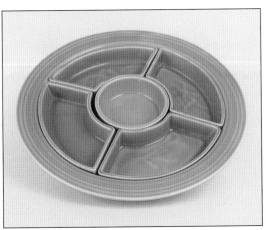

Relish tray and inserts in light green, as it would have come from the factory. **$295-$310/set**

Tidbit tray in ivory, light green, and cobalt blue. **$100-$200**

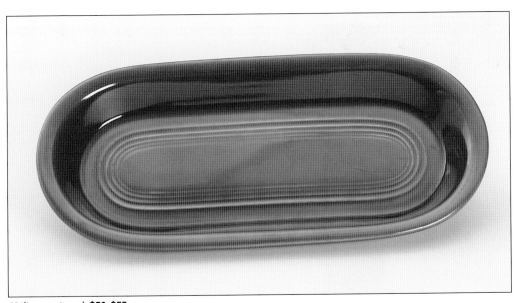

Utility tray in red. **$50-$55**

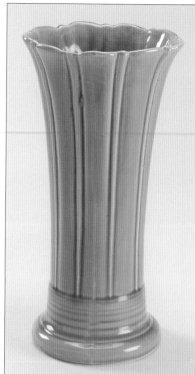

10" vase in light green. **$900-$975**

12" vase in light green. **$1,100-$1,200**

Bud vase in cobalt blue. **$100-$130**

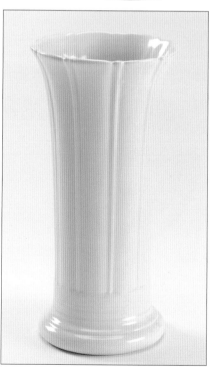

8" vase in ivory. **$740-$780**

Frankoma

John Frank was hired by the University of Oklahoma in 1927 to establish the school's first Ceramic Art Department. In 1933 he started his own business, Frank Potteries. His wife, Grace Lee, suggested that because it was Oklahoma's only commercial pottery, the company name should incorporate both their name and the state's name. The business became Frankoma Potteries, and moved to Sapulpa, a small town just southwest of Tulsa, in 1938. John Frank died in 1973, his wife in 1996. The business was sold in 1991 and is now operated by Joe Ragosta.

Vintage Frankoma squat vase in mottled blue glaze. Marked "Frankoma." Mint. 5" x 6" wide. **$23**

Belhorn Auction Services LLC

Early Frankoma Art Deco jug or pitcher and an Oklahoma National Youth Administration (NYA) cup. Both pieces are marked. Mint. 6 1/2" and 2 1/4". **$126 both**

Belhorn Auction Services LLC

Fulper Pottery Co.

The firm that became Fulper Pottery Co. of Flemington, N.J., originally made stoneware pottery and utilitarian wares beginning in the early 1800s. Fulper made art pottery from about 1909 to 1935.

The company's earliest artware was called the Vase-Kraft line (1910-1915). Its middle period (1915-1925) included some of the earlier shapes, but they also incorporated Oriental forms. Their glazing at this time was less consistent but more diverse. The last period (1925-1935) was characterized by Art Deco forms.

FULPER in a rectangle is known as the "ink mark" and dates from 1910-1915. The second mark, as shown, dates from 1915-1925; it was incised or in black ink. The final mark, FULPER, die-stamped, dates from about 1925 to 1935.

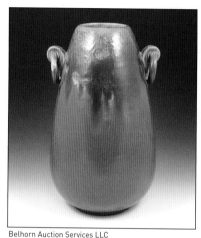

Belhorn Auction Services LLC

Fulper vase in green over rose flambe glaze with ring handles. Marked with vertical oval Fulper ink stamp. Mint. 12 3/4" h. **$450**

Belhorn Auction Services LLC

Fulper handled vase with turquoise over amber glaze treatment. Marked with vertical Fulper mark, incised by hand, couple small factory grinding nicks to the edge of the base. 8 3/4". **$402**

Fulper vase in Famille Rose glaze with four buttresses on a tapered form. Marked with remnants of two paper labels, 1/4" flake to the base. 8". **$241**
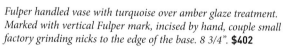
Belhorn Auction Services LLC

Grueby Faience Co.

William Grueby was active in the ceramic industry for several years before he developed his own method of producing matte-glazed pottery and founded the Grueby Faience Co. of Boston in 1897.

The art pottery was hand thrown in natural shapes, hand molded and hand tooled. A variety of colored glazes, singly or in combinations, was produced, but green was the most popular. In 1908, the firm was divided into the Grueby Pottery Co. and the Grueby Faience and Tile Co. The Grueby Faience and Tile Co. made art tile until 1917, although its pottery production was phased out about 1910.

Rago Arts and Auction Center

Grueby gourd-shaped vase with tooled and applied full-height ribbed leaves, covered in a superior feathered matte green glaze. (Extremely rare, one of Grueby's most important forms.) Professional restoration to small chip at rim and to a couple of leaf tips, several minor glaze nicks to leaf edges. Stamped GRUEBY. 9 1/4" h. **$84,000**

Grueby large matte green vase with yellow blossoms, glaze run on buds, a few manganese glaze lines, circular Faience stamp, 20 and green triangle, 13" x 8". **$5,185**

Rago Arts and Auction Center

Nan Hamilton

Potter Nan Hamilton founded Mudville Pottery in 1974 in Cambridge, Mass. It is now located in Somerville, Mass. Hamilton creates one-of-a-kind pieces, often with animal themes, especially Airedale motifs.

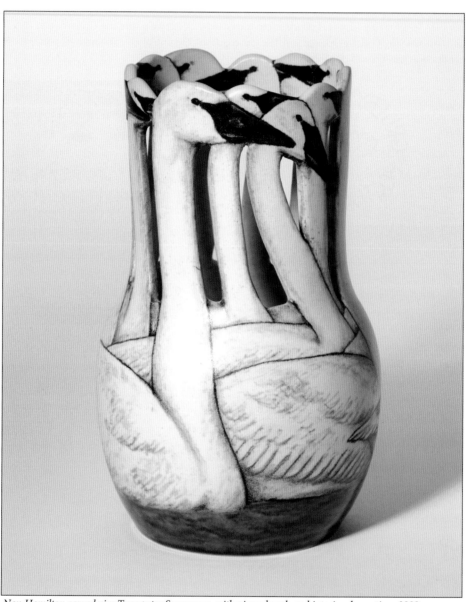

Nan Hamilton carved-rim Trumpeter Swan vase, with pierced neck and interior decoration, 2008, 7" x 4 1/2", marked on the bottom with stylized "Nh". **$600+**

Hampshire Pottery Co.

In 1871, James S. Taft founded the Hampshire Pottery Co. in Keene, N.H. Production began with redware and stoneware, followed by majolica in 1879.

Until World War I, the factory made an extensive line of utilitarian and artware, including souvenir items. After the war, the firm resumed operations, but made only hotel dinnerware and tiles. The company was dissolved in 1923.

Early Hampshire squat vase in dark brown under a dark orange glaze. A souvenir piece, remnants of Portsmouth, N.H., in gold leaf remain. Marked "JST & CO KEENE NH," 1 5/8" x 4 1/4". **$110**

Belhorn Auction Services LLC

Rago Arts and Auction Center

Hampshire vases (two) in fine blue and green frothy glazes. Both marked, 5 1/2" and 8 1/2". **$1,140 pair**

Arts & Crafts-style Hampshire vase in a matte blue glaze with feathered effect at the top of the vase. Marked with impressed "Hampshire Pottery 33" with an M in a circle and numbers in blue. Mint, 6 1/2". **$575**

Belhorn Auction Services LLC

Hull Pottery Co.

In 1905, Addis E. Hull purchased the Acme Pottery Co. of Crooksville, Ohio. In 1917, the A.E. Hull Pottery Co. began making art pottery, novelties, stoneware and kitchenware, later including the famous Little Red Riding Hood line. Most items had a matte finish, with shades of pink and blue or brown predominating.

After a flood and fire in 1950, the factory reopened in 1952 as the Hull Pottery Co. New pieces, mostly with a glossy finish, were produced. The firm closed in 1985.

Pre-1950 vases are marked "Hull USA" or "Hull Art USA" on the bottom. Many also retain their paper labels. Post-1950 pieces are marked "Hull" in large script or "HULL" in block letters.

Each pattern has a distinctive letter or number, e.g., Wildflower has a "W" and a number; Water Lily, "L" and number; Poppy, numbers in the 600s; Orchid, in the 300s. Early stoneware pieces are marked with an "H."

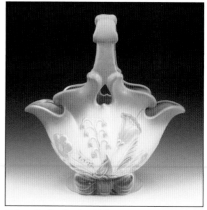

Belhorn Auction Services LLC

Hull Bow Knot basket in pink and blue. Marked USA Hull Art B-29-12". Mint. 11 3/4" h x 11" w. **$950**

Belhorn Auction Services LLC

Hull Ebb Tide E-5 fish basket in pink and turquoise. Unmarked. Mint. 6 5/8" h x 9 1/8" w. **$550**

Belhorn Auction Services LLC

Hull Continental #55 basket in mountain blue. Marked Hull USA 55. Mint. 12 3/8" h. **$325**

Belhorn Auction Services LLC

Hull Little Red Riding Hood baby feeding dish, exceptionally rare. Unmarked. 8" w x 4 3/4" h. **$1,400**

Warren MacKenzie

Warren MacKenzie (b. 1924) is a craft potter living outside Stillwater, Minn. MacKenzie studied with Bernard Leach from 1949 to 1952. His simple, wheel-thrown functional pottery is heavily influenced by the oriental aesthetic of Shoji Hamada and Kanjiro Kawai. He taught at the University of Minnesota beginning in 1952, and is now a professor emeritus.

Warren MacKenzie trumpet vase with dome top, made in 2000, unsigned, 10". **$200+**

Marblehead

This hand-thrown pottery was first made in 1905 as part of a therapeutic program introduced by Dr. J. Hall for the patients confined to a sanitarium located in Marblehead, Mass. In 1916, production was removed from the hospital to another site. The factory continued under the directorship of Arthur E. Baggs until it closed in 1936. Most pieces found today are glazed with a smooth, porous, even finish in a single color. The most desirable pieces have a conventional design with one or more subordinate colors.

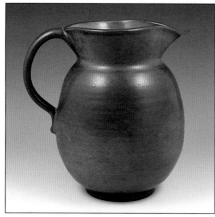

Belhorn Auction Services LLC

Marblehead hand-thrown pitcher signed by Arthur E. Baggs from 1936. Glazed in dark matte blue on the exterior with a lighter interior. Signed AEB by hand in script with the date. Mint, 7 3/4". **$550**

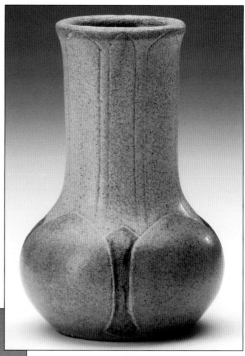

Rago Arts and Auction Center

Marblehead early bulbous vase by Arthur Baggs incised with a stylized design in blue-grays and pale yellow. Small glaze flake to rim. Incised M with seagull, AB. 4 3/4" x 3 1/4". **$45,000**

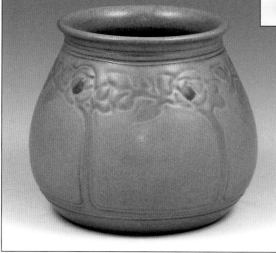

Marblehead vase with Arts & Crafts flower and tree decoration. Finished in four colors with a blue semi-gloss interior. Marked with impressed ship mark. Invisible restoration to a rim chip, 3 1/2". **$1,092**

Belhorn Auction Services LLC

McCoy

The first McCoy with clay under his fingernails was W. Nelson McCoy. With his uncle, W.F. McCoy, he founded a pottery works in Putnam, Ohio, in 1848, making stoneware crocks and jugs.

That same year, W. Nelson's son, James W., was born in Zanesville, Ohio. James established the J.W. McCoy Pottery Co. in Roseville, Ohio, in the fall of 1899. The J.W. McCoy plant was destroyed by fire in 1903 and was rebuilt two years later.

It was at this time that the first examples of Loy-Nel-Art wares were produced. The line's distinctive title came from the names of James McCoy's three sons, Lloyd, Nelson, and Arthur. Like other "standard" glazed pieces produced at this time by several Ohio potteries, Loy-Nel-Art has a glossy finish on a dark brown-black body, but Loy-Nel-Art featured a splash of green color on the front and a burnt-orange splash on the back.

George Brush became general manager of J.W. McCoy Pottery Co. in 1909. The company became Brush-McCoy Pottery Co. in 1911, and in 1925 the name was shortened to Brush Pottery Co. This firm remained in business until 1982.

W.F. McCoy 1-1/2-gallon crock, salt glaze with stenciled ink lettering: "W.F. McCoy Wholesale Dealer in Stoneware–Zanesville, O.," late 1800s, 9-1/4" h. **$1,000-$1,200**

Separately, in 1910, Nelson McCoy Sr. founded the Nelson McCoy Sanitary and Stoneware Co., also in Roseville. By the early 1930s, production had shifted from utilitarian wares to art pottery, and the company name was changed to Nelson McCoy Pottery.

Designer Sydney Cope was hired in 1934, and was joined by his son, Leslie, in 1936. The Copes' influence on McCoy wares continued until Sydney's death in 1966. That same year, Leslie opened a gallery devoted to his family's design heritage and featuring his own original art.

Nelson McCoy Sr. died in 1945, and was succeeded as company president by his nephew, Nelson McCoy Melick.

A fire destroyed the plant in 1950, but company officials—including Nelson McCoy Jr., then 29—decided to rebuild, and the new Nelson McCoy Pottery Co. was up and running in just six months.

Nelson Melick died in 1954. Nelson Jr. became company president, and oversaw the company's continued growth. In 1967, the operation was sold to entrepreneur David Chase. At this time, the words "Mt. Clemens Pottery" were added to the company marks. In 1974, Chase sold the company to Lancaster Colony Corp., and the company marks included a stylized "LCC" logo. Nelson Jr. and his wife, Billie, who had served as a products supervisor, left the company in 1981.

In 1985, the company was sold again, this time to Designer Accents. The McCoy pottery factory closed in 1990.

For more information on McCoy pottery, see *Warman's McCoy Pottery*, 2nd edition, by Mark F. Moran.

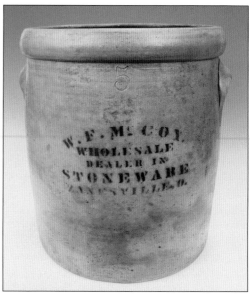

Leaves and Berries jardinière and pedestal in matte brown and green; jardinière, 7 1/2" diameter; pedestal, 6-3/4" h. **$225-$275/pair**

W.F. McCoy 5-gallon crock, salt glaze with stenciled ink lettering: "W.F. McCoy Wholesale Dealer in Stoneware–Zanesville, O.," with impressed "5," late 1800s, 13" h. **$1,200-$1,400 in mint condition**

Nelson McCoy Sanitary Stoneware jugs, 1910-20s, shield with M mark, 2- to 6-gallon sizes. **$75-$125, depending on size**

Three brown-top miniatures: plain crock, pickling crock, and jug, range from 3" to 3 3/4" h. **$175-$225 each**

Two jardinières with applied leaves and berries, late 1940s, McCoy USA mark, 7 1/2" h. **$200-$250 each**

Fish in Net jardinière in rare gray-green, late 1950s, McCoy mark, also found in brown, 7 1/2" h. **$250-$300**

Ivy jardinière in brown and green, early 1950s, unmarked, also found in a brighter glossy tan and green with matching pedestal, 8" h. **$350-$450**

Two sizes of the batter bowl with spoon rest in glossy green, late 1920s, shield mark #3, diameters without spouts and handles, 7 1/2", **$175-$225***; 9 1/2",* **$275-$325.**

Ring ware hanging salt box and covered jar (cheese or butter), both in glossy green, 1920s, shield mark "M." Saltbox, 6" h, **$250-$300***; covered jar, 5" h,* **$175-$200.**

Ring ware covered butter or cheese crock, 1920s, shield mark "M." **$90-$110**

Mixing bowl in the Wave or Sunrise pattern, size No. 7, from a set of six ranging in size from 5" to 11" diameter, 1920s, square bottom, also found in yellow and burgundy; and three 5" mixing bowls in green, yellow, and burgundy. Complete set, about **$1,200**; *individual sizes range from* **$175-$250 each.**

Raspberries and Leaves mixing bowl in glossy white, 1930s, unmarked, 9" diameter. **$200-$225**

Complete set of pink and blue banded nesting mixing bowls, 1930s, old mark, 4 1/2"-11 1/2" diameter, smallest bowls are hardest to find and most expensive. **$400-$500 set**

Cook-Serve Ware covered casserole and stickhandle creamer, late 1940s, McCoy mark; casserole, **$35-$40**; creamer, **$10-$15.**

Singing Bird planter in matte white, 1940s, USA mark, found in other colors, 4 1/2" h, **$30-$40.** Also found in 6 3/4" size.

Two Islander Line reamers in yellow and white, early 1980s. **$50-$60 each**

Five sizes of Stone Craft mixing bowls (called pink and blue) ranging in diameter from 7" to 14" (also a 5" size), mid-1970s, McCoy LCC mark. **$225-$250 for complete set**

Pine Cone planter, mid-1940s, McCoy USA mark, 8" wide, rare, **$500-$600.** (A slightly larger planter in rust glaze, **$1,800-$2,000**)

Small Stretch Lion in rare cobalt blue, 1940s, unmarked, 4" h. **$250-$300**

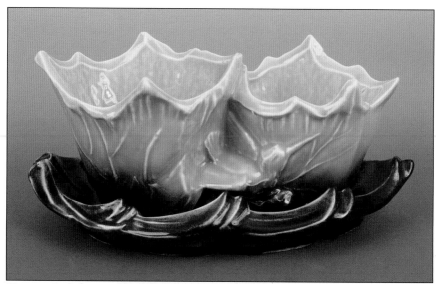

Humming Bird planter in blue, late 1940s, McCoy USA mark, 10 1/2" w. **$125-$150**

Butterfly hanging basket planter in non-production dark green glaze, early 1940s, NM mark; as shown, **$500-$600***; in pastel colors,* **$225-$250.**

Butterfly Line window box in matte aqua, 1940s, unmarked, hard to find this size, 9 1/4" l, **$150-$175***; if marked,* **$250.**

J.W. McCoy Olympia vase, with rare cream-drip glaze overflow, early 1900s, marked 28, 5 1/4" h. **$195-$225**

Lizard vase, stoneware, 1930s, unmarked, 9" h. **$350-$450**

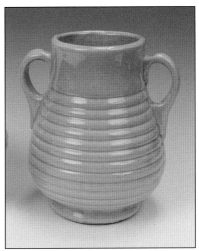

From left: "V" vase in glossy green glaze, mid-1920s, V2 mark, this style also found without handles, 9" h, **$90-$110.** *"Number 50" vase in glossy burgundy, 1930s, unmarked, 9" h,* **$100-$125**.

Ring ware vase, 1920s, unmarked, 9 1/4" h. **$100-$125**

Two Hourglass vases in matte yellow and pink, 1930s, unmarked, 8" h. **$90-$110 each**

Blossomtime handled vase with cobalt flowers (rare), 1940s, raised McCoy mark, 6 1/2" h. **$125+**

Leaves and Berries urn-form vase in matte white with small handles and unusual interior ring pattern, hard to find form, stoneware, 1930s, 8" h. **$300-$350**

Three Flower form wall pockets, late 1940s, unmarked, 6" h; the blue and coral are common colors, **$40-$50**; *the center pocket, with under-glaze decoration, is* **$175-$225.**

Three Flower form wall pockets, late 1940s, unmarked, 6" h; the blue and coral are common colors, **$40-$50**; *the center pocket, with under-glaze decoration, is* **$175-$225.**

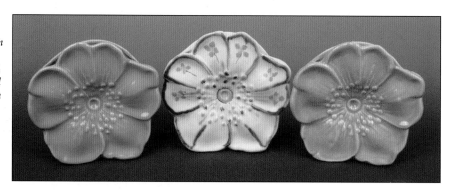

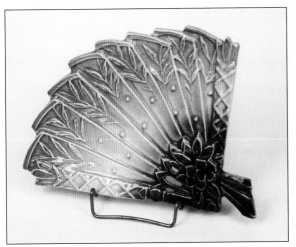

Fan wall pocket with crisp mold and unusual multicolor glaze, 1950s, McCoy USA mark, also signed by Nelson McCoy, 8 1/2" w; two hanging holes and no brace; no other example with these variations is known. **$5,000+**

Cuckoo Clock wall pocket in gold trim (comes with both Roman and Arabic numerals, and in a range of colors), 1950s, McCoy mark, 8" h without weights. **$200-$225**

Matthew Metz

Matthew Metz (b. 1961) is a ceramic artist living and working in Alfred, N.Y. His pots are created from porcelain or a porcelainous clay body and salt glazed. His influences include Asian pottery traditions, Greek and Roman pots, early American decorative arts (quilts, face jugs) and other folk traditions. Metz uses a variety of techniques in developing the surfaces of his pots, including carving, drawing, and "sprigging."

Matthew Metz platter with carved details of face looking out of trees, late 1990s, signed on bottom, 14" diameter. **$1,200+**

Matthew Metz bowl with carved details of plant growing out of pot, circa 2000, signed on bottom, 9" diameter. **$200+**

Muncie Pottery

Muncie Pottery started production of art pottery in 1919 as the Muncie Clay Products Co. This Indiana firm used a variety of glazes ranging from quality matte glaze to high gloss, drip glazes. Some of the most sought-after Muncie Pottery examples include the Ruba Rombic and Spanish lines. Both of these scarce patterns were designed by Reuben Haley.

Muncie Pottery can be found both marked and unmarked. Marked examples are usually stamped "Muncie" and/or marked with molder/finisher marks. These marks include a combination of letters (A, B, D, E, K, and M) and numbers (I, II, 2, 3, 4 and 5) such as 2-B, D-3, etc. Muncie went out of business in 1939.

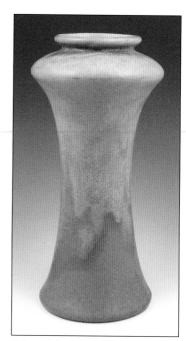

Belhorn Auction Services LLC

Muncie #U-2 Matte Green over Rose vase. Marked with an incised 2B. Mint with some minor factory grinding nicks to the edge of the base, 11 5/8". **$121**

Belhorn Auction Services LLC

Muncie handled vase in Peachskin. Marked D-3. Mint with a couple of small factory grinding nicks to the base. 6 7/8". **$57**

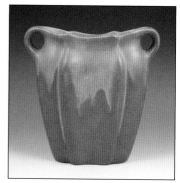

Belhorn Auction Services LLC

Muncie #192 handled vase in Matte Green over Pumpkin glaze. Marked MUNCIE with an incised IA and 192-9 in black crayon. Mint, 9" x 9". **$71**

Newcomb College

The Sophie Newcomb Memorial College, an adjunct of Tulane University in New Orleans, was originated as a school to train local women in the decorative arts. While metalworking, painting and embroidery were among the classes taught, the production of handcrafted art pottery remains its most popular and collectible pursuit.

Pottery was made by the Newcomb women for nearly 50 years, with earlier work being the rarest and most valuable. This is characterized by glossy finishes and broad, flat-painted and modeled designs. More common, though still quite valuable, are the matte-glaze pieces, often depicting bayou scenes and native flora. All bear the impressed NC mark.

Rago Arts and Auction Center

Newcomb College transitional chocolate set by Ora Reams, complete with six cups and saucers, carved with yellow daisies. Small chip to edge of two saucers, tight opposing lines to one cup. Chocolate pot marked NC/JM/B/ORA REAMS 1913/FH2. Pot: 10 1/2" x 6". **$15,600**

Newcomb College cabinet vase with Art Nouveau decoration from 1925 by Sadie Irvine (artist) and Joseph Meyer (potter). Marked with NC logo, OV28 and JM and SI (both faint), short and light glaze scratch, 3 1/2". **$1,265**

Newcomb College bulbous vase by Corinna Luria with ring handles in a stylized geometric design (rare form). Bruise to rim, firing line to shoulder. Marked NC/C.L./ KD18/192. 6" x 5". **$3,240**

Rago Arts and Auction Center

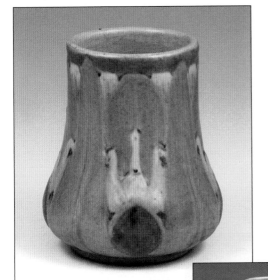

North Dakota School of Mines

The North Dakota School of Mines was established in 1890. Earle J. Babcock, a chemistry instructor, was impressed with the high purity level of North Dakota potter's clay. He tried to interest commercial potteries in the North Dakota clay, but had limited success.

In 1910, Babcock persuaded the school to establish a ceramics department. Margaret Cable, who studied under Charles Binns and Frederick H. Rhead, was appointed head. She remained until her retirement in 1949.

Decorative emphasis was placed on native themes, including flowers and animals. Art Nouveau, Art Deco and fairly plain pieces were made.

The pottery is often marked with a cobalt blue under-glaze circle of the words "University of North Dakota/Grand Forks, N.D./Made at School of Mines/N.D. Clay." Some early pieces are marked only "U.N.D." or "U.N.D./Grand Forks, N.D." Most pieces are numbered (they can be dated from University records) and signed by both the instructor and student. Cable-signed pieces are the most desirable.

North Dakota School of Mines fine bulbous vase by Margaret Cable with cutback daffodils in light brown on a deep brown ground. Circular ink mark/M. Cable/273. 8" x 5 1/2". **$3,120**

Rago Arts and Auction Center

Belhorn Auction Services LLC

UND School of Mines vase with cutout leaves, finished in a marbleized brown gloss glaze. Marked with UND circular stamp and "Minn" incised by the artist, 5 1/4" x 3 1/4". **$218**

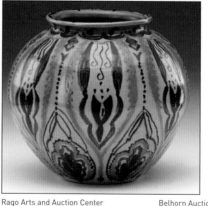

Rago Arts and Auction Center

North Dakota School of Mines bulbous vase painted in the Persian style in rich jewel tones. Indigo stamp, artist's cipher. 5" x 5 1/2". **$600**

Belhorn Auction Services LLC

UND School of Mines lamp base in blue matte from 1929. Marked with circular ink stamp and "Lila M. Argue Jan. 1929" (incised). There is a kiln kiss to the base, otherwise mint. The cap has a shallow flake to the underside, 10 3/4". **$99**

George E. Ohr

Ohr pottery was produced by George E. Ohr in Biloxi, Miss. There is a discrepancy as to when he actually established his pottery; some say 1878, but Ohr's autobiography indicates 1883. In 1884, Ohr exhibited 600 pieces of his work, suggesting that he had been a potter for some time.

Ohr's techniques included twisting, crushing, folding, denting and crinkling thin-walled clay into odd, grotesque and sometimes graceful forms. His later pieces were often left unglazed.

In 1906, Ohr closed the pottery and stored more than 6,000 pieces as a legacy to his family. The entire collection remained in storage until it was rediscovered in 1972.

Today, Ohr is recognized as one of the leaders in the American art-pottery movement.

Much of Ohr's early work was signed with an impressed stamp including his name and location in block letters. His later work was often marked with the flowing script designation "G. E. Ohr."

G.E. OHR, BILOXI.

George Ohr oversized teapot with an ear-shaped handle and serpentine spout on a dimpled body, covered in green and brown flambe glaze with gunmetal sponging. Small flat chip at rim, lid is original but not a match, as customary. (When Ohr's pottery was stored in 1907, the lids were packed separately from the teapots. As a result, perhaps a third were mismatched. This piece descended directly through Ohr family.) Stamped G. E. OHR Biloxi, Miss, twice. 7 1/4" x 8". **$10,800**

Rago Arts and Auction Center

Rago Arts and Auction Center

George Ohr squat vessel in raspberry volcanic glaze, a couple minor flakes, stamped G.E. OHR, Biloxi, Miss., 2 1/4" x 4". **$5,795**

Rago Arts and Auction Center

George Ohr vase with pinched top, covered in green speckled mustard glaze. Stamped GO. E. OHR BILOXI, MISS. 4" x 4 1/2". **$6,600**

Overbeck Pottery

Four Overbeck sisters – Margaret, Hannah, Elizabeth and Mary Frances – established the Overbeck Pottery in their Cambridge City, Ind., home in 1911. Production ended with the death of Mary Frances in 1955.

Overbeck early vase by Hannah and Elizabeth Overbeck with three panels carved and painted with owls on branches, in teals and purple against a brown ground. (A rare and early example decorated in the Arts & Crafts style, as opposed to the Art Deco influence more often seen.) Carved mark, OBK E H, 7 1/2" x 4". **$19,200**

Rago Arts and Auction Center

Overbeck vase incised with stylized figures of children amidst red hollyhock blossoms, on a matte mustard ground. (An important piece, pictured in The Chronicle of Overbeck Pottery *by Kathleen Postle, 1978, plate XXVIII.) Restoration to rim chip. Incised OBK F with paper label possibly covering E. 10 1/2" x 7".* **$72,000**

Rago Arts and Auction Center

Owens Pottery

J.B. Owens began making pottery in 1885 near Roseville, Ohio. In 1891, he built a plant in Zanesville and in 1897 began producing art pottery. After 1907, most of the firm's production centered on tiles.

Owens Pottery, employing many of the same artists and designs as its two cross-town rivals, Roseville and Weller, can appear similar to that of its competitors, e.g., Utopian (brown glaze), Lotus (light glaze) and Aqua Verde (green glaze).

There were a few techniques used exclusively at Owens. These included Red Flame ware (slip decoration under a high red glaze) and Mission (over-glaze, slip decorations in mineral colors) depicting Spanish Missions. Other specialties included Opalesce (semi-gloss designs in luster gold and orange) and Coralene (small beads affixed to the surface of the decorated vases).

Owens Matte Utopian jardiniere with tulip decoration and "pie crust" rim. Unmarked. Mint, 8" x 9 1/2". **$71**

Owens, matte blue Utopian jardiniere with slip-decorated tulips in white, unmarked. Mint. 7 5/8" h x 9 3/4" w. **$300**

Belhorn Auction Services LLC

Peters & Reed

J.D. Peters and Adam Reed founded their pottery in South Zanesville, Ohio, in 1900. Common flowerpots, jardiniéres and cooking wares comprised the majority of their early output. Occasionally, art pottery was attempted, but it was not until 1912 that their Moss Aztec line was introduced and widely accepted. Other art wares include Chromal, Landsun, Montene, Pereco and Persian.

Peters retired in 1921 and Reed changed the name of the firm to Zane Pottery Co.

Marked pieces of Peters & Reed pottery are extremely rare.

Belhorn Auction Services LLC

Peters & Reed marbleized vase in green, blue and yellow tones. Unmarked. There is a factory kiln kiss to the side of the vase and scratches to the glaze, 8 3/4". **$103**

Rago Arts and Auction Center

Peters & Reed Landsun vase finely decorated with a farm scene and cottage. Short under-glaze line to rim. Unmarked. 7 1/2" x 4". **$600**

Peters & Reed Shadow Ware pumpkin vase in blue and green drip over brownish orange. Mint, 8". **$178**

Belhorn Auction Services LLC

Red Wing Pottery

Various potteries operated in Red Wing, Minnesota, from 1868, the most successful being the Red Wing Stoneware Co., organized in 1877. Merged with other local potteries through the years, it became known as Red Wing Union Stoneware Co. in 1906 and was one of the largest producers of utilitarian stoneware items in the United States.

After a decline in the popularity of stoneware products, an art pottery line was introduced to compensate for the loss. This was reflected in a new name for the company, Red Wing Potteries, Inc., in 1936. Stoneware production ceased entirely in 1947, but vases, planters, cookie jars, and dinnerware of art pottery quality continued in production until 1967, when the pottery ceased operation altogether.

For more information on Red Wing pottery, see *Warman's Red Wing Pottery* by Mark F. Moran.

Transitional crocks with hand-lettered gallon markings, two with stamped birch leaves called "elephant ear" leaves. **$300-$1,000 each**

Close-up of the hand-decorated butterfly and flower on a 20-gallon salt-glaze crock. **$2,000-$2,500 signed**

One-of-a-kind 20-gallon stoneware crock/cooler with cover, jar form, but with bunghole, circa 1908. **No established value**

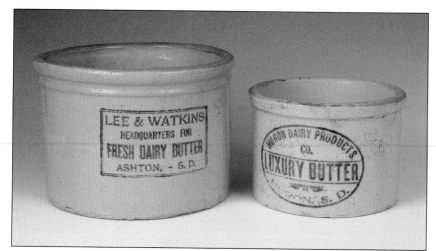

*White stoneware
advertising crocks,
5" and 3 3/4" tall,
unmarked.*
$900-$1,200 each

*Blue and white covered
butter crock in a daisy
pattern, left, 4 1/2" tall
with lid, 5 1/2" diameter.*
$400+
*Right, blue and white
bail-handle covered
butter crock with
advertising, 5 1/2" tall
without handle.* **$500+**

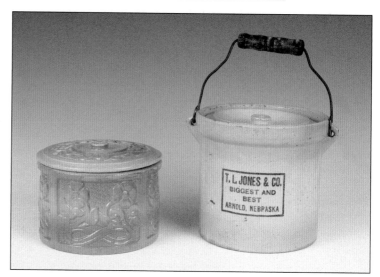

*White stoneware bail-
handle butter crock with
advertising (cover missing),
left, 7 1/4" tall without
handle, unmarked.* **$400+**
*Right, sponge-decorated
butter crock with lid, 7"
tall, unmarked.* **$300+**

One-gallon salt-glaze crock circa 1890, 8" tall, marked on bottom, "Minnesota Stoneware Co. Red Wing, Minn." Second photo shows rare one-gallon "petal" cover with Albany slip, 8" diameter. Crock, **$70+**; lid, **$400**

Two-gallon salt-glaze crock with strong cobalt decoration of "target with tail," circa 1890, marked on bottom, "Minnesota Stoneware Co. Red Wing, Minn." Second photo shows "petal" lid with glaze drippings known as "turkey droppings." Crock, **$175+**; lid, **$300**

Two-gallon crock with "elephant ears" stamp, and also with rare conjoined "MSW Co." stamp; raised bottom mark, "Minnesota Stoneware Co. Red Wing, Minn.," with correct petal lid impressed with a "2," 11 1/2" tall with lid. **$3,500-$4,000**

Two-gallon crock with "elephant ears" stamp and rare single-line "Minn. Stoneware Co." mark; raised bottom mark, "Minnesota Stoneware Co. Red Wing, Minn.," with correct petal lid impressed with a "2," 11 1/2" tall with lid. **$3,000-$3,500**

Two-gallon white stoneware crock with tilted birch leaves, 10" tall, impressed mark, "Minnesota Stoneware Co. Red Wing, Minn." **$70-$90**

Two-gallon crock with tilted birch leaves and oval stamp with "Minnesota Stoneware Company" (spelled out, commonly found as "Co."), 12" tall with lid, otherwise unmarked. **$1,500+**

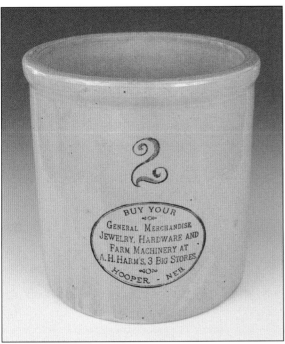

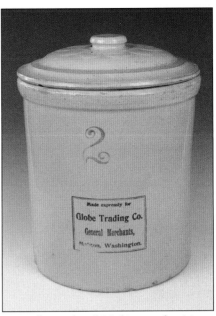

Two-gallon crock with Washington advertising and original lid, 12" tall with lid. **$2,500**

Two-gallon crock with atypical department stores advertising from Hooper, Neb., 9 3/4" tall, otherwise unmarked. **$4,500+**

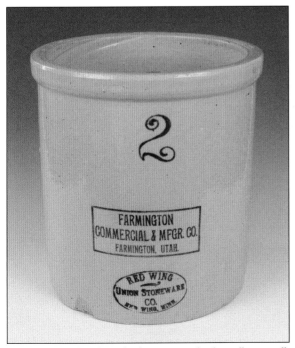

Two-gallon crock with double "elephant ears" stamp, 9 3/4" tall. (Collector tip: With double-stamped stoneware pieces, the proximity of the stamps to each other also determines value. The closer together the stamps, the higher the value.) **$1,500+**

Two-gallon crock with Utah advertising, with what collectors call the "ski oval," named for the mark between Red Wing and Union Stoneware, 10 1/8" tall. **$2,500+ if perfect**

Three-pound butter crock with Hormel advertising, 4 3/8" tall, soft impressed mark, "Red Wing Stoneware Co." **$2,500+**

Three-gallon white stoneware crock with tilted birch leaves and original lid, and rarely seen "Minnesota Stoneware Company" oval mark, 10 3/4" tall without lid; lid, 11" diameter. **$900+**

Three-gallon salt-glaze crock with cobalt decoration referred to as "double P ribcage" and "target," circa 1890, 10 1/4" tall, with impressed back stamp, "Minnesota Stoneware Co., Red Wing." Second photo shows "petal" lid with Albany slip glaze, 10 1/4" diameter. Crock, **$500+**; lid, **$300**

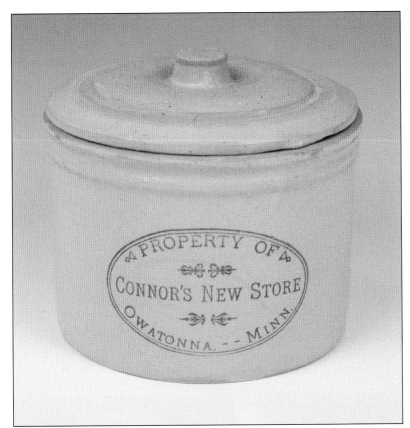

Three-pound butter crock with Owatonna, Minn., advertising, with button lid, 4 1/4" tall without lid, otherwise unmarked. **$2,500+**

Four-gallon salt-glaze crock with strong cobalt decoration of "target with tail," circa 1890, 12" tall. Second photo shows "petal" lid with glaze drippings known as "turkey droppings," 11" diameter. Crock, **$200+***; lid,* **$300**

Four-gallon white stoneware crock with "elephant ears," and original lid, 11 1/2" tall without lid. **$150+**

Five-gallon white stoneware crock with oval and large wing, the most commonly found size for crocks and jugs. **$70+**

Five-gallon crock with 6" wing, no oval, also with double trim line and a stamped "5" on base; base also shows a firing ring from the smaller crock it sat on in the kiln, 13" tall. **$250+**

Transitional five-gallon crock with hand-decorated blue-black number and "bowtie," circa 1900, the glaze on this crock is between white and tan, 13 1/4" tall, unmarked. **$300+**

Eight-gallon transitional zinc-glaze crock with stamped Minnesota oval and hand-decorated birch leaf. **$3,500+**. Twelve-gallon salt-glaze crock with large hand-decorated birch leaf pointing up. **$2,500**

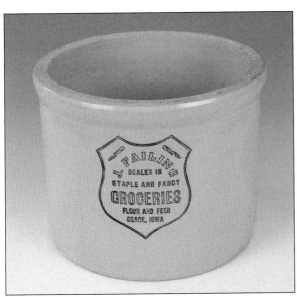

Ten-pound butter crock with Osage, Iowa, advertising, 6 3/4" tall, otherwise unmarked. **$1,500**

Detail of a 10-gallon crock with birch leaves and Nebraska advertising. **$2,800+**

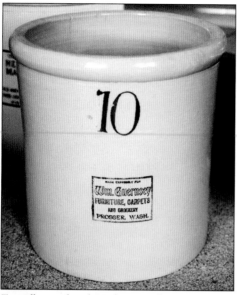

Ten-gallon crock with Washington advertising that includes crockery. (Collector tip: Strange as it may sound, it's unusual to find the word "crockery" on crockery.) **$1,500+ if perfect**

Detail of transitional 10-gallon zinc-glaze crock with hand-decorated leaf and "Union" oval. **$1,000**

Detail of a 10-gallon "double elephant ear" crock. **$3,000**

Fifteen-gallon salt-glaze crock with cobalt decoration of "bowtie" and double leaves, circa 1890, 18 1/2" tall, unmarked. (Collector tip: The leaves seen here are precursors to the stenciled or stamped birch-leaf decoration used on white hand-thrown stoneware made just a few years later.) **$800-$1,000**

White stoneware 20-pound butter crock with hand-decorated numbers, a transitional mark before stamping was regularly used, circa 1900, 8" tall, 11 1/2" diameter, raised mark on bottom, "Minnesota Stoneware Red Wing, Minn." **$800-$1,000**

Detail of 15-gallon crock with Storden, Minn., advertising and large wing. **$3,500+**

White stoneware 20-pound butter crock with 4" wing, 7 1/2" tall, 11 1/2" diameter. **$1,000+**

Twenty-gallon crock detail with double-stamped wing (red over blue), with original lid. **$600+**

Eight souvenir mini jugs commemorating outings, sports rivalries, businesses and communities, each 2 1/2" to 3" tall. **$250+ each**

Stoneware bread crock in glossy green glaze, also found with matte Brushed Ware surface, and in tan; lid missing, 11" tall, 14" diameter, rare. **$2,800+ (as is)**; *with lid,* **$4,000+**

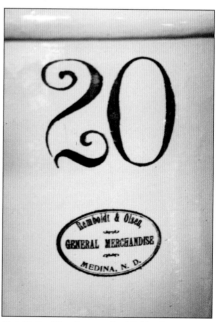

Detail of a 20-gallon crock with North Dakota advertising. **$3,000**

Eight souvenir mini jugs commemorating outings, sports rivalries, businesses and communities, and one marked "Mercury," each 2 1/2" to 3" tall, and a larger mercury bottle, 4" tall. **$250+ each, with a high range of $800 depending on markings**

Detail of a 25-gallon crock double-stamped. (Collector tip: With double-stamped stoneware pieces, the proximity of the stamps to each other also determines value. The closer together the stamps, the higher the value.) **$2,000**

Three brown-top mini jugs two with advertising and one a souvenir, each 4 1/4" tall, found unmarked and with raised "R.W.S.W. Co." **$250+ each, with a high range of $800 depending on markings**

Eighth-pint fancy jug with rare blue sponge decoration, 2 3/4" tall. **$1,800+**

Three small domed brown-top jugs, one with advertising; from left, 4 1/2", 6 1/4" and 5 1/2" tall. **Plain, $50-$75 each; advertising, $200+**

Two white stoneware shoulder jugs with advertising; left, 10 1/2" tall; right, 8 1/2" tall. **$275-$350 each**

White stoneware bail-handle jugs in three sizes with advertising; from left, 6", 10" and 7 1/2" tall. **$300-$400 each**

Two half-gallon shoulder jugs, one with a white top and one brown, late 19th and early 20th century, with advertising for the same liquor store in Lead, S.D., but identifying different owners, each 8 3/4" tall. White, **$500-$600**; *brown,* **$600-$800**

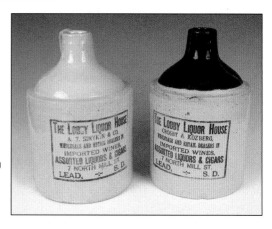

Two brown-top stoneware jugs with small red wings; left, half gallon, 9" tall; right, one gallon, wide mouth, 10 1/2" tall. **$150-$225 each**

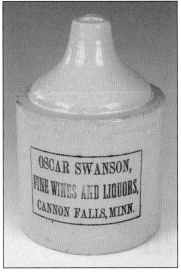

Half-gallon shoulder jug with Cannon Falls, Minn., advertising, 8 1/2" tall, impressed bottom mark, "Minnesota Stoneware Co. Red Wing, Minn." **$500+**

Two white stoneware shoulder jugs, one with elaborate advertising for a Chicago liquor store; left, 7 1/2" tall, with rare mark, "Minn. S. Co. Red Wing, Minn." **$70+**. *Right, 8 3/4" tall, unmarked.* **$300-$500**

White stoneware cone-top syrup (?) jug with pour lip, 10" tall, impressed mark, "Red Wing Stoneware Co." **$80+**

Wide-mouth, brown-top one-gallon jug left, with raised star on bottom, 10" tall. **$75+**
Right, dome-top one-gallon jug with unglazed top, with raised letters, "Wm. R. Adams Microbe Killer," 10 1/2" tall, unmarked. **$325+**

1915 Potters Excursion shoulder jug one gallon, 11" tall. **$7,000+**

Red Wing-produced one-gallon jugs in three styles, from left: funnel, dome and pear; each 10" tall. Second photo shows bottom marks of Minnesota Stoneware and North Star potteries. **$80-$110 each**

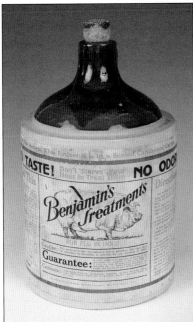

Two one-gallon white stoneware shoulder jugs with cobalt trim, with narrow and wide mouths, 11" and 10 1/4" tall, both marked on bottom, "Minnesota Stoneware Co. Red Wing, Minn." **$375-$450 each**

One-gallon brown-top stoneware jug with rare original paper label, 11" tall. **$300+**

Two white stoneware half-gallon jugs with advertising, each about 7 1/2" tall, found in scores of advertising variations. **$500-$700 each**

Two brown-top stoneware shoulder jugs with advertising, one-gallon and half-gallon sizes, 11 1/4" and 9 1/2" tall. **$500-$700 each**

Rookwood Pottery

Maria Longworth Nichols founded Rookwood Pottery in 1880. The name, she later reported, paid homage to the many crows (rooks) on her father's estate and was also designed to remind customers of Wedgwood. Production began on Thanksgiving Day 1880 when the first kiln was drawn.

Rookwood's earliest productions demonstrated a continued reliance on European precedents and the Japanese aesthetic. Although the firm offered a variety of wares (Dull Glaze, Cameo, and Limoges, for example), it lacked a clearly defined artistic identity. With the introduction of what became known as its "standard glaze" in 1884, Rookwood inaugurated a period in which the company won consistent recognition for its artistic merit and technical innovation.

Rookwood's first decade ended on a high note when the company was awarded two gold medals: one at the Exhibition of American Art Industry in Philadelphia and another later in the year at the Exposition Universelle in Paris. Significant, too, was Maria Longworth Nichols' decision to transfer her interest in the company to William W. Taylor, who had been the firm's manager since 1883. In May 1890, the board of a newly reorganized Rookwood Pottery Company purchased "the real estate, personal property, goodwill, patents, trade-marks… now the sole property of William W. Taylor" for $40,000.

Under Taylor's leadership, Rookwood was transformed from a fledgling startup to successful business that expanded throughout the following decades to meet rising demand.

Throughout the 1890s, Rookwood continued to attract critical notice as it kept the tradition of innovation alive. Taylor rolled out three new glaze lines—Iris, Sea Green and Aerial Blue—from late 1894 into early 1895.

At the Paris Exposition in 1900, Rookwood cemented its reputation by winning the Grand Prix, a feat largely due to the favorable reception of the new Iris glaze and its variants.

Over the next several years, Rookwood's record of achievement at domestic and international exhibitions remained unmatched.

Throughout the 1910s, Rookwood continued in a similar vein and began to more thoroughly embrace the simplified aesthetic promoted by many Arts and Crafts figures. Production of the Iris line, which had been instrumental in the firm's success at the Paris Exposition in 1900, ceased around 1912. Not only did the company abandon its older, fussier underglaze wares, but the newer lines the pottery introduced also trended toward simplicity.

Unfortunately, the collapse of the stock market in October 1929 and ensuing Depression dealt Rookwood a blow from which it did not recover. The Great Depression took a toll on the company and eventually led to bankruptcy in April 1941.

Rookwood's history might have ended there were it not for the purchase of the firm by a group of investors led by automobile dealer Walter E. Schott and his wife, Margaret. Production started once again. In the years that followed, Rookwood changed hands a number of times before being moved to Starkville, Miss., in 1960. It finally closed its doors there in 1967.

Early Wares

Large Limoges-style basket on lion's head feet, painted by A.R. Valentien with butterflies, 1882, stamped ROOKWOOD 1882 45 A.R.V., 9 3/4" x 20". **$800-$1,200**

Limoges-style humidor with double-lid by Maria Longworth Nichols, 1882, painted with spiders and bats on a mottled ground, stamped ROOKWOOD/1882/MLN, 6" x 6". **$2,000-$3,000**

Rare pitcher decorated by Laura Fry with incised fronds covered in indigo and dark green glaze, 1882, stamped ROOKWOOD 1882, incised Cincinnati Pottery Club, LAF, 7" x 5", **$1,500-$2,500**. Laura Fry was a member of the Women's Pottery Club of Cincinnati, a china-painting group, along with Clara Chipman Newton and Mary Louise McLaughlin, before joining the first generation of decorators at Rookwood. During her 10-year stay at the pottery, she developed and patented the atomizer for glazing purposes. From Rookwood, she moved on to the Lonhuda Pottery in Steubenville, Ohio.

Cincinnati Art Club/E. G. Winslow bulbous vase
with applied blue and red morning glories on
barbotine-painted ground, on Rookwood blank,
1882, stamped ROOKWOOD 1882, incised E.G.
Winslow, 1882, 11 1/2" x 7 1/2". **$700-$1,000**

Rare and important red clay "Indian" portrait charger
by H.F. Farny, 1881, with a Native American chief in
headdress painted in black surrounded by geometric and
abstract designs, 11" d, **$12,500-$17,500.** Henry Francois
Farny (1847-1916), a well-known Cincinnati artist,
designed the first trademark for Rookwood and was the
first to suggest "Indian designs" for its pottery. The charger
is recorded in the Shape Record Book as: "189. Red clay
plaque. Pressed. Decorated by H. Farny. Could not be
fired hard enough to set the colors in manner desired by
artist without destroying effect," (The Book of Rookwood
Pottery by Herbert Peck, 1968, p. 15).

Exceptional and rare tall Cameo cylindrical vase painted by
A.R. Valentien with a wisteria branch in white pate-sur-pate
on a dead matte indigo ground, 1893, flame mark/C/644/
A.R.V./W., 14 1/2" x 4". **$10,000-$15,000**

Standard Glaze Light large urn finely painted by Matt Daly with branches of yellow dogwood, a gently tooled underglaze design encircling the collar, 1888, flame mark/MAD/L/425/W, 13" x 10 1/2". **$3,000-$5,000**

Standard Glaze chocolate pot beautifully composed and painted by Caroline Steinle with orange and brown nasturtium, 1899, flame mark/772/CS, 9" x 6 1/4". **$850-$1,250**

Sea Green pillow vase with crescent rim, decorated by Edward Diers, 1899, with tall stems and leaves in green against a blue and celadon ground, wrapped in a bronze overlay of iris blossoms, 4 1/2" x 4". **$17,500-$25,000**

Tiger Eye vase, probably by Kitaro Shirayamadani, carved with full-length russet poppies on a silky brown, green and gold ground, mark obscured by glaze, 9 1/4" x 3 3/4". **$4,500-$6,500**

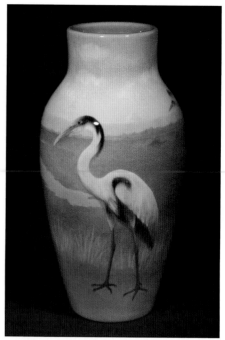

Iris Glaze vase painted by Carl Schmidt, 1902, with a blue and white water bird standing in tall grasses near a stream in tones of lavender, brown and green, 11" x 5 1/4". **$8,000-$12,000**

Rare Aerial Blue baluster vase painted by artist CW with a classical maiden as fertility goddess in front of a full moon on a blue ground, 1894, flame mark/E/538/273/CW/ crescents, 7 1/2" x 3 1/2". **$2,500-$3,500**

Iris Glaze scenic vase by Kitaro Shirayamadani, 1907, painted with a panoramic scene of tall trees and distant mountains around a lake in celadon, gray and pink, 9 1/4" x 5". **$18,000-$24,000**

Mat Glazes

Z-Line mug with wave pattern under a matt green glaze, 1902, marked, 5". **$600-$800**

Z-Line squat vessel by A. M. Valentien with reclining nude under a cherry red matte glaze, 1901, flame mark/?51Z/A.M.V., 3 1/2" x 4 1/2". **$2,000-$3,000**

Painted Mat vase by O.G. Reed with pink roses and yellow centers on an indigo-to-rose ground, 1906, flame mark/VI/907DD/O.G.R., 9 1/2" x 3 3/4". **$9,000-$13,000**

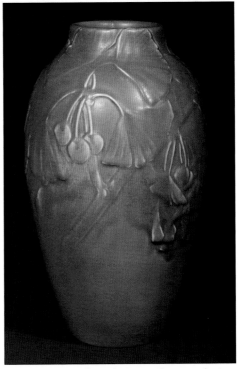

Modeled Mat ovoid vase by Kitaro Shirayamadani, 1905, with modeled branches of ginkgo leaves and berries in relief under a green and yellow mat glaze, 10 1/2" x 6 1/2". **$9,500-$12,500**

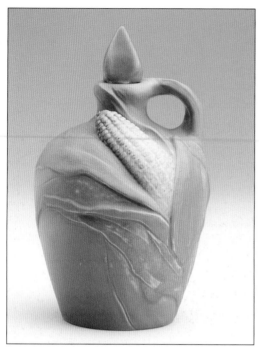

Incised Mat corn jug by Kitaro Shirayamadani in matte greens and browns, 1904, flame mark/IV/765BZ/X/artist cipher, 9" x 5 1/2". **$5,000-$6,000**

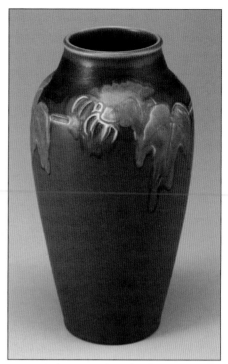

Fine Incised Mat ovoid vase by Elizabeth Lincoln, 1918, beautifully decorated with bright red fruit and green and purple leaves on a purple and umber butterfat ground, flame mark/XVIII/943C/LNL, 10 1/2" x 5 1/2". **$2,000-$3,000**

Incised Mat spherical vase decorated by Sallie Coyne with trillium in green on a matte red ground, 1905, flame mark/V/911E/artist's cipher, 4 1/4" x 5". **$800-$1,200**

Fine Incised Mat vase by unidentified artist MF, with stylized purple flowers on whiplash green stems on a green ground, 1909, flame mark/MF, 10". **$1,500-$2,500**

Ombroso vase by Elizabeth Barrett with large blue fruit and green leaves on a butterfat mustard ground, 1915, flame mark/XV/1917/artist's cipher, 6" x 6 1/4". **$900-$1,400**

Ombroso bulbous vase by William Hentschel with spade-shaped leaves in green on a flambe brown ground, 1911, flame mark, WEH, 7 1/2". **$2,000-$3,000**

New Porcelain Body

Fine Yellow Tinted vase by Sara Sax, 1923, with flaring rim decorated with honeysuckle blossoms and leaves on a yellow ground, uncrazed, flame mark/ XXIII/2545C/ artist's cipher, 10" x 3 1/4". **$2,500-$3,500**

Large Turquoise Blue bulbous vase painted by Sara Sax with birds and magnolia on a rich blue and black ground, 1917, flame mark/XVII/2272/ P/artist's cipher, 12 1/4" x 7 1/2". **$4,000-$6,000**

*Tiger Eye ovoid vase, beautifully painted by
Harriet Wilcox with stylized green poppies,
1929, flame mark/XXIX/2544/H.E.W., 8" x
3 3/4".* **$3,000-$4,000**

*Butterfat tall bottle-shaped vase painted by
Lorinda Epply with blue and green blossoms
under thick ivory curdled glaze, 1928, flame mark/
XXVIII/2983/LE, 15 1/2" x 8".* **$3,000-$4,000**

*Decorated Mat two-handled center bowl painted by Elizabeth Lincoln with red chrysanthemums and
pink flowers on a yellow butterfat ground, 1929, flame mark/XXVIV/2951/LNL, 5" x 10".* **$950-$1,250**

Fine and large Decorated Mat baluster vase incised and painted by Louise Abel with fleshy vermillion magnolias on a rich gold and orange butterfat ground, 1926, flame mark/XXVI/424B/ artist cipher, 14 1/4" x 7". **$2,750-$3,750**

French Red tall baluster vase enamel-decorated by Sara Sax with flowers on a gunmetal ground, 1921, flame mark/ XXI/2551/artist's cipher, 14" x 6". **$1,500-$2,000**

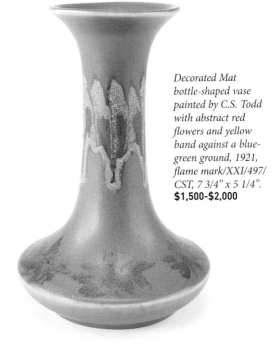

Decorated Mat bottle-shaped vase painted by C.S. Todd with abstract red flowers and yellow band against a blue-green ground, 1921, flame mark/XXI/497/ CST, 7 3/4" x 5 1/4". **$1,500-$2,000**

Decorated Mat vase painted by Sallie Coyne with abstract flowers in jewel tones on a vermillion ground, 1927, flame mark/XXVII/2785/artist's cipher, 13 1/4" x 5 1/2". **$1,500-$2,500**

Decorated Mat bulbous vase painted by unidentified artist with red hollyhocks in relief on a red and green ground, 1928, flame mark, 6 3/4". **$1,000-$2,000**

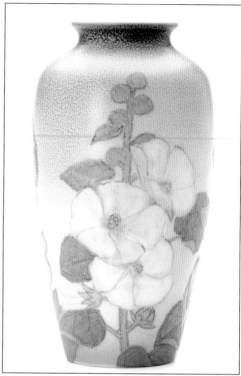

Decorated Mat vase beautifully painted by Kitaro Shirayamadani with purple and ivory hollyhocks, 1939, flame mark/XXXIX, 10" x 5 1/2". **$3,500-$4,500**

Large Decorated Mat vase by Jens Jensen with plums on a peach ground, 1930, flame mark/XXX/264OC/artist's cipher, 13 3/4" x 9 1/2". **$1,500-$2,000**

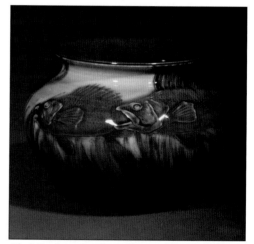

Black Opal vase by Kitaro Shirayamadani, 1925, its exterior painted and modeled with gray-green fish swimming through brown and red seaweed under a dripping cobalt glaze, and its interior in a deep mauve glaze, 5" x 7". **$8,500-$12,500**

Wax Mat bulbous vase painted by E.T. Hurley with orange roses and green foliage on ivory ground, 1933, uncrazed, flame mark/XXXIII/S/E.T.H. 6 1/4" x 4". **$1,000-$1,500**

Jewel Porcelain squat potpourri jar painted by Arthur Conant with rabbits in a Persian floral pattern, 1919, complete with two lids, flame mark/XIX/2337/C, 4 3/4" x 5". **$3,000-$5,000**

Jewel Porcelain plate painted by William Hentschel in blue and white Chinoiserie, 1924 (exhibited in "After the China Taste: China's Influence in America, 1730-1930," catalog #53, p. 69), flame mark/XXIV/K2A/artist's cipher, 10 1/4" d. **$1,250-$1,750**

Wax Mat flaring vase by Elizabeth Barrett with a geometric butterfat decoration in gray, black, and brown, 1943, flame mark/XLIII/2193/artist's cipher, 5" x 5 1/2". **$900-$1,400**

Jewel Porcelain squat vase by Sara Sax, 1922, its exterior painted with abstract circular designs in mauve, violet and gold, and its interior in bright green glaze, 6" x 7 1/4". **$4,500-$6,500**

Jewel Porcelain bulbous vase painted by Arthur Conant with an Oriental night landscape of flying bluebirds and small white rabbits around blooming trees by a mountain, 1918, flame mark/XVIII/1278F/ P/artist cipher, 7 1/4" x 3 3/4". **$4,500-$6,500**

Jewel Porcelain large, classically-shaped vase painted by Arthur Conant with peacocks perched on blooming apple branches and over paperwhites, in jewel tones on a gray ground, 1919, flame mark/XIX/2273/artist's cipher, 17 1/4" x 7 3/4". **$10,000-$15,000**

Jewel Porcelain ovoid vase decorated in a Persian floral pattern by Arthur Conant, 1921, flame mark/ XXI/551/artist cipher, 6 1/2" x 3". **$1,250-$1,750**

Jewel Porcelain vase painted by M.H. McDonald with branches of oak leaves and acorns on a butterfat ground, 1936, flame mark/XXXVI/621/MHM, 10" x 6 1/4". **$1,750-$2,500**

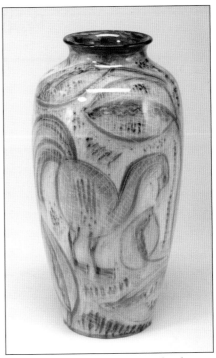

Jewel Porcelain baluster vase painted and incised by Jens Jensen with green and blue birds, fish and oversized leaves on a white and amber ground under a crackled overglaze, 1944, flame mark XLIV/614B/artist's cipher, 15 1/2" x 7 1/2". **$3,000-$4,000**

Jewel Porcelain hemispherical vessel painted by E.T. Hurley with large birds and blooming branches, 1929, flame mark/XXIX/2254D/E.T.H., 5 1/4" x 6 1/4". **$1,250-$1,750**

Production Wares

Early Production chamberstick in the form of a poppy in mustard and brown, 1903, flame mark, 8 1/4". **$550-$750**

Production Z-line cabinet vase, c. 1900, incised with key motif at rim and covered in a mottled mauve matte glaze, flame mark, 3 1/2" x 2 3/4". **$300-$400**

Rare Production rook inkwell covered in dark teal glaze, 1908, missing lid, flame mark, 7 1/2" x 12". **$700-$900**

Incised Mat ovoid vase by Cecil Duell, 1908, its rim carved with a band of free-form shapes, covered in a matte green glaze, flame mark/artist's cipher, 6 1/4" x 4 3/4". **$550-$750**

Production pitcher embossed with triangles under a good frothy mint green glaze, 1907, flame mark, 4 1/2". **$300-$400**

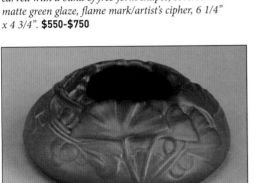

Rare and early Production squat bowl embossed with gingko leaves and fruit under purple and green matte glaze, 1913, flame mark/XIII/1680, 2 1/4" x 6 1/2". **$1,000-$1,500**

Production ovoid vase, 1916, embossed with panels of berries and leaves on a shaded green and umber matte ground, flame mark, 7 1/2" x 3". **$600-$900**

Large Production vase embossed with swirling blossoms under cobalt glaze, 1914, flame mark/XIV/516, 11" x 12". **$1,750-$2,250**

Production porcelain creamer and sugar bowl covered in glossy blue glaze, 1916, marked, 4". **$75-$125 each**

Production tall candlesticks, 1922, embossed with tulips and covered in a dark pink matte glaze, flame mark, 10 1/2". **$400-$600**

Production bookends with goddesses under matte indigo glaze, 1918, marked, 8". **$450-$650**

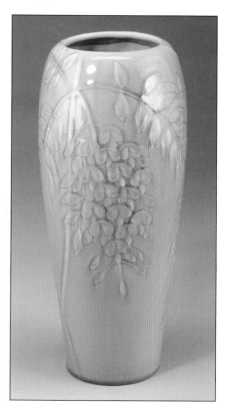

Production porcelain tall vase, 1947, embossed with wisteria under a crackled turquoise sheer glaze, flame mark/XLVII/6871, 13 3/4" x 6". **$350-$450**

Five Production
vessels in glossy
glazes: bulbous vase
with water lilies in
mauve, vase molded
with Southwestern
scene in ivory, two
cream pitchers in
yellow and blue, and
ribbed covered dish in
celadon, all marked,
tallest: 6 1/4"; pitchers
$50-$100 each; vases
$100-$250 each.

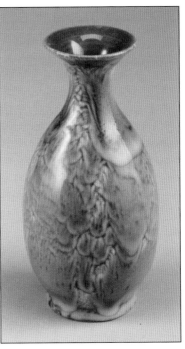

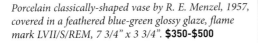

Production pair of urns covered in sky blue glaze dripping over dark
purple, 1951, complete with original factory boxes, flame marks,
7 1/4" x 7 1/4". **$150-$250 each**

*Porcelain classically-shaped vase by R. E. Menzel, 1957,
covered in a feathered blue-green glossy glaze, flame
mark LVII/S/REM, 7 3/4" x 3 3/4".* **$350-$500**

Roseville Pottery

Roseville is one of the most widely recognizable of potteries across the United States. Having been sold in flower shops and drug stores around the country, its art and production wares became a staple in American homes through the time Roseville closed in the 1950s.

The Roseville Pottery Company, located in Roseville, Ohio, was incorporated on Jan. 4, 1892, with George F. Young as general manager. The company had been producing stoneware since 1890, when it purchased the J. B. Owens Pottery, also of Roseville.

The popularity of Roseville Pottery's original lines of stoneware continued to grow. The company acquired new plants in 1892 and 1898, and production started to shift to Zanesville, just a few miles away. By about 1910, all of the work was centered in Zanesville, but the company name was unchanged.

Blackberry wall pocket, 1267-8", unmarked, 8 1/4". **$650-$950**

Young hired Ross C. Purdy as artistic designer in 1900, and Purdy created Rozane—a contraction of the words "Roseville" and "Zanesville." The first Roseville artwork pieces were marked either Rozane or RPCO, both impressed or ink-stamped on the bottom.

In 1902, a line was developed called Azurean. Some pieces were marked Azurean, but often RPCO. In 1904 at the St. Louis Exposition, Roseville's Rozane Mongol, a high-gloss oxblood red line, captured first prize, gaining recognition for the firm and its creator, John Herold.

Many Roseville lines were a response to the innovations of Weller Pottery, and in 1904 Frederick Rhead was hired away from Weller as artistic director. He created the Olympic and Della Robbia lines for Roseville. His brother Harry took over as artistic director in 1908, and in 1915 he introduced the popular Donatello line.

By 1908, all handcrafting ended except for Rozane Royal. Roseville was the first pottery in Ohio to install a tunnel kiln, which increased its production capacity.

Frank Ferrell, who was a top decorator at the Weller Pottery by 1904, was Roseville's artistic director from 1917 until 1954. This Zanesville native created many of the most popular lines, including Pine Cone, which had scores of individual pieces.

Many collectors believe Roseville's circa 1925 glazes were the best of any Zanesville pottery. George Krause, who had become Roseville's technical supervisor, responsible for glaze, in 1915, remained with Roseville until the 1950s.

Company sales declined after World War II, especially in the early 1950s when cheap Japanese imports began to replace American wares, and a simpler, more modern style made many of Roseville's elaborate floral designs seem old-fashioned.

In the late 1940s, Roseville began to issue lines with glossy glazes. Roseville tried to offset its flagging artware sales by launching a dinnerware line—Raymor—in 1953. The line was a commercial failure.

Roseville issued its last new designs in 1953. On Nov. 29, 1954, the facilities of Roseville were sold to the Mosaic Tile Company. For more information on Roseville, see *Warman's Roseville Pottery*, 2nd edition, by Denise Rago.

Pink Baneda urn, 589-6", unmarked, 6 1/2" x 4".
$350-$550

Green Bittersweet bowl, 829-12", raised mark. **$100-$150**

Blue Apple Blossom tall vase, 393-18", raised mark.
$400-$600

Pink Bleeding Heart jardinière and pedestal set,
651-8", both marked. **$750-$1,000**

Green Clemana vase, 753-8", impressed mark. **$250-$350**

Blended Iris jardinière, unmarked, 11" x 12". **$300-$500**

Blue Clematis cookie jar, 3-8", raised mark. **$150-$250**

Pink Cherry Blossom bulbous vase, 619-5", unmarked, 5 1/4" x 5". **$350-$550**

Blue Bushberry sand jar, 778-14", raised mark. **$700-$900**

Brown Columbine bulbous vase, 23-10", raised mark.
$200-$350

Tall blue Cosmos ewer, 957-15", unmarked. **$300-$400**

Crystalis ring-handle vase in an Egypto shape (E 58) with a mottled salmon and gold glaze, with "Rozane Ware/ Egypto" wafer, 14 7/8" h. **$1,500-$1,800**

Della Robbia teapot excised with stylized tulips and hearts in a two-tone green glaze, incised E Dutrow/medallion mark, 4 1/2" x 9". **$2,000-$3,000**

Pink Cremona flaring vase with two buttressed handles, 362-12" unmarked, 12" x 6". **$300-$400**

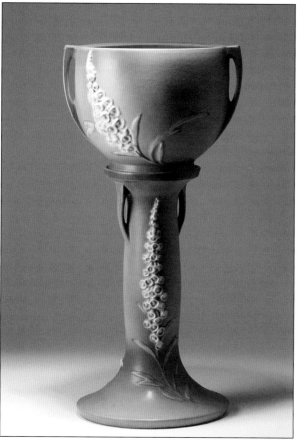

Green Foxglove jardinière and pedestal set, 659-8", raised mark. **$750-$1,250**

Dogwood I tall vase on squat base, unmarked, 15 3/4" x 6 1/2". **$350-$500**

Blue Falline vase with ribbed base and tapered neck, 652-9", unmarked. **$1,750-$2,250**

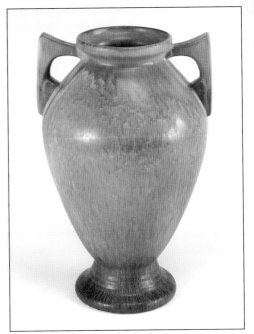

Fine and large Earlam two-handled vase, unmarked, 15 1/2" x 9 1/4". **$1,750-$2,500**

Donatello bulbous vase with two long, angular handles, a rare Donatello form, unmarked, 10 1/4". **$250-$400**

Red Ferella flaring two-handled vase, 501-6", unmarked, 6 1/4" x 4 1/2". **$600-$900**

Green Freesia bookends, #15, both marked, 5" each. **$125-$225**

Blue Iris jardinière and pedestal set, 647-8", impressed mark. **$650-$950**

Blue Fuchsia floor vase, 905-18", impressed mark. **$750-$1,000**

Fine Imperial II flaring vase covered in a curdled green over orange glaze, 476-8", unmarked. **$3,000-$4,000**

Futura hanging basket, 344-6", with leaves in polychrome on an orange ground, unmarked, 6 1/4" x 9 1/2". **$400-$600**

Ixia green vase, 064-12", some peppering to body, impressed mark and remnant of foil label to body. **$110-$140**

Pair of brown Gardenia bookends, #659, both marked. **$150-$250**

Green Laurel flaring vase, unmarked, 8" x 7". **$350-$500**

Jonquil large bulbous vase, this example has a very crisp mold, unmarked, 12 1/4". **$600-$900**

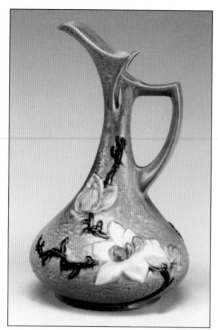

Blue Magnolia ewer, 15-15", raised mark.
$150-$250

Green Luffa 10" jardinière and pedestal set, unmarked.
$1,000-$1,500

*Ming Tree blue vase, 510-14", raised
mark.* **$150-$200**

Pink Mock Orange flaring vase, 985-12", raised mark. **$200-$300**

Pink Moss vase, 784-10", impressed mark.
$300-$400

Green Morning Glory bowl, unmarked, 5" x 11 1/2". **$350-$450**

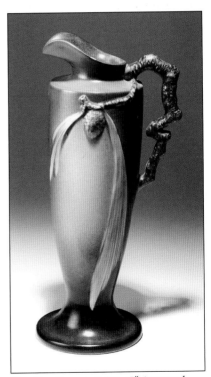

Blue Pine Cone ewer, 851-15", impressed mark. **$750-$1,250**

Normandy umbrella stand, blue ink stamp, 20" x 10". **$375-$425**

Large and rare brown Pine Cone urn, 912-15", impressed mark. **$1,500-$2,500**

Yellow Peony jardinière and pedestal set, 661-8", raised mark. **$450-$650**

Fine and large Pauleo vase covered in a mottled olive, red, and ochre, and brown glaze, unmarked, 24" x 13 1/2". **$6,000-$8,000**

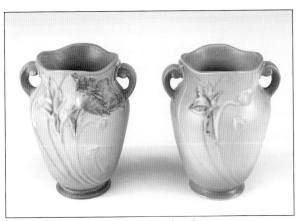

A pair of Poppy vases, 868-7", one pink and one green, both marked. **$125-$200 each**

Two Rozane 1917 pieces: green jardinière and ivory vase, Rozane stamp mark to one; jardinière: 9" h. **$150-$200/pair**

Pink Primrose sand jar, 772, impressed mark, 14" x 10". **$450-$650**

Blue Snowberry floor vase, IV-18", raised mark. **$300-$500**

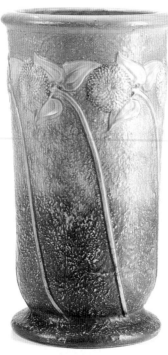

Tourmaline ribbed flaring vase, unmarked, 10". **$300-$500**

Sunflower umbrella stand, crisply decorated, strong color, unmarked, 20 1/4" x 11 1/2". **$3,000-$5,000**

Rare blue Velmoss II flaring vase with twisted leaves forming two handles, 119-10", unmarked, 10 1/2" x 6 1/4". **$850-$1,150**

Blue Thorn Apple vase, 324-16", impressed mark. **$450-$650**

Pink Tuscany four-sided vase, unmarked, 7 1/4" x 3 1/2". **$100-$200**

Rare blue Windsor basket with curved handle, paper label, 5" x 6 1/2". **$1,250-$1,750**

Velmoss Scroll jardinière, unmarked, 9" x 10 1/2". **$200-$300**

Pink White Rose floor vase, 994-18", raised mark. **$300-$400**

Green Zephyr Lily cookie jar, 5-8", raised mark. **$200-$300**

*Brown Water Lily ewer, 12-15", raised
mark.* **$300-$400**

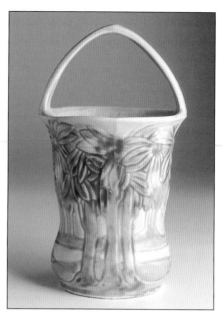

Rare Vista basket, unmarked, 10 1/2".
$600-$800

*Brown
Wisteria
wall pocket,
unmarked, 8
1/4".* **$700-
$1,000**

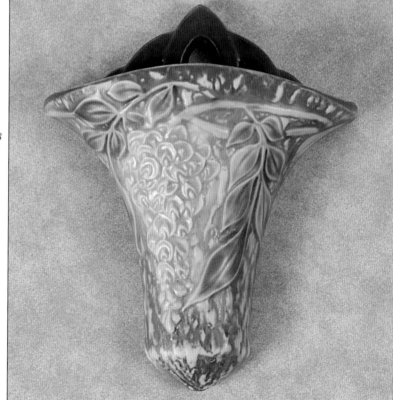

R.S. Prussia

Bob Welter has collected R.S. Prussia for 12 years, but his admiration for the porcelain china made by the Schlegelmilch family before 1917 dates back to his formative years, when he dished potato salad from a beautifully decorated bowl given to his grandparents as a wedding present in 1907.

In 2010, he discovered he had purchased a rare R.S. Prussia picture frame at a Woody Auction in August 2009. Welter said he bought the unmarked 8-inch by 10-inch frame thinking it was French, probably Limoges, even though Woody had listed it in his catalog as possibly being R.S. Prussia.

"I just thought it was so pretty that it would be something my wife would enjoy," said Welter, who asked auctioneer Jason Woody to hold it until they met up at the national convention in July.

"As soon as I saw it I said, 'Ooh!' and ran to our author in residence, Lee Marple, and said, 'Is it possible?' He looked at it and said, 'Oh, yes. That's R.S. Prussia.' I thought, 'A home run!'" said Welter.

Auctioneer Woody said he thought the unmarked frame was R.S. Prussia right from the start.

"R.S. Prussia collectors can tell by the style, the mold shape, the colors and decoration. Persons familiar with R.S. Prussia can identify it," said Woody.

Welter said that he thought Marple recognized the transfer decoration on the frame. Welter also suggested the frame was left unmarked because it was intended for the German market.

"Everybody knew who they were; they didn't need to mark it," said Welter.

Making the buy all the sweeter, the final auction price ended at only $225.

"I always ask the auctioneers what they think something will go for in their market. Woody said he thought it would go for $400 to $600. I bid (absentee) $750 and got it for $225," said Welter, adding, "It all depends on who's there and what they think."

— Tom Hoepf

R.S. Prussia & Related Marks

A selection of various R.S. Prussia marks.

R.S. Prussia embossed bowl with swan and landscape design, 10 3/4 inches in diameter. **$300**

Turkey Creek Auctions and Woody Auction

A photo of the frame in the auction catalog had Bob Welter thinking it was Limoges, but a hands-on inspection confirmed it was R.S. Prussia. **$225**

Group of four porcelain serving pieces, including an R.S. Prussia hand-painted, two-handled pastry tray in "Poppies" decor, 1904-1908; a smaller R.S. Prussia fruit bowl, also in "Poppies" decor; a German polychromed and parcel-gilt porcelain berry bowl in the R.S. Prussia style; and an Altrohlau richly decorated porcelain berry bowl in "Peonies" decor, 1884-1909; the R. S. Prussia and Altrohlau examples all signed; the largest diameter is 11 3/8 inches. **$70**

Dean Schwarz

Dean Schwarz (b. 1938) is a ceramic artist, painter, writer and teacher from Cedar Rapids, Iowa. While serving in the U.S. Navy in the early 1960s, he used his shore leaves to visit the studios of notable potters, including Shoji Hamada in Japan, and Bauhaus-trained Marguerite Wildenhain at Pond Farm near Guerneville, Calif. His work is represented in numerous private collections, and in the holdings of museums and universities around the world.

Dean Schwarz vase, mid-1990s, 10 1/2". **$350+**

Van Briggle

Artus Van Briggle, born in 1869, was a talented Ohio artist. He joined Rookwood in 1887 and studied in Paris under Rookwood's sponsorship from 1893 until 1896. In 1899, he moved to Colorado for his health and established his own pottery in Colorado Springs in 1901.

The Art Nouveau designs he had seen in France heavily influenced Van Briggle's work. He produced a wide variety of matte-glazed wares in this style. Colors varied. Artus died in 1904, but his wife, Anne, continued the pottery until 1912.

The "AA" mark, a date, and "Van Briggle" were incised on all pieces prior to 1907 and on some pieces into the 1920s. After 1920, "Colorado Springs, Colorado" or an abbreviation was added. Dated pieces are the most desirable.

Belhorn Auction Services LLC

Van Briggle floral plate made between 1907 and 1912 in red with gray overspray. Marked Van Briggle with logo, 17. Professionally restored, 8 1/4" diameter. **$63**

Belhorn Auction Services LLC

Van Briggle philodendron bowl with reticulated design in purple over blue matte. Marked Van Briggle with logo, Colo. Spgs. Colo. and the finisher's initials, AES. Mint, 5" x 4 1/4". **$71**

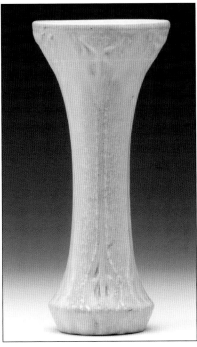

Rago Arts and Auction Center

Van Briggle, unusual flaring vase embossed with blossoms under a fine yellow and pearl gray frothy glaze, 1906. AA VAN BRIGGLE COLO. SPRINGS 1906 495. 9 1/2" x 4 1/2". **$1,320**

Van Briggle early bud vase embossed with trillium and covered in a frothy lime green glaze, the pale clay showing through, 1903. Incised AA VAN BRIGGLE 121 1903. 6 1/2" x 3". **$1,920**

Rago Arts and Auction Center

Weller Pottery

Weller Pottery was made from 1872 to 1945 at a pottery established originally by Samuel A. Weller at Fultonham, Ohio and moved in 1882 to Zanesville, Ohio.

Weller's famous pottery slugged it out with several other important Zanesville potteries for decades. Cross-town rivals such as Roseville, Owens, La Moro, and McCoy were all serious fish in a fairly small and well-stocked lake. While Weller occasionally landed some solid body punches with many of his better art lines, the prevailing thought was that his later production ware just wasn't up to snuff.

Samuel Weller was a notorious copier and, it is said, a bit of a scallywag. He paid designers such as William Long to bring their famous discoveries to Zanesville. He then attempted to steal their secrets, and, when successful, renaming them and making them his own.

After World War I, when the cost of materials became less expensive than the cost of labor, many companies, including the famous Rookwood Pottery, increased their output of less expensive production ware. Weller Pottery followed along in the trend of production ware by introducing scores of interesting and unique lines, the likes of which have never been created anywhere else, before or since.

In addition to a number of noteworthy production lines, Weller continued in the creation of hand-painted ware long after Roseville abandoned them. Some of the more interesting Hudson pieces, for example, are post-World War I pieces. Even later lines, such as Bonito, were hand painted and often signed by important artists such as Hester Pillsbury. The closer you look at Weller's output after 1920, the more obvious the fact that it was the only Zanesville company still producing both quality art ware and quality production ware.

For more information on Weller pottery, see *Warman's Weller Pottery Identification and Price Guide* by Denise Rago and David Rago.

Early Art Ware

Vase, Hunter, rare, slightly flared, incised with seagulls flying over waves, marked with impressed numbers, 7 1/4" x 3". **$600-$900**

Vase, Dickensware I, bulbous, beautifully decorated by Frank Ferrell with chrysanthemums in polychrome, impressed mark and signed Ferrell, 7" x 6 1/2", **$1,500-$2,500**

Jardinière, Etched Floral or Modeled Etched Matt, by Frank Ferrell with sunflowers in burnt orange on ivory over celadon ground, artist's signature, 10" x 13 1/2". **$450-$650**

Jardinière and pedestal set, Etna, painted with pink nasturtium, unmarked, 25 1/2". **$750-$1,000**

Ewer, Aurelian, ruffled rim, painted by T.J. Wheatley with nasturtium, 10". **$500-$700**

Vase, Fru Russet, bulbous, exceptionally decorated by Pickens with pink lilies on a heavily curdled pale green ground, 13". $3,000-$4,000

Vase, Fudzi, ovoid, leaves and berries around the rim, impressed numbers, 10 1/2". $1,500-$2,000

Vase, Rhead Faience, ovoid, blue with birds, signed Weller Faience with numbers, 11". $3,000-$5,000

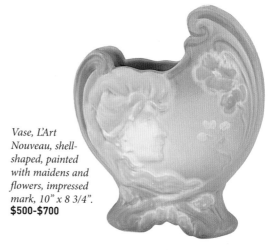

Vase, L'Art Nouveau, shell-shaped, painted with maidens and flowers, impressed mark, 10" x 8 3/4". $500-$700

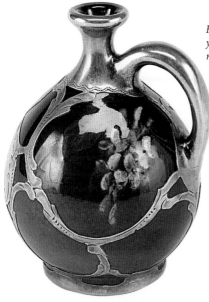

Fine cabinet jug, Louwelsa, painted with small yellow blossoms, overlaid with silver, impressed mark, 3 3/4" x 2 3/4". **$1,000-$1,500**

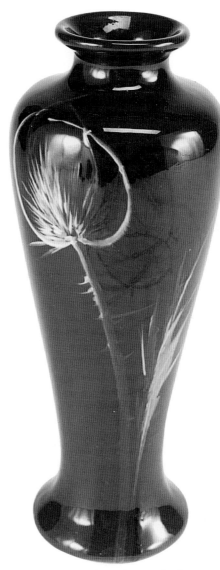

Vase, Louwelsa, red, painted with pink teasel in pink, ivory, and purple on a red ground, unmarked, 10 1/2" x 4". **$1,500-$2,000**

Floor vase, Sicard, fine and large, extensively decorated with flowers and leaves, signed on body and dated 1902, 25" x 13". **$5,000-$7,500**

Jardinière, Turada, massive with banded floral decoration in orange and ivory on an olive ground, impressed Turada 217 mark, 17" x 18".
$1,000-$1,500

Middle Period to Late Art Ware and Commercial Ware

Large Ardsley flaring bowl and Kingfisher flower frog, stamped mark, 9 1/2" x 16" diameter. Both are fine examples of these forms.
$650-$950

Batter jug, Ansonia, covered in a mottled green and yellow glaze, signed Weller in script, 10" x 8". **$100-$200**

Jardinière and pedestal set, Blue Drapery, unmarked, 29" overall. **$600-$900**

Umbrella stand, Bedford Matt, covered in the standard matt green glaze, unmarked, 20" h. **$600-$900**

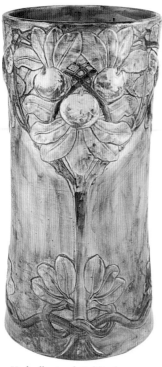

Umbrella stand, Baldin, brown, unmarked. **$1,000-$1,750**

Vase, White and Decorated Hudson, classically shaped, with branches of pink and ivory roses, impressed mark, 13" x 6 1/2". **$600-$800**

Vase, Blue and Decorated, faceted, painted with a bluebird and cherry blossoms, impressed mark, 11 1/2" x 5". **$1,000-$1,500**

Vase, Blue Ware, large, has maidens dancing and playing instruments, stamped mark, 12" x 6 1/2". **$300-$400**

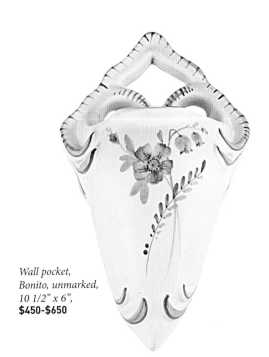

Wall pocket,
Bonito, unmarked,
10 1/2" x 6",
$450-$650

Pair of colorful parakeets on a branch, Brighton, 9".
$950-$1,450

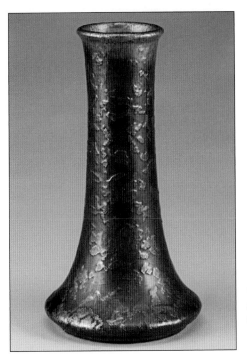

Two Cameo pieces: one blue and one orange, both marked
in script, 7 1/2" and 5 1/4". **$75-$150** and **$50-$75**

Vase, Bronze Ware, tall,
curdled reddish bronze glaze,
unmarked, 13". **$600-$800**

Figure, dancing frogs, Coppertone, extremely rare, 16 1/2". **$7,000-$9,000**

Bowl, Dupont, decorated with birds on a wire between puffy green trees, unmarked, 3 3/4" x 8".
$75-$150

Basket, Copra, painted with daisies, impressed mark, 10" x 7 1/2".
$250-$350

Vase, Frosted Matt, baluster, with heavily curdled pale lime green over sheer brown glaze, 13 1/2".
$1,500-$2,500

Jardinière, Flemish, decorated with colorful birds, leaves, and flowers, unmarked, 10 1/2" x 15". **$500-$700**

Vase, Stellar, bulbous, blue, painted by Hester Pillsbury, incised mark and artist's initials, 6" x 6 1/2". **$700-$900**

Wall pocket, Florala, conical, unmarked, 9 1/2" x 5". **$250-$350**

Vase, Cornish, blue, corseted, marked in script, 7 1/4" x 4 1/4". **$100-$200**

Vase, Glendale, baluster, embossed with birds, flowers, and butterflies, 12". **$850-$1,250**

Covered jar, Greora, marked in script, 6 1/4" x 5".
$450-$650

Vase, Juneau, bright pink, impressed mark, 10".
$150-$250

Vase, Kenova, two-handled, decorated with hanging branches of roses, unmarked, 10". **$800-$1,200**

Fine planter, Knifewood, carved with bluebirds in an apple tree, unmarked, 6" x 7". **$750-$1,250**

Four wall pockets: One Woodrose in pale blue, one basket-shaped Klyro, one tapered Klyro, and one Roma conical, all unmarked, 6 1/2", 5 1/2", 6 3/4", 7". **$75-$150 each**

Pair of bud vases, LaSa, corseted, unmarked, 7 1/4".
$200-$300 each

Pillow vase, Malverne, marked in script, 8" x 6".
$100-$200

*Vase, Manhattan, green with tall leaves,
marked in script, 9" x 5".* **$100-$250**

*Pitcher, Marvo, pink, unmarked,
8" x 8".* **$250-$350**

*Vase, Neiska, blue bulbous with twisted
handles, incised mark.* **$100-$200**

Form duck planter or bowl, Patricia, covered in an Evergreen glaze, incised mark, 8" x 16". **$150-$250**

Wall pocket, Orris, with flowers and trellis pattern, unmarked, 8" x 4 1/2". **$100-$200**

Vessel, Patra, handled, incised mark, 4 3/4" x 6". **$100-$200**

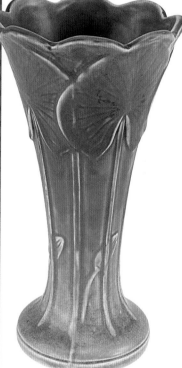

Vase, Pumila, brown, flaring, stamped mark, 10 1/4" x 6". **$150-$250**

Planter, Roma, large ovoid with clusters of red roses, unmarked, 5 1/2" x 16". **$300-$400**

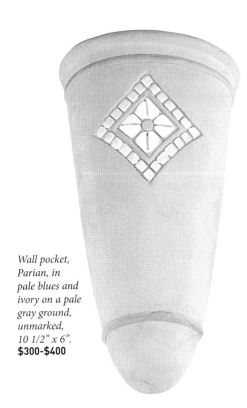

Wall pocket, Parian, in pale blues and ivory on a pale gray ground, unmarked, 10 1/2" x 6". **$300-$400**

Planter, Rosemont, unmarked, 7 1/2" x 9 1/2". **$600-$800**

Pillow vase, Sabrinian, sea horses along the sides, stamped mark, 7" x 7 1/2". **$200-$300**

Vase, Rochelle, bulbous, painted by Hester Pillsbury with blue and yellow flowers, a highly decorated example, incised mark and artist's initials, 6 1/2" x 3 1/4". **$700-$900**

Jardinière, Silvertone, has clusters of hydrangea, stamped mark, 11" x 10 1/2". **$600-$900**

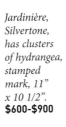

Vase, Turkis, flaring, marked in script and Turkis paper label, 8 3/4" x 6". **$100-$200**

Vase, Tutone, rare, green leaf design around the rim, 12 3/4". **$500-$800**

Vase or ginger jar, Velva, brown, lidded, marked in script, 11 1/4" x 6". **$350-$450**

Wall hanging, Woodcraft, rare, with branch-shaped pockets, decorated with large pink flowers and applied blue birds nesting in branches, impressed mark, 15" x 13". **$1,250-$1,750**

Potpourri jar, Warwick, lidded, 5". **$200-$250**

Two Wild Rose tall pieces: a bulbous vase and a ewer, in pale orange and green blended glaze, marked in script. **$75-$125 each**

Pitcher, Zona, with lightly colored panels of kingfishers and cattails, impressed mark, 8 1/2" x 9". **$200-$300**

Wall pocket, Woodrose, unmarked, 6 3/4" x 3". **$75-$120**

European

Select English, European Makers

The **Amphora Porcelain Works** was one of several pottery companies located in the Teplitz-Turn region of Bohemia in the late 19th and early 20th centuries. It is best known for art pottery, especially Art Nouveau and Art Deco pieces. Several markings were used, including the name and location of the pottery and the Imperial mark, which included a crown. Prior to World War I, Bohemia was part of the Austro-Hungarian Empire, so the word "Austria" may appear as part of the mark. After World War I, the word "Czechoslovakia" may be part of the mark.

Belleek is thin-bodied, ivory-colored, almost-iridescent porcelain, first made in 1857 in County Fermanagh, Ireland. Production continued until World War I, was discontinued for a period of time, and then resumed. The Shamrock pattern is most familiar, but many patterns were made, including Limpet, Tridacna and Grasses.

Several American firms made a Belleek-type porcelain. The first was Ott and Brewer Co. of Trenton, N.J., in 1884. Other firms producing this ware included The Ceramic Art Co. (1889), American Art China Works (1892), Columbian Art Co. (1893) and Lenox Inc. (1904). Irish Belleek bore specific marks during given time periods, which makes it relatively easy to date. Variations in mark color are important, as well as the symbols and words.

Capo-di-Monte: In 1743, King Charles of Naples established a soft-paste porcelain factory. The firm made figurines and dinnerware. In 1760, many of the workmen and most of the molds were moved to Buen Retiro, near Madrid, Spain. A new factory, which also made hard-paste porcelains, opened in Naples in 1771. In 1834, the Doccia factory in Florence purchased the molds and continued production in Italy.

Capo-di-Monte was copied well into the 20th century by makers in Hungary, Germany, France and Italy.

Capo-di-Monte

Figures (pair), Capo-di-Monte, classical females, one at desk with compass and scroll, other sculpting helmeted bust on stand, oval base, porcelain, Capo-di-Monte, 19th century, 6 1/2" h. **$510 pair**

Sanford Alderfer Auction & Appraisal

COPELAND

Copeland

Spode

In 1749, **Josiah Spode** was apprenticed to Thomas Whieldon and in 1754 worked for William Banks in Stoke-on-Trent, Staffordshire, England. In the early 1760s, Spode started his own pottery, making cream-colored earthenware and blueprinted whiteware. In 1770, he returned to Banks' factory as master, purchasing it in 1776.

Spode pioneered the use of steam-powered, pottery-making machinery and mastered the art of transfer printing from copper plates. Spode opened a London shop in 1778 and sent William Copeland there in about 1784. A number of larger London locations followed. At the turn of the 18th century, Spode introduced bone china. In 1805, Josiah Spode II and William Copeland entered into a partnership for the London business. A series of partnerships between Josiah Spode II, Josiah Spode III and William Taylor Copeland resulted.

In 1833, Copeland acquired Spode's London operations and seven years later, the Stoke plants. William Taylor Copeland managed the business until his death in 1868. The firm remained in the hands of Copeland heirs. In 1923, the plant was electrified; other modernization followed.

In 1976, Spode merged with Worcester Royal Porcelain to become Royal Worcester Spode, Ltd.

Delftware is pottery with a soft, red-clay body and tin-enamel glaze. The white, dense, opaque color came from adding tin ash to lead glaze. The first examples had blue designs on a white ground. Polychrome examples followed.

The name originally applied to pottery made in the region around Delft, Holland, beginning in the 16th century and ending in the late 18th century. The tin used came from the Cornish mines in England. By the 17th and 18th centuries, English potters in London, Bristol and Liverpool were copying the glaze and designs. Some designs unique to English potters also developed.

Skinner Inc.

Plate, Delftware, England, 18th century, with polychrome decorated floral and bird designs, (rim chips), 11 3/4" d. **$444**

Augustus II, Elector of Saxony and King of Poland, founded the Royal Saxon Porcelain Manufactory in the Albrechtsburg, **Meissen**, in 1710. Johann Frederick Boettger, an alchemist, and Tschirnhaus, a nobleman, experimented with kaolin from the Dresden area to produce porcelain. By 1720, the factory produced a whiter, hard-paste porcelain than that from the Far East. The factory experienced its golden age from the 1730s to the 1750s under the leadership of Samuel Stolzel, kiln master,

Dresden/Meissen

and Johann Gregor Herold, enameler.

The Meissen factory was destroyed and looted by forces of Frederick the Great during the Seven Years' War (1756-1763). It was reopened, but never achieved its former greatness.

In the 19th century, the factory reissued some of its earlier forms. These later wares are called "Dresden" to differentiate them from the earlier examples. There were several other porcelain factories in the Dresden region and their products also are grouped under the "Dresden" designation.

Many marks were used by the Meissen factory. The first was a pseudo-Oriental mark in a square. The famous crossed swords mark was adopted in 1724. A small dot between the hilts was used from 1763 to 1774, and a star between the hilts from 1774 to 1814. Two modern marks are swords with a hammer and sickle, and swords with a crown.

Gouda and the surrounding areas of Holland have been principal Dutch pottery centers for centuries. Originally, the potteries produced a simple utilitarian, tin-glazed Delft-type earthenware and the famous clay smoker's pipes.

Gouda

When pipe making declined in the early 1900s, Gouda turned to art pottery. Influenced by the Art Nouveau and Art Deco movements, artists expressed themselves with freeform and stylized designs in bold colors.

In 1842, American china importer David Haviland moved to Limoges, France, where he began manufacturing and decorating china specifically for the U.S. market. Haviland is synonymous with fine, white, translucent porcelain, although

Haviland

early hand-painted patterns were generally larger and darker colored on heavier whiteware blanks than were later ones.

Haviland revolutionized French china factories by both manufacturing the whiteware blank and decorating it at the same site. In addition, Haviland and Co. pioneered the use of decals in decorating china.

Haviland's sons, Charles Edward and Theodore, split the company in 1892. In 1936, Theodore opened an American division. In 1941, Theodore bought out Charles Edward's heirs and recombined both companies under the original name of H. and Co. The Haviland family sold the firm in 1981.

Charles Field Haviland, cousin of Charles Edward and Theodore, worked for and then, after his marriage in 1857, ran the Casseaux Works until 1882. Items continued to carry his name as decorator until 1941.

Thousands of Haviland patterns were made, but not consistently named until after 1926. The similarities in many of the patterns make identification difficult. Numbers assigned by Arlene Schleiger and illustrated in her books have become the identification standard.

Skinner Inc.

KPM porcelain plaque depicting the Duchess of Devonshire as the Vestal Virgin, Germany, late 19th century, after the original by Angelica Kauffmann, impressed KPM and scepter, paper label for "Henry Bucker, Painter on China, 5 Pragerstrasse Dresden", 9 3/8". **$2,015**

The **"KPM"** mark has been used separately and in conjunction with other symbols by many German porcelain manufacturers, among which are the Königliche Porzellan Manufactur in Meissen, 1720s; Königliche Porzellan Manufactur in Berlin, 1832-1847; and Krister Porzellan Manufactur in Waldenburg, mid-19th century.

Collectors now use the term KPM to refer to the high-quality porcelain produced in the Berlin area in the 18th and 19th centuries.

Creamware is a cream-colored earthenware created about 1750 by the potters of Staffordshire, England, which proved ideal for domestic ware. It was also known as "tortoiseshellware" or "Prattware" depending on the color of glaze used.

The most notable producer of creamware was Josiah Wedgwood. Around 1779, he was able to lighten the cream color to a bluish white and sold this product under the name "pearl ware." Wedgwood supplied his creamware to England's Queen Charlotte (1744-1818) and Russian Empress Catherine the Great (1729-1796), and used the trade name "Queen's ware."

Leeds Pottery

The **Leeds Pottery** in Yorkshire, England, began production about 1758. Among its products was creamware that was competitive with that of Wedgwood. The original factory closed in 1820, but various subsequent owners continued until 1880. They made exceptional cream-colored ware, either plain, salt glazed or painted with colored enamels, and glazed and unglazed redware.

Early wares are unmarked. Later pieces are marked "Leeds Pottery," sometimes followed by "Hartley-Green and Co." or the letters "LP."

Skinner Inc.

Coffeepot and cover, creamware, England, circa 1780, attributed to Liverpool, pear shape with black transfer "tea party" and "shepherd" prints, strap handle and ball knop, (spout restored, slight rim lines), 10" h. **$355**

Liverpool is the name given to products made at several potteries in Liverpool, England, between 1750 and 1840. Seth and James Pennington and Richard Chaffers were among the early potters who made tin-enameled earthenware.

By the 1780s, tin-glazed earthenware gave way to cream-colored wares decorated with cobalt blue, enameled colors and blue or black transfers.

Bubbles and frequent clouding under the foot rims characterize the Liverpool glaze. By 1800, about 80 potteries were working in the town producing not only creamware, but soft paste, soapstone and bone porcelain.

The reproduction pieces have a crackled glaze and often age cracks have been artificially produced. When compared to genuine pieces, reproductions are thicker and heavier and have weaker transfers, grayish color (not as crisp and black), ecru or gray body color instead of cream, and crazing that does not spiral upward.

In 1793, **Thomas Minton** joined other entrepreneurs formed a partnership to build a small pottery at Stoke-on-Trent, Staffordshire, England. Production began in 1798 with blueprinted earthenware, mostly in the Willow pattern. In 1798, cream-colored earthenware and bone china were introduced.

Minton

A wide range of styles and wares was produced. Minton introduced porcelain figures in 1826, Parian wares in 1846, encaustic tiles in the late 1840s, and majolica wares in 1850. In 1883, the modern company was formed and called Mintons Limited. The "s" was dropped in 1968.

Many early pieces are unmarked or have a Sevres-type marking. The "ermine" mark was used in the early 19th century. Date codes can be found on tableware and majolica. The mark used between 1873 and 1911 was a small globe with a crown on top and the word "Minton."

Mocha decoration usually is found on utilitarian creamware and stoneware pieces and was produced through a simple chemical action. A color pigment of brown, blue, green or black was made acidic by an infusion of tobacco or hops. When the acidic colorant was applied in blobs to an alkaline ground, it reacted by spreading in feathery designs resembling sea plants. This type of decoration usually was supplemented with bands of light-colored slip.

Types of decoration vary greatly, from those done in a combination of motifs, such as Cat's Eye and Earthworm, to a plain pink mug decorated with green ribbed bands. Most forms of mocha are hollow, e.g., mugs, jugs, bowls and shakers.

English potters made the vast majority of the pieces. Collectors group the wares into three chronological periods: 1780-1820, 1820-1840 and 1840-1880.

Moorcroft

William Moorcroft was first employed as a potter by James Macintyre & Co. Ltd. of Burslem, Staffordshire, England, in 1897. He established the Moorcroft pottery in 1913.

The majority of the art pottery wares were hand thrown, resulting in a great variation among similarly styled pieces. Colors and marks are keys to determining age.

Walter Moorcroft, William's son, continued the business upon his father's death and made wares in the same style.

The company initially used an impressed mark, "Moorcroft, Burslem;" a signature mark, "W. Moorcroft" followed. Modern pieces are marked simply "Moorcroft," with export pieces also marked "Made in England."

Sanford Alderfer Auction & Appraisal

Bowl, Moorcroft, china with fruit motif, grapevine and leaves in blue, purple and yellow on green ground, 8 3/4" d, 2 3/4" h. **$184**

In 1794, the Royal Bayreuth factory was founded in Tettau, Bavaria. Royal Bayreuth introduced its figural patterns in 1885. Designs of animals, people, fruits and vegetables decorated a wide array of tableware and inexpensive souvenir items.

Tapestry wares, in rose and other patterns, were made in the late 19th century. The surface of the pieces feel and look like woven cloth.

The Royal Bayreuth crest used to mark the wares varied in design and color.

Royal Bayreuth

Skinner Inc.

Royal Crown Derby bone china cockerel, England, circa 1952, polychrome enamel decorated, modeled standing on a tree stump, printed mark, 11 3/4". **$207**

Derby Crown Porcelain Co., established in 1875 in Derby, England, had no connection with earlier Derby factories that operated in the late 18th and early 19th centuries. In 1890, the company was appointed "Manufacturers of Porcelain to Her Majesty" (Queen Victoria) and since that date has been known as "Royal Crown Derby."

Most of these porcelains, both tableware and figural, were hand decorated. A variety of printing processes were used for additional adornment.

Derby porcelains from 1878 to 1890 carry only the standard crown printed mark. After 1891, the mark includes the "Royal Crown Derby" wording. In the 20th century, "Made in England" and "English Bone China" were added to the mark.

Doulton pottery began in 1815 under the direction of John Doulton at the Doulton & Watts pottery in Lambeth, England. Early output was limited to salt-glazed industrial stoneware. After John Watts retired in 1854, the firm became Doulton and Co., and production was expanded to include hand-decorated stoneware such as figurines, vases, dinnerware and flasks.

ROYAL
DOULTON
FLAMBE

Royal Doulton

In 1878, Doulton's son, Sir Henry Doulton, purchased Pinder Bourne & Co. in Burslem, Staffordshire. The companies became Doulton & Co., Ltd. in 1882. Decorated porcelain was added to Doulton's earthenware production in 1884.

Most Doulton figurines were produced at the Burslem plants, where they were made continuously from 1890 until 1978. After a short interruption, a new line of Doulton figurines was introduced in 1979.

Dickensware, in earthenware and porcelain, was introduced in 1908. The pieces were decorated with characters from Dickens' novels. Most of the line was withdrawn in the 1940s, except for plates, which continued to be made until 1974.

Character jugs, a 20th-century revival of early Toby models, were designed by Charles J. Noke for Doulton in the 1930s. Character jugs are limited to bust portraits, while Royal Doulton Toby jugs are full figured. The character jugs come in four sizes and feature fictional characters from Dickens, Shakespeare and other English and American novelists, as well as historical heroes. Marks on both character and Toby jugs must be carefully identified to determine dates and values.

WEDGWOOD

WEDGWOOD
c1900

WEDGWOOD
c1759-1769

Wedgwood

Doulton's Rouge Flambé (Veined Sung) is a high-glazed, strong-colored ware.

Production of stoneware at Lambeth ceased in 1956.

Beginning in 1872, the "Royal Doulton" mark was used on all types of wares produced by the company.

Beginning in 1913, an "HN" number was assigned to each new Doulton figurine design. The "HN" numbers, which referred originally to Harry Nixon, a Doulton artist, were chronological until 1940, after which blocks of numbers were assigned to each modeler. From 1928 until 1954, a small number was placed to the right of the crown mark; this number, when added to 1927, gives the year of manufacture.

In 1751, the Worcester Porcelain Co., led by Dr. John Wall and William Davis, acquired the Bristol pottery of Benjamin Lund and moved it to Worcester. The first wares were painted blue under the glaze; soon thereafter decorating was accomplished by painting on the glaze in enamel colors. Among the most-famous 18th-century decorators were James Giles and Jeffery Hamet O'Neal. Transfer-print decoration was developed by the 1760s.

A series of partnerships took place after Davis' death in 1783: Flight (1783-1793); Flight & Barr (1793-1807); Barr, Flight & Barr (1807-1813); and Flight, Barr & Barr (1813-1840). In 1840, the factory was moved to Chamberlain & Co. in Diglis, Worcester. Decorative wares were discontinued. In 1852, W.H. Kerr and R.W. Binns formed a new company and revived the production of ornamental wares.

Skinner Inc.

Wedgwood solid black Jasper Dancing Hours bowl, England, 20th century, applied white classical relief with running laurel border above figures, impressed mark, 7" diameter, 6" area of rim sprayed with rim chips repaired. **$119**

In 1862, the firm became the Royal Worcester Porcelain Co. Among the key modelers of the late 19th century were James Hadley, his three sons, and George Owen, an expert with pierced clay pieces. Royal Worcester absorbed the Grainger factory in 1889 and the James Hadley factory in 1905. Modern designers include Dorothy Doughty and Doris Lindner.

The principal patron of the French porcelain industry in early 18th-century France was Jeanne Antoinette Poisson, Marquise de Pompadour. She supported the Vincennes factory of Gilles and Robert Dubois and their successors in their attempt to make soft-paste porcelain in the 1740s. In 1753, she moved the porcelain operations to Sevres, near her home, Chateau de Bellevue.

The Sevres soft-paste formula used sand from Fontainebleau, salt, saltpeter, soda of Alicante, powdered alabaster, clay and soap.

In 1769, kaolin was discovered in France, and a hard-paste formula was developed. The baroque designs gave way to rococo, a style favored by Jeanne du Barry, Louis XV's next mistress. Louis XVI took little interest in Sevres, and many factories began to turn out counterfeits. In 1876, the factory was moved to St. Cloud and was eventually nationalized.

Louis XV allowed the firm to use the "double L" in its marks.

Spatterware generally was made of common earthenware, although occasionally creamware was used. The earliest English examples were made about 1780. The peak period of production was from 1810 to 1840. Firms known to have made spatterware are Adams, Barlow, and Harvey and Cotton.

The amount of spatter decoration varies from piece to piece. Some objects simply have decorated borders. These often were decorated with a brush, requiring several hundred touches per square inch to achieve the spatter effect. Other pieces have the entire surface covered with spatter. Marked pieces are rare.

Collectors today focus on the patterns—Cannon, Castle, Fort, Peafowl, Rainbow, Rose, Thistle, Schoolhouse, etc. The decoration on flatware is in the center of the piece; on hollow ware, it occurs on both sides.

Aesthetics and the colors of spatter are key to determining value. Blue and red are the most common colors; green, purple, and brown are in a middle group; black and yellow are scarce.

In 1754, Josiah **Wedgwood** and Thomas Whieldon of Fenton Vivian, Staffordshire, England, became partners in a pottery enterprise. Their products included marbled, agate, tortoiseshell, green glaze and Egyptian black wares. In 1759, Wedgwood opened his own pottery at the Ivy House works, Burslem, Staffordshire. In 1764, he moved to the Brick House (Bell Works) at Burslem. The pottery concentrated on utilitarian pieces.

Between 1766 and 1769, Wedgwood built the famous works at Etruria. Among the most-renowned products of this plant were the Empress Catherine of Russia dinner service (1774) and the Portland Vase (1790s). The firm also made caneware, unglazed earthenwares (drabwares), piecrust wares, variegated and marbled wares, black basalt (developed in 1768), Queen's or creamware, and Jasperware (perfected in 1774).

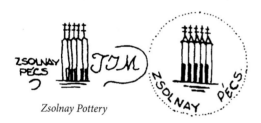

Zsolnay Pottery

Bone china was produced under the direction of Josiah Wedgwood II between 1812 and 1822 and revived in 1878. Moonlight Luster was made from 1805 to 1815. Fairyland Luster began in 1920. All luster production ended in 1932.

A museum was established at the Etruria pottery in 1906. When Wedgwood moved to its modern plant at Barlaston, North Staffordshire, the museum was expanded.

Vilmos Zsolnay (1828-1900) assumed control of his brother's factory in Pécs, Hungary, in the mid-19th century. In 1899, Miklos, Vilmos' son, became manager. The firm still produces ceramic ware.

The early wares are highly ornamental, glazed and have a cream-colored ground. Eosin glaze, a deep, rich play of colors reminiscent of Tiffany's iridescent wares, received a gold medal at the 1900 Paris exhibition.

Originally, no trademark was used, but in 1878 the company began to use a blue mark depicting the five towers of the cathedral at Pécs. The initials "TJM" represent the names of Miklos' three children.

Ceramic styles produced by many makers—including Flow Blue, Majolica and Quimper—are found at the end of this section. *Also see Oriental Objects and Tiffany.*

Majolica

In 1851, an English potter was hoping that his new interpretation of a centuries-old style of ceramics would be well received at the "Great Exhibition of the Industries of All Nations" set to open May 1 in London's Hyde Park.

Potter Herbert Minton had high hopes for his display. His father, Thomas Minton, founded a pottery works in the mid-1790s in Stoke-on-Trent, Staffordshire. Herbert Minton had designed a "new" line of pottery, and his chemist, Leon Arnoux, had developed a process that resulted in vibrant, colorful glazes that came to be called "majolica."

Trained as an engineer, Arnoux also studied the making of encaustic tiles, and had been appointed art director at Minton's works in 1848. His job was to introduce and promote new products. Victorian fascination with the natural world prompted Arnoux to reintroduce the work of Bernard Palissy, whose naturalistic, bright-colored "maiolica" wares had been created in the 16th century. But Arnoux used a thicker body to make pieces sturdier. This body was given a coating of opaque white glaze, which provided a surface for decoration.

Pieces were modeled in high relief, featuring butterflies and other insects, flowers and leaves, fruit, shells, animals and fish. Queen Victoria's endorsement of the new pottery prompted its acceptance by the general public.

When Minton introduced his wares at Philadelphia's 1876 Centennial Exhibition, American potters also began to produce majolica.

For more information on majolica, see *Warman's Majolica Identification and Price Guide* by Mark F. Moran.

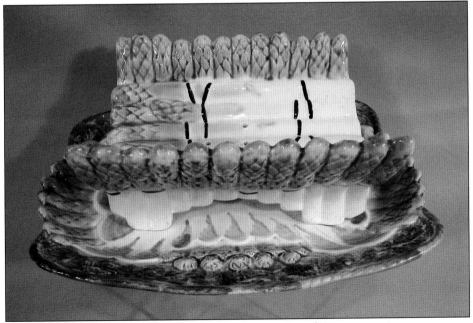

Longchamp French asparagus tray and cradle, good color, 13 1/2" long. **$250+**

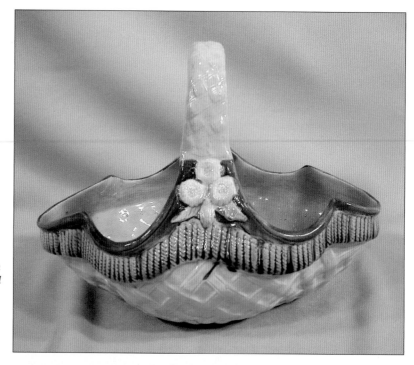

Yellow basket weave basket with flowers, attributed to Holdcroft, 10" long. **$300+**

Minton putti shell carriers on cobalt rimmed base, strong color and detail, 11" wide, 11" tall. **$3,000+**

Holdcroft pond lily foot cachepot strong color and detail, 7" diameter, 5 3/4" tall. (Collector tip: Joseph Holdcroft majolica ware was produced at Daisy Bank in Longton, Staffordshire, England, from 1870 to 1885. Items can be found marked with "JHOLDCROFT," but many items can only be attributed by the patterns and colors that are documented to have come from the Holdcroft potteries.) **$700+**

Pond lily and stork tall cake stand, good detail, 9 1/2" tall, 10 1/2" diameter. **$400+**

Minton dolphin candlestick professional repair to top, 8 1/4" tall. (Thomas Minton founded his factory in the mid-1790s in Stoke-on-Trent, Staffordshire, England. His son, Herbert Minton, introduced majolica pottery—with glazes created by Léon Arnoux—at England's Great Exhibition of 1851.) **$450+**

Minton rabbits under cabbage table centerpiece, shape no. 1451, date code for 1873, strong color and detail, 9 1/2" long, 4 1/2" tall. **$7,500-$10,000**

George Jones cobalt picket fence and daisy full-size cheese keeper, outstanding color, minor professional rim repair to under plate, 12" diameter, 12" tall. **$10,000+**

Etruscan cobalt daisy comport (compote), 8 1/2" diameter. **$250+**

Holdcroft mottled shell comport (or compote) with shells and seaweed on base, good detail, 9 1/2" diameter, 7" tall. **$325+**

Wardle floral and leaf covered sugar, 5" tall. **$130+**

Fielding bird and fan turquoise cup and saucer. (Collector tip: Railway Pottery, established by S. Fielding & Co., Stoke, Stoke-on-Trent, Staffordshire, England, 1879.) **$125+ pair**

Victoria Pottery Co. (VPC) basket weave game dish with mallard ducks on bed of ferns on cover, good color, with insert, professional repair to duck's wing, 12" wide. (Collector tip: Victoria Pottery Co., Hanley, Staffordshire, England, 1895 to 1927.) **$600+**

Copeland ewer with angel faces and birds in high relief, band of ivy and berries on cobalt ground, good color, professional spout and handle repair, 10 1/2" tall. (Collector tip: William T. Copeland & Sons pottery of Stoke-on-Trent, England, began producing porcelain and earthenware in 1847.) **$1,200**

Bird and fan turquoise humidor, 5 1/2" tall. **$150+**

Large French birds on branch, blackberry, floral and leaves oval jardinière, good detail, 15" wide, 8" tall. **$500+**

Thomas Sergent Palissy shells, fern and leaf jardinière, great detail, 7 1/2" tall, 10" diameter. (Collector tip: Thomas-Victor Sergent was one of the School of Paris ceramists of the late 19th century who was influenced by the works of Bernard Palissy, c. 1510-1590, the great French Renaissance potter.) **$800+**

Minton tower jug with jester finial on hinged pewter lid, shape no. 1231, 13" tall. **$850+**

"BB" figural match striker with mouse, melon, flowers and leaves, minor rim repair, 8" wide. **$550+**

George Jones apple blossom and basket weave mug, good color and detail, 5 1/2" tall. (Collector tip: The company started operations in the early 1860s as George Jones in Stoke, Staffordshire, England, and in 1873 became George Jones & Sons Ltd.) **$2,000+**

Fish oyster plate with large fish cracker well, 10" wide. **$800+**

Samuel Lear sunflower oyster plate with lavender rim, minor rim glaze wear, 9 3/4" diameter. (Collector tip: Samuel Lear, Hanley, Staffordshire, England, 1877 to 1886.) **$1,300+**

Wedgwood St. Louis pattern oyster plate with cobalt and turquoise wells, strong color and detail, 9" diameter. (Collector tip: Founded by Josiah Wedgwood in 1759 at Burslem, Staffordshire, England.) **$1,300+**

Cobalt wild rose pitcher with butterfly spout, good color, 9 1/2" tall. **$300+**

Holdcroft cobalt pond lily ice-lip pitcher, great color, 9 1/2" tall. (Collector tip: Joseph Holdcroft majolica ware was produced at Daisy Bank in Longton, Staffordshire, England, from 1870 to 1885. Items can be found marked with "JHOLDCROFT," but many items can only be attributed by the patterns and colors that are documented to have come from the Holdcroft potteries.) **$800-$1,200**

George Jones turquoise apple blossom and basket pitcher, strong color and detail, Bacall Collection, 8" tall.
$1,600+

Turquoise tree bark and blackberry pitcher, 4 1/2" tall.
$175+

Wild rose on mottled ground pitcher, 8" tall. **$180+**

Hugo Lonitz small dolphin footed planter with mythological faces on ends, cobalt accents, 6" wide, 5" tall. (Collector tip: Hugo Lonitz operated in Haldensleben, Germany, from 1868-1886, and later Hugo Lonitz & Co., 1886-1904, producing household and decorative porcelain and earthenware, and metal wares. Look for a mark of two entwined fish.) **$170+**

Begonia on basket plate with cobalt rope edge, good color, 8" diameter. **$250+**

Brownfield strawberry and leaf plate, 8 3/4" diameter. (Collector tip: W. Brownfield & Son, Burslem and Cobridge, Staffordshire, England, 1850 to 1891.) **$275+**

Fielding bird and fan cobalt plate, strong color, 7 1/2" diameter. (Collector tip: Railway Pottery, established by S. Fielding & Co., Stoke, Stoke-on-Trent, Staffordshire, England, 1879.) **$150+**

Geranium and floral plate with lavender flowers, strong color, 9 1/4" diameter. **$300+**

Holdcroft cobalt leaf plate strong color, 8 1/4" diameter. (Collector tip: Joseph Holdcroft majolica ware was produced at Daisy Bank in Longton, Staffordshire, England, from 1870 to 1885. Items can be found marked with "JHOLDCROFT," but many items can only be attributed by the patterns and colors that are documented to have come from the Holdcroft potteries.) **$385+**

George Jones pineapple plate good color, rim chip to back, 9" diameter. **$375+**

Samuel Lear floral and fan plate 8" diameter. (Collector tip: Samuel Lear, Hanley, Staffordshire, England, 1877 to 1886.) **$140+**

Wedgwood yellow grape and leaf plate, strong color, 9" diameter. **$350+**

Geranium platter with lavender flowers, outstanding color and detail, 12" wide. **$550+**

George Jones overlapping ferns and leaves platter with twig handles, strong color and detail, 14" wide. (Collector tip: The company started operations in the early 1860s as George Jones in Stoke, Staffordshire, England, and in 1873 became George Jones & Sons Ltd.) **$2,300+**

Wedgwood yellow salmon platter, extremely rare in this color, outstanding color, detail and condition, 25" long, 12 3/4" wide. (Collector tip: Founded by Josiah Wedgwood in 1759 at Burslem, Staffordshire, England.) **$12,500+**

Yellow sardine box with attached under plate. **$200+**

Etruscan cobalt sunflower sauce dish, strong color, 5" diameter. (Collector tip: Made by Griffen, Smith and Hill of Phoenixville, Pa., 1879 to about 1890.) **$250+**

George Jones strawberry server with cream and sugar, strong color and detail, 14 1/2" long. **$1,500-$2,000**

Fielding ribbon bow, daisy and wheat teapot, great detail, 6" tall. **$350+**

Minton "Spikey" fish figural teapot, extremely rare, professional repair to spout, base rim and rim of lid, outstanding color and detail, 9-1/2" long, 7" tall. **$26,000+**

Victoria Pottery Co. (VPC) floral three-piece tea set, professional spout repair to creamer. (Collector tip: The Victoria Pottery Co. of Hanley, Staffordshire, England, was active from 1895 to the late 1920s.) **$700+ all**

Cobalt fish and seaweed tray, strong color and detail, 13 1/2" wide. **$450+**

Fan-shaped dragonfly tray with cobalt ribbon handle, 10" long. **$225+**

George Jones turquoise butterfly, wheat and bamboo two-handled tray, outstanding color and detail, Bacall Collection, 13" wide. **$4,000+**

Wedgwood turquoise basket weave grape tray with twig handles, 9-1/2" diameter. (Collector tip: Founded by Josiah Wedgwood in 1759 at Burslem, Staffordshire, England.) **$400+**

Lavender covered game tureen with liner, good color, professional rim repair to base and rim of lid, 9" wide. **$750+**

Holdcroft cobalt water lily and bamboo umbrella stand, strong color, 23" tall. (Collector tip: Joseph Holdcroft majolica ware was produced at Daisy Bank in Longton, Staffordshire, England, from 1870 to 1885. Items can be found marked with "JHOLDCROFT" but many items can only be attributed by the patterns and colors that are documented to have come from the Holdcroft potteries.) **$3,250+**

Czechoslovakia bird wall pocket, 7" tall. **$120+**

Minton turquoise wine cooler with mythological mask and snake handles, strong color, shape no. 946, date code for 1871, 8 1/2" tall, 7 1/2" diameter. (Thomas Minton founded his factory in the mid-1790s in Stoke-on-Trent, Staffordshire, England. His son, Herbert Minton, introduced majolica pottery—with glazes created by Léon Arnoux—at England's Great Exhibition of 1851.) **$1,500-$2,000**

Delphin Massier figural stork vase, good detail, 8 1/2" tall. (Collector tip: The Massier family began producing ceramics in Vallauris, France, in the mid-18th century.) **$350+**

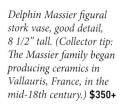

Pair of Copeland cobalt mantle vases with floral and leaf motif, strong color and detail, each 11 1/2" tall. (Collector tip: William T. Copeland & Sons pottery of Stoke-on-Trent, England, began producing porcelain and earthenware in 1847.) **$2,750+ pair**

W.S. & S. vase with mask feet and handles, 12 1/2", (Collector tip: Wilhelm Schiller and Sons, Bodenbach, Bohemia, established 1885.) **$500+**

Other Majolica Makers

John Adams & Co., Hanley, Stoke-on-Trent, Staffordshire, England, operated the Victoria Works, producing earthenware, jasperware, Parian, majolica, 1864-1873. (Collector's tip: Jasperware is a fine white stoneware originally produced by Josiah Wedgwood, often colored by metallic oxides with raised classical designs remaining white.)

Another Staffordshire pottery, Samuel Alcock & Co., Cobridge, 1828-1853; Burslem, 1830-1859, produced earthenware, china and Parian.

The W. & J.A. Bailey Alloa Pottery was founded in Alloa, the principal town in Clackmannanshire, located near Edinburgh, Scotland.

The Bevington family of potters worked in Hanley, Staffordshire, England, in the late 19th century.

W. Brownfield & Son, Burslem and Cobridge, Staffordshire, England, 1850-1891.

T.C. Brown-Westhead, Moore & Co., produced earthenware and porcelain at Hanley, Stoke-on-Trent, Staffordshire, from about 1862 to 1904.

The Choisy-le-Roi faience factory of Choisy-le-Roi, France, produced majolica from 1860 until 1910. The firm's wares are not always marked. The common mark is usually a black ink stamp "Choisy-le-Roi" pictured to the right with a large "HBm" which stands for Hippolyte Boulenger, a director at the pottery.

William T. Copeland & Sons pottery of Stoke-on-Trent, Staffordshire, England, began producing porcelain and earthenware in 1847. (Josiah Spode established a pottery at Stoke-on-Trent in 1770. In 1833, the firm was purchased by William Copeland and Thomas Garrett. In 1847, Copeland became the sole owner. W.T. Copeland & Sons continued until a 1976 merger when it became Royal Worcester Spode. Copeland majolica pieces are sometimes marked with an impressed "COPELAND," but many are unmarked.)

Jose A. Cunha, Caldas da Rainha, southern Portugal, also worked in the style of Bernard Palissy, the great French Renaissance potter.

Julius Dressler, Bela Czech Republic, company founded 1888, producing faience, majolica and porcelain. In 1920, the name was changed to EPIAG. The firm closed about 1945.

Eureka Pottery was located in Trenton, N.J., circa 1883-1887.

Railway Pottery, established by S. Fielding & Co., Stoke, Stoke-on-Trent, Staffordshire, England, 1879.

There were two Thomas Forester potteries active in the late 19th century in Staffordshire, England. Some sources list the more famous of the two as Thomas Forester & Sons Ltd. at the Phoenix Works, Longton.

Established in the early 19th century, the Gien pottery works is located on the banks of France's Loire River near Orleans.

Joseph Holdcroft majolica ware was produced at Daisy Bank in Longton, Staffordshire, England, from 1870 to 1885. Items can be found marked with "J HOLDCROFT," but many pieces can only be attributed by the patterns and colors that are documented to have come from the Holdcroft potteries.

George Jones & Sons Ltd., Stoke, Staffordshire, started operation in about 1864 as George Jones and in 1873 became George Jones & Sons Ltd. The firm operated the Trent Potteries in Stoke-on-Trent (renamed "Crescent Potteries" in about 1907).

In about 1877, Samuel Lear erected a small china works in Hanley, Staffordshire. Lear produced domestic china and, in addition, decorated all kinds of earthenware made by other

manufacturers, including "spirit kegs." In 1882, the firm expanded to include production of majolica, ivory-body earthenware and Wedgwood-type jasperware. The business closed in 1886.

Robert Charbonnier founded the Longchamp tile works in 1847 to make red clay tiles, but the factory soon started to produce majolica. Longchamp is known for its "barbotine" pieces (a paste of clay used in decorating coarse pottery in relief) made with vivid colors, especially oyster plates.

Hugo Lonitz operated in Haldensleben, Germany, from 1868-1886, and later Hugo Lonitz & Co., 1886-1904, producing household and decorative porcelain, earthenware and metalwares. Look for a mark of two entwined fish.

The Lunéville pottery was founded about 1728 by Jacques Chambrette in the city that bears its name, in the Alsace-Lorraine region of northeastern France. The firm became famous for its blue monochromatic and floral patterns. Around 1750, ceramist Paul-Louis Cufflé introduced a pattern with animals and historical figures. Lunéville products range from hand-painted faience and majolica to pieces influenced by the Art Deco movement.

The Massier family began producing ceramics in Vallauris, France, in the mid-18th century.

François Maurice, School of Paris, active 1875-1885, also worked in the style of Bernard Palissy.

George Morley & Co., East Liverpool, Ohio, 1884-1891.

Morley & Co. Pottery was founded in 1879, Wellsville, Ohio, making graniteware and majolica.

Orchies, a majolica manufacturer in northern France near Lille, is also known under the mark "Moulin des Loups & Hamage," 1920s.

Faïencerie de Pornic is located near Quimper, France.

Quimper pottery has a long history. Tin-glazed, hand-painted pottery has been made in Quimper, France, since the late 17th century. The earliest firm, founded in 1685 by Jean Baptiste Bousquet, was known as HB Quimper. Another firm, founded in 1772 by Francois Eloury, was known as Porquier. A third firm, founded by Guillaume Dumaine in 1778, was known as HR or Henriot Quimper. All three companies made similar pottery decorated with designs of Breton peasants, and sea and flower motifs.

The Rörstrand factory made the first faience (tin-glazed earthenware) produced in Sweden. It was established in 1725 by Johann Wolff, near Stockholm.

The earthenware factory of Salins was established in 1857 in Salins-les-Bains, near the French border with Switzerland. Salins was awarded with the gold medal at the International Exhibition of Decorative Arts in Paris in 1912.

Sarreguemines wares are named for the city in the Lorraine region of northeastern France. The pottery was founded in 1790 by Nicholas-Henri Jacobi. For more than 100 years, it flourished under the direction of the Utzschneider family.

Wilhelm Schiller and Sons, Bodenbach, Bohemia, established 1885.

Thomas-Victor Sergent was one of the School of Paris ceramists of the late 19th century who was influenced by the works of Bernard Palissy.

St. Clement: Founded by Jacques Chambrette in Saint-Clément, France, in 1758. Chambrette also established works in Lunéville.

The St. Jean de Bretagne pottery works are located near Quimper, France.

Vallauris is a pottery center in southeastern France, near Cannes. Companies in production there include Massier and Foucard-Jourdan.

Victoria Pottery Co., Hanley, Staffordshire, England, 1895-1927.

Wardle & Co., established 1871 at Hanley, Staffordshire, England.

Josiah Wedgwood was born in Burslem, Staffordshire, England, on July 12, 1730, into a family with a long pottery tradition. At the age of nine, after the death of his father, he joined the family business. In 1759, he set up his own pottery works in Burslem. There he produced cream-colored earthenware that found favor with Queen Charlotte. In 1762, she appointed him royal supplier of dinnerware. From the public sale of "Queen's Ware," as it came to be known, Wedgwood was able to build a production community in 1768, which he named Etruria, near Stoke-on-Trent, and a second factory equipped with tools and ovens of his own design. (Etruria is the ancient land of the Etruscans, in what is now northern Italy.)

Unless otherwise indicated, all majolica listings in this edition come courtesy of Strawser Auction Group, Wolcottville, Ind., *www.strawserauctions.com*, facilitated by Artfact, *www.artfact.com*.

Flow Blue

Flow Blue is the name applied to china of cobalt blue and white, whose color, when fired in a kiln, produced a flowing or blurred effect. The color varies from dark royal cobalt blue to navy or steel blue. The flow may be very slight to a heavy blur, where the pattern cannot be easily recognized. The blue color does not permeate through the body of the china. The amount of flow on the back of a piece is determined by the position of the item in the "sagger" (a case of fire clay) during firing.

Known patterns of flow blue were first produced around 1830 in the Staffordshire area of England. Credit is generally given to Josiah Wedgwood, who worked in that area. Many other potters followed, including Alcock, Davenport, Grindley, Johnson Brothers, Meakin, Meigh and New Wharf. They were attempting to imitate the blue and white wares brought back by the ship captains of the tea trade. Early flow blue, 1830s to 1870s, was usually of the pearlware or ironstone variety. The later patterns, 1880s to 1900s, and the modern patterns after 1910, were of the more delicate semi-porcelains. Most flow blue was made in England but it was made in many other countries as well. Germany, Holland, France, Spain, Wales and Scotland are also known locations. Many patterns were made in the United States by several companies: Mercer, Warwick, Sterling and the Wheeling Pottery to name a few.

Collector's Note: The Flow Blue International Collectors' Club Inc. has studied new vs. reproduction flow blue. There are still areas of personal judgment as yet undetermined. The general rule has been "new" indicates recent or contemporary manufacture and "reproduction" is a copy of an older pattern. Problems arise when either are sold at "old" flow blue prices.

The club continues to inform members through its conventions, newsletters and the Web site: www.flowblue.com.

The following is a listing of "new" flow blue, produced since the 1960s.

Blossom: Ashworth Bros., Hanley, 1962. Washbowl and pitcher made for many years now.

Iris: By Dunn, Bennett, Burslem, has been reproduced in a full chamber set.

Romantic Flow Blue: Blakeney Pottery, 1970s. Resembles Watteau. The old patterns never had the words "flow blue" written on them.

Touraine: By Stanley, by far the most prolific reproduction made recently, in 2002. Again, the "England" is missing from the mark, and it is made in China. Nearly the entire dinnerware set has been made and is being sold.

Victoria Ware: Mark is of lion and uniform, but has paper label "Made in China," 1990s. Made in various patterns and designs, but the giveaway is the roughness on the bottoms, and much of it has a pea-green background.

Vinranka: Upsala-Ekeby, Sweden, 1967-1968. Now discontinued and highly collectible, a full dinnerware set.

Waldorf: By New Wharf, cups and saucers are found, but missing "England" from their mark and are made in China.

Floral pitchers (jugs) and teapots bearing a copied "T. Rathbone England" swan mark.

Williams-Sonoma and Cracker Barrel have released a vivid blue-and-white line. Both are made in China. One line is a simplified dahlia flower on white; the other has summer bouquets. Both are well made and readily available, just not old. The reproductions are more of a threat to collectors.

In all cases, regarding new pieces and reproductions, be aware of unglazed areas on the bottoms. The foot rings are rough and too white. The reproductions, particularly the Touraine, are heavier in weight, having a distinctive thick feel. The embossing isn't as crisp and the pieces are frequently slightly smaller in overall size than the originals.

Check the Flow Blue International Collectors' Club, Inc. Web site. Join the club, study the books available, and always work with a trusted dealer. Good dealers guarantee their merchandise and protect their customers.

Flow Blue, pitcher, Stag and Hound, unknown maker, 1850, 8". **$425**

Flow Blue, Polychrome, plate, unknown maker, 1855, 9". **$110**

Flow Blue pitcher, John Westwood, Low Toryburn, 1866. **$575**

Flow Blue bowl, La Belle, Wheeling, orange, 1890. **$2,550**

Quimper

Quimper faience, dating back to the 17th century, is named for Quimper, a French town where numerous potteries were located. Several mergers resulted in the evolution of two major houses—the Jules Henriot and Hubaudière-Bousquet factories.

The peasant design first appeared in the 1860s, and many variations exist. Florals and geometrics, equally popular, also were produced in large quantities. During the 1920s, the Hubaudière-Bousquet factory introduced the Odetta line, which used a stone body and Art Deco decorations.

The two major houses merged in 1968, the products retaining the individual characteristics and marks of the originals. The concern suffered from labor problems in the 1980s and was purchased by an American group.

The "HR" and "HR Quimper" marks are found on Henriot pieces prior to 1922. The "Henriot Quimper" mark was used after 1922. The "HB" mark covers a long time span. Numbers or dots and dashes were added for inventory purposes and are found on later pieces. Most marks are in blue or black. Pieces ordered by department stores, such as Macy's and Carson Pirie Scott, carry the store mark along with the factory mark, making them less desirable to collectors.

Contributor: Al Bagdade.

Additional Terms:

A la touche border decor—single brush stroke to create floral

Breton Broderie decor—stylized blue and gold pattern inspired by a popular embroidery design often used on Breton costumes, dates from the 1920s.

Croisille—criss-cross pattern

Decor Riche border—acanthus leaves in two colors

Fleur-de-lys—the symbol of France.

Condiments, 5 1/4" h,
HB Quimper marks.
$350 pair

*Cake plate, 11 1/2"
handle to handle,
Breton Broderie, HB
Quimper mark, circa
1925.* **$300**

*Plate, 13 1/2", square-
on-square design, "HR
Quimper" mark.* **$295**

Civil War Collectibles

The Civil War began April 12, 1861, at Fort Sumter, the Confederates surrendered at Appomattox Courthouse on April 9, 1865, and all official fighting ceased on May 26, 1865.

For some Civil War enthusiasts, collecting war relics is the best way to understand the heritage and role of the thousands who served.

It has become commonplace to have major sales of Civil War artifacts by a few major auction houses, in addition to the private trading, local auctions, and Internet sales of these items. These auction houses handle the majority of significant Civil War items coming to the marketplace.

The majority of these valuable items are in repositories of museums, universities, and colleges, but many items were also traded between private citizens. Items that are being released by museums and from private collections make up the base of items currently being traded and sold to collectors of Civil War material culture. In addition, many family collections amassed over the years have been recently coming to the marketplace as new generations have decided to liquidate some of them.

Civil War items are acquired by collectors in the same fashion as any material cultural item. Individuals interested in antiques and collectibles find items at farm auction sales, yard sales, estate sales, specialized auctions, private collectors trading or selling items, and the Internet and online auction sales.

Provenance is important in Civil War collectibles—maybe even more important than with most other collectibles. Also, many Civil War items have well-documented provenance as they come from family collections or their authenticity has been previously documented by auction houses, museums, or other experts in the field.

For more information on Civil War memorabilia, see *Warman's Civil War Collectibles Identification and Price Guide*, 3rd edition, by Russell L. Lewis.

Middle Tennessee Relics

Excavated, Leech & Rigdon, Memphis, Tennessee, C.S.-molded officer's cavalry spur. **$1,850-$2,000**

James D. Julia Auctioneers '07

Extremely rare Bartholomae patent filter canteen, cover and partial strap. Invented and patented by Charles Bartholomae, the tin canteen is about 6" h. x 6" w. and is kidney-shaped in cross section with a wide, funnel-like spout with an applied brass label reading "PATENTED JULY 3rd 1861" and two other lead spouts (one retaining its lead cap and chain). In his patent, Bartholomae described his invention "as a canteen which may be worn with greater facility than those of usual construction, more readily filled and more convenient to drink from, and one supplied with an efficient filtering device, which may be used whenever necessity requires". This example retains its original brown wool cover and part of its narrow brown bridle leather strap. These canteens, mostly private purchase, saw actual use in the field, which accounts for their rarity today. Good condition. $3,737

A limber was a two-wheeled carriage used to transport a cannon and its carriage. This U.S. field artillery limber retains 50 percent of its original paint. **$6,000-$10,500**

James D. Julia Auctioneers

James D. Julia Auctioneers

Privately purchased McClellan-style saddle attributed to Confederate General A.R. Lawton. The entire seat, pommel, and cantle are covered in black bridal leather. The pommel has a stamped brass shield reading "11 inch seat." **$7,500-$9,000**

S.E.L.L. Antiques/Paul Goodwin

This officer's-grade sword belt plate was made for troops from Ohio; rare. **$2,800-$3,000**

British 6.4" Armstrong bolt, non-excavated. This shell was imported by the Confederates. Written in old lettering on the shell is "CONFEDERATE RIFLE PROJECTILE, NORFOLK NAVY YARD, C.S.A." On the opposite side is "CSA 100." **$6,800-$7,350**

James D. Julia Auctioneers

S.E.L.L. Antiques/Paul Goodwin

Marine Corps cuff-size button made by Horstmann. **$275**

S.E.L.L. Antiques/Paul Goodwin

Confederate General Staff coat-size button, marked "S&K Rivet'd & Solder'd." **$1,100**

Authentic signature of "A. LINCOLN MARCH 4, 1864" on a sheet of plain yellow stationery measuring approximately 7" by 9" folded to the approximate size of an envelope. The autograph is accompanied by a copy print of a photograph of Lincoln originally taken by C.G. German of Springfield, Illinois. Near excellent condition. **$2,012**

James D. Julia Auctioneers

James D. Julia Auctioneers

Two autographs by Confederate General J.E.B. Stuart. An envelope addressed to Mrs. J.E.B. Stuart in J.E.B. Stuart's hand. There is an added, clipped autograph from letter placed on envelope to show that the other signature was an in situ autograph. Hinged above the address line is this clip. Envelope has 5¢ Jefferson Davis stamp from 1862 and an imprint, "Headquarters Cavalry Brigade / Army of the Potomac." Attached, clipped autograph has been closely trimmed, removing portion of the "S" in Stuart. Hinge has stained paper. Envelope is soiled with numerous small tears and reductions. Stamp is partially missing. **$2,530**

Wisconsin Veterans Museum

Nickel-plated brass E-flat alto horn made by E.G. Wright, a Boston maker of fine instruments. The horn was used by Merrill Sherman, 24th Wisconsin Infantry. **$2,950**

Diary in a small fold-over booklet, 1864, kept by Corporal J.R. Braley, Co. G, 30th Maine Regiment. **$1,410**
Skinner, Inc.

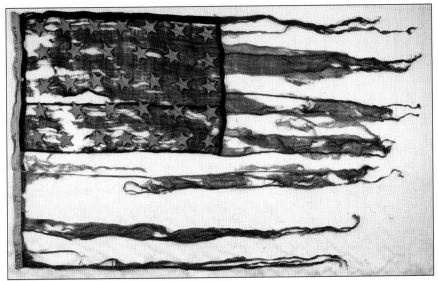

James D. Julia Auctioneers

The first American flag captured. "This flag was hauled down by secessionists on January 12, 1861, fully three months before the firing on Fort Sumter, and so far as known was the first United States flag so desecrated in the Great Conflict"–so reads the provenance from the Soldier and Sailors Memorial, where this flag has been since 1912, just being de-accessed in 2007. Much of the stripes are worn and missing; however, the canton is fairly complete with all 33 stars. The hoist is sound. Markings on hoist are very good. Attached pennant is intact with one approximately 2" x 2" hole and several large stains. **$33,350**

James D. Julia Auctioneers

Captured Confederate drum. Standard military drum used by both North and South; 16" x 14" with about 2" high red-painted hoops, a natural wood body with a geometric design, a bone vent hole plug, and original tied-on carrying strap. The drum came from a direct descendant of the soldier, who captured this drum and carried it home as a souvenir. There is a 15-line ink inscription on the top head that is no doubt contemporary to the capture of the drum. Because of its bulk, a drum would have been a difficult souvenir for a soldier to obtain, unless he were stationed on a ship such as soldiers fighting at Port Royal, at Hilton Head Island, South Carolina, where other large souvenirs have been known to have been collected. The inscription, though worn and weathered, is still mostly discernible as follows: "This drum was found 3 miles from Fort Walker, Hilton Head, S.C. on the 8th of November 1861, by WM. Car.... the Steward of Steamship Manion. The drum was left in that spot by one of the drummers of the Berry Infantry of ... 7th day of ... Georgia on the named month..... after their defeat in the battle for Port Royal. The drummer ... in the hand during his... was on the drum...SECESSION DRUM FROM PORT ROYAL, S.C.". **$20,700**

Cavalry items seem to be a favorite area among collectors. This pair of sergeant chevrons made of yellow worsted tape sewn to a wool backing sold for **$3,737**

James D. Julia Auctioneers

Confederate Southern Cross of Honor was made by Charles Crankshaw of Atlanta in the late 19th century. The United Daughters of the Confederacy gave these medals to any Confederate soldier who was honorably discharged or surrendered with his army or died during the Civil War. These medals were not issued named, and it was up to the soldier to have a jeweler inscribe or scratch his name himself into the name bar. "R. W. Jenkins" inscribed his name quite nicely. R. W. Jenkins appears on the rolls of the 6th and 8th South Carolina Infantry as a sergeant and later lieutenant. Medal is in "as found" condition with pleasant patina on all surfaces. **$805**

James D. Julia Auctioneers

Dr. Michael Echols

Tourniquet, petit brass screw frame, fabric strap, maker. **$200-$270**

Cowan's Auctions, Inc.

Brown leather medical saddle bags owned by Dr. E. Karn M.D., an assistant surgeon in the 93rd Indiana Infantry.
$750-$1,000

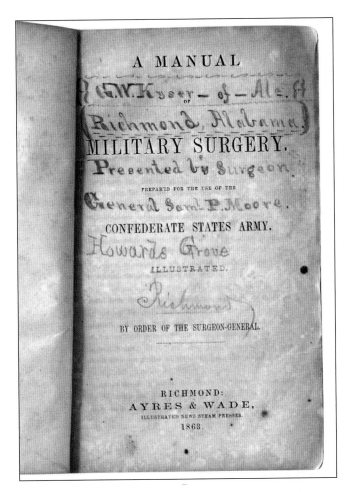

A Manual of Military Surgery, *by Samuel Moore, M.D., Richmond: Ayres & Wade, 1863. With 30 plates and 174 figures, this was the first of only two illustrated military surgical manuals to have been compiled and printed in the Confederacy. During the Civil War, Dr. Moore was the surgeon general of the Confederate States Army Medical Department.* **$4,500**

Dr. Michael Echols

Quarter-plate tintype of an African-American Union soldier uniformed in standard nine-button frock coat and slouch hat. **$2,800-$3,300**

Cowan's Auctions, Inc.

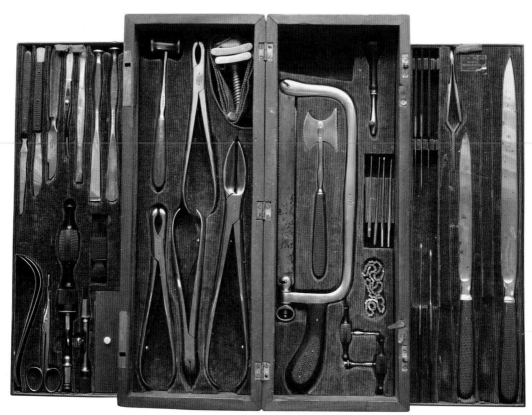

Dr. Michael Echols

A Civil War military issue set by Kolbe, Philadelphia, marked "U.S.A., Hosp. Dept." for amputation and major bone surgery. **$15,500**

Soldiers spent far more time in camp passing time than they did marching or fighting. A variety of board games can be a fine representation of one of the ways soldiers passed their hours. This checkerboard belonged to George Stinchfield, a member of Company G, 12th Maine Volunteer Infantry. **$750**

Tommy Haas/Paul Goodwin

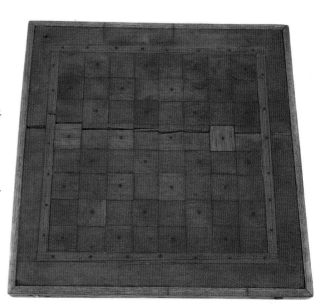

Skinner, Inc.

Bells in sight musical box by Bremond with American Civil War Tune, No. 24245, playing "Stonewall Jackson, La Fille du Regiment" and six other airs, Gamme No. 518, accompanied by nine optional engine-turned bells with finial strikers, with zither attachment, flat-topped winding lever and tune-sheet, in burl walnut veneered case with tulipwood banding and retailer's transfer of "Alfred Hays, Manufacturer & Importer of Musical Instruments, 4 Royal Exchange Buildings and 82 Cornhill," 23" wide, cylinder 13". The second track is named after the Confederate general of the American Civil War, Thomas Jonathan "Stonewall" Jackson (1824-1863). Its inclusion on a musical box retailed by an English firm, whose program also includes French, German, and Scottish tunes, is unusual, suggesting a special order from an original owner with broad musical tastes. Movement has been recently cleaned and overhauled and plays well. Case has old finish with an attractive mellow patina. Inner glass replaced. **$4,444**

James D. Julia Auctioneers

Colt Navy carried by Captain Thomas Chubb of the Confederate schooner Royal Yacht. Serial number 23167. This Model 1851 Colt Navy was recently found in the state of Vermont, where Chubb died at his summer home in 1886. Chubb's son had a business of manufacturing fishing rods and reels with the Thomas H. Chubb brand, which are highly collectible today. This business was near Chubb's summer home in Post Mills, Vermont. The commemorative inscription on backstrap of gun reads "CAPT T. H. CHUBB, 1861-1865" and "CSN ROYAL YACHT" back of trigger guard. Accompanying this gun is a large folio of history. Mechanically fine, tight with sharp edges in "as found" condition. Gun overall is gray with scattered pitting over 20% or 30%, bright blue on barrel. Cylinder scene is complete but with scattered pitting. Backstrap and trigger guard retain a portion of silver plate. Stocks are very good with original varnish; a small chip is present on inside toe of left stock. **$9,200**

Skinner, Inc.

Quilt, appliquéd cotton made by Margaret Hazzard, Bainbridge Township, Berrien County, Michigan, 1864. **$82,250**

James D. Julia Auctioneers

Military portrait / Lincoln-signed Congressional resolution to Commander John L. Worden of the U.S.S. Monitor. Portrait is oil on board and is a copy of an identical portrait hanging in the U.S. Naval Academy Museum in Annapolis, Maryland, by Philipp Albert Gliemann (1822-1871). This portrait and genre painter was born in Germany in 1822 and died in 1871. The portrait measures 19 3/4" x 24" (slightly smaller than the signed portrait in the Naval Academy Museum), and is unsigned, but obviously from the hand of the same artist. He is depicted in U.S. Navy, regulation uniform of dark blue with brightly highlighted, gold, full dress epaulets on each shoulder, bearing a single star. On his right sleeve is the regulation braid for a rear admiral, being two slightly raised bands on a broad band of gold embroidered lace with a five-pointed gold star above. Cuff of his white shirt is showing. Both of his hands hold the grip and knuckle bow of his elaborate, gold-plated, eagle pommel sword. Frame is of fancy gilded gesso and wood measuring 28" x 32". Portrait is accompanied by Worden's Congressional Resolution, which is a framed, partially printed document on vellum, measuring 15" x 18". Framed oil painting is in very good condition but unrestored. Scratches on Worden's forehead and chipped paint loss on canvas near corners. Light paint flaking at the upper left hand corner and in the lower right hand corner. Painting has darkened with the age of its varnish. No defects affect the subject. Frame is in excellent condition with one broken scroll at the bottom. Partially printed Congressional Resolution is framed and in very good condition with some fading to the ink and signatures. **$40,250**

James D. Julia Auctioneers

Civil War engraved and inscribed Smith & Wesson No. 2 Army revolver. Serial number 14456. Cal. 32 RF. Usual configuration with 6" octagonal barrel with integral rib and German silver front sight and two-piece rosewood grips numbered to this revolver. Frame, cylinder and barrel are engraved in period chiseled foliate arabesque patterns with punch dot background and a wave and dot pattern on each side of barrel. Backstrap is inscribed in period script "Col. John T. Wilder". Both sides of receiver have an engraved lightning bolt representing Col. Wilder's "Lightning Brigade". Col. Wilder joined the Indiana 17th Infantry as a lieutenant colonel on June 4, 1861, and resigned on Oct. 5, 1864, as a brevette brigadier general. He was born Jan. 31, 1830, and died Oct. 20, 1917. Good to very good condition. Metal retains a dark plum/brown patina with blue in some of very sheltered places. Grips are fine. Good mechanics, strong dark bore. **$20,125**

Wisconsin Veterans Museum

This dark blue wool forage cap features an embroidered infantry bugle insignia with regiment number "2" in the center. The cap was worn by Col. Lucius Fairchild, 2nd Wisconsin Infantry during the Gettysburg campaign. Because of the association with the famous Iron Brigade, this cap, which would normally sell for around $3,850, is valued at about **$22,000.**

South Carolina major's frock coat worn by Robert Jefferson Betsill, 18th South Carolina Volunteer Infantry. It is double breasted with 14 large three-piece U.S. staff officer buttons. The coat suffered major losses, particularly on one side of the breast. Numerous holes in the sleeves, skirts, and back have been professionally conserved and backed with a similar appearing gray wool cloth. Buttons and rank insignia are modern replacements. **$20,000-$25,000**

James D. Julia Auctioneers

Clocks

The clock is one of the oldest human inventions. The word clock (from the Latin word clocca, "bell"), suggests that it was the sound of bells that also characterized early timepieces.

The first mechanical clocks to be driven by weights and gears were invented by medieval Muslim engineers. The first geared mechanical clock was invented by an 11th century Arab engineer in Islamic Spain. The knowledge of weight-driven mechanical clocks produced by Muslim engineers was transmitted to other parts of Europe through Latin translations of Arabic and Spanish texts.

In the early 14th century, existing clock mechanisms that used water power were being adapted to take their driving power from falling weights. This power was controlled by some form of oscillating mechanism. This controlled release of power—the escapement—marks the beginning of the true mechanical clock.

Pook & Pook Inc.

Ansonia porcelain mantel clock with Royal Bonn "La Vendee" case and open escapement, 14 3/4" h. **$793**

Heritage Auction Galleries

Cartier diamond, jade, pearl, coral and rock crystal "Mystery Clock," No. 202085. Case: upper mother of pearl, coral and rock crystal case measuring 6" diameter with gold-set diamonds at the hour positions, silver and gold framework, atop a diamond-set, onyx and jade Oriental motif pedestal, jade and pearl base measuring 6" by 4 1/2" with coral-set silver feet, bottom sterling movement cover, 14 3/8". Dial: tapered yellow gold and black enamel hands with diamond-encrusted center. Movement: base-mounted 3/4-plate eight-day lever movement, 15 jewels, wound and set through the base, mono-metallic balance with circular gear-toothed regulator, gold finish to the plates. Signed, with original red and gold fitted box, movement signed Cartier, base signed Cartier N. 202085. (The mystery effect achieved by this timepiece has the clock hands seemingly floating in space without any connection to the movement. The hands are set on two clear revolving discs with toothed metal outer rims that are propelled by gears hidden in the outer clock frame.) **$155,350**

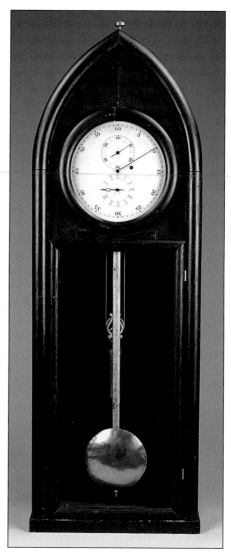

James D. Julia Auctioneers

New England Jeweler's Astronomical Regulator Clock. Mid-19th century. Originating probably in Massachusetts or in central New Hampshire, this example is in a walnut Gothic beehive case, the circular upper door with half-round molding and conforming glass panel hinged and opening upwards, the white enamel painted steel dial with hour and seconds dials within the minutes dial on the outer perimeter, the brass works weight-driven and pendulum regulated with maintaining power and dead-beat escapement, with original brass pendulum and weight behind the rectangular, half-round, molded, glass panel lower door; the case sides with viewing windows to the movement; the case edge with half-round moldings; all raised on a molded plinth. 60 1/2" h x 20 1/2" w x 6 1/2" d. Case and movement both in fine original condition, showing fine patina; dial with crackle and some early repainting. **$4,600**

Pook & Pook Inc.

Chelsea "Gothic" silver over brass time only desk clock retailed by Van Dusen & Stokes Co., Philadelphia, 5 1/4" h. **$263**

Pook & Pook Inc.

Swiss enamel decorated sterling silver peacock desk clock, marked "Yocs Paris", 3 1/4" h. **$2,808**

Pook & Pook Inc.

Marlow's Atlantic advertising clock by the Electric Neon Clock Co., Cleveland, 31" h, 36" w. **$549**

Heritage Auction Galleries
Will Rogers Character Clock (United Clock Co., 1930s). Electric personality clock features three likenesses of the great American humorist: Will Rogers the radio star, humorist and movie star. Cast in base metals, it measures 12" x 14". Original lightbulbs still in place. **$143**

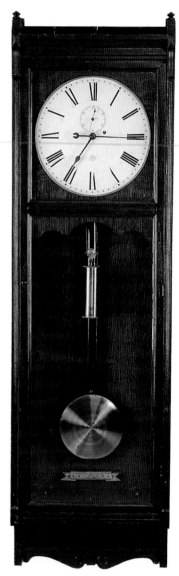

Heritage Auction Galleries
Mickey Mouse alarm clock, Ingersoll, circa 1930s. Classic wind-up alarm clock with moving-head Mickey and pointing hands. Clock housing and base are painted green; listed on base as "Made in the U. S. A.", in style of later Bayard clock. **$69**

James D. Julia Auctioneers
Seth Thomas Wall Regulator, quartersawn oak cabinet with reeded moldings, and crest with turned finials. Large door in front with glass window allows viewing of large pendulum. Clock face (possible replacement) is marked with Seth Thomas logo and separate second indicator, 66 1/2" h x 19 1/2" w. Appears complete with exception of bottom finials (holes plugged), and small piece that hooks pendulum into mechanism is broken. **$1,610**

Heritage Auction Galleries

Pook & Pook Inc.

Black man figure with clock, circa 1910. Made of cast spelter, the figure is a jolly African native sporting feathers on his head and pierced ears. His large belly holds the works of a 30-hour clock that is missing its glass and is not functional. It is 12" tall and shows remnants of highlighted areas in gold with good patina. **$300**

Waterbury Sage eight-day repeater carriage clock, 5 1/2" h. **$214**

Heritage Auction Galleries

Archibald Knox for Liberty & Co., silver hammered metal and enamel "Tudric" clock, circa 1902-1905, impressed "English Pewter 01126/ Made By Liberty & Co", 8" x 12" x 3". **$2,390**

Henri Marti mirrored glass, palmwood and chromium-plated brass mantel clock, circa 1925, 13". **$1,290**

Zachary Taylor mantel clock with reverse-on-glass portrait. From the 1830s through the 1850s, a number of companies produced clocks that incorporated reverse-on-glass portraits of presidents and statesmen into their design. Taylor's profile is flanked by draped American flags, while an eagle above clutches both the arrows of war and the olive branch of peace. Minor flaking on the original dial, and a few scattered paint flakes on the flags and eagle. Taylor's portrait has flaking on his white hair. The original maker's label inside indicates that the clock was made and sold by William S. Johnson of New York City. The works and pendulum are present, but not the weights; there is one broken hinge on the door, 19". **$1,135**

LeCoultre gilt brass and glass perpetual-motion Atmos clock, circa 1960s. Case: gilt brass glazed on four sides and the top, 9" x 8" x 6 1/2", stepped plinth base with canted corners, leveling screws and spirit level in the base, locking lever for the circular disc pendulum. Dial: white ring with golden Arabic numerals and applied dart indexes, golden Dauphine hands. Movement: 15 jewels, gilt with lever escapement, vacuum chamber winding the going barrel, annular tension pendulum, powered by barometric changes, signed LeCoultre. **$956**

Heritage Auction Galleries

English painted and gilt wood tall-case clock, late 18th century; dial signed "John Burges Gosport," 86" x 19 1/2" x 10". The bonnet with shaped and arched crown over glazed door flanked by colonettes, waist with shaped door, raised on bracket feet, decorated all over in black paint with gilt chinoiserie motifs. **$4,182**

Pook & Pook Inc.

French painted mantel clock with ormolu mounts, 16" h. **$439**

Jeffrey S. Evans & Associates

New Jersey Federal inlaid mahogany tall-case clock, unsigned, painted iron moon-phase dial and eight-day brass works, hood with broken-arch pediment, brass finials and reeded columns, waist with reeded quarter columns and inlaid ovals, string-inlaid base raised on replaced bracket feet. Weights and pendulum present. First quarter 19th century, 100" overall, base 9 1/2" x 20 1/2", top 10" x 20 7/8", with some small repairs to case. **$4,600**

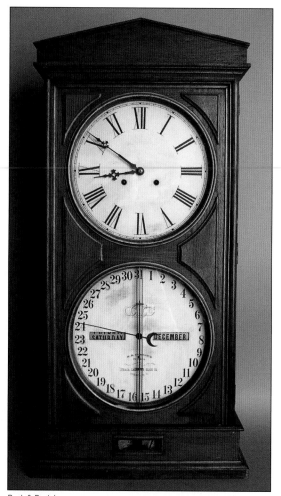

Pook & Pook Inc.

Ithaca No. 3 calendar clock, circa 1875, 38 1/2" h. **$1,404**

Pook & Pook Inc.

Swiss Omega square eight-day brass desk clock, #10600650, 5 1/2" h. **$1,404**

Coca-Cola Collectibles

— By Allan Petretti

Organized Coca-Cola collecting began in the early 1970s. The advertising art of The Coca-Cola Company, which used to be thought of as a simple area of collecting, has reached a whole new level of appreciation. Because of their artistic quality, these images deserve to be considered true Americana.

Coca-Cola art is more than bottles and trays, more than calendars and signage, more than trinkets, giveaways, and displays. It incorporates all the best that America has to offer. The Coca-Cola Company, since its conception in 1886, has taken advertising to a whole new level. So much so that it has been studied and dissected by scholars as to why it has proved to be so successful for more than 120 years.

Can soda pop advertising be considered true art? Without a doubt! The very best artists in America were an integral part of that honorary place in art history. Renowned artists like Rockwell, Sundbloom, Elvgren, and Wyeth helped take a quality product and advance it to the status of an American icon and all that exemplifies the very best about America.

Allan Petretti

This beautiful advertising directly reflects the history of our country: its styles and fashion, patriotism, family life, the best of times, and the worst of times. Everything this country has gone through since 1886 can be seen in these wonderful images.

For more information on Coca-Cola collectibles, see *Petretti's Coca-Cola Collectibles Price Guide*, 12th edition, by Allan Petretti.

1940s, 20" x 36", cardboard sign with gold wood frame. **$1,500**

1936 calendar. **$1,000**

1891 calendar, 6 1/2" x 9". **$25,000**

1910 calendar, 15" x 26",
"Happy Days." **$15,000**

1897, 9 1/4", serving tray. **$37,000**

1903, 5 1/2", bottle tray. **$12,000**

1931, 10 1/2" x 13 1/4", serving tray. **$900**

1916, 8 1/2" x 19", serving tray. **$500**

*1953-60, 10 1/2" x 13 1/4",
serving tray.* **$45**

*1908, 14" x 22", "Good to the Last Drop," paper
sign, metal strip top and bottom, very rare.*
$19,000

*1897, 6 1/2" x 10 1/2", "Victorian Girl,"
hanging sign, cardboard.* **$25,000**

Coca Cola: advertising sign picturing Lillian Nordica, 1904. Long considered one of the most important pieces of Coca Cola advertising. Picturing the 1904 "Yankee Diva" of the American opera scene, this lithographed paper sign is certainly one of the most beautiful. Deep, rich colors with a very Victorian border, the sign is in very near mint condition. **$7,170**

1936, 29" x 50", "50th Anniversary," cardboard sign. **$3,000**

1957, 16" x 27", cardboard sign
with gold wood frame. **$600**

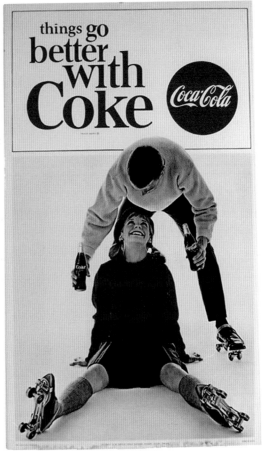

1960s, 16" x 27",
cardboard sign. **$200**

1950, 10" x 12", Phil Rizzuto,
cardboard cutout. **$1,000**

1964, 20" x 28", tin sign. **$300**

Circa 1912, 30" x 46", cardboard cutout. **$12,000**

"SATISFIED"

1907, 8" x 10", celluloid, manufactured by Whitehead and Hoag Co., Newark, N.J. **$20,000**
The celluloid "Satisfied" sign is very rare. The price range is for examples in high quality
collector condition and complete with ornate corners as shown. Examples in lesser
condition will be valued much lower.

1941, 32" x 42", cardboard Santa Claus cutout. **$1,600**

Pre-1900, 8" x 24", porcelain sign, rare. **$10,000**

1950s, metal and Masonite menu board. **$400**

Late 1930s, 12" x 14" reverse glass sign, The Brunhoff Mfg. Co., near mint condition. **$5,000** Note: This Brunhoff sign is highly desirable to collectors. In Mint condition at auction, it has been known to bring above the value listed.

Circa 1941, 9 1/2", stamped composition sign, rare. **$2,000**

Early 1900s, reverse glass sign, gold foil backing, beveled edge, very rare. **$25,000**

1948, Buddy-L, wood truck. **$5,000**

1930-31, 36", Coca-Cola Flyer, three-wheel scooter. **$2,500**

1978, Japanese R2D2 radio, mint in box, toy made by Takara. **$1,200**

1950s, 12" Buddy Lee, plastic or composition doll. **$1,200**
Must be complete and all original to warrant value shown.

1933, 24",
bottle radio.
$7,500

Early 1900s,
ceramic jug,
paper label.
$3,000
Label must
be at least
90% intact
to warrant
this value.

1903-08, paper label
amber, first paper
label, rare. **$600**

1960s, 10 oz., diamond paper label. **$550**

1958, Acton No. 10 Jr. picnic cooler, different versions. **$325**

1950s, 12-bottle carrier, aluminum. **$125**

Circa 1929, Glascock cooler, single case, junior size. **$1,600**

1960, first domestic can. **$400**

1940s, six bottle carrier, wood, rare. **$600**

Circa 1892, 3 1/2" x 5 1/2", trade card. **$2,000**

1914, Verigraph (early 3-D) glasses. **$825**

1900, fan, showing both sides. **$225**

Circa 1920, 4", hat pin, chrome. **$300**

*1908, pocket mirror, "Bastian Bros. Co.,
Rochester, NY, Duplicate Mirrors 5¢ Postage,
Coca-Cola Company, Atlanta, GA."* **$700**

*Circa 1929, 12 1/2", axe, "For Sports Men,"
mint in original box.* **$2,800**

1940s, "Bullet" cigarette lighter, Monroe Coca-Cola Bottling Co. **$400**

*1910, "The Coca-Cola Girl"
matchbook, shows both sides.* **$1,600**

1940s, match holder, tin. **$385**

Circa 1913-1915, brass door knob. **$500**

Coin-Operated Devices

Coin-operated devices fall into three main categories: amusement or arcade games, trade stimulators and vending machines.

James D. Julia Auctioneers

Little Dream, gum machine, penny drop, trade stimulator with walnut case with glass front, behind which is a series of pins. Drop a penny in and it would fall to any one of several baseball-related outcomes (runs, outs, etc.). Retains original directions card, 14" w x 18 1/2" h x 9 1/2" deep. Lacking key, front door is locked. Lacking marquee. Overall good to very good condition with some old chips. **$230**

James D. Julia Auctioneers

Match vendors (two) by Advance Machine Co., Chicago, with cast-iron bases with ornate feet. Insert penny and pull lever. Matches fall to tray below. One with original dome (cracked), one without. Stacks with what appear to be original cardboard marquees, other with painted lettering (paint is redone), 14" h each. Some wear and corrosion to cast iron. Lacking keys to padlocks. **$1,437 pair**

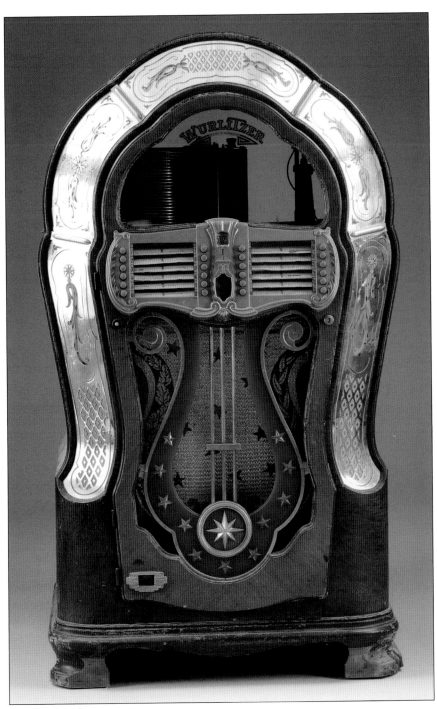

James D. Julia Auctioneers

Wurlitzer, Victory Model 1080 jukebox, walnut case with decorative mirrors on front and music lyre and stars on front, 24-selection changer, 58" h x 34" w x 25" deep. Appears complete except for back panel and one tube. Light corrosion, finish is generally good. Two small pieces and one large piece of molding missing from base. Accompanied by box of records. **$6,325**

Morphy Auctions

Watling 25-Cent Cherry Rol-a-Top slot machine, 26" t. **$5,500**

Morphy Auctions

Dilling's Butter Scotch 1-cent candy dispenser, patented July 25, 1899. Includes key and weights, very rare. **$15,500**

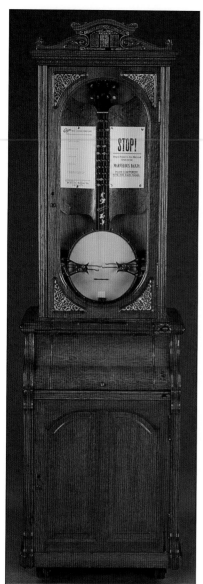

James D. Julia Auctioneers

Encore coin-operated automated banjo. Features a banjo inside an elaborate oak case. When a coin is deposited, the banjo would play a tune. A paper roll similar to those used on player pianos was responsible for the action of the banjo. Curved metal "fingers" pluck away at the banjo. The cabinetry is oak with detailed inset panels, fancy trims and moldings, serpentine opening front, and cast-metal grilles in place on front and sides. Extremely rare, 83" x 26" x 24". Machine has had total overall restoration inside and out. Internal wood barrel covering the mechanics and music roll has been replaced. Wood panel at the rear of the machine is also of newer vintage. Machine is functional, but should be tuned. **$54,625**

James D. Julia Auctioneers

5-Cent/25-Cent Caille Double with original music. All the original linkage is intact except wire rods to trip music. The crank on the side and the lever to deactivate music are still present. The original iron castings have substantial nickel plating, and painted highlighting to head is almost all intact. The iron legs have little nickel left, which is typical, and often over the years the legs were painted silver. Dials are intact and in fine condition, original reverse glasses are present; one has three cracks, the others are intact and are flaking to blue background paint. Wood cabinet needs cleaning and some re-gluing. Lacking partial rounded molding around center dials and a few pieces of trim. Back doors are present with original locks; one door missing section of wood. Musical containment area is present including rear containment door. Approximately 47" x 14" x 63". Left-side handle plate is intact, handle missing. Mechanisms appear to be complete. Iron castings are intact, and the only visible damage is a hairline crack in iron plate surrounding the right side coin head. **$80,500**

James D. Julia Auctioneers

Mills Wizard Fortune Teller. With Mills trademark owl on the front casting, which is covered in card symbols, signs of the zodiac, flaming urn, and a wise man/wizard. Customer selected the question; upon depositing a penny and plunging the lever on the right side of the machine, the answer would appear. Professionally restored, 13 1/2" x 6" x 18 1/2". **$2,070**

James D. Julia Auctioneers

Seeburg Style "KT Special" Orchestrion. Produced from approximately 1918 until the late 1920s. This particular model has piano, xylophone, mandolin, base drum, snare drum, tympani (base drum attachment), cymbal, castanets, triangle, tambourine and Chinese wood block. According to Q. David Bowers (Encyclopedia of Automatic Instruments), this particular style was a top-of-the-line model with the most instruments of any cabinet-style orchestrion. Encased in a fancy veneered-oak cabinet with a leaded art glass front exposing a few of the instruments, 48 1/2" x 24 1/2" x 65 1/2". Art glass does have some cracks. **$12,650**

James D. Julia Auctioneers

Groetchen "Poison This Rat" arcade machine. From the 1940s, featuring Hitler on the front facade. A penny is deposited and the player gets five "poison" pills to be dispensed to the Fuhrer in hopes of killing him off. The game uses slopes and runways to get the small red balls into Hitler's mouth. It retains much of its original finish and is in working order, 16 1/2" x 11" x 24". Couple of minor splits to wooden cabinet. Lacking original wooden back door. Original directions on interior panel. Needing additional small wooden pills/balls. **$7,475**

James D. Julia Auctioneers

A.J. Stephens dice game, circa 1930s. A player would deposit a nickel, depress the level, and watch the dice flip. Various award cards (four included) could be changed by the operator/bartender. Displayed also would be the beer of choice that the player could win. Overall in as-found, original condition and finish. Glass possibly incorrect, 11" x 7 1/2" x 5" (excluding bottle and glass). Padlock lacking key. **$1,035**

James D. Julia Auctioneers

Pulver's wooden cased "Yellow Kid" gum machine. A clockwork turn-of-the-century gum vendor features the Yellow Kid. Activated by a penny, the Yellow Kid bows, then turns to the gum column, raising his hand to his mouth and then turns back. A pot-metal head with original paint and a polished cotton gown (frail, fabric loss) adorn the Yellow Kid figure. Cabinet is constructed of oak with a glass front window and two smaller glass windows on either side. An oval brass tag is mounted to the front panel/door and all paper adorning the front window is original, 12" x 10 1/2" x 24 1/4". In as-found working condition with a couple minor splits to wood case, lacking lock on back door. **$10,350**

Comics

Riding a rising tide

— By Brent Frankenhoff, Comics Buyer's Guide

Four comics selling for more than $1 million each in the past couple of years has caused increased interest in the field once again. In early 2010, three comics from the late 1930s, the early days of comic-book publishing, made headlines as they sold for progressively higher numbers within a few weeks of each other. *Action Comics* #1 (cover-dated June 1938), featuring the first appearance of Superman, and graded 8.0 (Very Fine) by third-party grading service Certified Guaranty Company, sold for $1 million Feb. 22. On Feb. 25, an identically graded copy of *Detective Comics* #27 (cover-dated May 1939) and featuring the first appearance of Batman, sold for $1,075,500. On March 29, another copy of *Action Comics* #1, this one graded 8.5 (Very Fine+) by CGC, sold for $1.5 million.

Brent Frankenhoff

Those record-setting sales of early examples of comics history could be seen as singular events in the overall collecting and investing picture, but events since then have shown that prices realized continue to increase on other comics as well, especially those containing first appearances or other key events (deaths, weddings, etc.). That was borne out with the sale of *Amazing Fantasy* #15 (Aug 62), the first appearance of Spider-Man, which sold for $1.1 million March 7, 2011. The issue was graded considerably higher than those other million-dollar comics, coming in at 9.6 (Near Mint+) from CGC.

Interest generated by that sale helped another copy of the issue, this one graded 8.0 by CGC, sell for $83,650 in Heritage Comic Auctions Signature Sale Aug. 17 and 18, 2011.

While there are collectors investing large sums of money in such key issues, there are also plenty willing to pay premiums for comics from their childhood. Just as the 1990s saw prices move rapidly upward for many comics of the 1960s as children from that era had more disposable income, the 2000s saw a similar rise in comics of the 1970s. With the economic downturn, there are both plenty of collectors cashing in their earlier investments and new collectors looking to invest in those same books. In addition, collectors who had to settle for lesser-grade comics previously now are able to upgrade their collections with an influx of higher-grade material coming to the market, including that of late Minnesota collector Gary Dahlberg, whose high-grade Marvels commanded stellar prices in a May 2011 Heritage sale as the first offerings from what's been dubbed "The Twin Cities Pedigree." Heritage Vice President of Auctions Ed Jaster said, "The mood among collectors seems to be to grab strong copies of major key issues before they get even more expensive."

But, beware of over-investing in comics of more recent vintage. With few exceptions, comics produced from the early 1990s to today have little investment value. First issues and special editions have proliferated in the past 20 years and most everyone who wanted a copy has got one (or more) in high grade. Special editions with extremely low print runs, especially ones produced for comics retailer meeting giveaways, have investment potential and do their best when they're CGC-graded so that both buyer and seller can agree on the condition.

One part of the market that is dying off at least for comics collectors, is the TV and movie tie-in genre as well as the many Western comics that were heavily produced by such publishers as Dell in the 1950s and early 1960s. The same copies populate dealer shelves for years and continue to deteriorate as potential buyers handle them, but don't buy them. Part of that decline can be attributed to the aging of that group's usual collector.

Super Bad

Be wary of oversized reprints

Action Comics #1 is historically significant because it contains the first appearance of Superman, written by Jerry Siegel and drawn by Joe Shuster.

With Superman jump-starting the super-hero genre and what is known as The Golden Age of comics, the issue has been reprinted several times in the past 72 years, so collectors should be wary of copies presented as the original printing. This is *especially* true of an oversized reprint from the early 1970s that was one of DC's *Famous First Editions* titles. That reprint was roughly the size of a *Life* magazine, and there have been several cases of buyers being told, "Comics back then were that much bigger than comics of today," and informed that the reprint was the original. (Such sellers would remove the cardboard identifying outer cover, leaving what appeared to be a complete copy of *Action* #1,

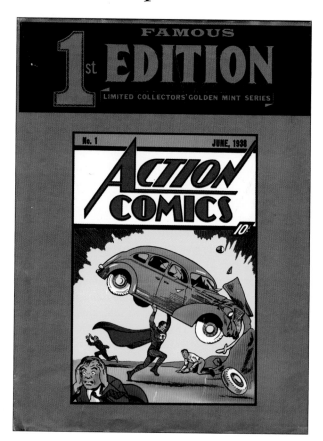

including the glossy cover and all the original ads.)

Action Comics was an anthology series, containing several stories featuring other characters, and The Man of Steel's first outing was actually a late addition to the package. Long considered one of the "holy grails" of the collecting hobby, copies of the issue in collectible condition have been selling at gradually higher and higher prices over the years. These 2010 sales surpassed all previous sales by a wide margin. It is estimated that, of its 200,000 copy initial print run, around 100 copies still exist — and approximately half of those have been graded by CGC.

Just shy of a year after Superman's introduction, Batman (written by Bill Finger and drawn by Bob Kane) first appeared in *Detective Comics* #27, another anthology title — and the series whose initials gave DC its identity.

Initially an anthology of mystery stories, *Detective* quickly embraced super-heroes with The Caped Crusader's adventures. The issue hasn't been reprinted as often as *Action* #1, but there is an oversized early 1970s *Famous First Edition* out there, as well as a 1984 reprint. It's estimated that 175,000 copies of this key issue were printed in 1939, with approximately 100 copies surviving and 50 being CGC-graded.

— Brent Frankenhof, Maggie Thompson, Peter Bickford

All images and prices courtesy of Heritage Comic Auctions (http://comics.ha.com)

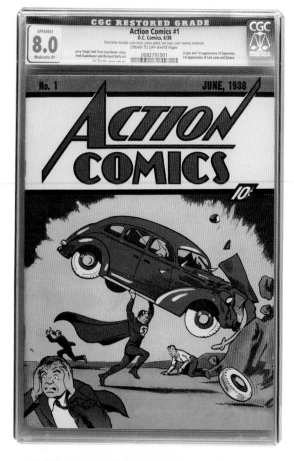

Action Comics #1 (1938), a restored copy CGC-graded an apparent 8.0 (Very Fine). **$149,375**

Action Comics #1-24, two bound volumes. **$131,450**

Adventure Comics #40 (1939), CGC-graded 7.0 (Fine/Very Fine). **$38,837**

All Winners Comics #1 (1941), Chicago Pedigree, CGC-graded 9.6 (Near Mint+). **$49,293**

Amazing Fantasy #15 (1962), CGC-graded 8.0 (Very Fine). **$83,650**

Amazing Spider-Man #1 (1963), CGC-graded 9.0 (Very Fine/Near Mint). **$38,837**

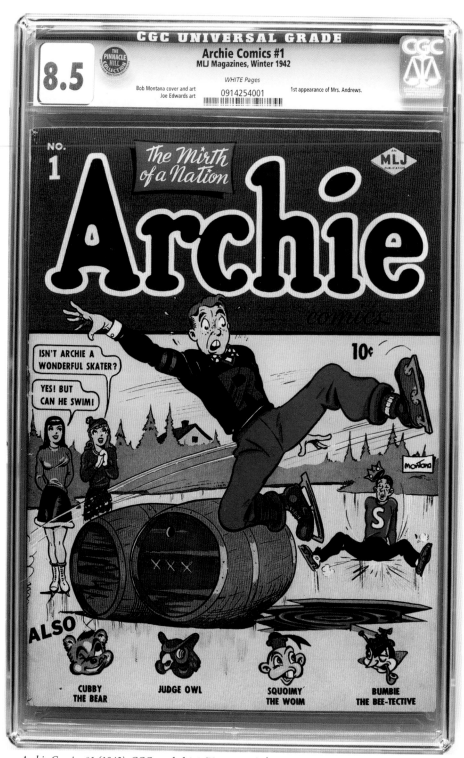

Archie Comics #1 (1942), CGC-graded 8.5 (Very Fine+). **$167,300**

Amazing Spider-Man #2 (1963), Twin Cities
Pedigree copy, CGC-graded 9.6 (Near Mint+).
$65,725

Amazing Spider-Man #4 (1963), Twin Cities
Pedigree copy, CGC-graded 9.6 (Near Mint+).
$77,675

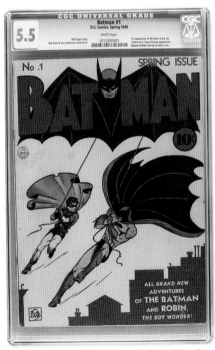

Batman #1 (1940), CGC-graded 5.5 (Fine-).
$55,268

Fantastic Four #1 (1961), CGC-graded 8.0
(Very Fine). **$47,800**

Detective Comics #27 (1939), CGC-graded 8.0 (Very Fine). **$1,075,500**

Flash #105 (1959), CGC-graded 9.4 (Near Mint). **$38,837**

Flash Comics #2 (1940), Mile High Pedigree copy, CGC-graded 9.4 (Near Mint). **$40,331**

Green Lantern #1 (1960), CGC-graded 9.4 (Near Mint). **$50,787**

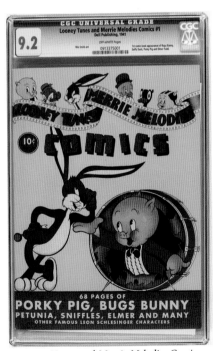

Looney Tunes and Merrie Melodies Comics #1 (1941), CGC-graded 9.2 (Near Mint-). **$38,837**

Marvel Comics #1 (1939), CGC-graded 6.0 (Fine). **$71,700**

More Fun Comics #52 (1940), Larson Pedigree copy, CGC-graded 9.2 (Near Mint-). **$89,625**

More Fun Comics #53 (1940), Rockford Pedigree copy, CGC-graded 9.6 (Near Mint+). **$47,800**

Sensation Comics #1 (1942), CGC-graded 9.4 (Near Mint). **$83,650**

Showcase #4 (1956), Bethlehem Pedigree copy, CGC-graded 9.0 (Very Fine/Near Mint). **$38,837**

Superman #1 (1939), restored copy, CGC-graded an apparent 8.5 (Very Fine+). **$44,812**

Superman #24 (1943), CGC-graded 9.4 (Near Mint). **$41,825**

Tales of Suspense #39 (1963), Twin Cities Pedigree copy, CGC-graded 9.2 (Near Mint-). **$56,762**

Wonder Woman #1 (1942), Crowley Copy Pedigree, CGC-graded 8.5 (Very Fine). **$53,775**

Cookie Jars

Cookie jars, colorful and often whimsical, are popular with collectors. They were made by almost every manufacturer in all types of materials. Figural character cookie jars are the most popular with collectors.

Cookie jars often were redesigned to reflect newer tastes. Hence, the same jar may be found in several different variations, and these variations can affect the price.

Many cookie-jar shapes were manufactured by more than one company and, as a result, can be found with different marks. This often happened because of mergers. Molds also were traded and sold among companies.

For more information on cookie jars, see *Warman's Cookie Jars Identification and Price Guide* by Mark F. Moran.

Humpty Dumpty by Abingdon, 10 1/2" tall, late 1940s, ink-stamped on bottom, "Abingdon USA," and impressed "663." **$500+**

Dutch Shoe by American Bisque, 10 1/4" long, 1950s, unmarked, very rare. **$3,000+**

Casper the Friendly Ghost (candy jar, with lollipops) by American Bisque, 11 3/4" tall, early 1960s, impressed mark on reverse, "U.S.A." Beware of reproductions. **$2,500+**

Cow with Cat Finial by Brush, 12 1/2" long, 1950s, raised mark, "Brush USA" in an artist's palette, and "W10." Prices vary widely depending on colors used, from about $200 for typical tan and yellow, to near $2,000 for purple or blue combinations, or with gold trim. **$200-$2,000**

Mammy by Brayton Laguna, in rare red dress, 11 3/4" tall, 1940s, hand inscribed, "Brayton 2"; Adding to the confusion caused by reproductions is the fact that the genuine Brayton Laguna Mammy has been found in sizes up to almost 13" tall. With red dress, **$800-$900; other colors $600+**

Lady in the Blue Dress, unmarked. According to collector Kathleen Moloney, "This jar is rare, valuable, and shrouded in mystery. It was obviously produced by Brush. The pottery is pure Brush; the colors are identical to those of the Little Girl, Little Angel, and Little Boy Blue jars, to name a few; and the base of the jar is similar to the Clown Bust." There is only one of these jars known to exist, but there are probably more out there. **$3,500+**

Pinocchio by California Originals, 12 1/4" tall, 1950s (?), impressed mark on bottom, "Calif. Orig. G-131 USA." Also found unmarked or with only an impressed "USA." **$1,200+**

Cookie Tug with cold-paint decoration, 1950s, McCoy USA mark. **$8,000-$10,000**

Little Red Riding Hood by Hull, with open basket, with transfer-decorated flowers, 13" tall, 1940s, marked on the bottom, "967 Hull Ware Little Red Riding Hood—Patent Applied For USA." **$400+**

Grapes with bird on lid in air-brushed colors, non-production piece, McCoy mark, 9 1/2" tall. **$7,000+**

Bluebird on Pine Cone by Metlox, 11 1/2" tall, marked on bottom, "Made in USA," and gold and brown foil label, "Metlox Manufacturing Co." **$350+**

Brownie by Metlox, 9 1/4" tall, made from 1963 to 1967, with gold and brown foil label, "Metlox Manufacturing Co." **$2,000+**

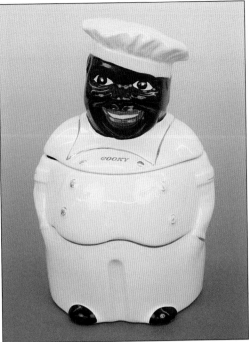

Black Chef by Pearl China, marked in gold on front, "Cooky," 10 1/4" tall, 1940s, stamped on bottom, "Pearl (in a seashell) China Co. Hand decorated 22 Kt. Gold U.S.A." and impressed, "639." (A companion to the Chef was a Mammy jar, same marks, $900+.) **$600+**

Carousel by Pfaltzgraff, lid 9 1/2" wide, 1950s, unmarked. **$500+**

Cattails by Red Wing, in glossy blue and tan, with "Cookies" in raised lettering, very crisp mold, 8 5/8" tall, late 1930s, ink-stamped, "Red Wing Union Stoneware Co.-Red Wing Minn." **$600+**

Uncle Mistletoe by Regal China, 11 1/2" tall, early 1960s, marked on back, "Uncle Mistletoe Cookie Jar Patent D. 1-50028." **$3,000+**

Frightened Alice in Wonderland by Regal China, 13 1/4" tall, late 1950s, marked "Walt Disney Productions Copyright (symbol) Alice in Wonderland." **$4,000+**

Whale by Robinson Ransbottom, 8" tall, 1950s, impressed mark, "RRPCo. USA Roseville O." **$900+**

Cottage House by Shawnee, 7" tall, 1940s, impressed mark, "U.S.A. 6." (Other Cottage-theme pieces include teapot, sugar bowl, and salt and pepper shakers.) **$1,400+**

Woven Bowl of Fruit by Shawnee, 8 1/2" tall, 1940s, raised mark, "Shawnee U.S.A." and an impressed "84." **$150-$200**

Tuggles by Sierra-Vista, 9" tall, late 1940s, impressed mark, "Sierra-Vista California." **$300+**

Rocking Horse by Starnes, 10 1/2" tall, late 1950s, unmarked. **$350+**

Champ designed by Don Winton, 11 1/4" tall, 1960s, also found with green or yellow sweater, unmarked. **$2,500+**

Cross-eyed Chick by Ungemach, 10 3/4" tall, late 1950s, impressed mark, "CJ-6 USA." **$600+**

Winkie by Vallona-Starr, 8 1/4" tall, marked "Vallona-Starr 302 Copyright (symbol) 51 California." This jar is widely available as a reproduction. **$1,000-$1,200**

Dinosaurs

This dinosaur skull of a triceratops horridus was discovered on a private ranch in Montana. The skull measures 7 1/2 feet in length from the beak to the frill. Triceratops (meaning three-horned face) was a rhinoceros-like dinosaur that had a short, pointed tail, a bulky body, and walked on short, sturdy, column-like legs with hoof-like claws. They grew in lengths up to 30 feet, up to 10 feet tall, and weighed up to 12 tons, making it the largest dinosaur in the ceratopsians family. **$250,950**

Heritage Auction Galleries

The Fighting Pair: *Allosaurus* vs. *Stegosaurus*

In the spring of 2007, on a ranch located near the foothills of the Big Horn Mountains in Ten Sleep Wyoming, this pair of Jurassic dinosaur icons – an Allosaurus and Stegosaurus – was discovered together virtually complete. It has been hypothesized that the pair got stuck in mud and died in combat; forever locked in death. The Allosaurus and Stegosaurus, deadly carnivore and armored herbivore, were often speculated to have fought pitched battles across the savannahs of Upper Jurassic North America but never before had they been found together. **$2,748,500**

Folk Art

— By Tim Chambers, Missouri Plain Folk, Sikeston, Mo.

Most folk art, by definition, refers to goods made by hand. In one form or another, it can be found almost anywhere we are. It is generally accepted from its earliest origins up to the mid-20th century.

Countless objects were made down on the farm, up in the city, or somewhere in between. Whether driven by necessity or a desire to create, folks hooked rugs, sewed quilts, painted game boards or constructed a whirligig just to see which way the wind was blowing. It is human nature to create, and most of those objects created fall somewhere in the definition of folk art.

Experts have a difficult time agreeing on a conclusive definition of what constitutes folk art but can agree on the attraction to be found in its many forms. Folk art often represents a slower, less complicated time, which resonates with many of us.

What is considered the most desirable in this abundance of choices? That varies from person to person. However, it is safe to say the best example of anything in its field becomes the standard by which all other examples are judged.

Skinner Inc.

"Black Hawk," running horse, molded copper, "Harris & Co." Boston, late 19th century, flattened full-body figure with zinc ears, mounted on a copper rod over a small sphere, maker's mark impressed on side, no stand, dents, seam separations, 20 1/2" h, 26 1/2" l. **$3,081**

Green Valley Auctions

Figure of a rooster, carved and painted wood, attributed to S.F. Welsh, Grayson County, Va., in a standing position with boldly carved tail, inset metal eyes, one retaining a quartz-stone pupil, red-painted comb and wattles, applied legs mortised into original block-form stand, original dry crackled varnished surface; with a letter of provenance and a group of research material. Fourth quarter 19th century, 13 1/2" h, 11 3/4" l, old (possibly when produced) repair to lower tip of beak, minor loss/wear to top of comb, slight wear and flaking to surface. **$41,800**

Skinner Inc.

Figure, polychrome carved bird, American, 19th century, with applied carved agate eyes, copper feet, mounted on a wall bracket, repair to crack on beak, overall 26 1/4" h. **$1,896**

Game board, Parcheesi, American, late 19th century, square wooden panel with polychrome-painted playing field, the "Home" area at center with black-painted scrolled foliage on a red ground, the board is composed of two thin wide square panels sandwiched together, surrounded by a thin applied molding, the boards are a little bowed causing three cracks on the playing surface, 20 1/4" square. **$3,081**

Skinner Inc.

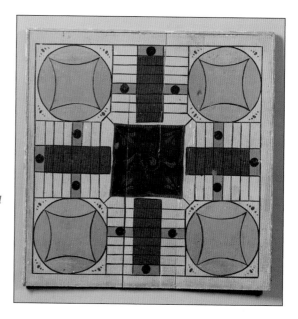

Picture frame, Shenandoah
Valley, carved walnut, diminutive
slightly arched top surmounted by
boldly scrolled ears and a central
crosshatched inverted heart, original
yellow pine backboard, original
dry surface. Contains a cutout and
woven paper heart in hand mounted
on lined paper. Second half 19th
century, 6 1/4" h, 4 1/8" w. **$4,950**

Green Valley Auctions

Whirligig figure, carved and painted
wood, "Dewey Boy" sailor, possibly
Nantucket, Mass., late 19th/early
20th century, with tin hat brim,
mounted on a wooden stand,
lacking paddles, shrinkage crack on
right-facing leg, overall 15 1/4" h.
$1,422

Skinner Inc.

Carved hand, originally an Odd Fellows staff head, with heart in palm and shirt cuff, 7 3/4". **$732**

Leslie Hindman Auctioneers

Pineapple carving by Eugene "Nick" Nielsen (1921-2009), circa 1995, carved and painted pine board, inscribed on reverse "N.N.", 18" x 10" x 2". This is one of a series of pineapples that Nielsen carved in the 1980s and '90s, though it was unusual for him to paint them. He also carved three-dimensional fruit and vegetables. **$300+**

Canes & Walking Sticks

Canes and walking sticks have existed through the ages, first as staffs or symbols of authority. They evolved into a fashion accessory that might incorporate carved ivory, precious metals, jewels, porcelain and enamel.

Canes have also been a favorite form of expression for folk artists, with intricate pictorial carving on shafts and handles.

Another category of interest to collectors features gadget canes or "system sticks" that contain hidden objects, from weapons to drinking flasks, telescopes, compasses and even musical instruments.

Cane with detailed riding-boot-form handle and brass collar, deeply carved shaft with eagle (brass tack eye), bird with brass tack eye, hollowed diamond, leaf stem, potted plant, acorn, hearts, turtle, salamander, arrow (some loss), flower, frog, cutlass, snake, raised diamonds, metal ferrule, painted highlights, circa 1880. **$1,200**

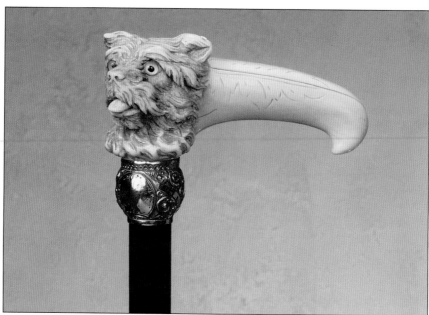

Tradewinds Antiques & Auctions

Dog motif, substantial elephant ivory "L" handle is 2 1/8" high and 5" to the side. It is incised with two long leaves and is carved at the shaft end with the shaggy head of a terrier with yellow glass eyes and tongue protruding. There is a 1 1/8" blown-out gold-filled collar that is decorated and initialed "C.G.H." The shaft is ebony with a 1" replaced brass ferrule. The overall length is 35 3/4". Possibly American, circa 1880. **$3,450**

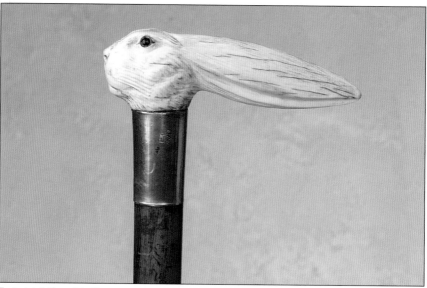

Tradewinds Antiques & Auctions

Hare motif, elephant ivory "L" handle is 4 1/2" to the side and 1 1/4" at its widest. It depicts a detailed long-eared hare with brown glass eyes. There is a 1 1/2" smooth sterling collar Chester hallmarked for 1862. The shaft is malacca with a 1 1/2" burnished brass and iron ferrule. The overall length is 34". **$690**

Weathervanes

James D. Julia Auctioneers

Banner, from the Universalist Unitarian Church of Waterville, Maine, branded "S. H. & W. C. Hunneman". In the shape of an arrow having a cast zinc/lead front part, which includes an arrow flanked by two C-scrolls attached to a cast-zinc rectangular area set for rod insert. The back section has two open S-scrolls leading to an 11-rayed star with four round cutouts. Back section appears to be flat sheet metal. Central rod receiving area has a hand-forged top with open prongs. The maker's brand on the central pole receiving area, 61" l x 21 1/2" h (without wrought-iron rod). Bend in one cast scroll, a break 1" from the central vertical support, several bends and loss of green patina throughout. Remnants of the original gilt can be seen. The weathervane has a green over-paint. **$6,612**

James D. Julia Auctioneers

Chicken, carved and painted wood, three-dimensional fully sculpted chicken stands on a wood ball resting on a long wood and sheet-metal arrow. White and green body with red tail. Ball is painted green and the arrow a light blue. Weathervane with ball is 16" h; chicken is 17 1/2" l; arrow is 60" l. Some wear to paint, some cracking at lamination, cracks in ball. **$2,588**

Green Valley Auctions

Fish, carved wood, Virginia, second quarter 19th century, flat body with V-shape open mouth, faint eyes, crescent-shape gills and simple tail, fins mortised into upper and lower edges of body and secured with wooden pins, top to bottom mounting hole located to the rear of the front fins, weathered natural surface 48" l, 11" h. Loss to upper rear fin, small hole below upper front fin, expected wear. **$17,600**

Fishing trawler, gilt copper, Massachusetts, early 20th century, molded sheet copper and wirework vessel, including stand, gilt wear, overall 32" h, 25" l. **$3,851**

Skinner Inc.

Bull weathervane, 19th century. Molded copper with a long tail, applied horns and ears. Verdigris patina, 18" x 30". Two bullet holes. **$10,350**

James D. Julia Auctioneers

Furniture

Furniture styles

Furniture styles can be determined by careful study and remembering what design elements each one embraces. To help understand what defines each period, here are some of the major design elements for each period.

William and Mary, 1690-1730: The style is named for the English King William of Orange and his consort, Mary. New colonists in America brought their English furniture traditions with them and tried to translate these styles using native woods. Their furniture was practical and sturdy. Lines of this furniture style tend to be crisp, while facades might be decorated with bold grains of walnut or maple veneers, framed by inlaid bands. Moldings and turnings are exaggerated in size. Turnings are baluster-shaped and the use of C-scrolls was quite common. Feet found in this period generally are round or oval. One exception to this is known as the Spanish foot, which flares to a scroll. Woods tend to be maple, walnut, white pine or southern yellow pine. One type of decoration that begins in the William and Mary period and extends through to Queen Anne and Chippendale styles is known as "japanning," referring to a lacquering process that combines ashes and varnish.

Queen Anne, 1720-1760: Evolution of this design style is from Queen Anne's court, 1702 to 1714, and lasted until the Revolution. This style of furniture is much more delicate than its predecessor. It was one way for the young Colonists to show their own unique style, with each regional area initiating special design elements. Forms tend to be attenuated in New England. Chair rails were more often mortised through the back legs when made in Philadelphia. New England furniture makers preferred pad feet, while the makers in Philadelphia used triffid feet. Makers in Connecticut and New York often preferred slipper and claw and ball feet. The most popular woods were walnut, poplar, cherry, and maple. Japanned decoration tends to be in red, green and gilt, often on a blue-green field. A new furniture form of this period was the tilting tea table.

Chippendale, 1755-1790: This period is named for the famous English cabinetmaker, Thomas Chippendale, who wrote a book of furniture designs, *Gentlemen and Cabinet-Maker's Director*, published in 1754, 1755 and 1762. This book gave cabinetmakers real direction and they soon eagerly copied the styles presented. Chippendale was influenced by ancient cultures, such as the Romans, and Gothic influences. Look for Gothic arches, Chinese fretwork, columns, capitals, C-scrolls, S-scrolls, ribbons, flowers, leaves, scallop shells, gadrooning and acanthus leaves. The most popular wood used in this period was mahogany, with walnut, maple and cherry also present. Legs become straight and regional differences still existed in design elements, such as feet. Claw and ball feet become even larger and more decorative. Pennsylvania cabinetmakers used Marlborough feet, while other regions favored ogee bracket feet. One of the most popular forms of this period was a card table that sported five legs instead of the four of Queen Anne designs.

Federal (Hepplewhite), 1790-1815: This period reflects the growing patriotism felt in the young American states. Their desire to develop their own distinctive furniture style was apparent. Stylistically it also reflects the architectural style known as Federal, where balance and symmetry were extremely important. Woods used during this period were mahogany and mahogany veneer, but other native woods, such as maple, birch or satinwood, were used. Reflecting the architectural ornamentation of the period, inlays were popular, as was carving and even painted highlights. The motifs used for inlay included bellflowers, urns, festoons, acanthus leaves and pilasters, to name but a few. Inlaid bands and lines were also popular and often used in combination with other inlay. Legs

of this period tend to be straight or tapered to the foot. The foot might be a simple extension of the leg, or bulbous or spade shaped. Two new furniture forms were created in this period. They are the sideboard and the worktable. Expect to find a little more comfort in chairs and sofas, but not very thick cushions or seats.

When a piece of furniture is made in England, or styled after an English example, it may be known as Hepplewhite. The time frame is the same. Robert Adam is credited with creating the style known as Hepplewhite during the 1760s and leading the form. Another English book heavily influenced the designers of the day. This one was by Alice Hepplewhite, and titled *The Cabinet Maker and Upholsterer's Guide*, published in 1788, 1789 and 1794.

Sheraton, 1790-1810: The style known as Sheraton closely resembles Federal. The lines are somewhat straighter and the designs plainer than Federal. Sheraton pieces are more closely associated with rural cabinetmakers. Woods would include mahogany, mahogany veneer, maple and pine, as well as other native woods. This period was heavily influenced by the work of Thomas Sheraton and his series of books, *The Cabinet Maker and Upholsterer's Drawing Book*, from 1791-1794, and his *The Cabinet Directory*, 1803, and *The Cabinet-Maker, Upholsterer, and General Artist's Encyclopedia* of 1804.

Empire (Classical), 1805-1830: By the beginning of the 19th century, a new design style was emerging. Known as Empire, it had an emphasis on the classical world of Greece, Egypt and other ancient European influences. The American craftsmen began to incorporate more flowing patriotic motifs, such as eagles with spread wings. The basic wood used in the Empire period was mahogany. However, during this period, dark woods were so favored that often mahogany was painted black. Inlays were popular when made of ebony or maple veneer. The dark woods offset gilt highlights, as were the brass ormolu mountings often found in this period. The legs of this period are substantial and more flowing than those found in the Federal or Sheraton periods. Feet can be highly ornamental, as when they are carved to look like lion's paws, or plain when they extend to the floor with a swept leg. Regional differences in this style are very apparent, with New York City being the center of the design style, as it was also the center of fashion at the time.

New furniture forms of this period include the sleigh bed, with the headboard and footboard forming a graceful arch. Several new forms of tables also came into being, especially the sofa table. Because the architectural style of the Empire period used big, open rooms, the sofa was now allowed to be in the center of the room, with a table behind it. Former architectural periods found most furniture placed against the outside perimeter of the walls and brought forward to be used.

Victorian, 1830-1890: The Victorian period as it relates to furniture styles can be divided into several distinct styles. However, not every piece of furniture can be dated or definitely identified, so the generic term "Victorian" will apply to those pieces. Queen Victoria's reign affected the design styles of furniture, clothing and all sorts of items used in daily living. Her love of ornate styles is well known. When thinking of the general term, think of a cluttered environment, full of heavy furniture, and surrounded by plants, heavy fabrics and lots of china and glassware.

French Restoration, 1830-1850: This is the first sub-category of the Victoria era. This style is best simplified as the plainest of the Victorian styles. Lines tend to be sweeping, undulating curves. It is named for the style that was popular in France as the Bourbons tried to restore their claim to the French throne, from 1814 to 1848. The Empire (Classical) period influence is felt, but French Restoration lacks some of the ornamentation and fussiness of that period. Design motifs continue to reflect an interest in the classics of Greece and Egypt. Chair backs are styled with curved and concave crest rails, making them a little more comfortable than earlier straight-back chairs. The use of bolster

pillows and more upholstery is starting to emerge. The style was only popular in clusters, but did entice makers from larger metropolitan areas, such as Boston and New Orleans, to embrace the style.

The Gothic Revival period, 1840-1860: This is relatively easy to identify for collectors. It is one of the few styles that celebrates elements found in the corresponding architectural themes: turrets, pointed arches and quatrefoils—designs found in 12th through 16th centuries that were adapted to this mid-century furniture style. The furniture shelving form known as an étagère was born in this period, allowing Victorians to have more room to display their treasured collections. Furniture that had mechanical parts was also embraced by the Victorians of this era. The woods preferred by makers of this period were walnut and oak, with some use of mahogany and rosewood. The scale used ranged from large and grand to small and petite. Carved details gave dimension and interest.

Rococo Revival, 1845-1870: This design style features the use of scrolls, either in a "C" shape or the more fluid "S" shape. Carved decoration in the form of scallop shells, leaves and flowers, particularly roses, and acanthus further add to the ornamentation of this style of furniture. Legs and feet of this form are cabriole or scrolling. Other than what might be needed structurally, it is often difficult to find a straight element in Rococo Revival furniture. The use of marble for tabletops was quite popular, but expect to find the corners shaped to conform to the overall scrolling form. To accomplish all this carving, walnut, rosewood, and mahogany were common choices. When lesser woods were used, they were often painted to reflect these more expensive woods. Some cast-iron elements can be found on furniture from this period, especially if it was cast as scrolls. The style began in France and England, but eventually migrated to America where it evolved into two other furniture styles, Naturalistic and Renaissance Revival.

Elizabethan, 1850-1915: This sub-category of the Victorian era is probably the most feminine-influenced style. It also makes use of the new machine-turned spools and spiral profiles that were fast becoming popular with furniture makers. New technology advancements allowed more machined parts to be generated. By adding flowers, either carved or painted, the furniture pieces of this era had a softness to them. Chair backs tend to be high and narrow, having a slight back tilt. Legs vary from straight to baluster-turned forms to spindle turned. This period of furniture design saw more usage of needlework upholstery and decoratively painted surfaces.

Louis XVI, 1850-1914: One period of the Victorian era that flies away with straight lines is Louis XVI. However, this furniture style is not austere; it is adorned with ovals, arches, applied medallions, wreaths, garlands, urns and other Victorian flourishes. As the period aged, more ornamentation became present on the finished furniture styles. Furniture of this time was made from more expensive woods, such as ebony or rosewood. Walnut was popular around the 1890s. Other dark woods were featured, often to contrast the lighter ornaments. Expect to find straight legs or fluted and slightly tapered legs.

Naturalistic, 1850-1914: This furniture period takes the scrolling effects of the Rococo Revival designs and adds more flowers and fruits to the styles. More detail is spent on the leaves—so much that one can tell if they are to represent grape, rose or oak leaves. Technology advances enhanced this design style, as manufacturers developed a way of laminating woods together. This layered effect was achieved by gluing thin layers together, with the grains running at right angles on each new layer. The thick panels created were then steamed in molds to create the illusion of carving. The woods used as a basis for the heavy ornamentation were mahogany, walnut and some rosewood. Upholstery of this period is often tufted, eliminating any large flat surface. The name of John Henry Belter is

often connected with this period, for it was when he did some of his best design work. John and Joseph W. Meeks also enjoyed success with laminated furniture. Original labels bearing these names are sometimes found on furniture pieces from this period, giving further provenance.

Renaissance Revival, 1850-1880: Furniture made in this style period reflects how cabinetmakers interpreted 16th- and 17th-century designs. Their motifs range from curvilinear and florid early in the period to angular and almost severe by the end of the period. Dark woods, such as mahogany and walnut, were primary with some use of rosewood and ebony. Walnut veneer panels were a real favorite in the 1870s designs. Upholstery, usually of a more generous nature, was also often incorporated into this design style. Ornamentation and high relief carving included flowers, fruits, game, classical busts, acanthus scrolls, strapwork, tassels and masks. Architectural motifs, such as pilasters, columns, pediments, balusters and brackets, are another prominent design feature. Legs are usually cabriole or have substantial turned profiles.

Néo-Greek, 1855-1885: This design style easily merges with both the Louis XVI and Renaissance Revival. It is characterized by elements reminiscent of Greek architecture, such as pilasters, flutes, column, acanthus, foliate scrolls, Greek key motifs and anthemion high-relief carving. This style originated with the French, but was embraced by American furniture manufacturers. Woods are dark and often ebonized. Ornamentation may be gilded or bronzed. Legs tend to be curved to scrolled or cloven hoof feet.

Eastlake, 1870-1890: This design style is named for Charles Locke Eastlake, who wrote a popular book in 1872 called *Hints on Household Taste*. It was originally published in London. One of his principles was the relationship between function, form and craftsmanship. Shapes of furniture from this style tend to be more rectangular. Ornamentation was created through the use of brackets, grooves, chamfers and geometric designs. American furniture manufacturers were enthusiastic about this style, since it was so easy to adapt for mass production. Woods used were again dark, but more native woods, such as oak, maple and pine, were incorporated. Legs and chair backs are straighter, often with incised decoration.

Art Furniture, 1880-1914: This period represents furniture designs gone mad, almost an "anything goes" school of thought. The style embraces both straight and angular with some pieces that are much more fluid, reflecting several earlier design periods. This era saw the wide usage of turned moldings and dark woods, but this time stained to imitate ebony and lacquer. The growing Oriental influence is seen in furniture from this period, including the use of bamboo, which was imported and included in the designs. Legs tend to be straight; feet tend to be small.

Arts & Crafts, 1895-1915: The Arts & Crafts period of furniture represents one of the strongest trends for current collectors. Quality period Arts & Crafts furniture is available through most of the major auction houses. And, for those desiring the look, good quality modern furniture is also made in this style. The Arts & Crafts period furniture is generally rectilinear and a definite correlation is seen between form and function. The primary influences of this period were the Stickley brothers (especially Gustav, Leopold and John George), Elbert Hubbard, Frank Lloyd Wright and Harvey Ellis. Their furniture designs often overlapped into architectural and interior design, including rugs, textiles and other accessories. Wood used for Arts & Crafts furniture is primarily oak. Finishes were natural, fumed or painted. Hardware was often made in copper. Legs are straight and feet are small, if present at all, as they were often a simple extension of the leg. Some inlay of natural materials was used, such as silver, copper and abalone shells.

Art Nouveau, 1896-1914: Just as the Art Nouveau period is known for women with long hair, flowers and curves, so is Art Nouveau furniture. The Paris Exposition of 1900 introduced furniture styles reflecting what was happening in the rest of the design world, such as jewelry and silver. This style of furniture was not warmly embraced, as the sweeping lines were not very conducive to mass production. The few manufacturers that did interpret it for their factories found interest to be slight in America. The French held it in higher esteem. Legs tend to be sweeping or cabriole. Upholstery becomes slimmer.

Art Deco, 1920-1945: The Paris "*L'Exposition International des Arts Décorative et Industriels Modernes*" became the mantra for designs of everything in this period. Lines are crisp, with some use of controlled curves. The Chrysler Building in New York City remains among the finest example of Art Deco architecture and those same straight lines and gentle curves are found in furniture. Makers used expensive materials, such as veneers, lacquered woods, glass and steel. The cocktail table first enters the furniture scene during this period. Upholstery can be vinyl or smooth fabrics. Legs are straight or slightly tapered; chair backs tend to be either low or extremely high.

Modernism, 1940-present: Furniture designed and produced during this period is distinctive, as it represents the usage of some new materials, like plastic, aluminum and molded laminates. The Bauhaus and also the Museum of Modern Art heavily influenced some designers. In 1940, the museum organized competitions for domestic furnishings. Designers Eero Saarien and Charles Eames won first prize for their designs. A new chair design combined the back, seat and arms together as one unit. Tables were designed that incorporated the top, pedestal and base as one. Shelf units were also designed in this manner.

Legs

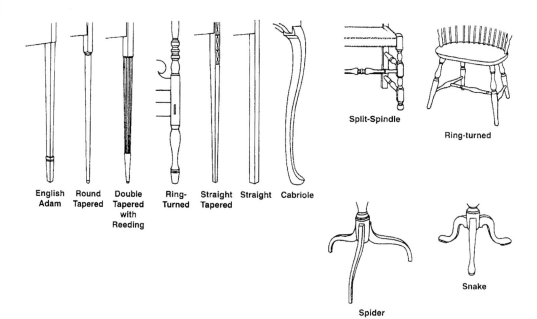

English Adam   Round Tapered   Double Tapered with Reeding   Ring-Turned   Straight Tapered   Straight   Cabriole

Split-Spindle

Ring-turned

Spider

Snake

Hardware

Bail Handle

Teardrop Pull

Oval Brass

Brass

Pressed Glass

Wooden Knob

Eagle Brass

Construction Details

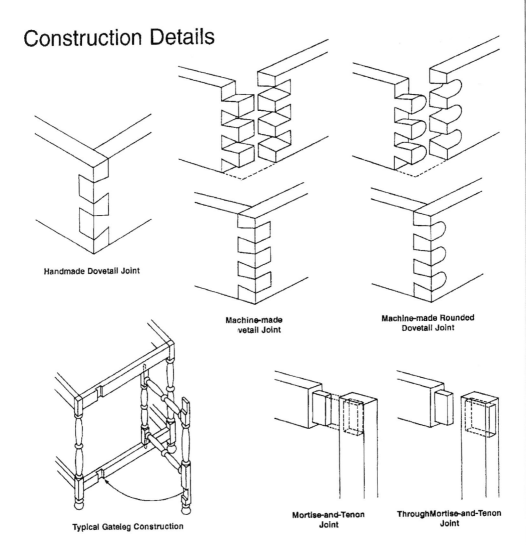

Handmade Dovetail Joint

Machine-made ⌄vetail Joint

Machine-made Rounded Dovetail Joint

Typical Gateleg Construction

Mortise-and-Tenon Joint

ThroughMortise-and-Tenon Joint

Feet

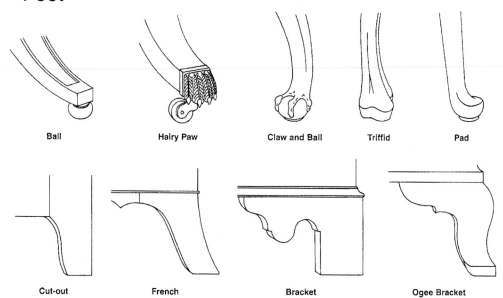

Ball   Hairy Paw   Claw and Ball   Triffid   Pad

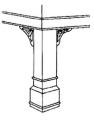  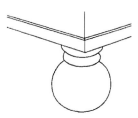

Cut-out   French   Bracket   Ogee Bracket

Marlborough   Spanish   Turmed Ball

Spider   Spade   Snake

Modernism

— By Zac Bissonnette

Mid-century modern has been the hottest style over the past decade – often at the expense of period furniture.

Guy Regal, a dealer with New York City-based Newell Antiques, a leading furniture dealer with a $50 million inventory says that it's been "red hot" – but also sees the category evolving as top decorators look to mix mid-century pieces with period objects.

"People don't collect by period as much anymore over the past 20-30 years," he says. "Now, as with everything else, you're starting to see an eclecticism happen again. People are far more interested in putting art on their walls than mirrors or anything else, and they're looking for things that complement that."

The success of AMC's "Mad Men" – with its mid-century modern sets – has certainly helped to drive interest in the category. Mid-century modern furniture is defined by clean lines, often industrial-age materials, and mass production. Traditionally defined as running from the years 1933 to 1965, the term mid-century modern is more of an after-the-fact description of a period than an actual self-contained movement. Consequently, there is no one standard definition of what mid-century modern is and what it isn't, and many dealers will label almost anything mid-century modern in the hopes of attracting a higher price.

"You're starting to see stuff from the '70s and '80s. It's not just '50s and '60s anymore," Regal says, noting that in his view the true mid-century modern pieces don't have much further to run in terms of values. One sign of concern? Pieces that were once considered second- or third-tier fetching extremely high prices. A couple of things to be aware of for collectors, dealers, and decorators interested in mid-century modern furniture:

• Reproductions are very common. The nature of products like the Eames Plywood Lounge Chair is that they were mass-produced and affordable. In the beginning of the mid-century modern comeback, that was a key draw: The furniture had a sleek, contemporary look that didn't look like your parent's house, and you could buy it on a budget. But now that prices have risen, so have reproductions, with companies like Crate & Barrel and even Macy's offering reproductions. Many buyers don't care because they're more interested in creating a "look" than in connoisseurship, but it's something to be aware of if you have higher aspirations for your purchases.

• Within mid-century, certain designers and styles are gaining momentum. Over the past year or so, Italian designers have seen interest skyrocket, with leading names including Gio Ponti, Paolo Buffa and Osvaldo Borsani.

And if top-tier mid-century modern objects are out of your price range, there's always Plan B: Furnish your house at IKEA, but tell everyone it's the real deal, straight off the set of "Mad Men."

Bedroom Furniture

Peter Hvidt, daybed by France and Sons, 75" x 29.5" x 16". **$500**

Dresser and mirror, 1940s, Italy; cabinet 62" x 23" x 36", mirror 50" x 31", overall 67". **$1,200**

Paul Laszlo, vanity in green lacquered finish, with pink embossed leather top, fitted with single drawer and lift-up mirror, the matching chair with pink ultra-suede cushions, circa 1952; vanity 29" x 37" x 24", chair 33" x 20" x 22".
$4,000 set

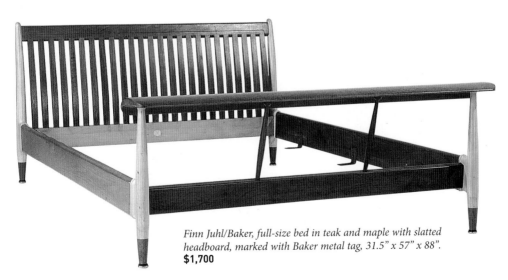

Finn Juhl/Baker, full-size bed in teak and maple with slatted headboard, marked with Baker metal tag, 31.5" x 57" x 88".
$1,700

Jean Royere, daybed with tan cushion and bolster pillows on oak frame with inset cobalt glass panels, 32.5" x 65" x 32.75".
$4,000

Desks/Credenzas

Edward Wormley, desk with inset leather top, 43.75" x 24" x 30.5". **$75**

Desk, single-drawer, in wood veneer, one end faceted, the other curved, 29.5" x 45.5" x 22.5". **$1,000**

Gordon Bunshaft desk, 66" x 30" x 30". **$1,500**

Hans Wegner/Ry Mobler, Oak credenza with two sliding doors enclosing four sliding trays and four adjustable shelves, with contrasing oak feet, stamped RY, 31" x 78.75" x 19.25". **$2,500**

Jean Prouve, oak and painted steel student desk and chair unit, with sliding iron inkwell, 25.5" x 23.5" x 32". **$1,900**

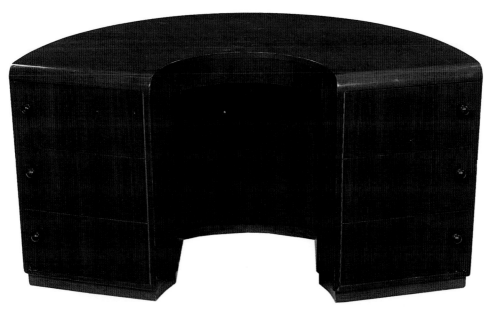

Edward Wormley, kneehole desk, curved form, 58.25" x 30" x 29.25". **$3,250**

Jean Prouve, double-seat school desk with oak shelf and top, on green enameled metal base, 27" x 45" x 32". **$5,000**

F *Furniture*

Portenzac, single-pedestal desk covered in composite with six shaped drawers and steel leg, 30" x 63" x 26.75". **$6,500**

George Nakashima, walnut credenza, with two grass cloth-backed grilled doors enclosing two drawers, 28.5" x 22" x 20". **$7,500**

Gio Ponti/Singer & Sons, two-drawer rosewood desk with tooled leather top and integrated magazine rack, circa 1950, 28.75" x 53.25" x 25.5". **$19,000**

Seating

Le Corbusier, LC/1 Basculant chairs brown leather, 25" x 27.5" x 26". **$550 pair**

George Nelson, Steelframe chair, 29" x 27" x 27". **$375**

Hans Wegner, CH25 armchairs, 28" x 28" x 28". **$2,000 pair**

Shiro Kuramato/XO, "Sing, Sing, Sing" anodized steel armchairs, marked XO, 33.5" x 20.5" x 23.5". **$2,700 pair**

Edward Wormley, vanity seat by Dunbar, 28" x 20" x 22.5". **$850**

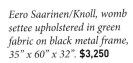

Eero Saarinen/Knoll, womb settee upholstered in green fabric on black metal frame, 35" x 60" x 32". **$3,250**

Vladimir Kagan, omnibus sofa upholstered in striped Knoll fabric on Plexiglas base, reupholstered in Knoll fabric, 27.5" x 72" x 32". **$1,000**

Parzinger, "American Modern" sectional sofa, leopard print fabric, 109" x 30.5" x 28". **$5,000**

Charles and Ray Eames, shell chair, 25" x 24.5" x 27.5". **$600**

Arne Jacobsen, Seagull chairs in original white finish, marked in Denmark by Fritz Hansen 1972, 31.5" x 21.5" x 18". **$3,000 pair**

Phillip Lloyd Powell, New Hope chair in walnut with webbed seat support, 32" x 29.5" x 30.5". **$7,500**

Lounge chair, possibly Milo Baughman, 1960s, 42" x 38" x 34". **$900**

Charles and Ray Eames, 670/671 lounge chair and ottoman, chair 33" x 35" x 32", ottoman 26.5" x 21" x 17.5". **$1,500**

Poul Kjaerholm/E. Kold Christensen, PK22 lounge chairs covered in tan leather on steel bases, impressed marks, set of four, 28" x 25" x 25". **$4,250 set**

Isamu Noguchi/ Knoll, teak rocking stool with steel wire frame, circa 1954, 10.5" x 14". **$5,500**

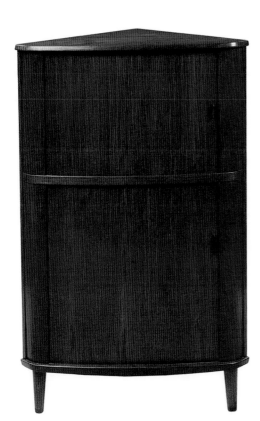

Shelving & Storage

Skovmand & Andersen, corner cabinet, 36.5" x 25.5" x 61.25". **$375**

George Nelson, cabinet by Herman Miller, 40" x 18.5" x 39.75". **$1,100**

Edward Wormley, sideboard,
59.25" x 18" x 28.25". **$1,600**

Paul Evans, Aluco Bond
cabinet with burled walnut
doors, 30" x 39.5" x 18".
$3,750

Osvaldo Borsani, mahogany
mirrored sideboard with beige
marble top and brass-capped feet,
77.5" x 107.25" x 17.75". **$7,500**

Charlotte Perriand and Jean
Prouve, bibliotheque with
enameled aluminum and pine
shelving unit on pine long bench,
1953, 63.5" x 138" x 21". **$70,000**

Tables

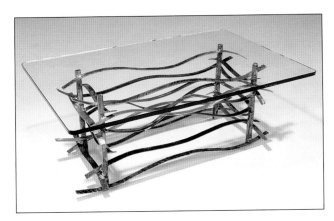

Silas Seandel, ribbon coffee
table with glass top on copper,
brass, bronze and steel base,
16" x 42" x 27". **$7,000**

Jens Risom Design Inc. coffee table, 40" x 18". **$300**

Coffee table, 1960s, 43" x 14.75". **$500**

Patio set, round table top and three benches, 1950s, table 48" x 30", benches 41" x 16" x 17.5". **$1,200 set**

Donald Deskey/W. & J. Sloane, 10-piece dining suite in Madrone burl veneer and Macassar ebony, extension table with six fabric-upholstered chairs and two 15" leaves, server with interior drawers and shelves, bar cabinet and china cabinet circa 1936; table (closed) 29.5" x 66" x 40", armchairs 34.5" x 23" x 20", server 36" x 66" x 20", bar 32" x 29" x 18", china cabinet 60" x 32.5" x 16". **$14,000 set**

Jonathon Singleton, dining table with "cerused" (pickled) oak top on curvaceous steel base, metal tag, Jonathan Singleton SIG Furniture, 31" x 89" x 55". **$4,000**

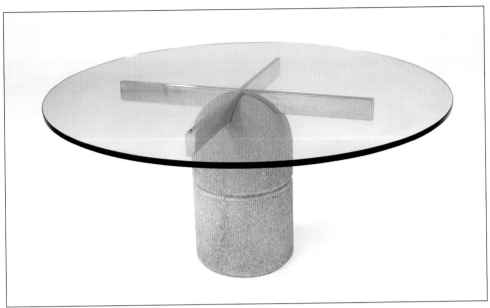

Saporiti, dining table with concrete and chrome pedestal base under a circular plate glass top, 27.75" x 60". **$4,250**

Vladimir Kagan, tri-symmetric side table with biomorphic plate glass top on sculpted walnut base, 19" x 31" x 24". **$2,100**

Jay Spectre, occasional table, wedge shaped, 15.5" x 15.5" x 18". **$125**

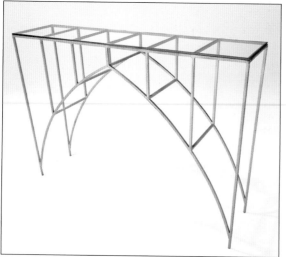

Philippe Starck, steel console table with glass top, 16" x 47" x 18". **$2,000**

George Nakashima, early walnut side table with round top on four tapered, angular legs, 26" x 24". **$2,700**

Eliot Noyes, telephone stand, 15.5" x 13.5" x 23". **$550**

Isamu Noguchi/Herman Miller, chess table with rotating, inlaid biomorphic top over cast-aluminum tray and ebonized base, 20.75" x 25" x 25". **$65,000**

Glass

Art Glass

Green Valley Auctions

Durand, Lustre Ware vase, gold iridescent, polished pontil mark signed "Durand / V / 1982-14." Vineland Flint Glass Works. First quarter 20th century. 14" h. **$920**

Durand cocktail shaker. Green cut to clear Art Deco design on a large cocktail shaker with nickel-plated top. The shaker comes with a note on Farber's Antiques paper stating that the green cocktail shaker was the personal property of Victor Durand. The note is signed by Samuel Farber. 12 1/4" t. **$1,437**

James D. Julia Auctioneers

Durand ginger jar. Decorated with bright white hearts and vines on a shaded platinum-blue to deep mirror-blue iridescent ground. Jar is topped with transparent maize-colored fluted knop resting on a matching lid. Unsigned. Overall 9" t. **$3,600**

James D. Julia Auctioneers

English cameo footed vase, white cut to yellow, intricate floral decoration on body, stylized scrollwork on neck, polished rim, slightly concave base. Probably Thomas Webb & Sons. Fourth quarter 19th century. 9" h, 3 1/4" d overall. **$3,737**

Green Valley Auctions

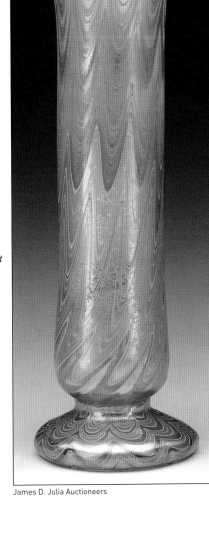

Loetz decorated vase. With platinum iridescent wave design against an amber background. The cylindrical body gives way to a slightly flaring lip. Unsigned. 6 1/8" t. **$517**

James D. Julia Auctioneers

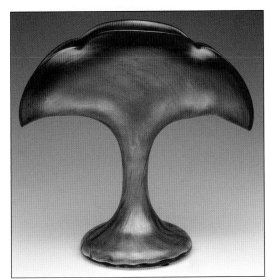

Green Valley Auctions

Loetz, giant clam-like fan vase, red to yellow green swirling mottled iridescent, unmarked, partially polished pontil mark. Late 19th/early 20th century. 12" h, 5 1/2" x 12 1/4" rim, 6" d base. **$488**

James D. Julia Auctioneers

Nash art glass vase. Chintz decorated with fine Cypriot texture to the decoration. Engraved "GD 72 NASH" on the foot rim. 7 1/4" t. **$805**

Steuben figural flower frog. Moonstone double-tier flower frog with clear glass figural insert. Insert depicts a standing Oriental woman with long gown and bouquet of flowers. Overall 9" h. Some chips to peg of insert. **$862**

Cameo Glass

*Cameo glass vase, peach cylindrical shouldered body,
cascading blue leafy branches, pastoral scene of shepherd,
flock, and farmhouse with surrounding trees, slight rim
grinding, signed in cameo, Devez, 12" h.* **$1,650**

Early Auction Co. LLC

*Cameo glass vase, soft rose and white
leaf pattern on clear and frosted
ground, 12 1/2" h.* **$1,500**

Early Auction Co. LLC

Cameo glass vase, cylindrical form, footed, frosted glass decoration with elongated stemmed flowers towering over pond scene, signed Gallé, 13" h. **$1,500**

Early Auction Co. LLC

Cameo glass vase, blossoming carnations in deep red and yellow on polished and mottled red ground, engraved signature, Muller Freres, circa 1900, 17". **$3,120**

David Rago Auctions Inc.

Early Auction Co. LLC

Cameo glass vase, three color canoe shape, citron body, crimson and yellow pond scene of water lilies and foliage, signed in cameo Gallé, 16" l. **$2,600**

Carnival Glass

— By Ellen T. Schroy

Carnival glass is what is fondly called mass-produced iridescent glassware. The term "carnival glass" has evolved through the years as glass collectors have responded to the idea that much of this beautiful glassware was made as giveaway glass at local carnivals and fairs. However, more of it was made and sold through the same channels as pattern glass and Depression glass. Some patterns were indeed giveaways, and others were used as advertising premiums, souvenirs, etc. Whatever the origin, the term "carnival glass" today encompasses glassware that is usually pattern molded and treated with metallic salts, creating that unique coloration that is so desirable to collectors.

Ellen Schroy

Early names for iridescent glassware, which early 20th century consumers believed to have all come from foreign manufacturers, include Pompeiian Iridescent, Venetian Art, and Mexican Aurora. Another popular early name was "Nancy Glass," as some patterns were believed to have come from the Daum, Nancy, glassmaking area in France. This was at a time when the artistic cameo glass was enjoying great success. While the iridescent glassware being made by such European glassmakers as Loetz influenced the American market place, it was Louis Tiffany's Favrile glass that really caught the eye of glass consumers of the early 1900s. It seems an easy leap to transform Tiffany's shimmering glassware to something that could be mass produced, allowing what we call carnival glass today to become "poor man's Tiffany."

Carnival glass is iridized glassware that is created by pressing hot molten glass into molds, just as pattern glass had evolved. Some forms are hand finished, while others are completely formed by molds. To achieve the marvelous iridescent colors, a process was developed where a liquid solution of metallic salts was put onto the still hot glass form after it was unmolded. As the liquid evaporated, a fine metallic surface was left, which refracts light into wonderful colors. The name given to the iridescent spray by early glassmakers was "dope."

Many of the forms created by carnival glass manufacturers were accessories to the china American housewives so loved. By the early 1900s, consumers could find carnival glassware at such popular stores as F. W. Woolworth and McCrory's. To capitalize on the popular fancy for these colored wares, some other industries bought large quantities of carnival glass and turned them into "packers." This term reflects the practice where baking powder, mustard, or other household products were packed into a special piece of glass that could take on another life after the original product was used. Lee Manufacturing Co. used iridized carnival glass as premiums for its baking powder and other products, causing some early carnival glass to be known by the generic term "Baking Powder Glass."

Classic carnival glass production began in the early 1900s and continued about 20 years, but no one really documented or researched production until the first collecting wave struck in 1960. It is important to remember that carnival glasswares were sold in department stores as well as mass merchants, rather than through the general store often associated with a young America. Glassware by this time was mass-produced and sold in large quantities by such enterprising companies as Butler Brothers. When the economics of the country soured in the 1920s, those interested in purchasing iridized glassware were not spared. Many of the leftover inventories of glasshouses found their way to wholesalers who, in turn, sold the wares to those who offered the glittering glass as prizes at carnivals, fairs, circuses, etc. Possibly because this was the last venue people associated the iridized glassware with, it became known as "carnival glass."

Acorn vase, maybe U.S. Glass or possibly Millersburg, green, one of two known. **$9,000**

April Showers vase, amethyst opalescent, 11 1/4" h, made by Fenton. **$1,450**

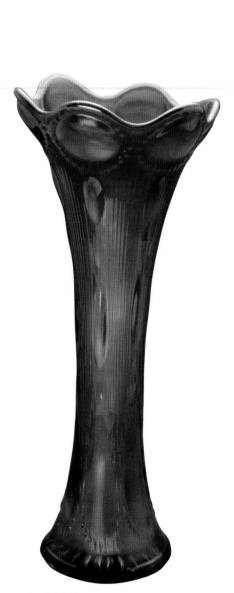

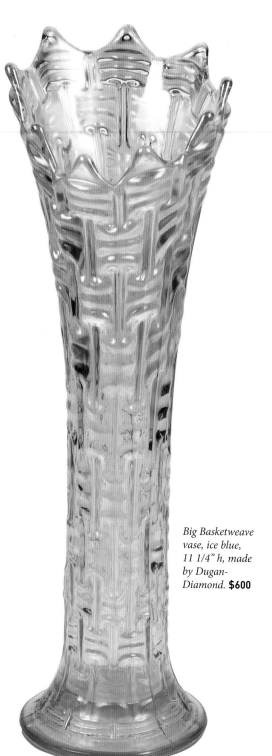

Beaded Bullseye vase, emerald green, 11", made by Imperial. **$700-$1,100** *Outstanding example* **$2,300**

Big Basketweave vase, ice blue, 11 1/4" h, made by Dugan-Diamond. **$600**

U.S. Glass Big Butterfly tumbler,
one of four known, green. **$10,000**

Blackberry Block water pitcher and one
tumbler, green, made by Fenton. **$4,000**

Blackberry Wreath large bowl, ruffled,
purple, made by Millersburg. **$40**

Blueberry water pitcher and three tumblers (one shown), white, made by Fenton. **$1,450**

Bouquet water pitcher and six tumblers (one shown), marigold, made by Fenton. **$265**

Broken Arches punch bowl and base, purple, 13" d, made by Imperial. **$1,000-$1,300**
Outstanding example **$2,000**

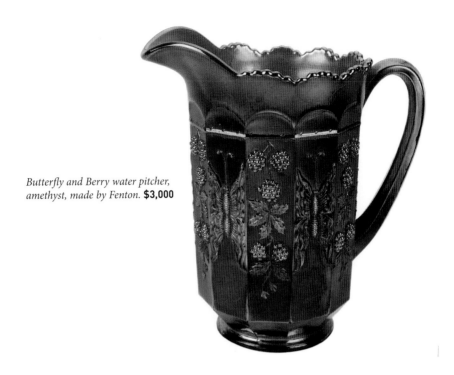

Butterfly and Berry water pitcher, amethyst, made by Fenton. **$3,000**

Butterfly and Fern water pitcher and six tumblers, amethyst. **$1,050**

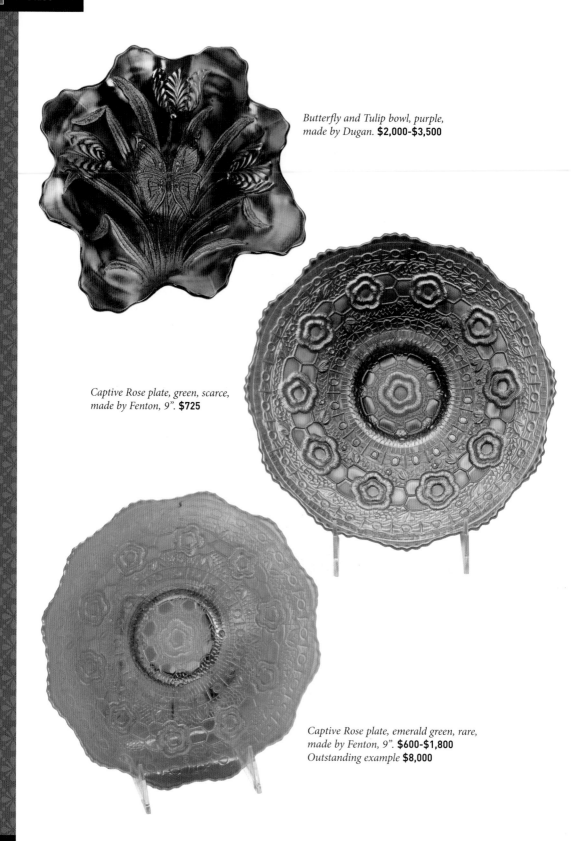

Butterfly and Tulip bowl, purple, made by Dugan. **$2,000-$3,500**

Captive Rose plate, green, scarce, made by Fenton, 9". **$725**

Captive Rose plate, emerald green, rare, made by Fenton, 9". **$600-$1,800** Outstanding example **$8,000**

Captive Rose bowl with 3-in-1 edge, electric blue, made by Fenton. **$500**

Captive Rose plate with great detail, amethyst, made by Fenton, 9". **$575**

Farmyard ruffled bowl, purple, made by Dugan. **$5,500-$8,000** *Outstanding example* **$12,500**

*Fentonia water pitcher
and one tumbler, blue,
made by Fenton.* **$875**

*Fluffy Peacock water pitcher and six
tumblers, amethyst, made by Fenton.* **$1,050**

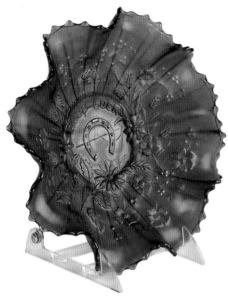

Good Luck eight-ruffled bowl with ribbed back, sapphire, by Northwood, 8 1/2". **$1,600-$2,300**

Good Luck stippled plate with ribbed back, purple, 9", made by Northwood. **$1,000-$1,500** *Outstanding example* **$2,200**

Imperial Grape carafe, emerald green, 9" h, made by Imperial, **$2,000-$3,000** *Outstanding example* **$4,300 (rare)**

Imperial Morning Glory funeral vase, purple, 14 1/4" h, 8 1/2" mouth. **$700-$1,000** *Outstanding example* **$2,400**

Imperial Morning Glory vase, purple, 12 1/2" h. **$500-$800**

Imperial Morning Glory miniature vase, vaseline, 5" h. **$600-$800 (very rare)**

Peacocks on the Fence stippled plate, electric blue, 9", made by Northwood. **$800-$1,200** *Outstanding example* **$2,500**

Peacocks on the Fence ruffled bowl, ribbed back, aqua opalescent, 8 1/2" d, made by Northwood. **$950-$1,500** *Outstanding example* **$3,200**

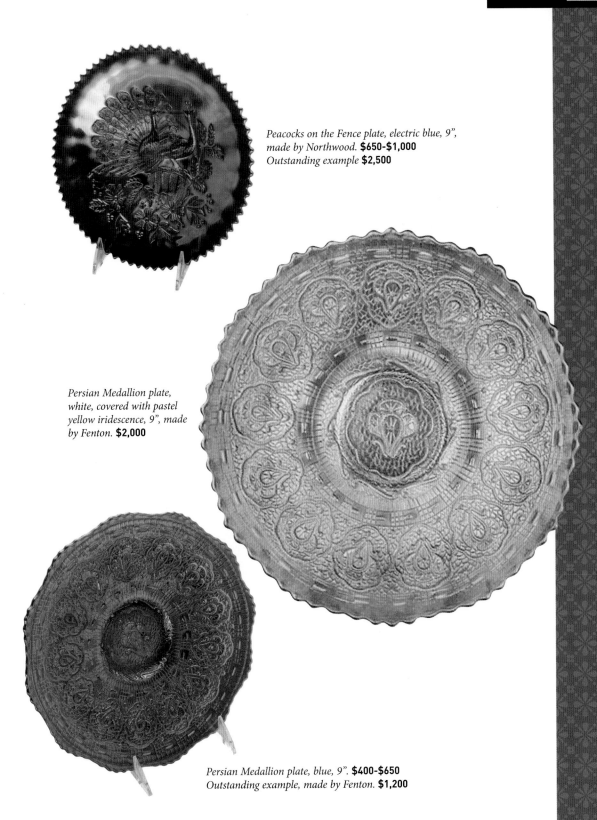

*Peacocks on the Fence plate, electric blue, 9",
made by Northwood.* **$650-$1,000**
Outstanding example **$2,500**

*Persian Medallion plate,
white, covered with pastel
yellow iridescence, 9", made
by Fenton.* **$2,000**

Persian Medallion plate, blue, 9". **$400-$650**
Outstanding example, made by Fenton. **$1,200**

Persian Medallion tri-fold bowl, amethyst, 6 3/4", made by Fenton. **$250-$300.**

Persian Medallion bonbon, two handles, red, made by Fenton. **$700**

Persian Medallion bonbon with two handles, celeste blue, 7". **$650-$950** *Outstanding example, made by Fenton.* **$1,800**

Northwood Poppy Show plate, electric blue, 9". **$5,000-$8,000**

Northwood Poppy Show flared plate, ice blue. **$1,700**

Northwood Poppy Show ruffled bowl, electric blue. **$1,500**

Northwood Poppy Show bowl, ruffled, white. **$400**

Ripple funeral vase, marigold, 11 1/2" h, made by Imperial. **$200-$400**

Ripple squat vase, purple, 6 1/2" h, with a 3" base, made by Imperial. **$150-$250**

Ripple vase, blue, 10" h x 3" base, made by Imperial. **$800-$1,200 (rare)**

Rose Show bowl, purple, 8 1/2" d, made by Northwood. **$500**

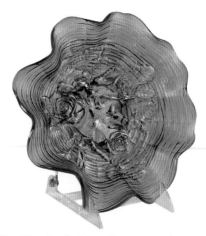

Rose Show bowl, eight ruffles, aqua opalescent, 8 1/2" d, made by Northwood. **$900-$1,600** *Outstanding example* **$3,000**

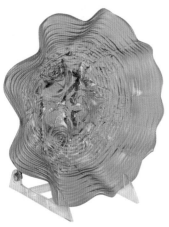

Rose Show bowl, eight ruffles, ice green opalescent, made by Northwood. **$2,800-$3,700 (rare)**

Rose Show plate, blue, 9" d, made by Northwood. **$1,100-$1,600**

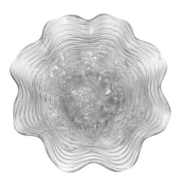

Rose Show ruffled bowl, ice blue, made by Northwood. **$1,300**

Strawberry Scroll water pitcher and six
tumblers, marigold, made by Fenton. **$2,500**

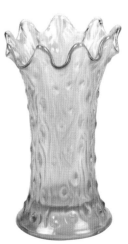

Tree Trunk vases, ice blue,
squatty 7" and 11". **$400 each**

Tree Trunk jester's cap
vase, marigold, 7 1/2".
$3,000-$4,500 (rare)

Tree Trunk funeral vase, mid-size,
aqua opalescent. **$19,000**

Tree Trunk elephant's foot funeral
vase, purple, 13" h. **$1,800-$3,400**
Outstanding example **$11,000**

Daum Nancy

Daum Nancy fine glass, much of it cameo, was made by Auguste and Antonin Daum, who founded a factory in 1875 in Nancy, France. Most of their cameo and enameled glass was made from the 1890s into the early 20th century.

Cameo glass is made by carving into multiple layers of colored glass to create a design in relief. It is at least as old as the Romans.

French art glass vase, Daum Frères, Nancy, France, circa 1900, marked Daum, Nancy, (cross of Lorraine), 12", with varied and vibrant coloration, the shaded orange ground featuring a town scene in one panel. **$9,560**

Heritage Auction Galleries

Heritage Auction Galleries

French art glass footed goblet, Daum Frères, Nancy, France, circa 1895, marked Daum, Nancy, (cross of Lorraine), 7" x 7 1/2", patterned with a frieze of field mice in shades of red and orange over shaded and frosted sky. **$5,078**

Heritage Auction Galleries

French art glass box and cover, Daum Frères, Nancy, France, circa 1900, marked Daum, Nancy, (cross of Lorraine), 3 3/4" x 5 1/2", squared box with round cover patterned with conforming landscape of birch trees in naturalistic spring palette over frosted, opalescent pink ground. **$3,585**

Heritage Auction Galleries

French art glass vase, Daum Freres, Nancy, France, circa 1910, marked DAUM, FRANCE, (cross of Lorraine), 11 3/4" x 4 3/4" x 3", with pattern of berried branches in dark mauve shades on dark blue and green modeled ground, surface showing multiple stress lines. **$310**

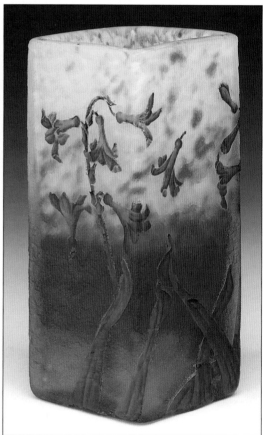

James D. Julia Auctioneers

Daum Nancy cameo and enamel floral vase. With delicate blue enameled flowers and green foliage that rest against a mottled background of blue, purple and green. Signed on the underside "Daum Nancy" with the Cross of Lorraine in gold. 5" h. Minor enamel loss to stems. **$2,400**

James D. Julia Auctioneers

Daum Nancy Art Deco vase. With deep acid cut-back Art Deco design against a smoky gray glass. The design has a textured finish in contrast with the polished glass highlights. Signed on the underside with engraved "Daum Nancy France" with Cross of Lorraine. 4" t. **$460**

James D. Julia Auctioneers

Monumental Daum Nancy cameo vase. With decoration of swans and birch trees. Decoration adorns both from and back of the vase and is finished with enameled scene of islands and trees in the background. A superior example. Signed in enamel on the foot rim "Daum Nancy". 25 1/4" t. **$18,400**

James D. Julia Auctioneers

Daum Nancy cameo and enameled vase. Square vase is decorated on each side with a cameo poppy, stem and leaves against a mottled yellow shading to orange background. Each poppy, in various stages of bloom, is enameled with bright orange flowers and subtle green and brown stems and leaves. The foot of the vase is trimmed with a simple gold gilt line. Signed on the side in cameo "Daum Nancy" with the Cross of Lorraine. 4 3/4" t. **$4,200**

Daum Nancy cameo cruet. Winter scene in rare shape. Signed in enamel on the underside "Daum Nancy" with Cross of Lorraine. 3" t. **$3,220**

James D. Julia Auctioneers

*Daum Nancy cameo vase. Acid
etched and enameled winter scene.
Signed in enamel on the underside
"Daum Nancy" with the Cross of
Lorraine. 4" t.* **$6,325**

James D. Julia Auctioneers

*Daum Nancy snail
vase. Design of
grapes, leaves and
vines in autumn-
colored vitreous glass
against a mottled
yellow, orange and
brown background.
The unusually large
egg-shaped vase is
finished with two
applied glass snails
(second view). Vase
is signed on the side
in cameo "Daum
Nancy" with the
Cross of Lorraine.
8 3/4" t.* **$10,925**

James D. Julia Auctioneers

Daum Nancy cameo vase. Winter scenic banjo vase. Unusual shape. Signed in enamel on the underside "Daum Nancy" with Cross of Lorraine. 12" t. **$10,350**

Daum Nancy cameo rose bowl. Winter scenic decoration, strongly colored and detailed. Engraved signature "Daum Nancy" with Cross of Lorraine on underside. 3 3/4" t x 5" diameter. **$8,625**

Daum Nancy cameo vase. Canoe shape with acid-etched and enameled winter scene. Enameled signature on the underside "Daum Nancy" with the Cross of Lorraine. 6 3/4" w. **$6,325**

James D. Julia Auctioneers

Daum Nancy rain scene vase. Extremely rare, square form is enameled with earthen-hued trees with green grass and foliage in the background. This design is set against a gray, rose and green ground. The "rain" effect is created by scoring the glass down to its transparency. Signed "Daum Nancy" with the Cross of Lorraine. 4 1/4" h. **$8,625**

Daum Nancy cameo vase. Spring scenic vase with acid-etched and enameled trees. Signed in enamel on the side "Daum Nancy" with the Cross of Lorraine. 10 1/2" h. **$6,325**

James D. Julia Auctioneers

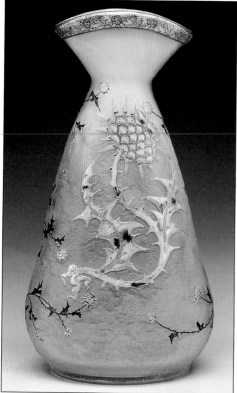

James D. Julia Auctioneers

Early Daum cameo and enameled vase. Decorated with a large, central heavily enameled thistle and flower with gold highlights. The flower is set against an acid-etched background of creamy yellow shading to clear. The back and sides of the vase are decorated with all-over cameo thistle design with black enamel highlighting the stems and leaves with gold gilt thistle flowers and red enamel highlights. The vase is finished with an enameled floral band at the lip. Signed on the underside in red enamel "Daum Nancy" with the Cross of Lorraine. 8" h. Some minor wear to gilt trim on lip. **$5,750**

Daum Nancy cameo vase. Acid etched and enameled pillow vase with red berries and green leaves on a yellow to brown mottled background. Vividly colored. Signed on the side in enamel "Daum Nancy France" with the Cross of Lorraine. 4 3/4" h. **$5,175**

James D. Julia Auctioneers

James D. Julia Auctioneers

Daum Nancy floral french cameo vase. Pillow-shaped vase has a frosted mottled ground which flows into a golden yellow hue. Accenting this is a pattern of violets enameled in purple with green foliage front and back. Signed "Daum Nancy" with Cross of Lorraine. 4 1/2" x 4 1/2". **$4,312**

James D. Julia Auctioneers

Daum Nancy cameo and enameled floral vase. Cornflowers in blue are accented by russet stamens with green foliage. This pattern wraps itself around the entire vase. The background glass is a softly mottled frost rose and green with an electric cobalt blue base. Signed "Daum Nancy" with the Cross of Lorraine. 3 3/4" h x 4" w. **$4,255**

James D. Julia Auctioneers

Daum Nancy cameo vase. Acid etched and enameled vase with red berries and green leaves on a yellow to brown mottled background. Vividly colored. Signed on the side in enamel "Daum Nancy France" with the Cross of Lorraine. 15 1/4" h. **$8,050**

Daum Nancy French cameo berry vase. Deep blue berry decoration with foliage in colors of amber and green atop a muted yellow mottled ground. Unusual tapered bulbous form. Signed "France" and also "Daum Nancy" in cameo with the Cross of Lorraine. 4 1/2" h. **$1,380**

James D. Julia Auctioneers

Daum Nancy cameo vase. Green acid-etched pendulous flowers on green to sky blue wheel-carved background and foot with simulated hammered texture, the entire vase fire-polished. Engraved signature on the underside "Daum Nancy" with the Cross of Lorraine enhanced with gilding. 11 3/4" h. **$8,400**

James D. Julia Auctioneers

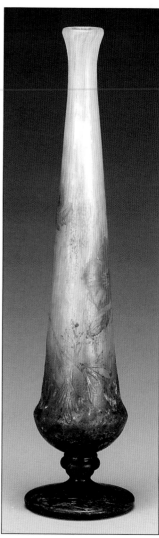

James D. Julia Auctioneers

Daum Nancy padded and wheel-carved vase. Orange poppies on striated blue to green wheel-carved background with simulated hammered texture, brown and yellow mottled foot. Intaglio carved signature on the foot "Daum Nancy" with the Cross of Lorraine. 16 1/4" h. **$9,200**

Daum Nancy cameo and applied covered jar. Rare example with one green-gold applied cabochon, one green applied insect and one red applied leaf on body with acid-etched maple leaves. The lid with applied and wheel-carved handle with red applied insect on top (second view). Signed on the underside with engraved and gilded "Daum Nancy" with the Cross of Lorraine. 4 1/2" h. **$9,200**

James D. Julia Auctioneers

Daum Nancy cameo vase. Padded and wheel-carved lavender and brown iris flowers and buds on a frosted to chartreuse background together with acid-etched, deep purple leaves. Acid etched signature on the side "Daum Nancy" with the Cross of Lorraine. 12" h. **$7,200**

James D. Julia Auctioneers

Daum Nancy cameo vase. Acid-etched green daffodils on wheel-carved green to frosted to green background with simulated hammered texture and foot with opalescent interior. Signed on the underside with engraved "Daum Nancy" with the Cross of Lorraine. 7 3/4" h. **$6,000**

James D. Julia Auctioneers

Daum Nancy cameo vase. Single wheel-carved parrot tulip in shades of purple with wheel-carved leaves on a shaded clear to purple background with simulated hammered texture. Signed on the underside with engraved "Daum Nancy" with the Cross of Lorraine. 6" h. **$6,000**

James D. Julia Auctioneers

Depression Glass

— By Ellen T. Schroy

Depression glass is the name of colorful glassware collectors generally associated with mass-produced glassware found in pink, yellow, crystal, or green in the years surrounding the Great Depression in America.

The housewives of the Depression-era were able to enjoy the wonderful colors offered in this new inexpensive glass dinnerware because they received pieces of their favorite patterns packed in boxes of soap, or as premiums given at "dish night" at the local movie theater. Merchandisers, such as Sears & Roebuck and F. W. Woolworth, enticed young brides with the colorful wares that they could afford even when economic times were harsh.

Ellen Schroy

Because of advancements in glassware technology, Depression-era patterns were mass-produced and could be purchased for a fraction of what cut glass or lead crystal cost. As one manufacturer found a pattern that was pleasing to the buying public, other companies soon followed with their adaptation of a similar design. Patterns included several design motifs, such as florals, geometrics, and even patterns that looked back to Early American patterns like Sandwich glass.

As America emerged from the Great Depression and life became more leisure-oriented again, new glassware patterns were created to reflect the new tastes of this generation. More elegant shapes and forms were designed, leading to what is sometimes called "Elegant Glass." Today's collectors often include these more elegant patterns when they talk about Depression-era glassware.

Depression-era glassware is one of the best-researched collecting areas available to the American marketplace. This is due in large part to the careful research of several people, including Hazel Marie Weatherman, Gene Florence, Barbara Mauzy, Carl F. Luckey, and Kent Washburn. Their books are held in high regard by researchers and collectors today.

Regarding values for Depression glass, rarity does not always equate to a high dollar amount. Some more readily found items command lofty prices because of high demand or other factors, not because they are necessarily rare. As collectors' tastes range from the simple patterns to the more elaborate patterns, so does the ability of their budget to invest in inexpensive patterns to multi-hundreds of dollars per form patterns.

The Depression-era glassware researchers have many accurate sources, including company records, catalogs, magazine advertisements, oral and written histories from sales staff, factory workers, etc.

For more information on Depression glass, see *Warman's Depression Glass Identification and Price Guide, 5th Edition*, or *Warman's Depression Glass Field Guide, 4th Edition*, both by Ellen T. Schroy.

Depression Glass Identification Guide

Depression-era glassware can be confusing. Many times, one manufacturer came up with a neat new design, and as soon as it was successful, other companies started to make patterns that were similar. To help you figure out what pattern you might be trying to research, here's a quick identification guide. The patterns are broken down into several different classifications by design elements. Try comparing your piece to these. For more information, prices and identification, read Warman's Depression Glass, 5th edition, by Ellen Schroy, available at Shop. Collect.com or 800-258-0929.

· · · · · · · · ·

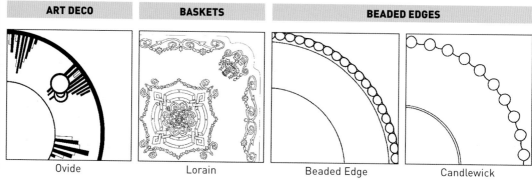

ART DECO	BASKETS	BEADED EDGES	
Ovide	Lorain	Beaded Edge	Candlewick

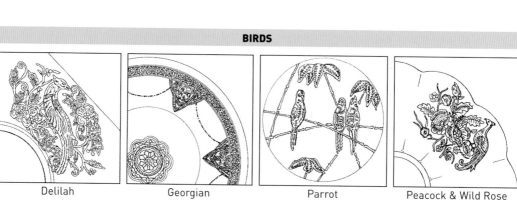

BIRDS

| Delilah | Georgian | Parrot | Peacock & Wild Rose |

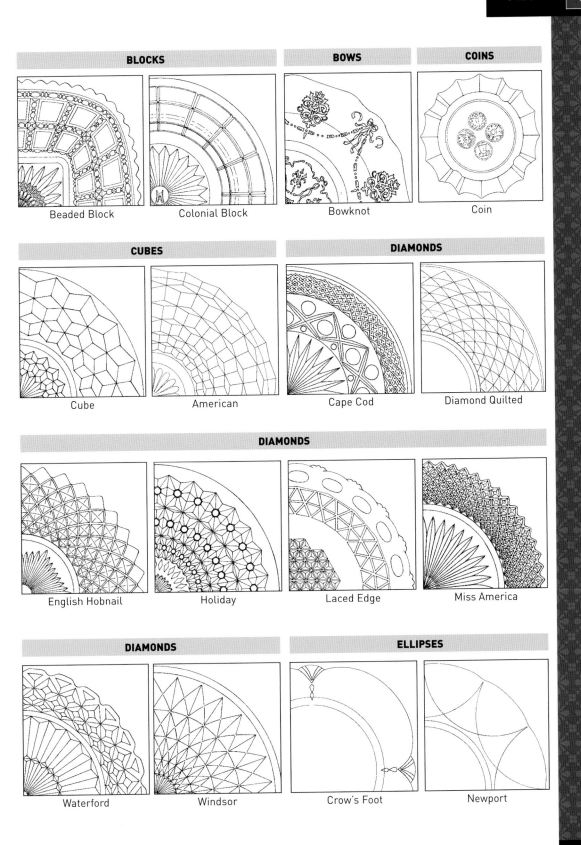

BLOCKS

Beaded Block

Colonial Block

BOWS

Bowknot

COINS

Coin

CUBES

Cube

American

DIAMONDS

Cape Cod

Diamond Quilted

DIAMONDS

English Hobnail

Holiday

Laced Edge

Miss America

DIAMONDS

Waterford

Windsor

ELLIPSES

Crow's Foot

Newport

ELLIPSES

FLORALS

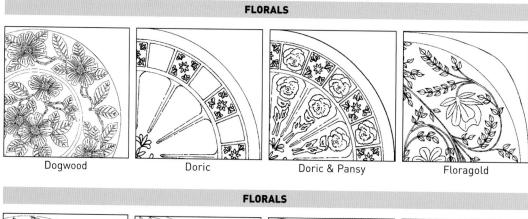

Romanesque

Cherry Blossom

Cloverleaf

Daisy

FLORALS

Dogwood

Doric

Doric & Pansy

Floragold

FLORALS

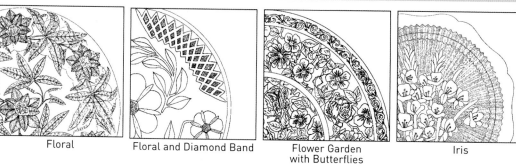

Floral

Floral and Diamond Band

Flower Garden with Butterflies

Iris

FLORALS

Jubilee

Mayfair

Mayfair (Open Rose)

Normandie

FLORALS

Pineapple & Floral

Rose Cameo

Rosemary

Royal Lace

FLORALS

Sharon

Sunflower

Thistle

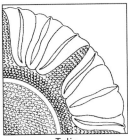
Tulip

FIGURES

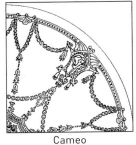
Cameo

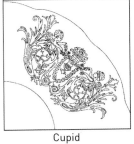
Cupid

FRUITS

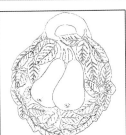
Avocado

Cherryberry

FRUITS

Della Robbia

Fruits

Paneled Grape

Strawberry

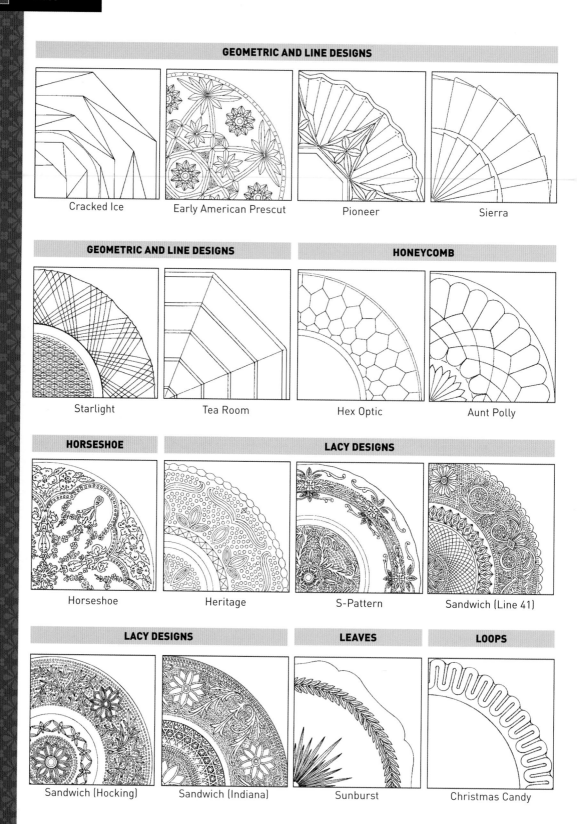

GEOMETRIC AND LINE DESIGNS

Cracked Ice

Early American Prescut

Pioneer

Sierra

GEOMETRIC AND LINE DESIGNS

HONEYCOMB

Starlight

Tea Room

Hex Optic

Aunt Polly

HORSESHOE

LACY DESIGNS

Horseshoe

Heritage

S-Pattern

Sandwich (Line 41)

LACY DESIGNS

LEAVES

LOOPS

Sandwich (Hocking)

Sandwich (Indiana)

Sunburst

Christmas Candy

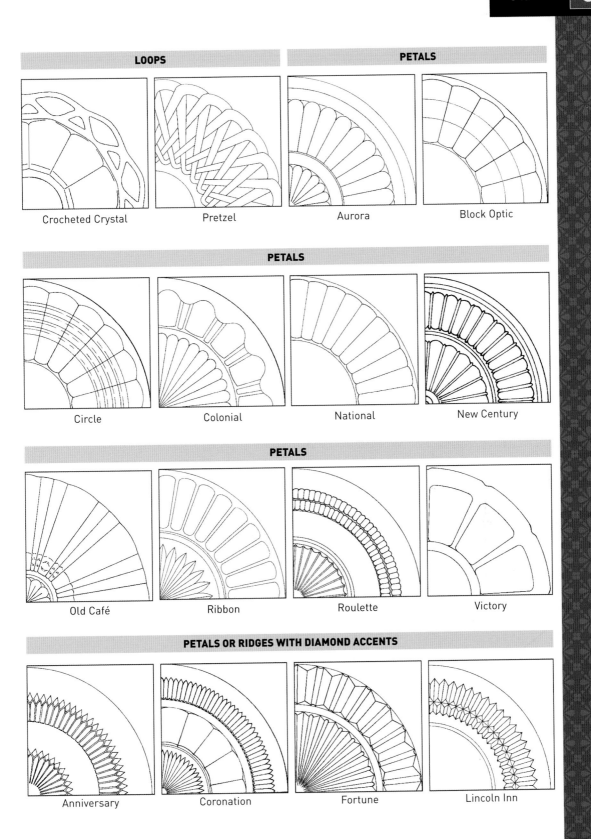

LOOPS

Crocheted Crystal

Pretzel

PETALS

Aurora

Block Optic

PETALS

Circle

Colonial

National

New Century

PETALS

Old Café

Ribbon

Roulette

Victory

PETALS OR RIDGES WITH DIAMOND ACCENTS

Anniversary

Coronation

Fortune

Lincoln Inn

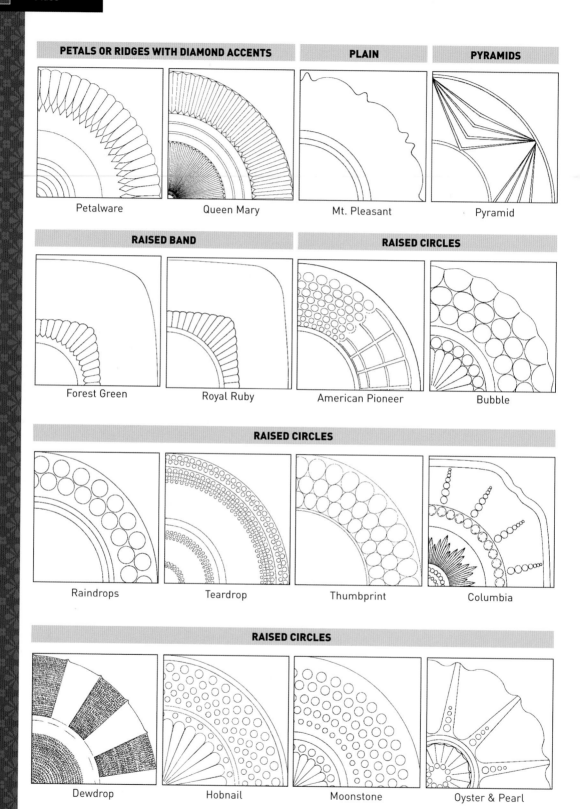

PETALS OR RIDGES WITH DIAMOND ACCENTS

Petalware

Queen Mary

PLAIN

Mt. Pleasant

PYRAMIDS

Pyramid

RAISED BAND

Forest Green

Royal Ruby

RAISED CIRCLES

American Pioneer

Bubble

RAISED CIRCLES

Raindrops

Teardrop

Thumbprint

Columbia

RAISED CIRCLES

Dewdrop

Hobnail

Moonstone

Oyster & Pearl

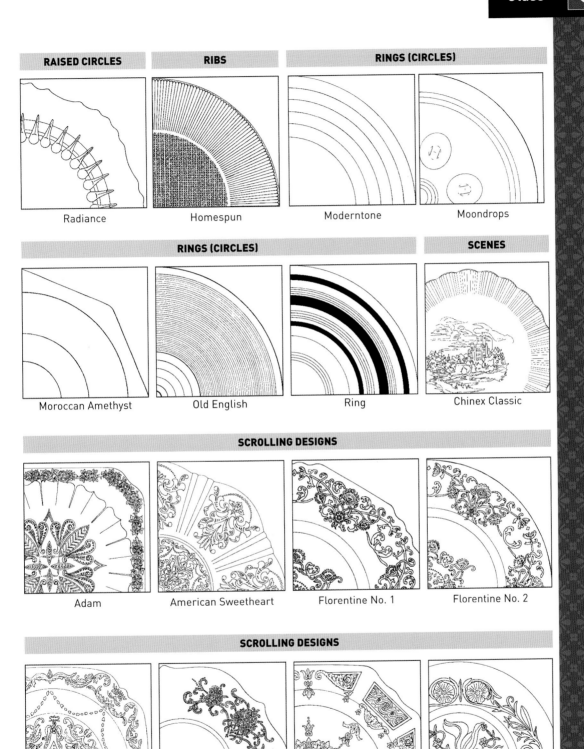

RAISED CIRCLES

Radiance

RIBS

Homespun

RINGS (CIRCLES)

Moderntone

Moondrops

RINGS (CIRCLES)

Moroccan Amethyst

Old English

Ring

SCENES

Chinex Classic

SCROLLING DESIGNS

Adam

American Sweetheart

Florentine No. 1

Florentine No. 2

SCROLLING DESIGNS

Madrid

Patrick

Princess

Rock Crystal

SCROLLING DESIGNS

SWIRLS

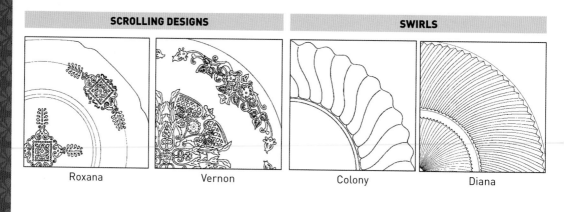

Roxana

Vernon

Colony

Diana

SWIRLS

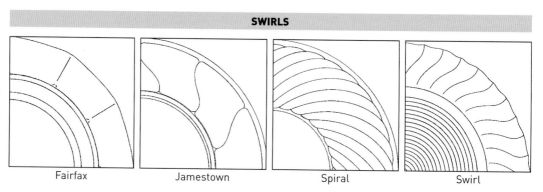

Fairfax

Jamestown

Spiral

Swirl

SWIRLS

TEXTURED

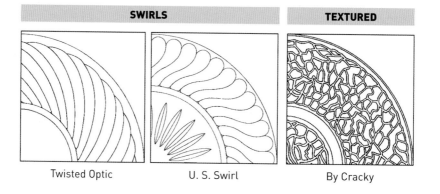

Twisted Optic

U. S. Swirl

By Cracky

Adam, pink covered casserole. **$80**

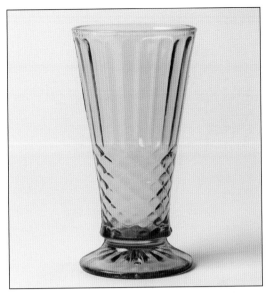

Aunt Polly, blue vase, 6 1/2" h. **$40**

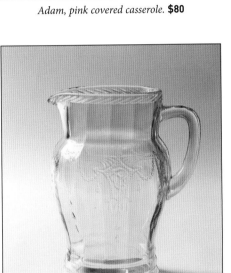

Cameo, green 56 oz pitcher. **$90**

Cherry Blossom, pink sugar. **$35**

Capri, azure blue swirled bowl, 8 3/4" d. **$12**; swirled berry bowl 4 3/4" d. **$7.50**

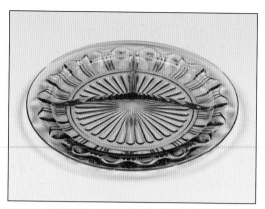

Colonial, pink divided grill plate. **$27**

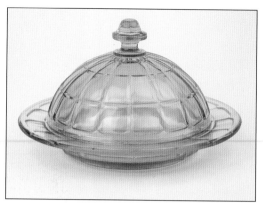

Colonial Block, green covered butter dish. **$50**

Coronation, royal ruby handled berry bowl. **$20**

Cracked Ice, pink creamer. **$35**; pink covered sugar. $35

Cupid, pink low pedestal-foot comport, 6 1/4". **$290**

Daisy, amber luncheon plate. **$10**

Doric and Pansy, ultramarine child's sugar. **$60**. Ultramarine child's creamer. **$50**

English Hobnail, green 6" mayonnaise. **$22** *Green 6 1/2" plate.* **$10**

Floral and Diamond Band, green luncheon plate. **$40**

Florentine No. 1, pink sherbet. **$15**
Pink cup. **$12**

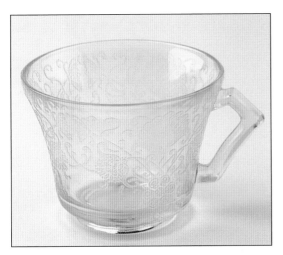

Florentine No. 2, yellow cup. **$14.50**

Hobnail, pink sherbet. **$5**

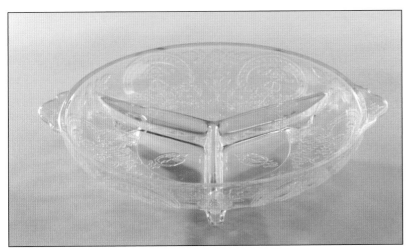

Horseshoe, yellow three-part footed relish dish. **$24**

Jamestown, blue footed creamer. **$25**

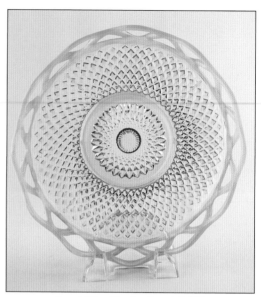

Laced Edge, blue bowl, 5 1/2". **$42**

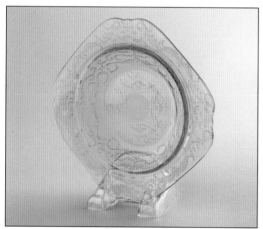

Madrid, amber bowl. **$17.50**

Mayfair Federal, amber dinner plate. **$20**

Mayfair, Open Rose ice blue sweet pea vase. **$160**

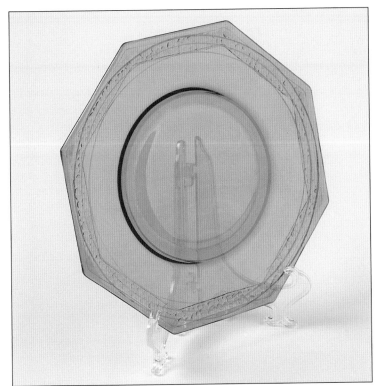

Melba, amethyst luncheon plate. **$9**

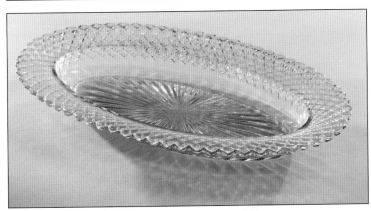

Miss America, pink 10 1/2" oval celery dish. **$45**

Moondrops, red sugar. **$18**
Red creamer. $16

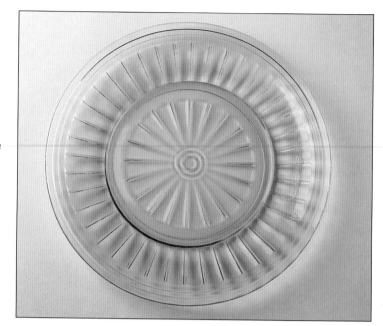

New Century, green dinner plate. **$24**

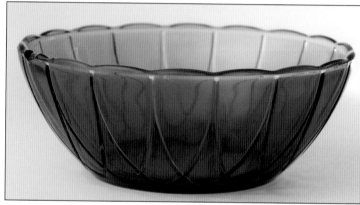

Newport, cobalt blue 5 1/4" d cereal bowl. **$45**

Normandie, iridescent cup. **$6**

Old Colony Lace Edge, pink 7 3/4" d salad bowl. **$60**

Old English, green compote. **$24**

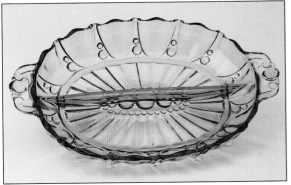

Oyster and Pearl, pink relish. **$35**

Patrician, amber covered butter. **$95**

Pioneer, pink luncheon plate, fruit center. **$8**

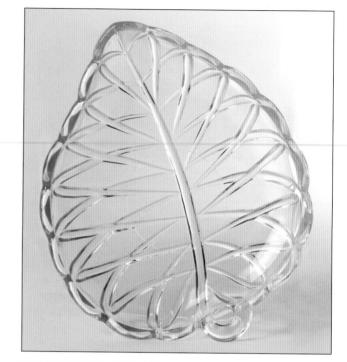

Pretzel, crystal leaf-shaped olive dish. **$7**

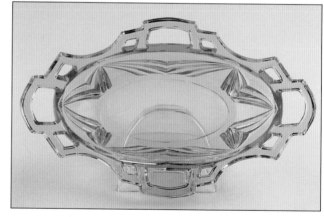

Pyramid, green pickle dish. **$35**

Radiance ice blue 6" comport with ruffled edge. **$35**

Ribbon green covered candy dish. **$45**

Rock Crystal, amber plate, 8 1/2" d. **$12**

Rosemary, amber vegetable bowl. **$18** *Amber berry bowl.* **$7**

Roulette, green 9" fruit bowl. **$25**

Sandwich, Hocking, smooth desert gold bowl, 6 1/2" d. **$9**

Sharon, pink 10 1/2" fruit bowl. **$50**

Sierra Pinwheel, green butter dish. **$80**
Pink cup. **$17.50**
Pink saucer. **$10**

Sunburst, crystal candelabra, two-light. **$20**

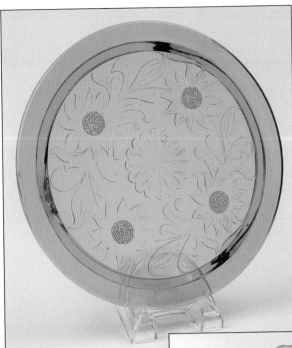

Sunflower, green cake plate. **$20**

Swirl, ultramarine cup and saucer. **$22.50**

Tea Room, green sugar and creamer on tray with center handle. **$95**

Twisted Optic, green covered flat candy dish. **$40**

Waterford, crystal 7 1/8" d salad plate. **$9**
Crystal 5 1/4" h goblet. **$18**

Windsor, pink 11 1/2" oval platter (in back). **$25**
Pink 10 1/2" oval bowl with pointed ends. **$32**
Pink 8 1/2" l oval bowl. **$30**

Yorktown, yellow sandwich server with gold metal center handle. **$8**

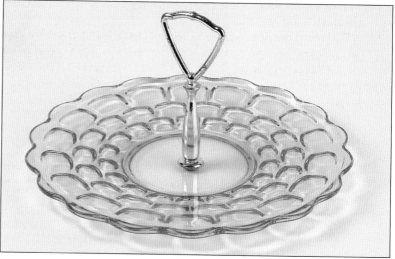

Fenton Art Glass

The Fenton Art Glass Co. was founded in 1905 by Frank L. Fenton and his brother, John W., in Martins Ferry, Ohio. They initially sold hand-painted glass made by other manufacturers, but it wasn't long before they decided to produce their own glass. The new Fenton factory in Williamstown, W.V., opened on Jan. 2, 1907. From that point on, the company expanded by developing unusual colors and continued to decorate glassware in innovative ways.

Two more brothers, James and Robert, joined the firm. But despite the company's initial success, John W. left to establish the Millersburg Glass Co. of Millersburg, Ohio, in 1909. The first months of the new operation were devoted to the production of crystal glass only. Later iridized glass was called "Radium Glass." After only two years, Millersburg filed for bankruptcy.

Fenton's iridescent glass had a metallic luster over a colored, pressed pattern, and was sold in dime stores. It was only after the sales of this glass decreased and it was sold in bulk as carnival prizes that it came to be known as carnival glass.

Fenton became the top producer of carnival glass, with more than 150 patterns. The quality of the glass, and its popularity with the public, enabled the new company to be profitable through the late 1920s. As interest in carnival subsided, Fenton moved on to stretch glass and opalescent patterns. A line of colorful blown glass (called "off-hand" by Fenton) was also produced in the mid-1920s.

During the Great Depression, Fenton survived by producing functional colored glass tableware and other household items, including water sets, table sets, bowls, mugs, plates, perfume bottles and vases.

Restrictions on European imports during World War II ushered in the arrival of Fenton's opaque colored glass, and the lines of "Crest" pieces soon followed.

In the 1950s, production continued to diversify with a focus on milk glass, particularly in Hobnail patterns.

In the third quarter of Fenton's history, the company returned to themes that had proved popular to preceding generations, and began adding special lines, such as the Bicentennial series.

Innovations included the line of Colonial colors that debuted in 1963, including amber, blue, green, orange and ruby. Based on a special order for an Ohio museum, Fenton in 1969 revisited its early success with "Original Formula Carnival Glass." Fenton also started marking its glass in the molds for the first time.

The star of the 1970s was the yellow and blushing pink creation known as Burmese, which remains popular today. This was followed closely by a menagerie of animals, birds, and children.

In 1975, Robert Barber was hired by Fenton to begin an artist-in-residence program, producing a limited line of art-glass vases in a return to the off-hand, blown-glass creations of the mid-1920s.

Shopping at home via television was a recent phenomenon in the late 1980s when the "Birthstone Bears" became the first Fenton product to appear on QVC (established in 1986 by Joseph Segel, founder of The Franklin Mint).

In the latter part of the century, Fenton established a website—www.fentonartglass.com—as a user-friendly online experience where collectors could learn about catalog and gift shop sales, upcoming events and the history of the company.

In August 2007, Fenton discontinued all but a few of its more popular lines.

For more information on Fenton Art Glass, see *Warman's Fenton Glass Identification and Price Guide, 2nd edition*, by Mark F. Moran.

1905-1930

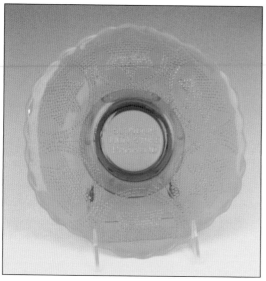

Blue Opalescent footed advertising plate in Beaded Stars, marked "Souvenir Lyon Store Hammond" (Ind.), circa 1910, 8 1/2" diameter. **$50+**

Blue Opalescent swung vase in Fenton Drapery, circa 1910, 14" h. **$45+**

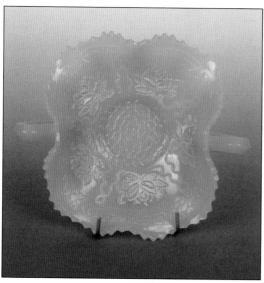

Persian Blue handled bonbon, 1915, in Pond Lily with enamel decoration, 7" diameter. **$35**

Celeste Blue stretch-glass covered jug and tumbler with cobalt handles, base and coaster, part of a lemonade set that would have included six tumblers, 1920s; jug, 11 1/4" h with base; tumbler, 5" h not including coaster, which is 3 1/4" diameter; **$700+ for complete set.**

Ruby dolphin-handle comport in Diamond Optic, late 1920s, 6" h. **$110+**

Tangerine stretch-glass tidbit tray in Diamond Optic, late 1920s, 10" diameter. **$125+**

Fenton Carnival Glass

The golden era of carnival glass was from about 1905 to the mid-1920s. It is believed that by 1906 the first cheap, iridized glass to rival the expensive Tiffany creations was in production. Carnival glass was originally made to bridge a gap in the market by providing ornamental wares for those who couldn't afford to buy the fashionable, iridized pieces popular at the height of the Art Nouveau era. It wasn't until much later that it acquired the name "carnival glass." When it fell from favor, it was sold off cheaply to carnivals and offered as prizes. Fenton made about 150 patterns of carnival glass.

Here are some of the basic colors:

Amethyst: A purple color ranging from quite light to quite dark
Aqua opalescent: Ice blue with a milky (white or colored) edge
Black amethyst: Very dark purple or black in color
Clam broth: Pale ginger ale color, sometimes milky
Cobalt blue (sometimes called royal blue): A dark, rich blue
Green: A true green, not pastel
Marigold: A soft, golden yellow
Pastel colors: A satin treatment in white, ice blue, ice green
Peach opalescent: Marigold with a milky (white or colored) edge
Red: A rich red, rare
Vaseline (Fenton called it topaz): Clear yellow/yellow-green glass

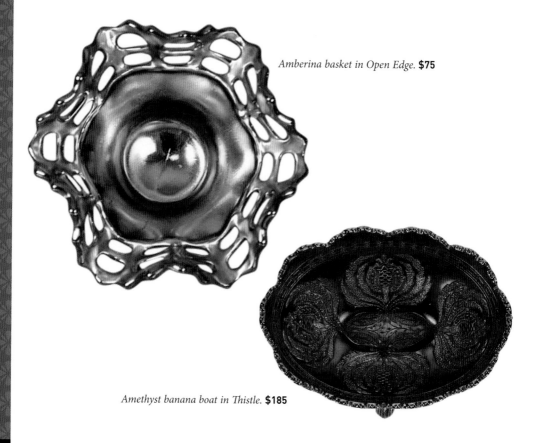

Amberina basket in Open Edge. **$75**

Amethyst banana boat in Thistle. **$185**

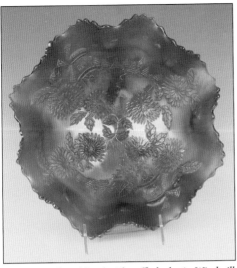

Cobalt Blue footed bowl with ruffled edge in Windmill and Mums, with wide-panel back, 11" d. **$500+**

White jug in Orange Tree Orchard, 10" h. **$500+**

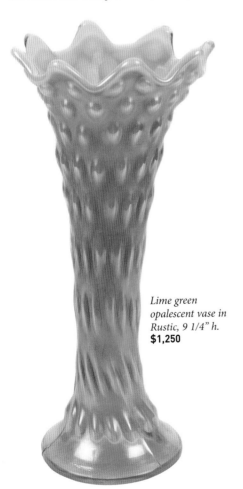

Lime green opalescent vase in Rustic, 9 1/4" h. **$1,250**

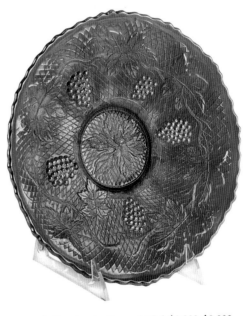

Purple flat plate in Concord, 9" d. **$2,000-$3,000**

1930-1955

*Nymph in footed bowl in Green Transparent, 1930s,
7 1/2" h.* **$275+ set**

Blue Opalescent biscuit jar in Hobnail, 1940s, 7 1/2" h.
$900+

*Cranberry Opalescent covered candy in Hobnail, with
clear lid, 1940s, 5 1/2" diameter.* **$300+**

*New World shakers, two sizes, in Cranberry Opalescent
Rib Optic, 1953, 5" h and 4" h.* **$175 pair**

*Emerald Green platter in Priscilla, early 1950s, 12"
diameter.* **$40+**

Ruby basket in Hobnail, circa 1950, 12". **$100+**

*Peach Crest melon-form vase with Charleton decoration by
Abels, Wasserberg of New York, mid-1950s, 5 1/2" h.* **$75+**

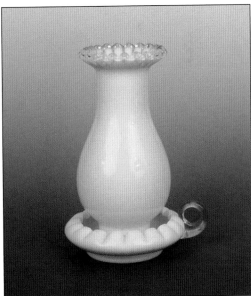

Silver Crest hurricane lamp, 8 1/2" h. **$250+**

1955-1980

Cranberry Polka Dot and Milk-glass covered butter with twig-form handle, 1955-56, 5 1/4" h and 8 1/4" diameter (base). **$400**

Jamestown Blue Overlay ribbed pillar vase, late 1950s, 5" h. **$45**

Ruby candleholders in Thumbprint, 1950s, each 9" h. **$125+**

Topaz Opalescent crimped bowl in Hobnail, 1959-60, 8" diameter. **$75**

Plum Opalescent and Green Opalescent footed covered candy jars in Hobnail, late 1950s to early 1960s, 8 1/2" h.
Plum **$175**
Green **$100**

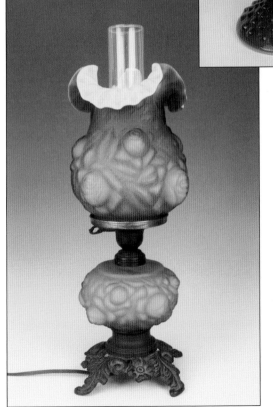

Wild Rose cased-glass electric lamp in Blown Out Roses, 1960s, made for L.G. Wright, 18 1/2" h with chimney. **$400+**

*Leaves on Burmese fairy lamp, 1970s,
6" h.* **$200+**

*Blue Opalescent creamer and covered sugar in Cactus, 1979, 5" h
and 6" h.* **$100+ pair**

*Burmese apothecary jar with hand-painted flowers,
mid-1970s, made for L.G. Wright, 10" h.* **$300+**

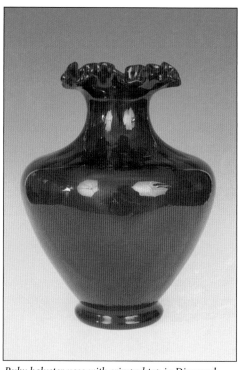

*Ruby baluster vase with crimped top in Diamond
Optic, 1970s, 11" h.* **$80+**

Cameo Opalescent basket in Lily of the Valley, 1979, 7 1/2" h. **$45**

Original Formula Carnival Glass swan candleholder, 1971, 6 1/2" h. **$50+**

Wisteria bell in Threaded Diamond Optic, 1977, 5 1/2" h. **$50**

Rosalene cracker jar in Cactus, circa 1980, 8" h. **$115**

1980-2007

Black (Ebony) miniature basket novelty with pink crest, 1980s, 4 1/4" h. **$90+**

Original Formula Carnival Glass Red wine decanter and wine goblet in Hobnail, purchased from the "special" room at the Fenton factory, early 1980s, 12" h and 4 1/2" h. **$300+ pair**

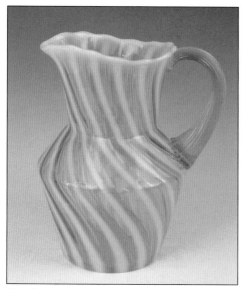

Blue Opalescent 44-ounce pitcher in Spiral Optic, circa 1980, 8" h. **$100+**

Lamp with interior and exterior hand-painted autumn-scene shade by Michael Dickinson, 1992, 21" h. **$500**

Cranberry cameo glass platter with sand-carved floral decoration by Martha Reynolds, 1994, one of 500, 14 1/2" diameter. **$275+**

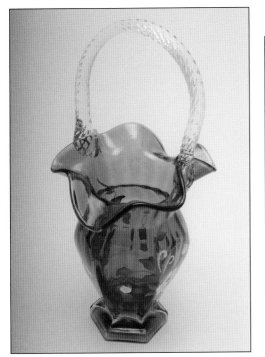

Burmese ginger jar, three pieces with base, decorated with butterflies, 2000, designed by J.K. (Robin) Spindler, with facsimiles of Fenton family signatures, 8 1/2" h. **$275**

Roselle on Cranberry basket, 1990s, 11 1/2" h. **$160+**

Pink Iridized trinket box made for Cracker Barrel, 2000, 4 1/2" l. **$50+**

Green iridized vase with hand-painted flowers, 2000 QVC Designer Showcase Series, signed by Bill Fenton, 8 1/2" h. **$100+**

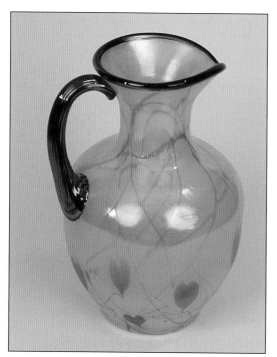

Dave Fetty handmade pitcher in Willow Green Opalescent Hanging Hearts, with iridized cobalt trim and handle, Connoisseur Collection, 2003, 8 1/2" h. **$425**

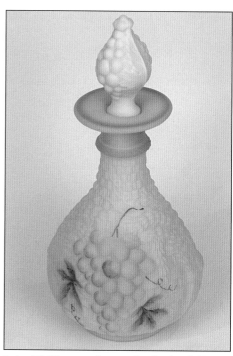

Lotus Mist Burmese decanter, hand painted, 2004, 11 1/2" h. **$120**

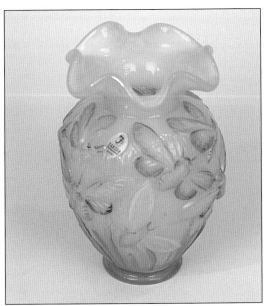

Topaz Blue Overlay Grasshopper vase made for QVC, 2004, hand painted, 6 3/4" h. **$50**

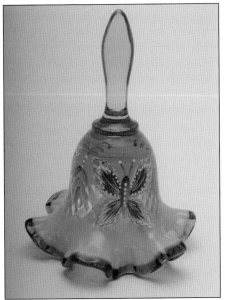

Mulberry Crest bell with ruffled edge, hand-painted, Designer Series, 2003, 7" h. **$90+**

Ruby Iridized paneled pitcher, 2002, 4 1/2" h. **$55+**

Aubergine Overlay covered candy in Wave Crest, with hand-painted decoration and applied metal trim, 2005, 5" h. **$150**

Lalique

René Jules Lalique was born on April 6,1860, in the village of Ay, in the Champagne region of France. In 1862, his family moved to the suburbs of Paris.

In 1872, Lalique began attending College Turgot where he began studying drawing with Justin-Marie Lequien. After the death of his father in 1876, Lalique began working as an apprentice to Louis Aucoc, who was a prominent jeweler and goldsmith in Paris.

Lalique moved to London in 1878 to continue his studies. He spent two years attending Sydenham College, developing his graphic design skills. He returned to Paris in 1880 and worked as an illustrator of jewelry, creating designs for Cartier, among others. In 1884, Lalique's drawings were displayed at the National Exhibition of Industrial Arts, organized at the Louvre.

At the end of 1885, Lalique took over Jules Destapes' jewelry workshop. Lalique's design began to incorporate translucent enamels, semiprecious stones, ivory, and hard stones. In 1889, at the Universal Exhibition in Paris, the jewelry firms of Vever and Boucheron included collaborative works by Lalique in their displays.

In the early 1890s, Lalique began to incorporate glass into his jewelry, and in 1893 he took part in a competition organized by the Union Centrale des Arts Decoratifs to design a drinking vessel. He won second prize.

Lalique opened his first Paris retail shop in 1905, near the perfume business of François Coty. Coty commissioned Lalique to design his perfume labels in 1907, and he also created his first perfume bottles for Coty.

In the first decade of the 20th century, Lalique continued to experiment with glass manufacturing techniques, and mounted his first show devoted entirely to glass in 1911.

During World War I, Lalique's first factory was forced to close, but the construction of a new factory was soon begun in Wingen-sur-Moder, in the Alsace region. It was completed in 1921, and still produces Lalique crystal today.

In 1925, Lalique designed the first "car mascot" (hood ornament) for Citroën, the French automobile company. For the next six years, Lalique would design 29 models for companies such as Bentley, Bugatti, Delage, Hispano-Suiza, Rolls Royce, and Voisin.

Lalique's second boutique opened in 1931, and this location continues to serve as the main Lalique showroom today.

René Lalique died on May 5, 1945, at the age of 85. His son, Marc, took over the business at that time, and when Marc died in 1977, his daughter, Marie-Claude Lalique Dedouvre, assumed control of the company. She sold her interest in the firm and retired in 1994.

For more information on Lalique, see *Warman's Lalique Identification and Price Guide* by Mark F. Moran.

(In the descriptions of Lalique pieces that follow, you will find notations like this: "M p. 478, No. 1100." This refers to the page and serial numbers found in *René Lalique, maître-verrier, 1860-1945: Analyse de L'oeuvre et Catalogue Raisonné* by Félix Marcilhac, published in 1989 and revised in 1994. Printed entirely in French, this book of more than 1,000 pages is the definitive guide to Lalique's work, and listings from auction catalogs typically cite the Marcilhac guide as a reference. A used copy can cost more than $500. Copies in any condition are extremely difficult to find, but collectors consider Marcilhac's guide to be the bible for Lalique.)

Ashtrays

"Archers" in deep red glass, circa 1922, 5 1/2" diameter. (M p. 269, No. 278) **$2,500+**

"Irene" in deep green glass, circa 1929, stenciled R. LALIQUE FRANCE, 3 3/4" diameter. (M p. 276, No. 304) **$1,200-$1,500**

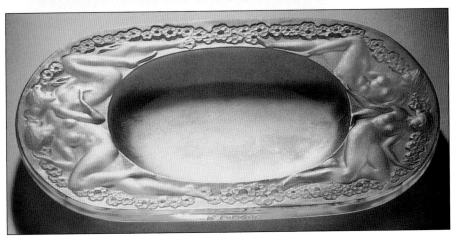

"Medicis" in blue glass, circa 1924, molded R. LALIQUE, 5 3/4" long. (M p. 270, No. 280) **$1,500-$1,600**

Bowls

*"Marguerites"
a center bowl,
circa 1941, in
clear and frosted
glass with green
patina, stenciled
R. LALIQUE
FRANCE,
4 3/4" diameter. (M
p. 312, No. 10-404)*
$900-$1,000

*"Nemours" circa
1929, in clear and
frosted glass with
sepia patina and
brown enameled
highlights, molded R.
LALIQUE FRANCE,
10" diameter.
(M p. 299, No. 404)*
$900-$1,000

*"Perruches" circa
1931, in opalescent
glass with blue
patina, stenciled R.
LALIQUE FRANCE,
9 5/8" diameter.
(M p. 302, No. 419)*
$4,000-$4,500

Boxes

"Cleones" circa 1921, in amber glass, molded R. LALIQUE, engraved France, 6 3/4" diameter. (M p. 231, No. 9) **$900-$1,100**

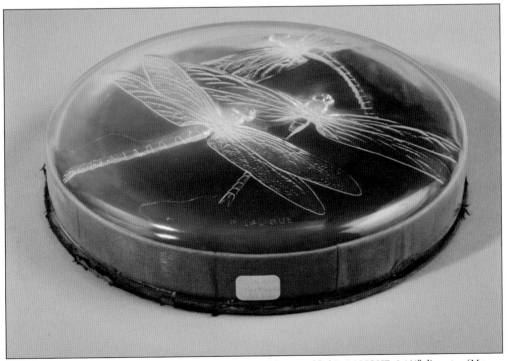

"Georgette" circa 1922, in opalescent glass with satin and card base, molded R. LALIQUE, 8 1/4" diameter. (M p. 30, No. 45) **$1,700-$2,000**

*"Quatre Scarabees" in cobalt blue glass with white patina, circa 1911, engraved R. Lalique France, No.15, 3 3/8"
diameter. (M p. 225, No. 15)* **$2,500-$2,800**

Car Mascots (Hood Ornaments)

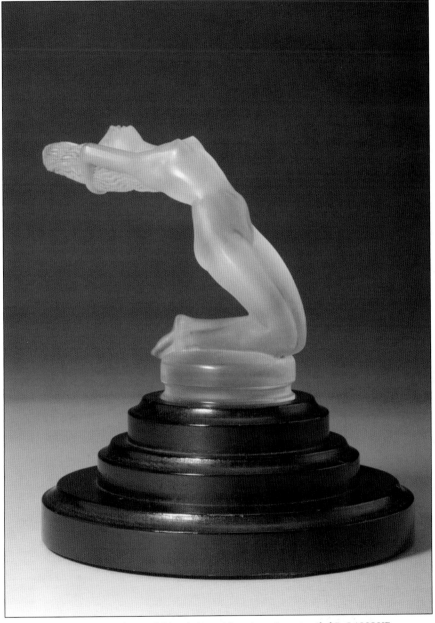

"Chrysis" in clear and frosted glass with sepia patina, stenciled R. LALIQUE, with an ebonized wood display stand. (M p. 505, No. 1183.) **$5,000-$6,000**

"Libellule" Grande Modele, circa 1928, in clear and frosted glass with pale amethyst tint, molded R. LALIQUE FRANCE and engraved R. Lalique France, 8 1/4" t, accompanied by a letter authenticating the mascot as the one formerly used by Gary Cooper on his Duesenberg, and presented by Cooper as a gift. (M p. 501, No. 1145)
$9,000-$12,000

"Victoire" circa 1928, in clear and frosted glass, molded R. LALIQUE FRANCE, 10 1/4" l, together with an original Lalique wood display mount. (M p. 502, No. 1147)
$24,000-$26,000

Figures

"Groupe de Six Moineaux" a decoration, in clear and frosted glass with gray patina, circa 1933, 11 5/8" l. (M p. 492, No. 1218) **$2,500+**

"Suzanne" a statuette, in amber glass, with original bronze illuminating stand, molded R. LALIQUE, statuette 9 1/8" t. (M p. 399, No. 833) **$30,000+**

Paperweights

"Toby" circa 1931, in clear and frosted glass, stenciled R. LALIQUE FRANCE, 3 1/3" t. (M p. 391, No. 1192) **$1,700-$2,000**

"Deux Tourterelles" circa 1925, in topaz glass, stenciled R. LALIQUE FRANCE, 4 3/4" t. (M p. 381, No. 1128) **$2,200-$2,600**

Perfume Bottles

"Bouchon Mures" bottle in clear glass with enamel decoration, stopper in amber glass, circa 1920, 4 1/3" t. (M p. 329, No. 495) **$3,000+**

"Clairefontaine" in clear
and frosted glass, circa
1931, 4 3/4" t. (M p. 338,
No. 526) **$1,800+**

"Clamart" in smoky satin glass with
black patina, circa 1927, 4 1/2" t. (M
p. 336, No. 517) **$1,800+**

"Helene" (Lotus), a perfume bottle, circa 1928, in clear and frosted glass, stenciled R. LALIQUE FRANCE, 2 5/8" t. (M p. 337, No. 522) **$1,800-$2,100**

"La Violette" a perfume bottle for Gabilla, circa 1925, in clear glass with violet enamel, molded LALIQUE, 3 1/3" t. (M p. 940, No. 2) **$3,000-$3,500**

"Roses" a clear and frosted glass perfume bottle for D'Orsay, circa 1912, molded LALIQUE, 4" t. (M p. 933, No. 3) **$2,700-$3,200**

Vases

"Acanthes" circa 1921, in red glass, 11 1/1/2" t. (M p. 417, No. 902) **$15,000+**

"Archers" circa 1921, in cherry red glass with strong white patina, 10 3/8" t. (M p. 415, No. 893) **$24,000+**

"Bacchantes" in topaz glass, with original (?) display stand, circa 1927, vase 9 7/8" t. (M p. 438, No. 997) **$15,000+**

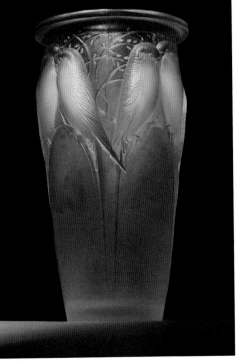

"Ceylan" circa 1924, in opalescent glass, wheel-cut R. LALIQUE FRANCE, 9 1/2" t. (M p. 418, No. 905) **$5,500-$6,000**

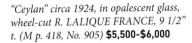

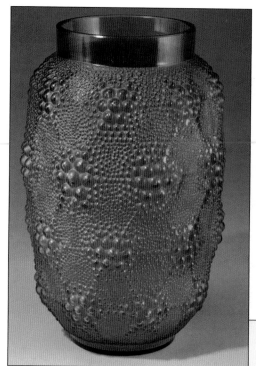

"Davos" circa 1932, in amber glass, engraved R. Lalique, 11 1/2" t. (M p. 455, No. 1079) **$3,500-$4,000**

"Escargot" in dark red glass, circa 1920, 8 5/8" t. (M p. 424, No. 931) **$15,000+**

"Languedoc" circa 1932, in cased green glass with white patina, engraved R. Lalique France, 8 3/4" t. (M p. 443, No. 1041) **$30,000+**

"Oranges" circa 1926, in clear and frosted glass with brown enamel decoration, molded R. LALIQUE, 11 1/2" t. (M p. 431, No. 964) **$30,000+**

"Penthivere" circa 1926, in cobalt blue glass with white patina, engraved R. LALIQUE, 10 1/4" t. (M p. 441, No. 1011) **$15,000+**

"Serpent" in purple glass, circa 1924, 10 1/4" t. (M p. 416, No. 896) **$40,000**

Early American Pattern Glass, Flint, Etc.

Early pattern glass (flint) was made with a lead formula, giving many items a ringing sound when tapped. Lead became too valuable to be used in glass manufacturing during the Civil War, and in 1864, Hobbs, Brockunier & Co., Wheeling, W.V., developed a soda lime (non-flint) formula. Pattern glass also was produced in transparent colors, milk glass, opalescent glass, slag glass and custard glass.

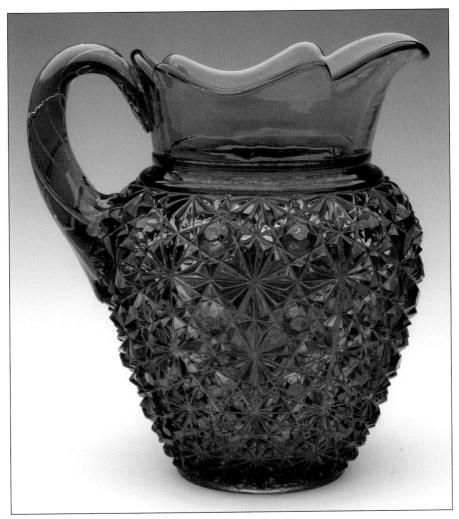

Green Valley Auctions

Belmont, No. 100 / Daisy and Button – Scalloped Edge, water pitcher, amber, applied air-twist handle with pressed fan design to upper terminal. Belmont Glass Co. Fourth quarter 19th century. 8 3/4" h overall. Two pattern chips. **$192**

Green Valley Auctions

Daisy and Button with Ornament, celery vase, vaseline. Fourth quarter 19th century. 6 3/4" h, 4 7/8" d overall. **$108**

Green Valley Auctions

Leaf Umbrella, Northwood No. 263 cracker jar, ruby/ cranberry, colorless applied finial, 8 3/4" h overall, 6" greatest d. Small area of polishing and several interior flakes to rim of cover, finial with roughness to tip; base having minor flaking/roughness to exterior rim. **$2,090**

Green Valley Auctions

Early Thumbprint, salver/cake stand, colorless flint glass, curved rim with 32 even scallops, double-step hollow stem with 12 flutes, circular foot with 24 scallops, single band of 24 thumbprints under foot, wafer construction. Bakewell, Pears & Co. Third quarter 19th century. 6" h, 11 1/2" d rim, 5 3/8" d foot. Small area of pattern roughness under the plate and a flake on one point of the stem. **$1,073**

Green Valley Auctions

Loop and Crystal tumbler, cobalt blue lead glass, faint pontil ring. Probably Pittsburgh. Mid-19th century. 3 1/2" h. **$138**

Green Valley Auctions

Riverside, No. 135 / Cabbage Leaf, water pitcher, amber, twisted-rib applied amber handle. Riverside Glass Works. Fourth quarter 19th century. 9 3/4" h overall, 6 3/4" d overall. Area of wear to un-patterned portion. **$1,685**

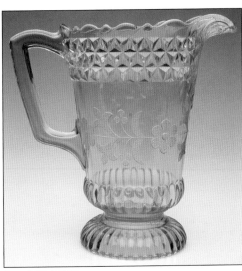

Green Valley Auctions

Wildflower, water pitcher, blue. Adams & Co. Fourth quarter 19th century. 8 3/4" h overall, 5 1/4" d rim. **$69**

Green Valley Auctions

Swirled Feather and Diamond Point, covered nappy/butter, fiery opalescent flint, cover with acorn-like finial, base with alternating large and medium scallop rim, eight-petal rosette in base. Possibly Boston & Sandwich Glass Co. Mid 19th century. 6 1/8" d overall. Some light mold roughness. **$226**

Quezal

The Quezal Art Glass Decorating Co., named for the quetzal—a bird with brilliantly colored feathers found in tropical regions of the Americas—was organized in 1901 in Brooklyn, N.Y., by Martin Bach and Thomas Johnson, two disgruntled Tiffany workers. They soon hired Percy Britton and William Wiedebine, two more former Tiffany employees.

The first products, unmarked, were exact Tiffany imitations. Quezal pieces differ from Tiffany pieces in that they are more defined and the decorations are more visible and brighter. No new techniques were developed by Quezal.

Johnson left in 1905. T. Conrad Vahlsing, Bach's son-in-law, joined the firm in 1918, but left with Paul Frank in 1920 to form Lustre Art Glass Co., which in turn copied Quezal pieces. Martin Bach died in 1924, and by 1925, Quezal had ceased operations.

The "Quezal" trademark was first used in 1902 and placed on the base of vases and bowls and the rims of shades. The acid-etched or engraved letters vary in size and may be found in amber, black or gold. A printed label that includes an illustration of a quetzal was used briefly in 1907.

Quezal flower form vase, corset shaped, flaring ruffled rim, green pulled feathers tipped in iridescent gold decoration, signed Quezal N 397, 6 1/2" h. **$3,250**

Early Auction Co. LLC

Quezal ovoid vase, deep iridescent green, blue graduating to gold hooked feather on opal ground, signed Quezal NY, 4 1/2" h. **$5,750**

Early Auction Co. LLC

Quezal vase, iridescent, opal footed urn form, everted rim with gold luster coil design, signed Quezal, 6 1/2" h. **$1,400**

Early Auction Co. LLC

Early Auction Co. LLC

Quezal cabinet vase, agate, cylindrical shouldered form, variegated gray green and amber glass, signed Quezal, 4 1/2" h. **$2,250**

Tiffany Glass

Tiffany & Co. was founded by Charles Lewis Tiffany (1812-1902) and Teddy Young in New York City in 1837 as a "stationery and fancy goods emporium." The store initially sold a wide variety of stationery items, and operated as Tiffany, Young and Ellis in lower Manhattan. The name was shortened to Tiffany & Co. in 1853, and the firm's emphasis on jewelry was established.

The first Tiffany catalog, known as the "Blue Book," was published in 1845. It is still being published today.

In 1862 Tiffany & Co. supplied the Union Army with swords, flags and surgical implements.

Charles' son, Louis Comfort Tiffany (1848-1933) was an American artist and designer who worked in the decorative arts and is best known for his work in stained glass. Louis established Tiffany Glass Co. in 1885, and in 1902 it became known as the Tiffany Studios. America's outstanding glass designer of the Art Nouveau period produced glass from the last quarter of the 19th century until the early 1930s. Tiffany revived early techniques and devised many new ones.

James D. Julia Auctioneers

Tiffany Studios blown-glass candelabra. Six-arm candelabra is made of bronze and has patina finish of brown with hints of green and red. From the oval-shaped platform base arises a single center stem with three candle cups on either side. Each of these candle cups has green blown-glass ornamentation and a bobeche. In the center stem of the candlestick rests a Tiffany snuffer that is concealed when in place. Signed on the underside "Tiffany Studios New York 1648." 15" x 21". One tight hairline to blown glass and one blown glass insert is slightly different color. **$6,900**

Tiffany Studios picture frame, circa 1906, in the Grapevine pattern with green and white opalescent glass, easel back, 7 3/8" x 8 3/4". **$1,673**

Heritage Auction Galleries

Tiffany Studios rose-water sprinkler, circa 1900, goose-neck form in iridescent Favrile glass with pink undertones, marked "L.C. Tiffany - Favrile W2714," 10" x 4". **$5,078**

James D. Julia Auctioneers

Tiffany Blue Favrile cabinet vase. Blue iridescence at the foot shading to platinum iridescence at the shoulder and neck. Signed on the bottom "L.C.T. D3473." 2-1/2" h. minor scratches to iridescence. **$805**

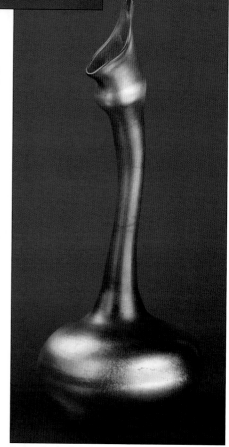

Heritage Auction Galleries

James D. Julia Auctioneers

Tiffany Studios Fireball lamp. One of two known examples. Exceptional early Tiffany Studios leaded orb shade has flame design in mottled red and orange glass against a textured green and brown swirled background. The flames are made up of numerous types of glass, including heavily rippled to lightly textured, giving the effect of dancing flames when lit. The shade rests atop a bronze saucer base with single socket. Base is finished with rich brown patina with green highlights. Shade and base are unsigned. Shade is 12" diameter. Overall 15" h. Few tight hairlines. **$48,875**

Tiffany Studios, nine Favrile glass tiles, circa 1900, four with molded "PAT. APPL'D. FOR," largest 4" square, four tiles with chips to the prongs on the reverse. **$1,195 all**

Heritage Auction Galleries

James D. Julia Auctioneers

Tiffany Studios Lemon Leaf table lamp. Heavily mottled apple-green background glass with heavily mottled maize-colored lemon-leaf band. Shade is signed "Tiffany Studios New York 1470." Base is signed "Tiffany Studios New York 531." Original patina on base and shade. Shade is 18" diameter. Overall 25 1/2" h. Some tight hairlines primarily in lower border with no missing glass. Slight lead separation in one small area where lemon-leaf band meets lower geometric bands. Slight dent in heat cap. **$17,250**

Tiffany Studios ruffled bowl. Deep gold iridescent finish with magenta, blue and pink highlights. Signed on the underside "L.C.T." 4 1/2" diameter. **$287**

James D. Julia Auctioneers

Tiffany Studios Geometric table lamp. Colors of butterscotch and caramel striated with white. Shade is supported by a Colonial-style, four-socket base with inverted saucer foot. Shade is signed "Tiffany Studios NY 1469". Base is marked "Tiffany Studios New York 532." Shade is 18" diameter. Overall 25" h. Base has replaced pull chains and has been cleaned down to copper finish. **$8,050**

James D. Julia Auctioneers

Tiffany Studios footed candy dish. With applied gold iridescent border on opaque blue body and foot. Scratched in "59" on the underside. 6" diameter. Multiple chips to foot rim, some scratches on interior. **$60**

James D. Julia Auctioneers

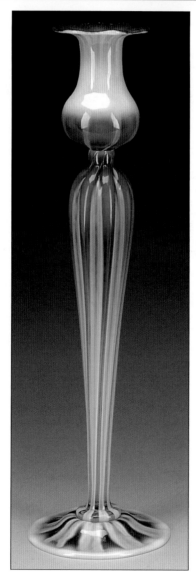

Tiffany pastel tulip candlestick. With raspberry opalescent cup applied to blue-to-green opalescent stem with white pulled striping and applied raspberry foot with opalescent ribbing. Signed on the underside "1845 L.C. Tiffany-Favrile." 16" t. **$6,612**

James D. Julia Auctioneers

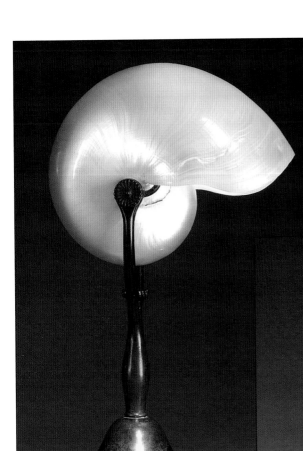

Tiffany Studios Nautilus lamp. Natural shell shade on a patina harp base with additional hook on the underside for possible wall hanging as well as five ball feet. Impressed on underside "403 Tiffany Studios New York." 12 1/2" h. Minor wear to patina. **$6,900**

James D. Julia Auctioneers

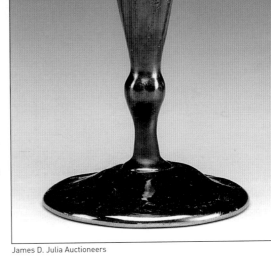

Tiffany Studios mini flower-form vase. Blue iridescent with vertical ribbing and applied foot. Irregular iridescence to top quarter of the vase shading down to deep purple mirror iridescence on the foot. Engraved signature "7311N 1522 L.C. Tiffany-Inc Favrile" on the underside. 6 1/4" t. **$2,400**

James D. Julia Auctioneers

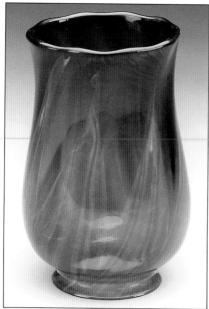

James D. Julia Auctioneers

Tiffany reactive glass shade. Green and orange flame design extending from the foot to near the rim. The smokey gray body of the shade has a slightly swirling rib running vertically. When shade is lit in a darkened room, it appears like a dancing flame. Shade is unsigned. 5" t x 2 1/4" fitter. **$4,025**

James D. Julia Auctioneers

Tiffany Studios art glass shade. Vertical ribbing and deep gold with purple and blue iridescence. Shade is finished with a gently scalloped border. Signed "L.C.T. Favrile" in rim. 2 1/4" fitter x 4 3/4" h. **$862**

James D. Julia Auctioneers

Tiffany Studios flower-form vase. Pulled-feather vase on opalescent ground with everted rim and decorated foot. Engraved signature "L.C. Tiffany Favrile 539A." 11 1/4" h. Some staining to the interior. **$3,680**

James D. Julia Auctioneers

Tiffany Studios Lily & Prism chandelier. With six gold lily shades and 19 prisms in colors of oyster, gold, amber and green with a deep iridescence over the lilies and complementary prisms. All of this Tiffany glass surrounds a decorated stalactite Tiffany shade with deep vertical ribbing and a hooked-feather pattern. The shade is supported by a bronze collar, three chains and hooks. The shades are supported by a Moorish-style bronze hanging fixture with openwork at the top, medallions of roping above six lily shade holders, 19 prism hooks and a single stem for the stalactite shade. Further accenting this lamp, alternating between the prisms, are 19 beaded chains that end in bronze balls. This entire lamp is supported by a bronze decorated ceiling cap, chain and S hook. Stalactite shade is signed "S323" and one lily shade is signed "L.C.T. Favrile" and another is signed "L.C.T." and the remainder are unsigned. Overall 42" l. Some parts are authentic while other parts are exact replications of Tiffany Studios hardware. Three lily shades have broken fitter rims, one has roughness to fitter rim. Stalactite shade has chips to fitter rim that are concealed when in place. All prisms either have chips or are cracked. **$32,775**

James D. Julia Auctioneers

Tiffany Studios Favrile desk lamp. Gold Favrile shade with rainbow iridescent finish with stretched edge. The cased white-lined shade is supported by a three-arm, leaf-decorated base with a statuary finish. The lamp is completed with a top cap in a patina finish. Shade is signed on the fitter "L.C.T. Favrile" and base is signed on the underside "Tiffany Studios New York 426". Shade is 7" diameter. Overall 14" t. $4,200

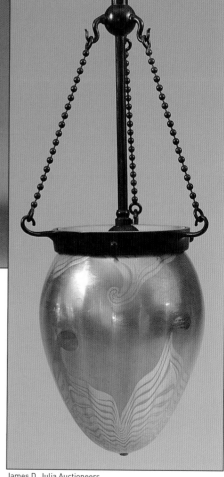

James D. Julia Auctioneers

Tiffany stalactite hanger. Shade has gold iridescent hooked-feather design extending from the bottom of the shade. There is an additional hooked-feather design descending from the fitter. Design is set against a lighter gold iridescent background of the vertically ribbed body of the shade. Interior of the shade has a light chartreuse color. Shade is unsigned and numbered "L2400." It is suspended from three chains attached to hooks on a center light post that terminates to a ceiling cap having beaded rim. The bronze replacement hardware is finished in a rich brown patina with strong red and green highlights. Shade is 8" l x 6" diameter x 4 3/4" fitter. Overall 24" h. $7,187

James D. Julia Auctioneers

Tiffany Studios mosaic pentray. Inlaid blue decorated Favrile glass. Impressed on the underside "TIFFANY STUDIOS NEW YORK 24336" together with the monogram of the Tiffany Glass & Decorating Co. 7 3/4" l. Patina may be enhanced. **$8,000**

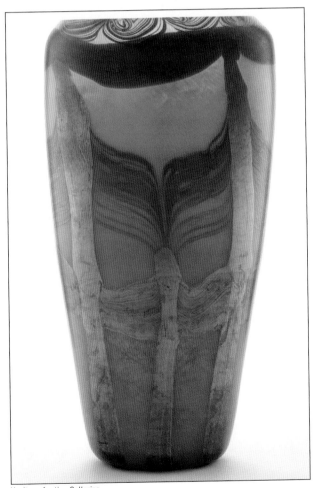

Tiffany Studios early experimental Favrile glass vase lamp base, circa 1900, engraved "X103 Louis C. Tiffany-Favrile," 14 3/4", significant surface scratches along interior, flaw on the body about a third of the way down from rim with some losses. **$3,585**

Heritage Auction Galleries

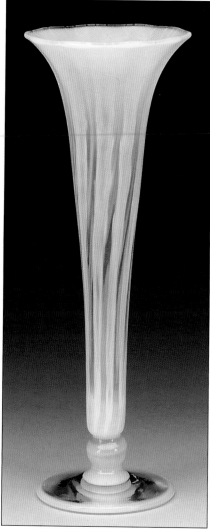

James D. Julia Auctioneers

Tiffany Studios pastel vase. Clear foot with white opalescent rim. Foot gives way to a white opalescent stem with white opalescent ribs vertically extending to the slightly flaring lip. Interior of the mouth is finished with a rich pastel yellow. Signed on the underside "L.C. Tiffany Favrile 1886." 9 3/4" t. **$1,380**

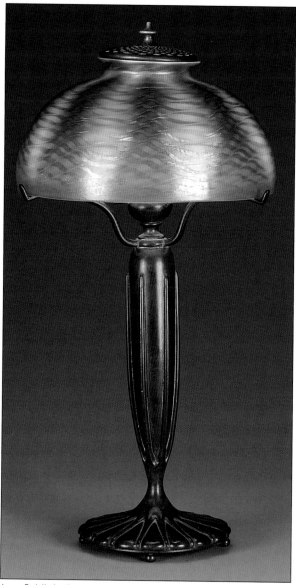

James D. Julia Auctioneers

Tiffany Studios Damascene table lamp. Green Favrile shade with a damascene-wave pattern decoration in gold shading to platinum having eight vertical ribs, which give it highlights of blue. The cased lined shade is supported by a patinated single-socket, three-arm bronze base with elongated rib decoration over an ornate root-style foot resting on four ball feet. Lamp is completed with a bronze heat cap. Shade is signed on the fitter rim "L.C.T.". Base is signed "Tiffany Studios New York 431." Shade is 9 1/2" diameter x 3 3/4" fitter. Overall 19 1/2" t. **$6,612**

James D. Julia Auctioneers

Tiffany Studios bell shade. Decorated with a translucent green pulled-feather motif with gold trim on an oyster ground. Signed "L.C.T.". 2 1/4" fitter rim x 4 1/2" h. Minor grinding to fitter rim. **$2,530**

James D. Julia Auctioneers

Tiffany Studios Blue Favrile vase. Classic Egyptian form with elongated neck and squared shoulder. Vase begins with a platinum iridescence over the neck area that recedes into a medium blue and a cobalt blue at the foot. Signed "L.C. Tiffany Inc. Favrile X1421024." 5 3/4" h. Tiny spot of missing iridescence on shoulder. **$920**

James D. Julia Auctioneers

Tiffany Studios Pine Needle card case. Constructed of green slag panels with darker striations. These panels are set in a bronze frame with decorative pine-needle decoration overall. Exceptional patina finish. Signed on underside "Tiffany Studios New York 875." 4" x 3" x 1". **$1,495**

James D. Julia Auctioneers

Tiffany Studios Favrile cabinet vase. Round squat body with pulled handles on each side and a slightly flaring mouth. The gold Favrile finish shows purple and blue highlights at foot and lip. Signed on the underside "L.C. Tiffany-Favrile 4014L." 2" t. **$540**

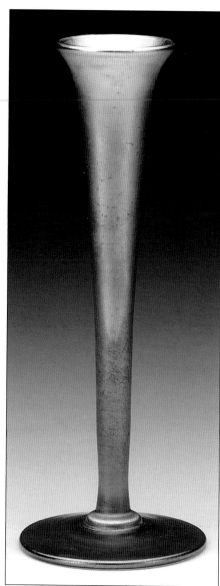

James D. Julia Auctioneers

Tiffany Studios Favrile Lily vase. Slender body, slightly flaring at the lip with saucer foot. Gold iridescence shows flashes of pink and blue at the foot. Signed on the underside "L.C. Tiffany Inc. Favrile 1504-7408M." 6" t. **$660**

James D. Julia Auctioneers

Tiffany Studios Tel El Amarna vase. With applied and decorated collar. Engraved "Exhibition Piece" and "6340N L.C. Tiffany – Favrile" on the underside. 5 3/4" h. Hairline crack to applied rim. **$5,750**

James D. Julia Auctioneers

Tiffany Studios Pomegranate table lamp. Shade has an allover geometric background of green striated glass with hints of blue, yellow and white. The shade is decorated with a single band of pomegranates in fiery mottled yellow and orange glass. Shade is supported by a three-socket, three-armed Grecian urn that is supported by four flaring feet on a pedestal stand. Shade is signed "Tiffany Studios New York" with a small early tag. Shade is 16" diameter. Overall 20" h. Several spider cracks. **$16,100**

James D. Julia Auctioneers

Tiffany Studios Geometric table lamp. With leaded "dichroic" glass shade glass (containing multiple micro-layers of metal oxides) that shows colors of green, tan and mauve when unlit. When lit, the glass turns a rich orange. Shade is signed "Tiffany Studios New York 1436" and rests atop an early Tiffany Studios base with an incised and slightly raised wave design. Base is finished with three attached arms to support the shade. Marked on the underside "25778." Shade is 16" diameter. Overall 20" h. A few tight hairlines in the shade. Bottom of font has been drilled. **$15,525**

Halloween

— By Mark B. Ledenbach, Halloween authority

Halloween came into its own in the late teens and early 1920s. Parties were all the rage then, but they were adult oriented. Tables and walls would be gaily decorated with a wide array of Halloween-themed items to set the party's mood. The games' winners would be given prizes to take home, like candy containers, nodders, lanterns, or noisemakers.

Many of the Halloween items most prized today were manufactured in Germany. The zenith of German Halloween production in terms of variety and design runs from about 1920 until 1935. After World War I, Germany was hampered in its recovery efforts by the Versailles Treaty. Under these circumstances, several American discount-merchandising magnates like Frank W. Woolworth and Sebastian S. Kresge encouraged German artisans to use their creative expertise to craft unique and wondrous paper items for export to the vast and growing American holiday market.

Mass-produced Halloween costumes did not appear in stores until the 1930s, and trick-or-treating did not become a fixture of the holiday until the 1940s.

For more information, see *Vintage Halloween Collectibles* by Mark Ledenbach.

Halloween authority Mark Ledenbach on the Martha Stewart Show.

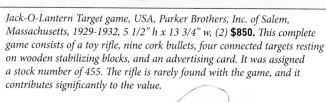

Jack-O-Lantern Target game, USA, Parker Brothers, Inc. of Salem, Massachusetts, 1929-1932, 5 1/2" h x 13 3/4" w, (2) **$850.** This complete game consists of a toy rifle, nine cork bullets, four connected targets resting on wooden stabilizing blocks, and an advertising card. It was assigned a stock number of 455. The rifle is rarely found with the game, and it contributes significantly to the value.

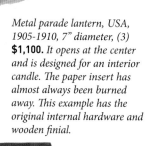

Metal parade lantern, USA, 1905-1910, 7" diameter, (3) **$1,100.** It opens at the center and is designed for an interior candle. The paper insert has almost always been burned away. This example has the original internal hardware and wooden finial.

Identical dual-sided JOL lantern with original inserts connected top and bottom supports, and honeycomb sides, USA, Beistle, (printed name), 1930-1931, 11" h x 3 3/4" w x 12" l, (2) **$800.** This stunning and much sought-after lantern represents the high-water mark of Beistle artistry in its sophistication and imaginative rendering. It was also made in an 8" size. Both are quite rare, especially when completely intact.

Morphy Auctions

Halloween cat figure squeaking mechanical toy with pumpkin mask. Press chest and cat lowers mask from face (below), 7". **$1,725**

JOL candy container with movable reticulated hat (opens at center), Germany, pre-1920s, 5-3/4" h x 3 1/2" w, (2) **$600.** *It is made of molded cardboard, fringed paper, and wood.*

Composition devil head candy container (bottom plug), Germany, 1920s, 3 3/4" h, (2) **$1,000.**

Porcelain devil creamer, Germany, Schafer & Vater, 1920s, 3 1/4" h x 3-1/2" w, (3) **$275.**

From the collection of Theresa Roberts

Key-wound mechanical, Germany, 1930s, 9" h, (1) **$1,450.**

Parade lantern, Germany, circa 1908-1912. This layered papier-mâché with compo wash lantern and its original inserts served as the focal point for a small town Halloween parade, probably in New Jersey. A stick would be placed in the wooden yoke surrounding the lantern before it was hoisted high to lead the festivities. This item transcends the singular Halloween genre, easily crossing into the wider world of folk art. The design was done by a gifted artist, with the great care taken in its creation obvious in how dramatic this item truly is to look upon. The parade lantern measures 7 1/4" high by 7 3/4" diameter and has a removable bottom plug candleholder. This is a one-of-a-kind item as to its size and intended purpose. There are fifteen or so of these small tabletop lanterns known to exist, many without bottoms. A cache of seven was discovered in Pennsylvania in 2003. They sell for around **$2,500 each. $12,000 to $15,000**

These mechanical items were made in Germany before 1920. Both of the items' faces are made from lithoed paper over cardboard. The handles, as well as the arms and legs, are wood. The multicolored outfits are made from thin cloth. The JOL-creature on the left holds a spun cotton carrot in one hand. Its arms and legs move whenever the ring attached to the bottom of the handle is pulled down. This item measures 10 1/2" high. The mechanical on the right is more intricate. Whenever the crank at the end of the handle is turned, the figure spins while a tune is played from the central ball. This item measures 13" high. **$1,300-$1,500 ea.**

Vegetable Halloween Man with movable glass eyes, with radish arms, zucchini legs, walnut feet and watermelon head with an expressive toothy grin. Clockwork mechanism contained within head, activates eyes, which move from right to left. Simulated apron and vest cover vegetable body. Most likely the only known example and probably originally used in a store as an trade stimulator. Some in-painting to right arm, removable stem on top of head was originally missing and one was recreated in papier-mache, 17 1/2". **$19,550**

Morphy Auctions

Morphy Auctions

None Such Mince Meat advertising lantern, 16" t, includes four decorative glass panels. **$5,200**

Morphy Auctions

Witch holding broom candy container, 7 1/2". **$2,300**

Halloween witch hanging decoration, USA, Beistle, (no mark), late 1930s-early 1940s, 43 1/2" h x 11 1/2" w. **$175**

Morphy Auctions

Arched-back black cat candy container, German, with glass eyes. Head comes off to reveal candy, 4". **$345**

Jewelry

Jewelry Styles

Jewelry has been a part of every culture throughout time. It is often reflective of the times, as well as social and aesthetic movements, with each piece telling its own story through hidden clues that, when interpreted, will help solve the mysteries surrounding them. Jewelry is generally divided into periods and styles.

Kathy Flood

Each period may have several styles, with some of the same styles and types of jewelry being made in both precious and non-precious materials. Additionally, there are recurring style revivals, which are interpretations of an earlier period. For example, the Egyptian Revival that took place in the early and late 1800s, and then again in the 1920s.

All jewelry in this year's edition comes courtesy *Warman's Jewelry 4th Edition* by Kathy Flood.

Georgian, 1760-1837. Fine jewelry from this period is quite desirable, but few good-quality pieces have found their way to auction in recent years. Sadly, much jewelry from this period has been lost.

Victorian, 1837-1901. Queen Victoria of England ascended the throne in 1837 and remained queen until her death in 1901. The Victorian period is a long and prolific one; abundant with many styles of jewelry. It warrants being divided into three sub-periods: Early or Romantic period dating from 1837-1860; Mid or Grand period dating from 1860-1880; and Late or Aesthetic period dating from 1880-1901.

Sentiment and romance were significant factors in Victorian jewelry. Often, jewelry and clothing represented love and affection, with symbolic motifs such as hearts, crosses, hands, flowers, anchors, doves, crowns, knots, stars, thistles, wheat, garlands, horseshoes and moons. The materials of the time were also abundant and varied. They included silver, gold, diamonds, onyx, glass, cameo, paste, carnelian, agate, coral, amber, garnet, emeralds, opals, pearls, peridot (a green gemstone), rubies, sapphires, marcasites, cut steel, enameling, tortoise shell, topaz, turquoise, bog oak, ivory, jet, hair, gutta percha and vulcanite.

Sentiments of love were often expressed in miniatures. Sometimes they were representative of deceased loved ones, but often the miniatures were of the living. Occasionally, the miniatures depicted landscapes, cherubs or religious themes.

Hair jewelry was a popular expression of love and sentiment. The hair of a loved one was placed in a special compartment in a brooch or a locket, or used to form a picture under a glass compartment. Later in the mid-19th century, pieces of jewelry were made completely of woven hair. Individual strands of hair would be woven together to create necklaces, watch chains, brooches, earrings and rings.

In 1861, Queen Victoria's husband, Prince Albert, died. The queen went into mourning for the rest of her life, and Victoria required that the royal court wear black. This atmosphere spread to the populace and created a demand for mourning jewelry.

Mourning jewelry is typically black. When it first came into fashion, it was made from jet, fossilized wood. By 1850, there were dozens of English workshops making jet brooches, lockets, bracelets and necklaces. As the supply of jet dwindled, other materials were used such as vulcanite, gutta percha, bog oak and French jet.

By the 1880s, the somber mourning jewelry was losing popularity. Fashions had changed and the clothing was simpler and had an air of delicacy. The Industrial Revolution, which had begun in the early part of the century, was now in full swing and machine-manufactured jewelry was affordable to the working class.

Edwardian, 1890-1920. The Edwardian period takes its name England's King Edward VII. Though he ascended the throne in 1901, he and his wife, Alexandria of Denmark, exerted influence over the period before and after his ascension. The 1890s was known as La Belle Epoque. This was a time known for ostentation and extravagance. As the years passed, jewelry became simpler and smaller. Instead of wearing one large brooch, women were often found wearing several small lapel pins.

In the early 1900s, platinum, diamonds and pearls were prevalent in the jewelry of the wealthy, while paste was being used by the masses to imitate the real thing. The styles were reminiscent of the neo-classical and rococo motifs. The jewelry was lacy and ornate, feminine and delicate.

Arts & Crafts, 1890-1920. The Arts & Crafts movement was focused on artisans and craftsmanship. There was a simplification of form where the material was secondary to the design. Guilds of artisans banded together. Some jewelry was mass-produced, but the most highly prized examples of this period are handmade and signed by their makers. The pieces were simple and at times abstract. They could be hammered, patinated and acid etched. Common materials were brass, bronze, copper, silver, blister pearls, freshwater pearls, turquoise, agate, opals, moonstones, coral, horn, ivory, base metals, amber, cabachon-cut garnets and amethysts.

Art Nouveau, 1895-1910. In 1895, Samuel Bing opened a shop called "Maison de lArt Nouveau" at 22 Rue de Provence in Paris. Art Nouveau designs in the jewelry were characterized by a sensuality that took on the forms of the female figure, butterflies, dragonflies, peacocks, snakes, wasps, swans, bats, orchids, irises and other exotic flowers. The lines used whiplash curves to create a feeling of lushness and opulence.

1920s-1930s. Costume jewelry began its steady ascent to popularity in the 1920s. Since it was relatively inexpensive to produce, there was mass production. The sizes and designs of the jewelry varied. Often, it was worn a few times, disposed of and then replaced with a new piece. It was thought of as expendable, a cheap throwaway to dress up an outfit. Costume jewelry became so popular that it was sold in both the upscale stores and the "five and dime."

During the 1920s, fashions were often accompanied by jewelry that drew on the Art Deco movement, which got its beginning in Paris at the "Exposition Internationale des Arts Décoratifs et Industriels Modernes" held in 1925. The idea behind this movement was that form follows function. The style was characterized by simple, straight, clean lines, stylized motifs and geometric shapes. Favored materials included chrome, rhodium, pot metal, glass, rhinestones, Bakelite and celluloid.

One designer who played an important role was Coco Chanel. Though previously reserved for evening wear, Chanel wore it during the day, making it fashionable for millions of other women to do so, too.

With the 1930s came the Depression and the advent of World War II. Perhaps in response to the gloom, designers began using enameling and brightly colored rhinestones to create whimsical birds, flowers, circus animals, bows, dogs and just about every other figural form imaginable.

Retro Modern, 1939-1950. Other jewelry designs of the 1940s were big and bold. Retro Modern had a more substantial feel to it and designers began using larger stones to enhance the dramatic pieces. The jewelry was stylized and exaggerated. Common motifs included flowing scrolls, bows, ribbons, birds, animals, snakes, flowers and knots.

Sterling silver now became the metal of choice, often dipped in a gold wash known as vermeil.

Designers often incorporated patriotic themes of American flags, the V-sign, Uncle Sam's hat, airplanes, anchors and eagles.

Post-War Modern, 1945-1965. This was a movement that emphasized the artistic approach to jewelry making. It is also referred to as Mid-Century Modern. This approach was occurring at a time when the Beat Generation was prevalent. These avant-garde designers created jewelry that was handcrafted to illustrate the artist's own concepts and ideas. The materials often used were sterling, gold, copper, brass, enamel, cabochons, wood, quartz and amber.

1950s-1960s. The 1950s saw the rise of jewelry that was made purely of rhinestones: necklaces, bracelets, earrings and pins.

The focus of the early 1960s was on clean lines: pillbox hats and A-line dresses with short jackets were a mainstay for the conservative woman. The large, bold rhinestone pieces were no longer the must-have accessory. They were now replaced with smaller, more delicate gold-tone metal and faux pearls with only a hint of rhinestones.

At the other end of the spectrum was psychedelic-colored clothing, Nehru jackets, thigh-high miniskirts and go-go boots. These clothes were accessorized with beads, large metal pendants and occasionally big, bold rhinestones. By the late 1960s, there was a movement back to mother nature and the "hippie" look was born. Ethnic clothing, tie dye, long skirts, fringe and jeans were the prevalent style and the rhinestone had, for the most part, been left behind.

Mexican Silver, 1930-1970. Mexican silversmiths first made jewelry for tourists. The jewelry had pre-Hispanic and traditional Mexican motifs as well as some abstract modern designs. Artisans used silver, a combination of silver with brass or copper, alpaca, amethysts, malachite, obsidian, sodalite, tiger eye, turquoise, abalone, ebony, rosewood and enameling to create their original designs. While hundreds of artists set up their shops in the town of Taxco, Mexico, in the 30s and 40s creating a silversmith guild, there are only a relatively small number of well-known artisans who gained their reputation for their designs and craftsmanship.

Pearls

Heritage Auction
Galleries

*Edwardian diamond, pearl,
white gold "jabot" (meaning an
ornamental cascade of ruffles
or frills), Cartier, French,
features mine-, single- and
rose-cut diamonds, highlighted
by a pearl measuring 4.00-
3.50mm, set in 18k white
gold. Marked Cartier Paris,
reference number 2463. French
hallmarks, gross weight 7.00
grams, 3 3/8" x 1".* **$8,365**

*Edwardian pearl and diamond brooch, 15k bar
and clasp are topped with a platinum-finished
oval, encircled with 12 natural Oriental pearls.
Rhomboid and fleur de lis diamond accents
frame the oval; 12 single-cut and rose-cut
diamonds, circa 1905.* **$900**

www.Topazery.com

Heritage Auction Galleries
Victorian glass, pearl, gold ring, featuring a cushion-shaped glass, enhanced by pearls measuring 3.00 - 2.50mm, set in 10k gold atop a 14k gold shank. **$77**

www.Topazery.com

Victorian Danish crucifix, 14k rose gold, the base has a punched surface for a textured effect. Rounded off into a fleur de lis at the four points, the cross culminates at the center with a starburst flower. A collection of 16 spherical and half spherical pearls are threaded down the middle, hallmark of the Netherlands, circa 1900. **$650**

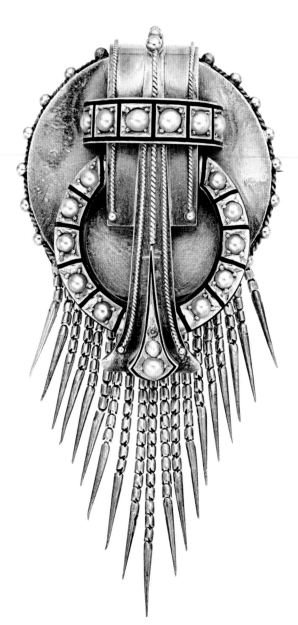

Heritage Auction Galleries
Victorian pearl, enamel, gold pendant-brooch, designed as an elaborate tassel, features half-pearls, enhanced by blue and black enamel applied on 14k yellow gold, completed by a retractable bail, pin stem and catch mechanism on the reverse, 3" x 1 3/8". **$480**

Heritage Auction Galleries

Mabé pearl, diamond, ruby, white gold ring, designed with a floral motif, features a mabé pearl, encircled by full-cut diamonds weighing a total of approximately 1.35 carats, accented by round-cut rubies weighing a total of approximately 0.95 carat, set in 14k white gold. **$450**

Pearl Society; Matthew Arden photo

Enamel, rubies, emerald drop brooch, gilded silver; "grape cluster" set with natural American pink and lavender pearls. 1 3/4", early 20th century. **$2,600**

Heritage Auction Galleries

Cultured pearl, diamond, emerald, white gold bracelet, features cultured pearls measuring 7.50 - 7.00mm, forming four knotted strands, completed by an ornate clasp enhanced by single-cut diamonds, accented by square-cut emeralds, set in 18k white gold. Total diamond weight is approximately 1.00 carat, 7 1/2" x 1 3/16". **$836**

© Eve Alfillé; Matthew Arden photo

*"Whimsy" bracelet from "Dream"
series, 14k gold, tourmaline and
peridot clasp, cultured Chinese
freshwater pearls (natural pink
and dyed black). Off-center
diagonal drilling shows Chinese
resourcefulness in offering new
options; 7 1/2" l, 3/4" w.* **$580**

Pearl Society; Matthew Arden photo

*Oriental pearls necklace sewn with white horsehair
to mother-of-pearl plates, given to Miss Constance
Wharton by her mother, late 19th century, with
a note (in her hand) indicating it had been
made circa 1820 for her great-grandmother.
Accompanying fitted case originally held matching
grand parure, likely dispersed to other members of
the family. Note small neck size, under 13", 3/4"
w. Members of this family included writer Edith
Wharton and founders of the Wharton School of
Economics.* **$2,150**

Heritage Auction Galleries

*South Seas cultured pearl, diamond, ruby, enamel, silver-
topped gold brooch designed as a bat, features a South Seas
cultured pearl measuring 21.00 x 12.00mm, highlighted
by rose-cut diamonds, enhanced by ruby cabochon eyes,
accented by plique-à-jour enamel, applied on silver-topped
18k yellow gold, completed by a pin stem and catch on the
reverse, 4 1/4" x 2".* **$3,585**

Jadeite

Milky Way Jewels; Rocky Day photo

Walter Lampl jadeite brooch and ring set, 14k gold, highly polished carved green jadeite imported from China, surrounded by tiny natural seed pearls, finished in 14k gold frame. Brooch marked WL 14k; ring marked 14k WL. Fine examples of Lampl jewelry. Pin 2", ring 7/8", 1920s. **$1,125 set**

Rocky Day photo

Walter Lampl jadeite dress clip, carved translucent green jadeite frog atop carved white jade leaf; natural seed pearl eyes; clip marked WL STERLING and PAT. 1852188, 1932, 1 1/2". **$150**

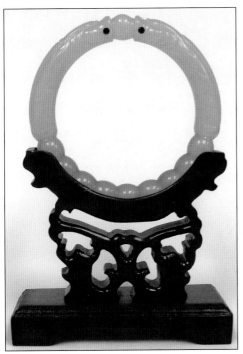

Animal bracelet, two dragon heads, white mutton-fat nephrite jade bangle, nine carved balls as tails, mouths hold pearl; very rare; 2 1/2" diameter, 19th century. **$2,000**

Jade bracelet, Chinese version of the gold-link bracelet, emerald green jadeite, 1970s, 7" x 2mm thick. **$1,000**

Milky Way Jewels; Rocky Day photo

Walter Lampl enameled sterling circus tent brooch, gold wash over sterling tent, roof finely enameled, polychrome colors. Two 20mm carved roosters, one amethyst, one jade, wired to small shelf so birds tremble slightly, appearing to peck at ground; marked Sterling by Lampl, 2 1/4", 1940s. **$400**

Mason-Kay, Inc..; Zalephoto.com photo

Ring with intense, fine lavender 3/5" cabochon, 18k white gold, .53ct pavé-set diamonds. **$15,500**

Kenneth Jay Lane

Carved-beads necklace, Asian-inspired, simulated jadeite and coral, first made in 1960s, continuing, 2000s, signed © Kenneth Lane, 28". **$305**

Jade ring, two 1/3" pear-shape fine red jade cabochons, 18k white gold, .26 carats diamonds. **$2,950**

Apple green jade cabochon, 1/3", set in "abstract sun" with blue sapphires and .22 carat diamonds. **$2,920**

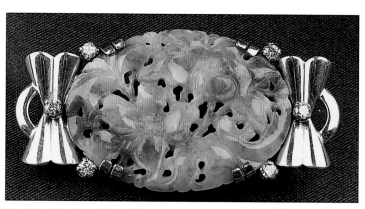

Bows brooch, jadeite, diamond, 14k gold, oval pierced, carved jadeite plaque flanked by gold bow designs highlighted by full-cut diamond mélée, maker's mark of Wordley, Allsopp & Bliss, retailed by Tiffany & Co., boxed, 2". **$3,000**

Pendant, fine almost 1" green jade drop, 18k white gold, .44 carat diamonds. **$10,200**

Esther Woo Jan; John F. Pipia photo

White jadeite pendant-pin, features ice or river jadeite, highly translucent and transparent, very rare because of the four matching high-dome cabochons; handcrafted 18k gold; approximately 3.00 total carat weight diamonds, 2000s. **$6,000**

Cameos

Rare antique Commesso cameo of mythological goddess; superb example using shell, coral, malachite, mother of pearl and mottled agate, incorporating multiple attributes of mythological goddesses, as well as Maenad (bacchante maiden). Base cameo is shell, different colored stones applied to create total artwork; great example of liberties some Victorian artists took with mythology, this cameo exhibiting attributes of four different mythological figures, all rolled into one: fruits or flowers in hair associated with Flora; crown associated with Hera; animal pelt associated with Omphale or maenads; bow associated with Diana; 14k gold mount; Italian, circa 1870, 2 1/4". **$2,500**

Exquisitely carved high relief hardstone cameo of the "Madonna" set in an equally fine 18k gold, pearl and black enamel brooch mount. Italian, circa 1880, 2". **$3,750**

Coral cameo habille of Athena Parthenos, Italian, late 19th century, well carved after a work by the Greek sculptor Phidias. Athena's helmet is adorned with a sphinx and horse and is inset with a diamond. She wears her aegis (breastplate) complete with head of Medusa. Set in gold pendant mount, 2 1/8". **$2,500**

Georgian/Victorian/Edwardian

Linda Lombardo, Worn to Perfection on Ruby Lane
Low-karat gold mourning pin with hair aperture and lock of hair, 1870s, 1 1/4". **$150**

Steve Fishbach Collection; Linda Lombardo photo
Victorian Etruscan two-color gold earrings on wires, circa 1880s, 1 3/4". **$1,800**

Steve Fishbach Collection; Linda Lombardo photo
Bohemian garnet necklace and brooch in low-karat gold setting, 1880s, 14 1/2" with 3 1/2" drop. **$3,500**

Steve Fishbach Collection; Linda Lombardo photo
European 18k gold, amethyst, rose diamond and purple enamel necklace, circa 1890s, 24" with chain. **$6,500**

Steve Fishbach Collection; Linda Lombardo photo
Bow brooch, silver face, gold back, turquoise and natural pearls, 1880s, 5". **$3,500**

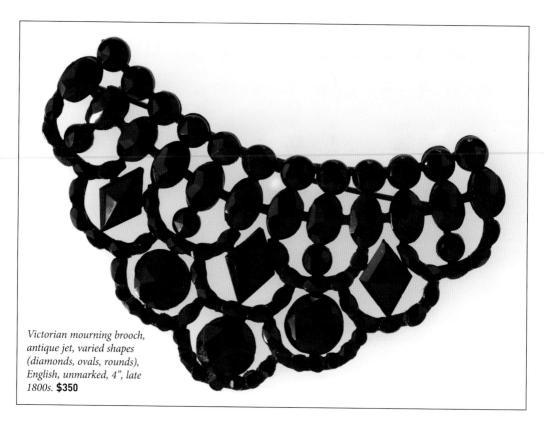

Victorian mourning brooch, antique jet, varied shapes (diamonds, ovals, rounds), English, unmarked, 4", late 1800s. **$350**

Steve Fishbach Collection; Linda Lombardo photo

Italian micro-mosaic bracelet in silver gilt setting, circa 1890, 7". **$700**

Steve Fishbach Collection; Linda Lombardo photo

Portrait brooch on porcelain, 1880s, 18k gold, 2 3/8". **$900**

Didier Antiques London; Adam Wide photo

Dorrie Nossiter comet brooch, pink tourmalines and pearl, 1920s, 2 1/3", British. **$2,735**

Steve Fishbach Collection; Linda Lombardo photo

*14k white gold pendant, blue and white enamel,
diamonds, from one of the Newark, N.J.,
jewelers, circa 1910, 19" chain with 1 1/2" drop.*
$3,500

Linda Lombardo, Worn to Perfection on Ruby Lane

*Late Edwardian pierced metal cameo
necklace, 18".* **$185**

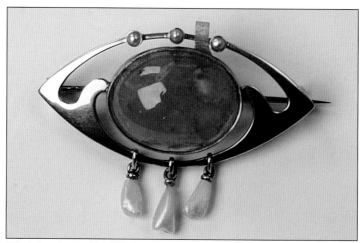

Didier Antiques London; Adam Wide photo

*Murlle Bennett and Co. pink tourmaline and pearl brooch, 15k gold,
circa 1900, Germany.* **$4,150**

Art Nouveau

Pin, diamond, enamel and 18k gold, Art Nouveau style, designed as a pair of large scrolled leaves enameled in bluish green and framed by looping leaves and arching blossoms and buds bead-set with single-cut diamond, suspending a freshwater pearl drop, early 20th century. **$2,250**

Pendant-necklace, plique-a-jour enamel, 18k gold and diamond, Art Nouveau style, designed as the gold dancing figure of a maiden wearing a swirled long gown enameled in turquoise and gold, the figure flanked by heavy gold vines curling up to suspend a pair of three-petal blossoms with blue and lavender plique-a-jour enamel and accented with old-European- and rose-cut diamonds, the base suspending a long freshwater pearl drop, the whole suspended by a pair of trace links joined to another three-petal blossom suspending a diamond drop, later trace-link chain, overall 18" l. **$8,000**

Earrings, pearl and 18k gold, Art Nouveau style, pendant-type, the top designed as an open flower and leaves centered by a small European-cut diamond and suspending a foliate designed gold framework enclosing a rounded blister pearl, European hallmarks, late 19th/early 20th century, each 2 5/8" l. **$4,994**

Art Deco

Art Deco potted plant pendant necklace, copy of an original in diamonds, rubies, topaz and enamels, this of silver-plated metal, rhinestones, enameling and glass, calibré cuts in necklace, pendant 4", necklace 15", 1991, signed Art Deco 89, B325. **$750**

Skinner Inc.

"Voodoo" necklace, 18k gold, platinum, emerald, diamonds, designed as textured, chased fringe highlighted by 17 cabochon emeralds and diamond-melée-set branches, approximate total diamond weight 6.22 carats, 15 1/4", signed Marianne Ostier. **$22,515**

Pagoda earrings, chalcedony, coral, marcasite, onyx, each designed as a shaped chalcedony tablet suspended from marcasite pagoda with coral bead accents, cabochon onyx tops, silver mounts, hallmark of Theodor Fahrner, circa 1930. **$3,000 pair**

*Art Deco necklace,
pink crystal demilune
stones, 1940s,
unsigned, 16".* **$150**

WornToPerfection.com; Linda Lombardo photo
Art Deco rhinestone buckle with triangular amber glass "stones," 4". **$195**

Art Deco winged dress clip, Egyptian influence, also converts to necklace pendant, 10 faceted oval emerald crystals, graduated chain fringe, deeply carved casting, bronze-finished base metal, 1930s, 4", stamped Reinad. **$200**

Plastics

Jelly sunflower brooch, Lucite and sterling silver, uncommon, Trifari, 3 1/4", 1944. **$750-$850**

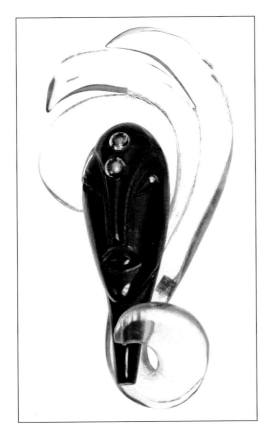

Man's head brooch, Lucite and ebony, unsigned, possibly Elzac, 3 3/4", 1940s. **$150-$250**

Jelly horse brooch, Lucite and base metal, rare, unsigned, 3 1/2", late 1930s. **$500-$600**

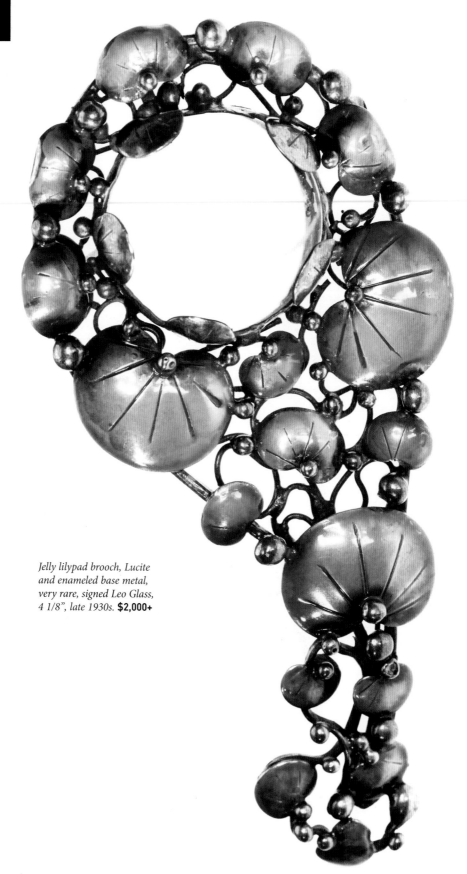

Jelly lilypad brooch, Lucite and enameled base metal, very rare, signed Leo Glass, 4 1/8", late 1930s. **$2,000+**

*Jelly acorn necklace,
Lucite and metal,
rare, signed Mazer,
16", mid-1940s.*
$800-$1,000

*Twin jelly birds
on branch brooch,
Lucite and base metal,
very rare, signed
"Trifari," 2", 1942.*
$1,500-$2,000

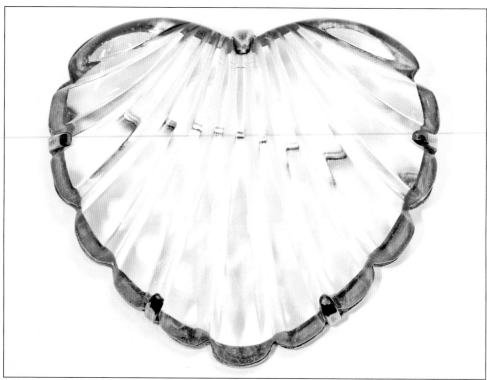

Jelly shell brooch, Lucite and sterling silver, uncommon, manufacturer unknown, unsigned, 2 3/8", 1944-46. **$250-$350**

Vintage pin, deeply carved black Bakelite, unsigned, 1940s, 3 1/4". **$375**

Leafy Bakelite bracelet, black with brass trim, hinged so fits larger wrists, leaves each 1 7/8", 1930s. **$850**

Rhinestones

Rhinestone set, clamper bracelet with buckle-effect design echoed in clip earrings. Pavé-set crystals with aurora-borealis treatment making stones reflect pastel pink-blue-lavender. Soldered rhinestone chain; clamper opens from side. Looks like a DeLizza & Elster product, but unconfirmed. Buckle motif 2 1/4"; earrings 1 1/2", 1960s. **$250 set**

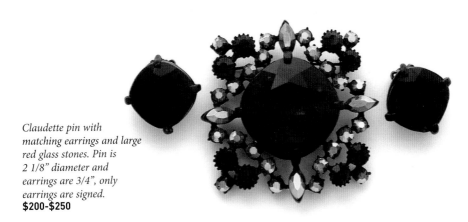

Claudette pin with matching earrings and large red glass stones. Pin is 2 1/8" diameter and earrings are 3/4", only earrings are signed.
$200-$250

DeLizza & Elster blue set with oval engraved flower stones from the mid-1960s.
$1,000-$1,300 set

DeLizza & Elster show-stopping bracelet with heliotrope stones, from the early 1960s,
a truly remarkable bracelet. **$400-$500**

DeLizza & Elster oval red cat's eye cabochon bracelet from the late 1950s. **$275-325**

Set with large, oval green and brown stones called "green heliotrope," necklace, bracelet, pin and earrings with other autumnal colors, mid-1960s. **$1,200-$1,400 set**

DeLizza & Elster set with stunning collar necklace and flat bracelet design with rivoli and margarita stones from the late 1960s. **$2,100-2,300+ set**

DeLizza & Elster chalk white and brown striped oval stone bracelet from the mid-1960s. **$250-$300**

DeLizza & Elster bracelet with blue and black beads that look like seed pods but are called "nugget beads," from the early 1960s, the set was called "Elegance." **$250-$300**

Calvaire sterling bracelet with large blue oval glass stones, gold wash over sterling. 7 1/2" x 3/4", marked Calvaire in block letters and Sterling. **$550-$650**

Unsigned brooch has a rose gold and gold washed appearance with amethyst and ruby glass stones, 2 3/4" x 2 1/8". **$100-$150**

Ciro fur clip with dark green ovals and clear chatons and baguettes, signed CIRO, 1 1/4" diameter. **$250-$275**

Rare "Original by Robert" ring with enormous opal like stone, ring has a uniquely adjustable shank and is marked with the artist's pallet "Original by Robert" mark, ring measures 1" across. **$125-$150**

Butler & Wilson rhinestone fruit clamper bracelet with tiny gold bee by the orange strawberry, signed inside the back of the apple. Bracelet is 1 1/2" tall. **$250-$300**

Trifari bracelet with aquamarine glass stones and chaton, tapered baguette and baguette clear stones, 7 1/2" x 1/2", marked with the crown Trifari mark. **$295-$350**

Rare Zoe Coste bracelet with black and clear Lucite stones, signed "Zoe Coste Made in France." 7 1/4" x 2". **$175-$195**

DeLizza & Elster heliotrope rhinestone pin with dangling beads. **$150-$200**

Les Bernard leaf pin with pearl center and colored glass cabochons and marcasites, with matching earrings, pin and one earring are marked Les Bernard, pin is 2 1/8" x 1 3/4", earrings are 7/8". Les Bernard was one of the first companies to mix rhinestones with marcasites in the same design. **$95-$125 set**

DeLizza & Elster jade matrix navette stones pin leaf from the early 1960s. **$95-$150**

DeLizza & Elster smoky topaz brooch with beads and stones called arrow stones, from 1959. **$175-$225**

DeLizza & Elster coral gold stippled cabochon set in peach from the early 1960s. Necklace, pin, bracelet and earrings; price depends on color. **$1,500-$2,500+ set**

DeLizza & Elster five-link bracelet with large green emerald-shaped glass stones accented with dark and light green chatons and navettes. **$250-$300**

DeLizza & Elster earrings with coral gold floral cabochons called "Rose Limoges," from the early 1960s. **$75-$150**

DeLizza & Elster brooch with hematite and topaz stones from 1963. **$175-$200**

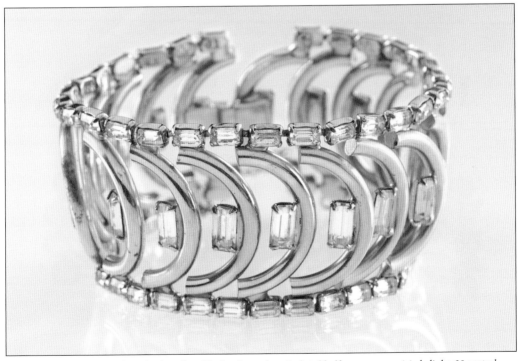

Semi-circles and baguettes bracelet, heavily gold-plated metal, articulated half moons or semicircle links, 20 central crystal baguettes, 58 smaller stones along perimeters, 7 3/4", 1950s, signed Trifari. **$150-$250**

Pair of geese in flight pin, highly dimensional, scattered rhinestone accents, sterling silver, 3", unsigned, 1942-46. **$50-$100**

Aquamarine arrangement of flowers in enameled-white gold basket, gilded pot metal, pink centerpiece stones in decorative raised prong settings, unsigned, 1940s, 3 1/2". **$150+**

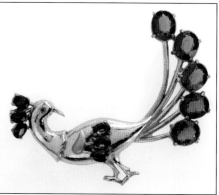

Jeweled peacock pin, gilded metal with flamboyant use of rhinestones, amethyst ovals in tail, emerald and ruby oval rhinestones on wing and head comb, signed Coro, 1940s, 3 1/4". **$150+**

Glass dress clip, gold-washed metal flowers centered with blue rhinestones set against highly detailed cast leaves, large, faceted crystal glass vase set into prongs; unsigned but has been found signed Mazer and Reinad; 1940s, 2 3/4". **$250**

Mechanical pelican pin, gilded, enameled pot metal, pavé-set rhinestone wing; pushing on head feather plume raises top of beak to reveal one fish; second fish dangles as charm from beak; 1940-42; unsigned; 3". **$500+**

Cross pendant-brooch, diamond and 18k gold, the gold mount set with 10 old European- and mine-cut diamonds weighing about 3.75 carats, each arm with a pointed and forked tip accented with black enamel, 2 1/8". **$3,525**

Floral hat brooch set (earrings not shown), gilded sterling silver (vermeil), 3-D, wire trim prong-set with multicolor rhinestones, unsigned other than hallmark but looks like CoroCraft; 2 3/4", 1940s. **$195 set**

Water lily brooch, huge gold-plated flower with tendril, purple-black pearlescent enamel, ruby-rose rhinestones, signed Eisenberg Original, 3", 1940s. **$500**

Glamorous butterfly brooch, enormous winged thing of heavy sterling silver, crystal accents, and large, horizontally faceted barrel glass stones in wings; hook and latch construction; signed Eisenberg Original Sterling (twice), 3", 1940s. **$1,500**

Branched arrangement, enameled leaves and flowers in gilded pitcher jardiniere, rhinestone and moonstone accents, from the "Gardenesque Series," rhodium reverse, signed Reja. 2 1/4", 1940s. **$150-$250**

GreatVintageJewelry.com; Veronica McCullough photo

Flower basket pin, silvery pot metal, 1930s thick, heavy urn with rhodium plating. Flower spray adorned with clear and amethyst rhinestones. Safety clasp, measures 3", unsigned, attributed to Reinad. **$110-$155**

Left to right, top to bottom:
- *Crystals green tree, icy crystals in varied shapes set into forest-green epoxy resin, unsigned Lianna, 1990s, 2 1/2".* **$25+**
- *Dove ribbon tree, metallic red epoxy, white dove, signed Lia, 1990s-2000s, 2 1/8".* **$50**
- *Floral-tinsel tree, glass flora ornaments set into golden tinsel and green epoxy tree, signed Lia, 1990s, 2 5/8".* **$50-$100.**
- *Ruby dots tree, red rhinestones in green tree, original made by Gem-Craft, signed Lia, 1990s, 2 1/2".* **$25-$50**
- *Modernist tree, original by Gem-Craft designer Gudrun, silver-plated metal, bright green metallic enamel, multicolor rhinestones, unsigned, date unknown, 3".* **$50-$100**
- *Meteorological tree, sun, moon and stars gold-plated against green epoxy resin, signed Lia, 1990s-2000s, 2 1/4".* **$25+**
- *Modern tree, band of red epoxy slanted across triangle, set with small crystal stones, unsigned Lia, 1990s, 2 3/8".* **$25+**
- *Pine tree, single crystal chaton in translucent epoxy overlay, early unsigned Lianna, sold at Accessory Lady, 1980s, 2".* **$50+**
- *Italian tree, 15 emerald, ruby and crystal navettes on five tiers, signed Lia, 1990s-2000s, 3".* **$50-$75**

Diamonds

Doyle New York

Diamond ring, platinum and vertically set European-cut diamonds, approximately 4.25 carats, elongated pierced openwork mount set throughout with numerous single-cut diamonds, circa 1915, approximately 4 dwt, 1 3/16" long. **$12,000**

Doyle New York

"Bird on a Rock" brooch, platinum, 18k gold, pavé-set with 70 round diamonds of 2.75 carats, polished gold beak, feathers and legs, ruby eye, perched atop cushion-cut citrine, 29.0mm, signed Schlumberger, Tiffany, approximately 18.3 dwt.; 2 1/2". Doyle catalog note: In the late 1950s, Jean Schlumberger was invited to design for Tiffany & Co., creating whimsical and surrealist pieces incorporating natural and organic forms in his work. This iconic design was originally created in the 1960s for the Tiffany yellow cushion-cut diamond of 128.50 carats. **$25,000**

Maidi Corp courtesy of Natural Color Diamond Association
Fancy natural pink marquise diamond earrings set in 18k rose gold and platinum, 4.97 carat weight. **$86,000**

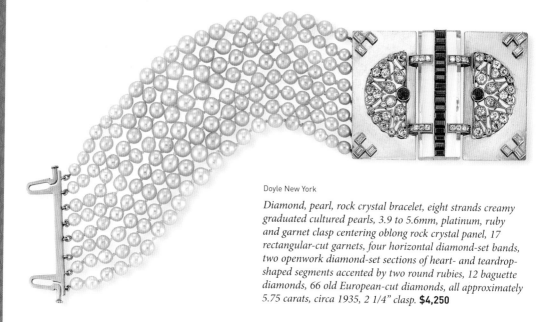

Doyle New York

Diamond, pearl, rock crystal bracelet, eight strands creamy graduated cultured pearls, 3.9 to 5.6mm, platinum, ruby and garnet clasp centering oblong rock crystal panel, 17 rectangular-cut garnets, four horizontal diamond-set bands, two openwork diamond-set sections of heart- and teardrop-shaped segments accented by two round rubies, 12 baguette diamonds, 66 old European-cut diamonds, all approximately 5.75 carats, circa 1935, 2 1/4" clasp. **$4,250**

Lamps and Lighting

Lighting devices have been around for thousands of years, and antique examples range from old lanterns used on the farm to high-end Tiffany lamps. The earliest known type of lamp was the oil lamp, mass-produced starting in the 19th century, which was then replaced by the kerosene lamp around 1850. In 1879, Thomas A. Edison invented the electric light, creating a new field for lamp manufacturers. Decorative table and floor lamps with ornate glass lampshades reached their height of popularity from 1900-1920. Companies like Tiffany and Handel became skillful at manufacturing electric lamps, and their decorators produced beautiful bases and shades.

Lamp, table, Bradley & Hubbard, its geometrical faceted shade with Greek key band, lined in green and yellow slag glass, over a three-socket base, covered in verdigris patina. One replaced socket, upper panels probably replaced. Unmarked, 22" x 15". **$900**

Rago Arts and Auction Center

Rago Arts and Auction Center

Lamp, table, Albert Berry, its four-panel shade of pierced and hammered copper with sylvan scenes lined in green and white slag glass, and garland chain suspending bone drops, over a single-socket mahogany base. Dark original patina, 3" break to one glass pane, two small corner chips to another. Unmarked, 20" x 8 3/4". **$6,600**

Lamp, table, Fulper, rare, its ceramic shade inset with small panels of blue-green leaded slag glass on a classically shaped, two-socket base, covered in a mirrored blue flambe glaze. Two short hairlines from rim to glass, original sockets and switch, overall excellent condition. Shade stamped 20 2 2, base has vertical stamped Fulper mark, PATENT PENDING US AND CANADA 20, 21 1/2" x 15 1/4". **$10,800**

Rago Arts and Auction Center

Lamp, table, Gorham, its leaded-glass shade in a foliate pattern over a three-socket fluted base in bronze patina. (Gorham's work in leaded glass is rare.) A few breaks to glass. Unmarked, 25 1/4" x 18 1/2". **$7,200**

Rago Arts and Auction Center

Rago Arts and Auction Center

Lamp, table, Handel, its large faceted shade with brown and green cattails against caramel slag glass, over a five-socket bronze base. Fine original patina, original sockets, cap and chains. Shade unmarked, base marked HANDEL 768?, 30 1/2" x 22 1/4". **$45,000**

Rago Arts and Auction Center

Lamp, table, Moe-Bridges, its hemispherical shade of acid-etched glass reverse-painted with a river landscape, on a two-socket bronze urn base. Shade signed MOE-BRIDGES CO. 186 HH, base unmarked, 23" x 18 1/4". **$4,200**
(Moe-Bridges Lamp Co., Milwaukee, early 20th century.)

Rago Arts and Auction Center

Lamp, table, Pairpoint, its "chipped ice" glass flaring shade obverse-painted with an autumnal landscape and reverse-painted in yellow, over a three-socket urn base in bronze patina. Base marked PAIRPOINT PD3034 MADE IN THE USA, 21" x 15 1/2". **$3,000**

Lamp, table, Lillian Palmer, hammered copper, its shade of four mesh panels painted with nasturtium blossoms in polychrome, its two-socket base incised with hollyhocks. Professionally enhanced patina on base. Unmarked, 18" x 19 1/4". **$13,200**
(The Lillian Palmer Shop, San Francisco, early 20th century.)

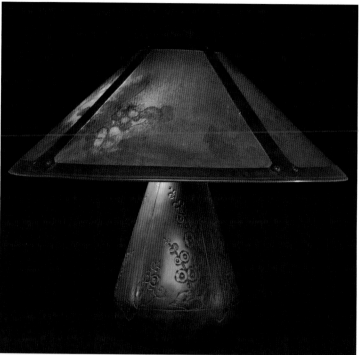

Rago Arts and Auction Center

Rago Arts and Auction Center

Lamp, table, Pittsburgh, its acid-etched glass shade reverse and obverse painted with autumnal maple leaves, over an organic two-socket base with bronze patina. A few minor flecks around rim. Unmarked, 23" x 18". **$4,200**
(Pittsburgh Lamp, Brass and Glass Co., 1901-1926.)

Rago Arts and Auction Center

Lamp, table, Roycroft, hammered copper, designed by Dard Hunter (1883-1966), flaring shade of bright green and purple leaded slag glass, over a three-socket base with ring pulls. Original patina, cap and finial. A couple of short breaks to glass pieces. Base has Orb & Cross mark, 22 1/4" x 18 3/4". **$20,400**

Rago Arts and Auction Center

Lamp, table, Roycroft, by Dard Hunter (1883-1966), its flaring shade of hammered copper lined in green textured glass, over a single-socket oak base with copper fittings. (Provenance: Charles Youngers, master bookbinder at the Roycrofters and close friend of the artist.) Glass replaced some 30 years ago with Roycroft-type material; replaced or missing screws to shade, some cleaning to copper. Unmarked, 23" x 16" sq. **$12,000**

Lamp, table, Tiffany, Russian #1910, 20" d shade has 4" aperture, "The Four Virtues" are depicted: Charitas, Veritas, Fides and Puritas. It is signed "Tiffany Studios New York #1916." Center panels are mottled in swirling multiple colors against a blue-purple background. The leading is finished in gold doré, The base is 23 1/2" h, signed "Tiffany Studios #567," finished in gold doré. Two or three hairlines in glass. **$155,000**

For more information on Tiffany, please see the Tiffany section of the Glass chapter.

Morphy Auctions

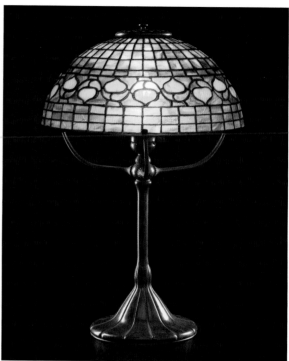

Lamp, table, Tiffany, Acorn, shade with blue, green and yellow slag glass over a three-arm, single-socket fluted bronze base. Fine original patina, several short breaks to glass. Shade and base stamped "Tiffany Studios New York," base with "TGDCo 259," 21" x 14". **$13,200**

Rago Arts and Auction Center

Lamp, table, Tiffany Studios, Red Tulip. The shade depicts the tulip flower in every stage of bloom. The colors used encompass the entire range of the red family from pink to purple. Some blossoms are entirely constructed of the softer colors, while others use striations of light, medium and dark to give a three-dimensional effect. There are other blossoms that used only the deepest colors and represent the flower in its later stage of bloom. This tulip pattern also shows the foliage in most every color of green. Glass used in this shade is also of a wide variety from striated to cat's paw to rippled and finally granular. The shade is completed with three geometric bands of rippled glass in earthen hues of fiery orange with hints of green. The shade is supported by a mock-turtleback base. This three-socket base is complete with riser, wheel and top cap all in a rich patina finish. Shade is signed "Tiffany Studios New York 1596." Base is signed "Tiffany Studios New York 587." Shade is 18" diameter. Overall 22 1/2" h. A few tight hairlines in shade. Patina has been enhanced on shade and base. **$109,250**

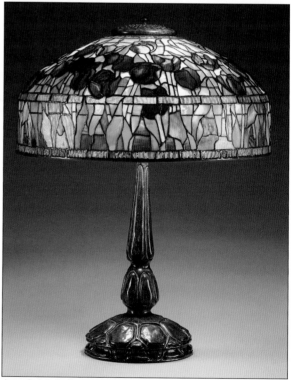

James D. Julia Auctioneers

Rago Arts and Auction Center

Lamp, table, Unique Lamp Co., leaded-glass shade with pink blossoms and green leaves on amber slag glass ground, over a two-socket fluted base with green leaves, 20" x 15". **$1,560**

Rago Arts and Auction Center

Lantern, Riviere, hanging copper in the style of Tiffany, its pierced sides in a floral pattern, lined in caramel slag glass. Unmarked, 14" x 8" sq. **$780**
(Riviere Studios, New York, early 20th century.)

Rago Arts and Auction Center

Sconces (pair), wall, Gustav Stickley, hammered copper lined in textured agate glass. Fine original dark patina, professionally re-glued glass of the period, which may not be original, one replaced pane. Unmarked, 17" x 6".
$9,600 pair

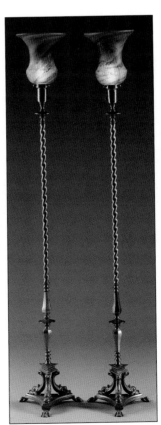

Pair of Steuben Moss Agate Torchieres. Acid-finished Moss Agate shades resting in a brass floor stand with lion paw feet, cast dolphin supports and twisted riser. The shades have a rich Moss Agate design in shades of green, red, brown and amber. The exterior of each shade is acid etched to give a frosted finish. Shades are 9" diameter x 9" t x 2 1/4" fitter. Overall 65 1/2" t.
$12,650 pair

James D. Julia
Auctioneers

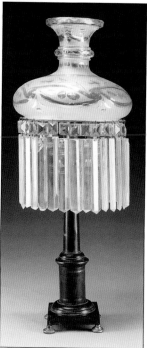

Early Sinumbra lamp. With four brass turned feet supporting a square base with pillar-type stem leading to the Sinumbra font. The lamp is finished with a frosted cut to clear shade with stylized floral design and large prisms. Lamp is signed with a square tag on the font "Stoutenburg & Morgan New York". 29" h. Lamp has been electrified and three prisms are missing. A few of the other prisms have chips. **$1,725**

James D. Julia Auctioneers

James D. Julia Auctioneers

Consolidated parrot lamp. Pressed-glass shade in the shape of a parrot perched atop a brown log. The parrot is painted in bright orange with green topknot. Shade screws on to a black glass footed base. 13" h. One tiny chip to bottom rim of shade. **$300**

Miniature Hanging Lamp. SII-381. Brass frame and chain with side arms depicting birds sitting on tree branches. Removable font marked "LP Lamp Co Sample" and "83" in the center. Green transparent prisms. Cosmos pattern clear glass shade flashed green. Acorn burner. Overall 12" l. **$1,840**

James D. Julia Auctioneers

Chandelier, brass and glass, four light with acid-etched glass panels, 20th century, 39" h, 18" d. **$900**

Candlestick, Tiffany, bronze floriform with blown-in green glass, complete with bobeche. Stamped "Tiffany Studios New York 91100," 20". **$2,280**

Rago Arts and Auction Center

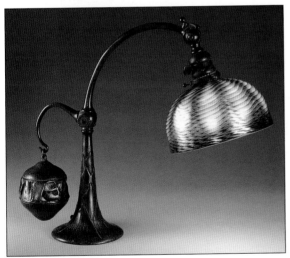

James D. Julia Auctioneers

Counterbalance lamp, desk, Tiffany Studios. With pendulous turtleback tile counterweight. Artichoke design stand and blue decorated damascene shade. Shade is signed "L.C.T. Favrile." Base is marked "Tiffany Studios New York." Shade is 8" diameter. Overall 14 1/2" h. Minor chips to three turtleback tiles in the counterweight, one tile with tight hairline, some minor wear to patina. **$32,775**

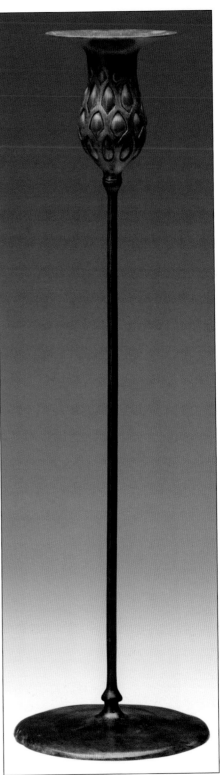

Rago Arts and Auction Center

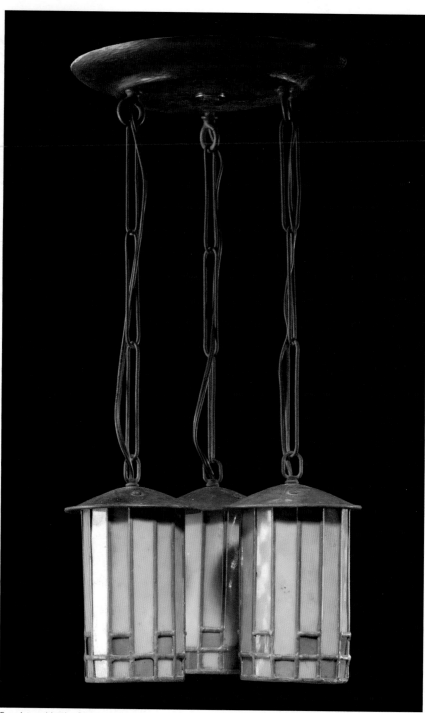

Rago Arts and Auction Center

Ceiling fixture, Roycroft, designed by Dard Hunter (1883-1966) with three cylindrical leaded-glass drops in bright green and purple glass, complete with chains and ceiling cap. Break to one piece of glass, missing finial and wear to patina on ceiling cap, 22" x 10 1/4" d. **$30,000**

Maps

Throughout the ages, pictorial maps have been used to show the industries of a city, the attractions of a tourist town, the history of a region or its holy shrines. Ancient artifacts suggest that pictorial mapping has been around since recorded history began. "Here be dragons" is a mapping phrase used to denote dangerous or unexplored territories, in imitation of the medieval practice of putting sea serpents and other mythological creatures in blank areas of maps.

All photos courtesy Heritage Auctions

Frederic De Wit map of the world, "NOVA ORBIS TABVLA IN LVCEM EDITA," 22.25" x 19", circa 1680, Amsterdam. Both hemispheres and the poles are depicted in this fine example of hand-colored Dutch engraving. Interestingly, De Wit still depicts California as an island when other cartographers were regarding it as part of the North American mainland. Each corner of this map carries a large tableaux representing one of the four seasons.
$3,883

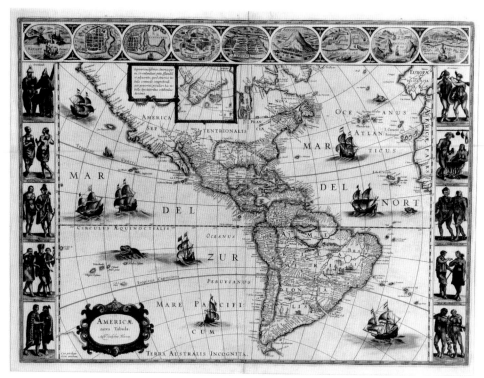

Willem Blaeu map of the Americas, " AMERICAE NOVA TABVLA," Amsterdam, circa 1635, 22.5" x 17", a spectacular early rendering of the Western Hemisphere by one of Holland's foremost Golden Age cartographers. Unlike many European cartographers of his day, Blaeu correctly shows California as part of the mainland with the Baja peninsula being well-defined. An upper register forms a top border composed of nine bird's-eye views of prominent American cities such as Havana, Potosi, Mexico City and Cartegena. Flanking the map are 10 panels showing indigenous peoples in native costume. **$4,780**

Map of Dayton by John W. Van Cleve, 1839, rare and early Dayton, Ohio, lithographed map, 34" x 34", designates numbered lots along city streets, all southeast of the convergence of the Miami and Mad Rivers. Also labeled are ponds, roads, the Miami Canal and basins. Dayton boasted a population of near 6,000 in 1839. John W. Van Cleve (1801-1858) was the first male of European decent born in Dayton. His father, Benjamin, had helped found the city in 1796. **$2,629**

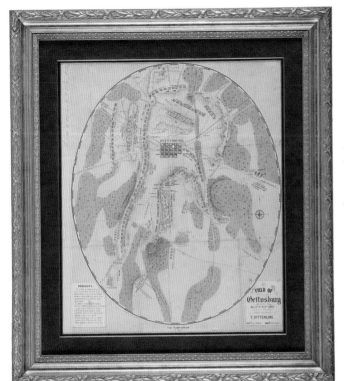

1863 Commercial Map of Gettysburg Battlefield with Booklet, Theodore Ditterline, Sketch of the Battles of Gettysburg with an Explanatory Map, (New York: C. A. Alford, 1863), 24 pp., blue cloth wrap, 7.25" x 5", plus colored map opening to approximately 16" x 19.5", the top margin of map and booklet's front endpaper are inscribed "Andrew W. Blocher Co. K 1st Regt P R I." **$2,270**

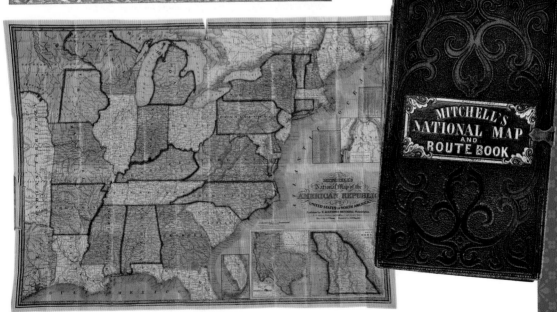

S[amuel] Augustus Mitchell. A Route-Book Adapted to Mitchell's National Map of the American Republic; Comprising Tables of the Principal Rail-road, Steam-boat and Stage Routes, Throughout the United States (1846); includes one large 34" x 24.5" hand-colored folding map of the eastern half of the United States drawn by J. H. Young and engraved by J. H. Brightly with four maps inset: "Map of the North-Eastern Boundary of the United States," "Map of Oregon Territory," "Map of the Southern Part of Florida," and "Map of the State of Texas." **$2,270**

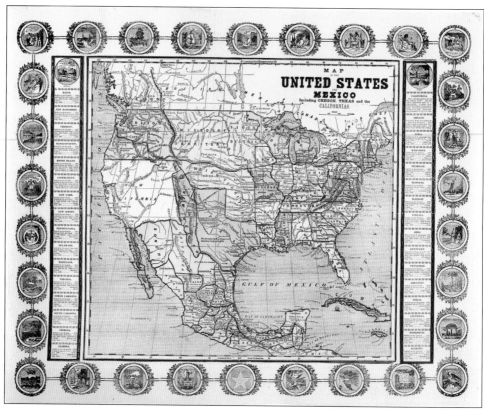

"Map of the United States and Mexico Including Oregon, Texas and the Californias," 1846, hand-colored map by John Haven, 23" x 19", statistical information on each U.S. state is included at the left and right edges of the map while 30 official state seals align the margins. **$2,151**

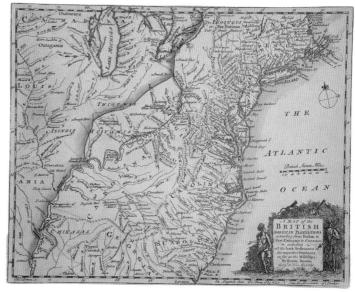

Early 1754 map of the American plantations commissioned by King George, titled "A Map of the British American Plantations extending from Boston in New England to Georgia; Including all the back settlements in the respective Providences as far as the Mississippi, By Eman: Bowen Geogr: to His Majesty"; one page, 11" x 9", 1754, beautiful and detailed map outlining the 13 original colonies as well as the French territory and forts including the Great Lakes Region, St. Louis, Illinois, the Ohio Valley and its western reaches; French boundaries and trade routes are colored in red and the eastern seaport of America is tinted in pale green. **$1,673**

"Pirates of the Caribbean: Dead Man's Chest" screen-used prop treasure map used by Johnny Depp in his role as Captain Jack Sparrow in the 2006 movie. Pivotal to the plot, the map was used by Sparrow as he raced to acquire the key to the chest containing Davy Jones' heart. **$1,195**

Celestial Chart from Harmonia Macrocosmica, ca. 1708, copper-engraved celestial map, 20" x 17", 23.25" x 19.25" overall. **$1,912**

Sebastian Munster map of Africa, AFRICA/ LYBIA/ MOZENLANDE MIT ALLEN KONIGREICHEN SO ZU UNSEREN ZEITEN DARIN GEFUNDEN WERDEN, 14.75" x 11", German, ca. 1550; an engaging masterpiece of late medieval cartography, hand-colored woodcut map presents a squat, wide Africa based on the Ptolemaic model of the 2nd century. Crowns with scepters denote known kingdoms amid a landscape of fantasized mountain ranges and jungles. According to Munster, the Nile rises from three lakes in the interior. Most jarring is the one-eyed giant - a "Monoculus" - shown in the vicinity of present-day Sierra Leone. Other creatures depicted are a grazing elephant and a quartet of parrots. **$896**

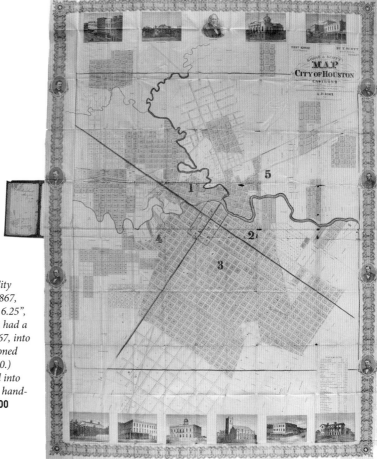

Kosse & Scott "Map of the City of Houston and Environs," 1867, 35" x 50" folding into 4.5" x 6.25", map divides Houston, which had a population near 8,000 in 1867, into five wards. (Houston abandoned the ward system around 1900.) Each ward is further divided into numbered lots, each brightly hand-colored pink or green. **$23,900**

Music Memorabilia

— By Susan Sliwicki, *editor*, Goldmine

Despite the Great Recession, which dates back to December 2007, the state of the hobby for those who collect music and related memorabilia is healthy, according to Jacques van Gool of Backstage Auctions.

Based in Houston, the boutique online auction house specializes in authentic rock memorabilia consigned directly by legendary musicians and entertainment professionals.

Jacques van Gool

"I have not seen a massive exodus or departure from collecting music memorabilia as a hobby," van Gool said. "I think the number of collectors and buyers is just as high as it was 3 or 5 years ago. But there is definitely a bigger interest for lower- to mid-range items."

Before the economy went south, multiple buyers might be in the market for a pricey item, such as a fully signed photo of The Beatles. The resulting bidding battle could drive that lot's price up to $10,000. These days, fewer people are looking for that type of lot to begin with, and those who are interested likely would pay less for it, too. Instead, buyers are gravitating toward low- to mid-price lots that previously might not have been considered for auction, van Gool said. And, the acts that buyers are interested in aren't necessarily your parents' favorites.

"There is definitely a new generation of collectors, which is people that currently age-wise are between 35 and 55, who didn't grow up listening to '60s music," van Gool said.

Artists from the late 1970s and 1980s, especially hard rock, heavy metal and pop acts, are poised to be the next generation of headlining acts for collectors, van Gool said. He listed Guns N' Roses, Motley Crüe, Bon Jovi, U2, Prince and Madonna as prime examples.

And just as the desired artists are changing, so, too, are some of the items that are being collected.

"Obviously, concert posters are becoming more and more extinct, because there hardly is a need to do concert posters anymore," van Gool said. "Back in the '60s, it was almost the only way to communicate that hey, there's a concert coming, and you would see these posters staple-gunned to phone poles. These days, you announce concerts via e-mail and websites and text messages and Facebook and Twitter and all of that."

Also on the endangered species list: ticket stubs, printed magazines, handbills and promotional materials. The sharp decline of many record companies and the rise of CD and digital formats have combined to reduce the production of promotional items, van Gool said.

T-shirts, on the other hand, have come into their own.

"T-shirts really didn't start taking off as either a promotion or concert merchandise item until the mid-'70s or beyond," van Gool said. "The whole T-shirt collection is more of a next-generation kind of thing. Of course, there are exceptions; there are old concert shirts for Led Zeppelin and the Stones. But in terms of sheer volume and numbers, that's not anything like the next decade."

And those reports you've heard about the pending demise of vinyl records in the wake of digital formats? Don't believe 'em.

"Vinyl is far from dead. Vinyl is alive and kicking," van Gool said. "Of '60s artists, vinyl is a prime collectible. But the same holds true for collectors of '80s bands or artists. They are just as intrigued and as interested in vinyl as the previous generation."

Whatever your interest in music and memorabilia, van Gool offers one key piece of advice.

"I have never looked at collecting music memorabilia as an investment," he said. Instead, he recommends building a collection around your passion, be it punk music, concert posters or all things Neil Diamond.

"If you just collect for the sheer and simple fact of pleasure and passion, then the money part, the investment part, becomes, at best, secondary," van Gool said. "In a way, collecting represents pieces of history. Whether it's an old handbill or a ticket stub or a T-shirt, every picture tells a story. When you buy that 1978 Blue Öyster Cult Wichita, Kansas, T-shirt, you've bought a piece of history."

Collecting Tips

There are a few things you should consider as you invest in your hobby, according to van Gool.

1. Condition, condition, condition. Strive to acquire items that are in the best condition possible, and keep them that way.

"One universal truth will always be condition," van Gool said. "Obviously, the more mint an item, the more it'll hold its value. That was true back then, it's true today, and it'll be true 40 years from now."

From poster frames to ticket albums to record storage sleeves, bags and boxes, there are ways to preserve basically every collectible you might seek.

"It's money well spent to make sure you preserve your items well," van Gool said.

2. Put a priority on provenance. Some collectors feel that personal items, like an artist's jewelry, stage-worn clothing or even a car, have more value than other pieces. But the personal nature of a piece doesn't matter if you can't prove its pedigree.

"Personal items are considered valuable, but you'd better have the provenance to back it up, and provenance is harder to come by than the actual item," van Gool said.

Working with reputable auctioneers and dealers is a great way to boost the likelihood that an item is everything you want. But even if you acquire a personal item with an impeccable provenance, keep in mind that doesn't necessarily make it more valuable than something of a less personal nature.

"What I've seen is that a fully signed Beatles item may be worth $10,000. But there's an enormous amount of nonpersonal items that are worth more. We've seen certain concert posters sell for $20,000, $50,000, even $100,000," van Gool said.

3. Weigh quantity and rarity. "You always want to collect those types of items that there are the fewest of — promotional items or items that are local, for instance," van Gool said. "Anything that is made in smaller quantities or made for promotional purposes or a local purpose, like a concert, eventually will be more collectible."

4. Take advantage of opportunities geared toward collectors. "Record Store Day is once a year, and I really think that it pays off to go to your local record store and buy the releases that will be unique for Record Store Day only," van Gool said. "The vinyl that is going to be offered is typically limited to 1,000 or 3,000 or 5,000 copies, and those limited editions will always become more valuable as time goes by."

Today, some bands release limited-edition vinyl LPs or singles in addition to CDs and MP3s. Van Gool recommends music lovers buy one format to enjoy (be it CD, vinyl or MP3) and buy a copy of the vinyl record to keep — still sealed, of course — in your collection.

"Because there are fewer records pressed, if you keep yours sealed, 20, 30 years from now, there's a good chance that you'll be happy you did that," he said.

5. Refine the focus of your collection. The hottest acts tend to have the most collectors and, by extension, the most items you can collect, van Gool said. If you try to collect everything that is available, you'll need a lot of time to chase pieces down and a lot of money to acquire them.

"Figure out what really excites you as a collector," van Gool said. "If you do that, you make the hobby a lot more fun for yourself. You set some parameters so you protect yourself from spending an enormous amount of money."

6. Think before you toss. Good-condition, once-common items that date back before World War II — like advertising posters, Coca-Cola bottles, 78 RPM records and hand tools — today are cherished by collectors.

"Nothing saddens me more than people going through their basements, garages, storage facilities, attics, etc., with big plastic bags and just putting it out for the trash," van Gool said. "Eventually, true historic treasures are just being thrown away. Why keep that concert poster? Well, you can pitch it, but that might be the only piece of evidence for that particular venue, and now it's gone."

Christie's

Louis Armstrong's trumpet. A Selmer trumpet stamped 46818, owned by Louis Armstrong, and given to the Harlem musical agent "Lady" Bertha Stewart. The trumpet is engraved "Henri Selmer Paris Made In France"; original hard case; accompanied by a letter concerning provenance. **$13,325**

Portion of Nirvana drumkit. A remnant of the TAMA bass drum from Nirvana's Dave Grohl's first drum-kit, as smashed on stage by Kurt Cobain at the end of a concert at the Cabaret Metro, Chicago, Oct. 12, 1991, and subsequently thrown out into the crowd; a handwritten set-list from the gig, black marker pen in an unknown hand on a paper plate; a Photostat flyer for the gig and a promotional flat for the album Nevermind as displayed at the venue; accompanied by a letter from the vendor concerning provenance and photographs of Grohl playing the kit. **$13,325**

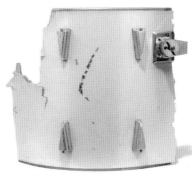

Christie's

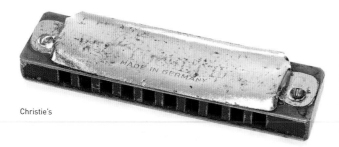

Christie's

A Hohner West Pocket Harp harmonica believed to have been given to Jimi Hendrix by Bob Dylan, when performing at Cafe Wha?, Greenwich Village, New York; 3 1/4" l; accompanied by a letter from the owner concerning provenance. **$7,790**

A small hand-carved wooden pipe, with glazed finish owned by Jimi Hendrix; accompanied by a letter concerning the provenance. Mike Quashie "performed with Led Zeppelin, was a constant companion to Lou Reed and became known, with a claim as quietly unchallenged as his title of Limbo King, as Jimi Hendrix's best friend." New York Times, Sept. 27, 2003. When they met, Jimi Hendrix was performing with Curtis Knight and the Squires and Trinidadian Mike Quashie was headlining at the African Room, drawing celebrity admirers with his rocking voodoo performance. Among the first to recognize Hendrix's talent, Mike invited Jimi to visit him in Greenwich Village and offered a place to stay whenever needed. When Jimi began to make it big and needed a place to get away, he hid out at Mike's place. When he left for the Isle of Wight, Jimi left two trunks full of his personal belongings in the front room, the room set aside for his use. **$5,740**

Christie's

Christie's

A mint green single-breasted fitted jacket with wide lapel, embellished with black sequin musical note and diamante treble clef motif to collar, sleeves and front, additional beading Rooty Toot! across the back, lined with black "art" silk, labeled inside "Mr. Freedom," worn by Marc Bolan in the 1972 Apple film "Born to Boogie"; accompanied by a DVD of the film and a letter concerning the provenance. **$15,375**

A very rare album "Double Fantasy," 1980, Geffen Records, signed, annotated, and dated on the inner lyric sleeve in blue marker pen "To KCPX love, Yoko Ono John Lennon 1980" with caricature portraits by John Lennon of himself and Yoko Ono; accompanied by two letters (one on Warner Brother Records headed paper, dated 12/16/80) and a newspaper clipping concerning the provenance; 12" x 12" (31.7 x 31.7 cm). **$38,950**

Christie's

Christie's

Multiple-autographed, outside broadcast script, five pages of mimeographed typescript, "The Beatles" insert into "Our World" BBC Television Service, EMI Recording Studios, 3 Abbey Road, N.W.8, rehearsals: Saturday, 24th June, 1967, LIVE TRANSMISSION: Sunday, 25th June, 1967, signed on the back of a page in blue ball-point pen by John Lennon, Paul McCartney, George Harrison, Ringo Starr, Mick Jagger, and Marianne Faithful; 13" x 8" (33 x 20.5 cm); accompanied by a letter concerning the provenance. **$19,475**

The Beatles' band-signed promotional photo from "A Hard Day's Night," this vintage black and white 14.5" x 11.5" picture is one of those rare pieces of Beatles memorabilia that bears the autographs of each member of the Fab Four: Paul McCartney has inscribed "Love" and signed in blue ballpoint, Ringo Starr signed in light green ballpoint that appears as gray against the image, John Lennon signed in black ballpoint, and George Harrison signed "To Louisea lovea froma Georgea Harrisonea" in black ballpoint. (A second, larger McCartney signature on the photo is printed on, not handwritten.) The autographs were obtained by acclaimed British actor Norman Rossington in March/April 1964 during the filming of the Beatles' motion picture debut, "A Hard Day's Night." This was one of many photos dropped from a helicopter during the filming of sequences of the Beatles on the playing fields; this is, to date, the only known autographed copy. **$19,120**

Heritage Auction Galleries

A pair of Jimi Hendrix's black leather calf-length boots, zipper inside, set of 19 eyelets to front with leather lace, owned and worn by Jimi Hendrix during his visits to New York and during performances at the Salvation Club, circa 1967-69; accompanied by a letter from Mike Quashie concerning the provenance. **$15,375**

Christie's

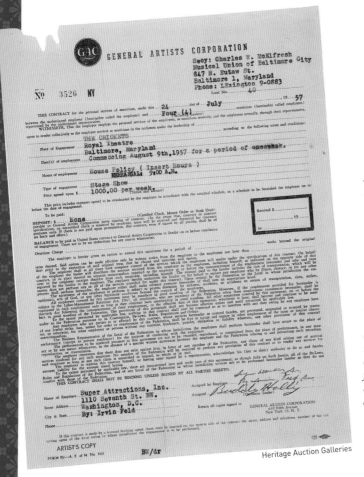

Heritage Auction Galleries

This rare signed contract from Buddy Holly engaged the rock and roll pioneer and his backing band, The Crickets, for a weeklong series of performances at the Royal Theatre in Baltimore, Md., that commenced on Aug. 9, 1957. The contract is dated July 24, 1957, very early in Holly's professional career. Holly had been dropped by Decca Records a few months earlier, and subsequently picked up by both Brunswick Records (with The Crickets) and Coral Records (as a solo artist), which put him in the unusual position of having two recording contracts at the same time. The week after these shows, Holly and The Crickets played their historic shows at the Apollo Theater in New York, and three months later, The Crickets' debut album, "The 'Chirping' Crickets," was released. The single-page standard agreement has two light fold creases and is missing a small piece from its top left edge. Signed by Holly in blue ink. Very fine condition. Accompanied by James Spence Authentication auction letter of authenticity. **$11,950**

Elton John's TV-worn costume designed by Bob Mackie for Sir Elton and worn by the musician while appearing on an unspecified episode of the 1975-76 "Cher" television series; this silver quilted-lamé, crystal-studded wrap coat is accompanied by a matching hat, aqua-and-silver jumpsuit and silver platform boots with crystal pave heels. In excellent condition. **$27,485**

Heritage Auction Galleries

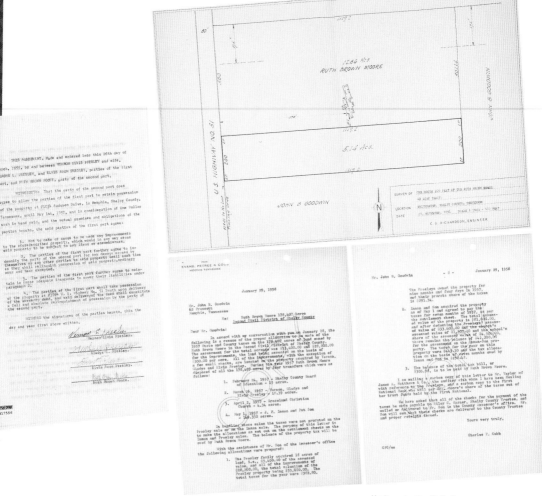

Heritage Auction Galleries

Graceland purchase agreement signed by Elvis Presley and his parents. A three-page real estate sales contract, each page measuring 8 1/2" x 14", for Graceland, dated March 26, 1957. Signed on the last page by Elvis (as "Elvis Aron Presley" with "Aron" added after initial signature), and Vernon and Gladys Presley, as well as real estate agent Ruth Brown Moore. Items signed by all three family members are extremely rare, due to Gladys Presley's untimely death on Aug. 14, 1958; the presence of Elvis' middle name in the signature makes it even more desirable. The Southern colonial-style house, situated on 13.5 acres of land in the then-rural outskirts of Memphis, was dubbed "Graceland" by its original owner, F.E. Toof, in honor of his daughter, Grace. As part of Elvis' offer of $102,500, the Presleys' home at 1034 Audubon Drive in Memphis was traded in for a value of $55,000. Also included is an 11" x 17" engineer's survey draft of the estate and surrounding acreage and a two-page letter from Shelby County regarding property taxes, dated Jan. 29, 1958. The documents are in overall very fine condition with some instances of staple and binder holes to the top edges, mild to moderate toning, and a fold crease to the drawing. Accompanied by certificates of authenticity from PSA/DNA and Rock Consola. **$38,837**

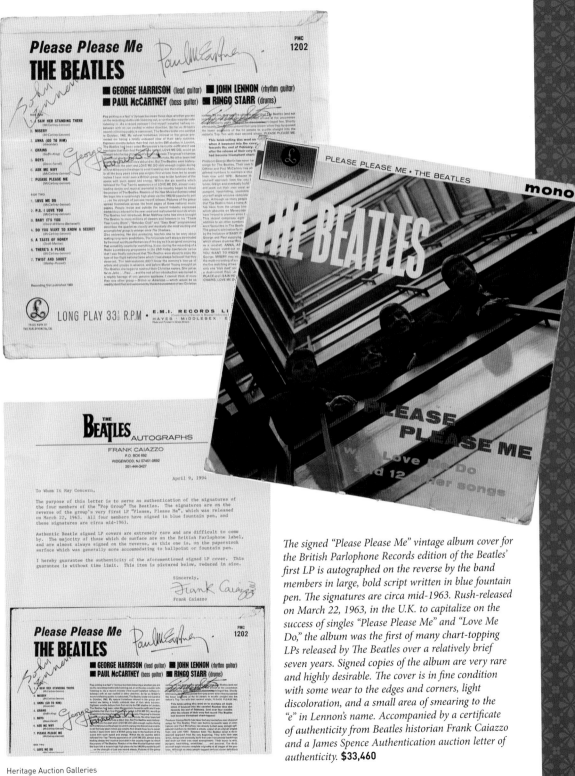

The signed "Please Please Me" vintage album cover for the British Parlophone Records edition of the Beatles' first LP is autographed on the reverse by the band members in large, bold script written in blue fountain pen. The signatures are circa mid-1963. Rush-released on March 22, 1963, in the U.K. to capitalize on the success of singles "Please Please Me" and "Love Me Do," the album was the first of many chart-topping LPs released by The Beatles over a relatively brief seven years. Signed copies of the album are very rare and highly desirable. The cover is in fine condition with some wear to the edges and corners, light discoloration, and a small area of smearing to the "e" in Lennon's name. Accompanied by a certificate of authenticity from Beatles historian Frank Caiazzo and a James Spence Authentication auction letter of authenticity. **$33,460**

Heritage Auction Galleries

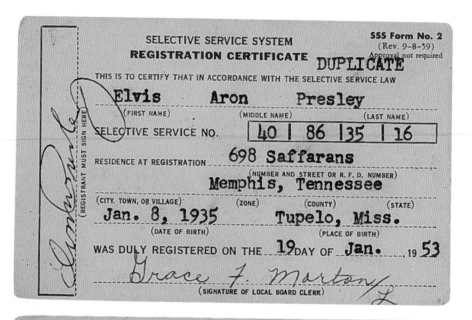

Heritage Auction Galleries

This is Elvis Presley's Selective Service registration certificate — more commonly referred to as a draft card — dated Jan. 19, 1953 (11 days after his 18th birthday). Signed along the left edge by Presley in blue ink and co-signed by a local board clerk along the bottom. Elvis had to put his professional music career on hold when he was called for active service. Elvis had been notified on Dec. 19, 1957, that he'd been inducted, but he got a deferment until March 1958 so he could complete the film "King Creole." Inducted into the U.S. Army as a private on March 24, a horde of photographers and reporters swarmed as he arrived at Fort Chaffee for basic training. Elvis told them that he was looking forward to his tour of duty, saying he did not want to be treated any differently from anyone else. "The Army can do anything it wants with me." After training at Fort Hood, Presley joined the 3rd Armored Division in Friedberg, Germany and was honorably discharged in 1960, at the rank of sergeant. **$26,290**

Heritage Auction Galleries

Heritage Auction Galleries

This Marine Band key of C harmonica by Hohner was signed by Bob Dylan across the top in black felt tip. The harmonica is one of a limited edition of 100 such harmonicas sold by Hohner in 2008. The harmonica is in excellent condition and is accompanied by a handcrafted inlaid ebony display box with a record of authenticity certificate by the president of Hohner, Inc., set inside the lid. These limited edition signed harmonicas sold for $5,000 each when originally released by Hohner. **$3,883**

A black and white 8" x 10" promotional photo issued by Sun Records circa the 1950s, signed by Johnny Cash—the Man in Black—in blue ink. In very fine condition with some toning along the right side. Pre-certified by PSA/DNA. From the collection of Rock and Roll Hall of Fame inductee Timothy D. Kehr. **$896**

Bill Graham concert poster for Jan. 13-15, 1967. Featured acts are Junior Wells' Chicago Blues Band, The Grateful Dead and The Doors. Measures 13 63/64" x 21 55/6". **$151**

Backstage Auctions

The first promotional handbill for "Sensational music with an irresistible beat Jerry Lee Lewis and his pumping piano," advertising Sun 259, "Crazy Arms" b/w "End of the Road." Includes a photo of Jerry Lee Lewis' face and shows his hands, holding a Sun 45. The flyer explains that Lewis is from Ferriday, La., and got his start as a fiddler, then switched to drums and tympani. "A year ago JERRY LEE sat down to a piano to play and sing and knew he had found his medium!" the handbill reads. **$600**

Backstage Auctions

This lot of four picks is comprised of three picks from the 1979 KISS Dynasty tour, featuring silver on white signature picks of Ace Frehley, Paul Stanley and Gene Simmons. Also included is a very rare black-on-white Gene Simmons pick from the same tour. The silver picks are in excellent condition. **$190**

Backstage Auctions

Backstage Auctions

Rare Pro-Mark Ringo Starr signature drumsticks. Signed with a fine black marker. In pristine condition.
$400

Backstage Auctions

The Who rare "SHOWCO" T-shirt. This size extra-large (vintage cut) T-shirt is an amazingly scarce specimen: a crew shirt from the band's March 11, 1976, concert at Madison Square Garden. It features a two-sided print and is overall in excellent condition. The shirt was made by Showco, Inc. for working personnel and crew only. Over the past years, Showco T-shirts have become highly collectible, and in some instances, are more valuable than the artist T-shirt for the same tour. **$320**

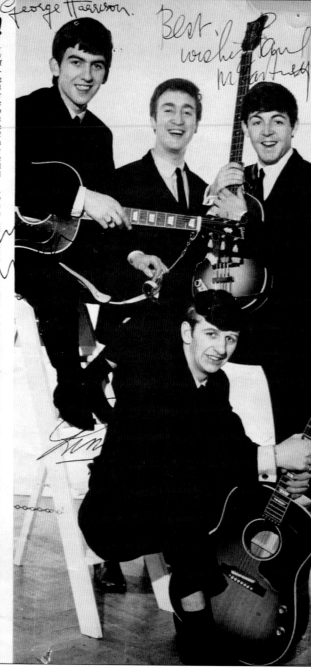

BEATLES BATTLE ON!

One group. Two hits. One sound—but whatta sound, plus some pretty cute vocalising as well!! They are, of course, the fabulous Beatles! An outstanding name—and an outstanding team who look certain for more chart entries in the very near—but near future! Their talent is obvious by the fact that they are the first British group to reach the charts with their first release—something which even the Tornados or Shadows could not do! Their first chunk of platter (as if you didn't know!) was the swingin' bouncy *Love Me Do*, which stayed around the charts for so long that the Beatles told me, "We felt like retiring there and then!"

Their latest single, *Please, Please Me*, vetted by experienced dee-jays who pronounced "one of the best seven inches of solid wax we've heard for some time!" The four lads, John Lennon, Paul McCartney, George Harrison, and Ringo Starr all write their own songs, work out their own stage acts, and can all play a variety of instruments. I asked them about their rather peculiar name, The Beatles. Drummer Ringo Starr said with a laugh, "I don't really know how it came about Dave. I think people put too much emphasis on the names for groups! We aren't really concerned when people think it funny."

John Lennon, however, had a different view of things. He said, "It came to me in a vision. A man astride a flaming pie said, 'From now on you will be known as the Beatles—with an "A"'!" Another unusual facet about this quartet is the fact that they all look rather like younger cousins to the Temperance Seven! About the only difference between them and the Temps is the fact that they are more inclined towards a touch of the old jollities! In fact when I had them in the office this is roughly how the interview went. John Lennon, "Wonder why we aren't in the charts? The Pop Weekly Popularity charts, I mean?"

Paul replied, "Perhaps it's because we're not all handsome." Flashed back George Harrison (lead guitar) "Speak for yourself!" Quipped Ringo Starr, "Yes, George is the handsome member of the group—but that's about all he does, isn't it?" George promptly sloshed, or attempted to slosh, Ringo with his guitar, but to no avail—as Ringo had by this time picked up his drum-sticks and was battling furiously! Then Paul McCartney told me about their combined ambitions, "You see, Dave, we think our success is due to the fact that we are *not* a copy of anyone else.

I mean, there are hundreds of professional and semi-professional acts who copy the Shadows, the Everlys, and various other people. We have a distinctive name, a distinctive sound, and a fresh stage act." I asked them what they had got in mind for the future, and they said, "To see our new platter *Please, Please Me* get to the No. 1 slot!"

POP Weekly   2/2/63

Backstage Auctions

Beatles fully signed Feb. 2, 1963, "Pop Weekly" U.K. magazine. Most of The Beatles' pre-1964 autographed pieces were from the U.K; this one was signed during the Helen Shapiro tour the band did that summer. Signatures are on the same page as the band's photo, which shows all four Beatles, with Ringo Starr, George Harrison and Paul McCartney holding guitars, next to an article titled "Beatles Battle On." John Lennon, Starr and Harrison signed their names; McCartney also signed "Best wishes." From the collection of heavy-metal music manager Walter O'Brien. **$6,030**

Musical Instruments

*Mandolin, Gibson Mandolin-Guitar Co., Kalamazoo, circa 1923, Model F4, labeled "GIBSON MANDOLIN STYLE F4, ...," etc., length of back 12 7/8", with case. Missing pick guard. Surface scratches and abrasions, 1 cm chip in face of headstock. Fracture near upper treble body point, approx. 3 cm, fracture below body scroll, approx. 3 cm. Wear to upper edge, back of headstock. **$3,081***

Guitars, Banjos, and Mandolins

The guitar has ancient roots and is used in a wide variety of musical styles. It typically has six strings, but four-, seven-, eight-, 10-, 11-, 12-, 13- and 18-string guitars also exist. The size and shape of the neck and the base of the guitar also vary. There are two main types of guitars, the electric guitar and the acoustic guitar. The banjo is a stringed instrument developed by enslaved Africans in the United States, adapted from several African instruments. The mandolin is part of the lute family (plucked or strummed). It is descended from the mandore, a soprano lute. It usually has a body with a teardrop-shaped soundboard, or one that is essentially oval in shape, with a soundhole, or soundholes, of varying shapes, which are open.

The instruments featured on this page and the next page are courtesy Skinner Inc., Boston and Marlborough, Mass., and Heritage Auctions, Dallas, Texas.

Harp guitar, Gibson Mandolin-Guitar Co., Kalamazoo, circa 1920, Style U, labeled "GIBSON STYLE U, NUMBER 78381 IS HEREBY, GUARANTEED..., etc., GIBSON MANDOLIN GUITAR CO, MANUFACTURERS, KALAMAZOO MICH, USA," length of back 26 1/2", width of lower bout 18 1/2", with case. Surface scratches and abrasions, wear to back of neck. Fracture to peg head of sympathetic tenth string. **$3,081**

Mandola, Lyon & Healy, Chicago, circa 1920, labeled "MADE BY, LYON & HEALY, CHICAGO, MAKERS OF HIGHEST GRADE MUSICAL, INSTRUMENTS, SOLD UNDER OUR UNLIMITED GUARANTEE NO 2 STYLE A, LYON & HEALY," length of back 15", width of back 11 3/8", with original case. **$7,110**

Tenor banjo, Weymann & Son, Philadelphia, circa 1930, labeled "WEYMANN, MANUFACTURED BY, WEYMANN & SON PHILA PA," serial number stamped on dowel stick, diameter of head 11", tarnish and mild corrosion to gold plating. $5,925

American Banjo, Vega Co., Boston, circa 1921, Model Tubaphone #9, stamped on the dowel stick "TUBAPHONE 45097, FAIRBANKS BANJO, MADE BY, THE VEGA COMPANY, BOSTON MASS, NO 9...," etc., and stamped "45097" on the inside rim, diameter of head 10 15/16", with later case. Very good condition. Later gold Grover tuners, wear to fingerboard at first and second position. $4,444

Following photos courtesy Heritage Auction Galleries

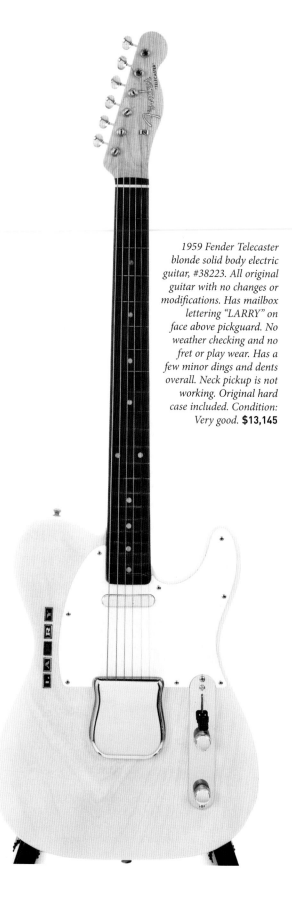

1959 Fender Telecaster blonde solid body electric guitar, #38223. All original guitar with no changes or modifications. Has mailbox lettering "LARRY" on face above pickguard. No weather checking and no fret or play wear. Has a few minor dings and dents overall. Neck pickup is not working. Original hard case included. Condition: Very good. **$13,145**

1952 Fender Telecaster butterscotch blonde solid body electric guitar, #N/A. Heavily weather checked and considerable finish wear with possible overspray. Neck date: TG10-20-52. Body date: 8-26-xx (year not legible). Bridge has been changed to six saddle modern style, and all electronics and pickups are non-original. Pickguard is probably not original. A couple of screws on tuners have been replaced. One non-original-type screw in pickguard. Control plate knobs, switch tip, and screws are all original. Neck mostly likely refretted and fingerboard refinished. Hard case included. Condition: Poor. **$13,145**

1956 Gibson Les Paul Goldtop solid body electric guitar, #68160. Les Paul Standard refinished and factory refurbished. Original serial number is stamped in back of headstock as Gibson would do when guitars were sent back to the factory. This guitar appears to have been re-necked, most likely by Gibson. Pot dates are 42nd week of 1955. Has one bumblebee and one grey tiger cap, which would be consistent for 1956. Pickups appear to be original to 1956 as well as knobs. Larger frets, which appear to be factory as well, have considerable wear and have been flattened down. Top mount Bigsby has been added, and may have been done when refurbishing occurred. Has metal jack plate, newer Schaller Keystone style tuners in gold. Has engraved Les Paul truss rod cover, similar to SG Les Paul covers. Poker chip has been replaced at switch. Pickguard and pickup covers appear to be original. No apparent breaks or repairs to guitar. Normal weather checking and greening of finish on top. Has a few dings and divots on back and one on neck, a good sized divot on treble side back of neck at ninth/tenth fret. Has chrome 1960s ABR-1 bridge missing wire. Control plates are not original to 1956, probably replaced with black plastic when refurbished. 1970s hard case included. Condition: Fair. **$11,053**

1956 Gibson Les Paul Special TV yellow solid body electric guitar, #6 9876. All original guitar, with no changes or modifications. Moderate weather checking overall. Original frets have moderate fret wear, missing one dot in finger board. Original tuners have deteriorating buttons and one is missing. Moderate finish wear through to wood first through fifth fret. Various dings, scuffs, and scrapes overall but non-severe. Original soft case included. Condition: Good. **$7,767**

1959 Gibson ES-355 cherry semi-hollow body electric guitar, #S606 22. Strong original cherry finish. Factory Bigsby, Grover tuners, and ABR-1 bridge are original. Both PAF pickups have strong output but have had their covers off and put back on. Ground wires from the bridge and varitone control appear to be re-soldered to the braided ground wire of the bridge pickup. There are two spliced wires coming from the varitone control. All pots have their covers with the exception of the bridge tone pot. All the electronics function as they should and the varitone is still wired up. There is slight fracture damage along the treble and bass sides of the neck binding area that extends from the non-original nut to the ninth fret. There is also a slight fracture behind the low E tuner where the wing is joined. There is some slight damage around the tuner bushings from over tightening, which is purely cosmetic. The frets have a lot of oxidation, but appear to have plenty of meat left. Interior orange label serial is A 31658. Original hard case included but is missing three feet. Condition: Good. **$9,261**

1963 Fender Jazz Bass Sunburst electric bass guitar, #89513. All original with moderate weather checking, light fret wear. Has some evidence of play with finish missing from back of upper horn from play. A few minor scuffs and dings overall, nothing major. Finish worn from play on treble side through 9th fret. Original, white hard case included. Condition: Good. **$9,261**

1952 Gibson Les Paul Goldtop solid body electric guitar, #N/A. Very early 1952 Goldtop, featuring diagonal pickup screw mount on bridge pickup and no serial number and no neck binding. Pots and caps appear original. Input jack wiring has been modified. Input jack plate is crude replacement with no extra holes, though the screws are larger than factory. The switch wiring has been modified and the bridge pickup does not function. The high E tuner is a later replacement with the same footprint as an original. The switch cover has larger than factory replacement screws. There are no visible breaks or repairs and the finish is original. Original hard case included. Condition: Good. **$10,755**

1958 Gibson Les Paul Special TV yellow solid body electric guitar, #83436. All original guitar with no apparent changes or modifications. A few minor dings on back of headstock as well as each corner on upper headstock of face. Some light pick scratching on front from play wear. Wear and scratches on sides of guitar in several locations, moderate but not severe. Minor weather checking overall. Guitar is stamped factory second. Odd touch up or discoloration on bass side near the end of finger board below binding at neck pickup. Original soft case included. Condition: Good. **$8,962**

1959 Fender Jazzmaster Sunburst solid body electric guitar, #33794. Neck date 12/58, probably a 1959 guitar. Appears all original except for changed knobs. Missing tremolo arm. Considerable weather checking overall. Various scuffs, dings, and scrapes overall, and cord rash on back. Hard case included. Condition: Good. **$6,871**

1980 Gibson Super 400 natural blonde semi-hollow body electric guitar, #83300007. All original guitar with moderate play wear and checking. Several dings on both sides of upper bout for no apparent reason. Has moderate gold wear. Has very small two-inch crack on top at waist on bass side bout. Considerable buckle or button damage on back, but only small area through to wood. Original frets have moderate wear. Pickguard is beginning to deteriorate at screw on bracket. Original hard case included. Condition: Good. **$7,170**

1967 Mosrite Ventures metallic blue solid body electric guitar, #D004. All original guitar with no changes or modifications. Missing spring from vibrato. Minimal weather checking and play wear. Original hard case included. Condition: Very good. **$3,585**

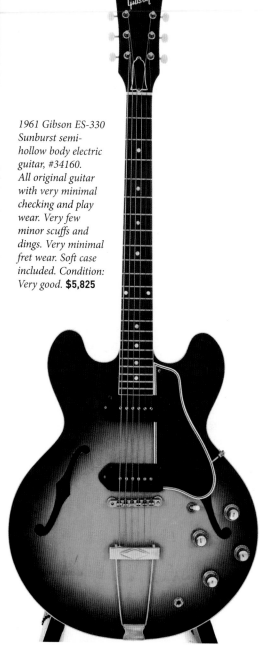

1961 Gibson ES-330 Sunburst semi-hollow body electric guitar, #34160. All original guitar with very minimal checking and play wear. Very few minor scuffs and dings. Very minimal fret wear. Soft case included. Condition: Very good. **$5,825**

1951 Gibson SJ-200 Sunburst acoustic guitar, #A7476. Bright, clean, original finish. Crack-free guitar. Beautiful flamed maple back. Original pickguard in excellent condition. Perimeter of all top surfaces, pickguard, bridge, and top binding have been coated and glued with sparkle. Decal stickers with sparkle "Dusty Rhodes" glued to lower treble bout area of top. Sparkle from body binding is gone, leaving glue residue. Condition of binding underneath glue unknown. Peghead crown coated with sparkle. Mustache bridge hollow areas filled with foreign material. Original frets in very good condition. Otherwise very nice guitar. Original hard case included. Condition: Good. **$6,273**

North American Indian Artifacts

— By Russell E. Lewis

This section covers collectible items commonly referred to as American Indian artifacts. Our interest in Native American material cultural artifacts has been long-lived, as was the Indian's interest in many of our material cultural items from an early period.

During recent years, it has become commonplace to have major sales of these artifacts by at least four major auction houses, in addition to the private trading, local auctions, and Internet sales of these items.

Anthropologists have written millions of words on American Indian cultures and societies and have standardized various regions of the country when discussing these cultures. Those standard regional definitions are continued here.

We have been fascinated with the material culture of Native Americans from the beginning of our contact with their societies. The majority of these valuable items are in repositories of museums, universities, and colleges, but many items that were traded to private citizens are now being sold to collectors of Native American material culture.

Native American artifacts are now acquired by collectors in the same fashion as any material cultural item. Individuals interested in antiques and collectibles find items at farm auction sales (an especially good place for farm family collections to be dispersed), yard sales, estate sales, specialized auctions, and from private collectors trading or selling items.

Native American artifacts are much more difficult to locate for a variety of reasons including the following: scarcity of items; legal protection of items being traded; more vigorous collecting of artifacts by numerous international, national, state, regional, and local museums and historical societies; frailties of the items themselves, as most were made of organic materials; and a more limited distribution network through legitimate secondary sales.

However, it is still possible to find some types of Native American items through the traditional sources of online auctions, auction houses in local communities, antique stores and malls, flea markets, trading meetings, estate sales, and similar venues. The most likely items to find in the above ways would be items made of stone, chert, flint, obsidian, and copper. Most organic materials will not have survived the rigors of a marketplace unless they were recently released from some estate or collection and their value was unknown to the previous owner.

For more information on Native American collectibles, see *Warman's North American Indian Artifacts Identification and Price Guide* by Russell E. Lewis.

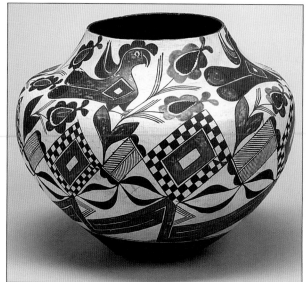

Skinner Inc.

Acoma polychrome olla, circa 1900. Concave base, rounded shoulder and tapered neck with black, red/brown and orange geometric, foliate motifs and a stylized parrots on a cream-colored ground, 11" high x 13 1/2" diameter. **$29,275**

Allard

Navajo weaving, late 1800s. Fine tapestry grade weaving of classic red, gold, brown, green, etc., 45" x 30". **$2,250**

Allard

Apache White Mountain moccasins, early 1900s. Full high top moccasins with toe tab in yellow ocher, 10" long x 30" high. **$475**

Louisiana polychrome twilled lidded basket, circa 1900. Chitimacha culture lidded form with damage to three corners, squares and rectangular designs, 5" high. **$2,350**

Skinner Inc.

Skinner Inc.

Rare Southeastern beaded cloth sash, Creek, second quarter of 19th c. Sash panel is 26 1/2" long. Black trade cloth backed with an early velvet and beaded on one side. The drops are natural dyed wool with white pony beaded edging and tassels at the ends that appear to have once been braided. Some bead loss and minor damage.
Provenance: Given in the 19th c. by Native Americans in Oklahoma to Rev. B. F. Tharpe for services rendered and then descended through his family. **$10,575**

Passamaquaddy basket, circa 1900. Woven split ash basket with bentwood handles in excellent condition, a style seen throughout both the Northeast and Great Lakes regions, 9 1/2" x 9 1/2". **$150**

Allard

Iroquois bag, early 1900s. Finely detailed two-sided flap pouch with floral design in small beads on brown velvet, some beads missing, 6 1/4" x 6". **$250**

Allard

Two Ojibwa spoons, circa 1870s. Two small carved spoons found in medicine bundles, 6" x 4 1/2". **$225**

Allard

Very rare and early Huron baby moccasins, circa 1780-1810. Excellent and original condition, 5" long. **$2,500**

Allard

Ball headed war club, Eastern Great Lakes, 19th c. Carved of hardwood, this is actually an example of a club that would have been carried denoting the bearer was on "men's business" and not a war club. However, the design of the war clubs was similar with ball end clubs being favored in the Great Lakes and the Northeastern Woodlands. **$1,725**

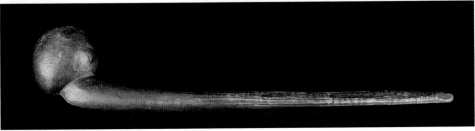

James D. Julia Auctioneers

Sauk Fox/Otoe beaded moccasins, early 1900s. Rare and in very fine condition, 10 1/2" long. Provenance: Richard Pohrt, Sr. Collection. **$3,000**

Allard

Mesquakie sash, circa 1890s. Finger woven yarn and pony bead sash with yarn and bead fringe, excellent condition, 6' 10" x 6" wide. Provenance: Pohrt collection. **$425**

Allard

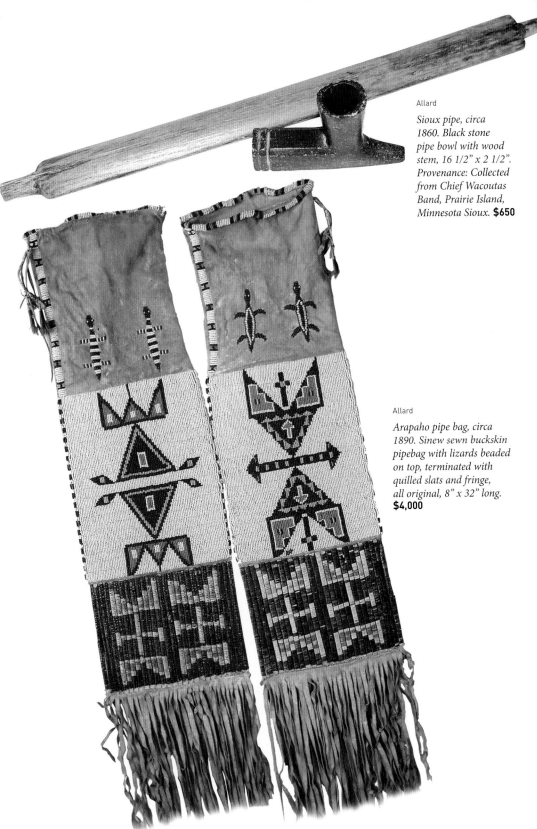

Allard

Sioux pipe, circa 1860. Black stone pipe bowl with wood stem, 16 1/2" x 2 1/2". Provenance: Collected from Chief Wacoutas Band, Prairie Island, Minnesota Sioux. **$650**

Allard

Arapaho pipe bag, circa 1890. Sinew sewn buckskin pipebag with lizards beaded on top, terminated with quilled slats and fringe, all original, 8" x 32" long. **$4,000**

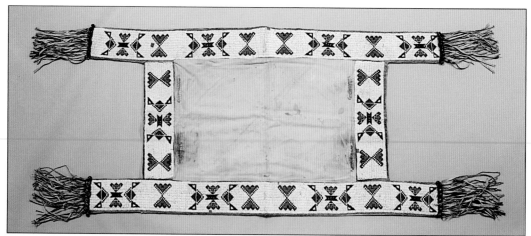

Skinner Inc.

Lakota Sioux beaded hide and cloth saddle blanket, late 19th c. Central panel is canvas, and beadwork is on recycled buffalo hide with cowhide fringe trim. Beads include metallic and glass seed beads and also used are brass hawk bells. **$2,585**

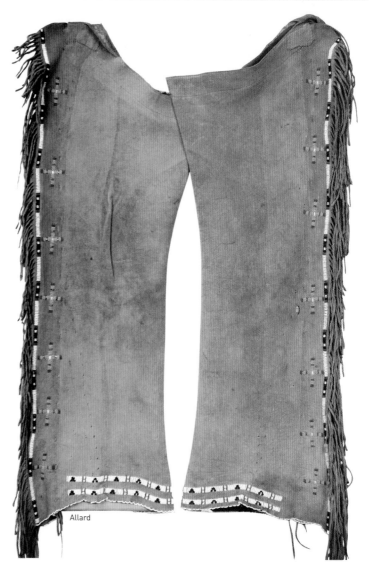

Southern Cheyenne leggings, 1870s. Sinew sewn beadwork on green and yellow ocher stained elk hide, trimmed with brass shoe buttons, 12" x 30". Provenance: Richard Pohrt, Sr. collection. **$3,250**

Allard

Apache bear claw necklace, late 19th c. Provenance: Moon collection. Consists of nine grizzly claws and eight black bear claws attached to buffalo hide and edged with red felt similar to that used for the backing on buffalo lap robes. The metallic and blue beads used as spacers are of an unknown origin.
$3,450

James D. Julia Auctioneers

Skinner Inc.

Plains tomahawk, circa third quarter 19th c. Handle has typical Plains adornment of tacks, original beaded drop has been repaired and a newer piece added to the buffalo hide original, head is forged; it is 23 1/2" l. **$10,575**

Blackfoot leggings, circa 1880. Calico-backed leggings with beaded panels, 13" x 13". **$1,300**

Allard

Crow moccasins, circa 1890. Buffalo hide soles, false vamps, partially beaded moccasins, museum quality, 10 1/2". Provenance: Honnen collection. **$1,900**

Allard

Skinner Inc.

Quilled cloth bag, Cree, first half 19th c. Made of blue trade cloth with silk applique details, decorated with tightly loomed geometric quillwork with quill wrapped hide loops and white seed bead spacers below the panels. It has a braided cloth strap and is lined with cloth ticking. An old paper label says, "This Indian bag was made by squaws and used by Titian Peale during Longs Rocky Mountain Expedition in 1819-1820." The reverse of the paper says, "Holmesberg Feb. 4, 1876." The bag has some minor loss and is 10 3/4" long. Provenance: Supposedly purchased from the direct descendants of the Peale family by Wesley Crozier of Red Bank, New Jersey. Exhibitions: Monmouth (NJ) County Library. **$94,000**

Skinner Inc.

Pictorial coiled basketry bowl, Yokuts, circa late 19th c. Flared form pictorial bowl with four rows of two color rattlesnake design and a top row of humans holding hands in alternating colors, some restoration done to this piece, 7 1/2" h x 17 1/4" diameter. **$14,100**

Allard

Hupa lidded basket, early 1900s. Rare fine-weave lidded basket with excellent black and red designs and top knot handle on lid, 10" h x 9 1/2" diameter. **$2,000**

Skinner Inc.

NW Coastal painted and carved wood mask, Tsimshian, second half 19th c. Apparently the provenance is solid and the age of the mask important, as well as the articulating mouth. The mask is a cedar form with both an articulated lower jaw and articulated eyes, part of the articulation device remains on the mask. It is in a form with both human and bird features, it has red lips and nostrils over a graphite-like black pigment. The outer edge of the mask is decorated with cedar bark bundles nailed to the edge, patina on mask from use, 14" high. Provenance: Collected by Garnet West in 1952 from Rev. Shearman, Kitkatla Reserve, Prince Rupert, British Columbia. Note: "Over 200 years old, worn by Chief Gum-I-gum, meaning 'Brave Man'." **$259,000**

Allard

Haida totem pole, 1890. Very detailed old hand-carved totem pole with six figures, concave back and covered in a reddish paint or stain, 16 1/2" h. **$1,000**

Aleutian basket, circa 1900. Extremely finely woven lidded treasure basket with checks done in blue and red yarns, 5 1/4" x 6 1/2". **$550**

Allard

Allard

Blackfoot telescope, 19th c. Brass telescope covered with beadwork. An old tag reads "Blackfeet Indian Spy Glass, Arrowwood, Alberta, Canada," 2" x 9". **$500**

Allard

Inuit basketry, circa 1900. Very rare lidded baleen basket tipped with a carved walrus head, 3 1/2" x 4 1/2". **$1,000**

Allard

Inuit moccasins, early 1900s. Rare pair of hard-soled seal skin child's boots, 4" x 5" x 2 1/2". **$70**

Outdoors

Bird Decoys

— By Russell E. Lewis, author, Warman's Duck Decoys

The origin of the decoy in America lies in early American history, pre-dating the American pioneer by at least 1,000, perhaps 2,000 years. In 1924, at an archeological site in Nevada, the Lovelock Cave excavations yielded a group of 11 decoys preserved in protective containers. The careful manner of their storage preserved them for us to enjoy an estimated 1,000 to 2,000 years later.

When the first settlers came to North America, their survival was just as dependent upon hunting wild game for food as it was for the Indians. They began to fashion likenesses of their prey out of different materials, ultimately finding that wood was an ideal raw material. Thus the carving of wildfowl decoys was born out of necessity for food.

Historical records indicate wooden decoys were in general use as early as the 1770s, but it seems likely that they would have been widely used before then.

Until the middle of the 1800s, there was not sufficient commercial demand for decoys to enable carvers to make a living selling them, so most decoys were made for themselves and friends. Then the middle of the 19th century saw the birth of the market gunners. During the market-gunning period, many carvers began making a living with their decoys, and the first factory-made decoys came into existence. The huge numbers of decoys needed to supply the market hunters and the rising numbers of hunters for sport or sustenance made commercial decoy carving possible.

The market hunters and other hunters killed anything that flew. This indiscriminate destruction of wildfowl was the coup de grace for many bird species, rendering them extinct.

The United States Congress, with the passage of the Migratory Bird Treaty Act in 1918, outlawed the killing of waterfowl for sale. Following the passage of the 1918 act came the demise of the factory decoys of the day.

Today a few contemporary carvers carry on their tradition. They produce incredibly intricate, lifelike birds. What these contemporary carvings represent is that decoy carving is one of the few early American folk arts that has survived into our modern times and is still being pursued.

Elmer Crowell's Preening Pintail drake, carved in 1915, is known as Crowell's finest and is the only known example. It was made for Crowell's friend, Dr. John C. Phillips of Beverly, Mass., for whom Crowell ran a gunning stand at the turn of the 20th century. **$801,500**

Guyette & Schmidt, Inc.

Pitt Collection

The Mason "snake-head" Pintail drake, in Standard Grade with glass eyes, is a very rare configuration. **$32,000**

Albert Laing, Stratford, Conn. (1811-1886), carved this Black Duck in the mid- to late- 19th century. This exceptional hollow-carved bird began life as a Canvasback by Albert Laing and it was then later converted to a Black Duck by Shang Wheeler also of Stratford, Conn. It is an old working repaint by Wheeler that comes from the Shelburne Museum collection and is so stamped. **$35,000-$40,000**

Guyette & Schmidt, Inc.

Hank and Judy Norman Collection

A Golden Plover is by William Bowman, Lawrence, Long Island, N.Y., circa 1880. **$25,000**

Guyette & Schmidt, Inc.

A rare and early Delaware River Pintail drake dates to the last quarter of the 19th century to early 20th century. By an unknown maker, it has hollow carving, "V" primaries and inserted hardwood tail, similar to work by John English. It has original paint with very minor touchup. **$27,500**

Guyette & Schmidt, Inc

Capt. Ed Phillips (1901-1964), Cambridge, Md., made this Pintail drake, circa first quarter of the 20th century. This rare decoy with lifted head and an extended tail sprig is in original paint with minor wear; underside of the body has a small old touchup. **$10,500**

A very rare summer plumage Old Squaw drake was the very last one of these made by the Ward Brothers in 1977. **$25,000-$30,000**

Pitt Collection

Ned Burgess, Churches Island, N.C., carved this Mallard hen. It is very rare, created in the early 20th century. It has original paint and a small dent in back. It is featured in Southern Decoys. **$21,000**

Guyette & Schmidt, Inc.

The Caines Brothers, Georgetown, S.C., made this very rare Mallard drake, circa turn of the 19th to 20th century. Carved with a peg placed to support a fragile bill, it has raised wings, tack eyes, working second coat of paint believed to have also been done by the Caines, and slight damage to the bill. **$35,000**

Guyette & Schmidt, Inc.

A rare Widgeon drake, Premier Grade, produced by the Mason factory early in the 20th century has original paint, several tiny dents, with original newspaper wrapping visible. **$55,000**

Guyette & Schmidt, Inc.

Lures and Fish Decoys

All fishing-related photos courtesy Lang's Sporting Collectibles, Waterville, N.Y.; www.langsauction.com.

Cargem Mignon No. 33 ultra-light reel. **$510**

Dame, Stoddard & Kendall reel. **$280**

Four Brothers Delite trout reel. **$172**

Hardy Elarex reel with box. **$150**

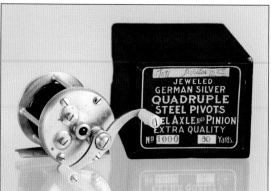

Jupiter casting reel with box. **$402**

Heddon 3-25 German-silver reel. **$300**

Hendryx aluminum trout reel. **$920**

6 1/2' Orvis Deluxe, with the original plaid bag and black tube with early Orvis label. Sold by Abercrombie & Fitch. **$1,035**

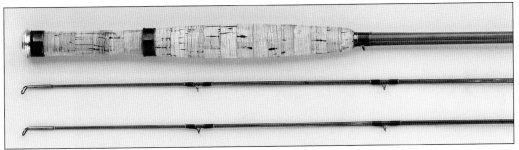

8' Payne sold by Abercrombie & Fitch, with original bag and tube with silver label. **$2,588** *(Rods may bring a premium with the A&F name applied.)*

Florida Shinner, from Frostproof, Fla., and F.L.B. Flood, measuring 5", finished in brown back with silver scales, in the correct cardboard box with original fragile instruction flyer. **$649**

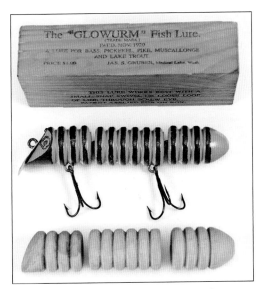

Gruber's Glowurm Fish Lure, patented November 1920, by J.S. Gruber of Medical Lake, Wash., finished in yellow with green stripes, in the correct wood box. Also included is an unassembled, unfinished Glowurm. **$265**

Copper minnow bucket. **$390**

Leather-covered tackle box. **$390**

Tackle shop fish sign, metal. **$2,990**

Native American Salish creel. **$4,255**

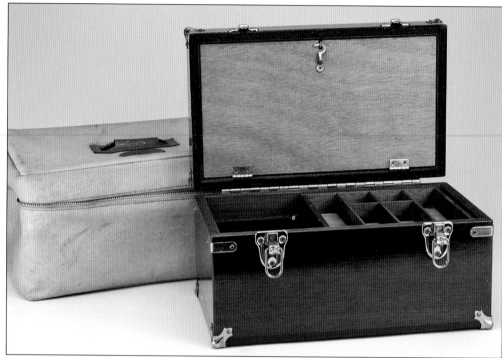

A&F tackle box, lift-out tray, 1945-65, 13" x 7 3/4" x 7", grained solid mahogany and finished with several coats of high-luster lacquer. Finished with brass corner protectors, piano hinge, latches and handle, with original custom-tailored canvas cover. **$767**

Early wooden A&F line dryer, having a 9" wide spool consisting of eight spindles, mahogany, overall length of 12" not including the wooden handle, with circular A&F label, mild chipping. **$590**

Perfume Bottles

— By Kyle Husfloen

Although the human sense of smell isn't nearly as acute as that of many other mammals, we have long been affected by the odors in the world around us. Science has shown that scents or smells can directly affect our mood or behavior.

No one knows for certain when humans first rubbed themselves with some plant or herb to improve their appeal to other humans, usually of the opposite sex. However, it is clear that the use of unguents and scented materials was widely practiced as far back as Ancient Egypt.

Some of the first objects made of glass, in fact, were small cast vials used for storing such mixtures. By the age of the Roman Empire, scented waters and other mixtures were even more important and were widely available in small glass flasks or bottles. Since that time glass has been the material of choice for storing scented concoctions, and during the past 200 years some of the most exquisite glass objects produced were designed for that purpose.

Kyle Husfloen

It wasn't until around the middle of the 19th century that specialized bottles and vials were produced to hold commercially manufactured scents. Some aromatic mixtures were worn on special occasions, while many others were splashed on to help mask body odor. For centuries it had been common practice for "sophisticated" people to carry on their person a scented pouch or similar accoutrement, since daily bathing was unheard of and laundering methods were primitive.

Commercially produced and brand name perfumes and colognes have really only been common since the late 19th and early 20th centuries. The French started the ball rolling during the first half of the 19th century when D'Orsay and Guerlain began producing special scents. The first American entrepreneur to step into this field was Richard Hudnut, whose firm was established in 1880. During the second half of the 19th century most scents carried simple labels and were sold in simple, fairly generic glass bottles. Only in the early 20th century did parfumeurs introduce specially designed labels and bottles to hold their most popular perfumes. Coty, founded in 1904, was one of the first to do this, and they turned to Rene Lalique for a special bottle design around 1908. Other French firms, such as Bourjois (1903), Caron (1903), and D'Orsay (1904) were soon following this trend.

People collect two kinds of perfume bottles—decorative and commercial. Decorative bottles include any bottles sold empty and meant to be filled with your choice of scent. Commercial bottles are any that were sold filled with scent and usually have the label of the perfume company.

The rules of value for perfume bottles are the same as for any other kind of glass—rarity, condition, age, and quality of glass.

The record price for a perfume bottle at auction is something over $200,000, and those little sample bottles of scent that we used to get for free at perfume counters in the 1960s can now bring as much as $300 or $400.

For more information on perfume bottles, see *Antique Trader Perfume Bottles Price Guide* by Kyle Husfloen.

Perfume bottle and stopper, shoe-shaped black glass with "jade" knot stopper and enameled and jeweled applied metalwork, Hoffman, stenciled "Made in Czechoslovkia," ca. 1920s, 41/2" l. **$18,000**

Perfume bottle and stopper, amber crystal in an oblong upright shape with a low angled shoulder to a short neck fitted with an amber facet-cut stopper, mounted in a gilt-metal base with decorative plaque on the side, paper label reads "TandB Austria," ca. 1920s, 8 1/2" h. **$3,000-4,000**

Perfume bottle and stopper, domed cylindrical cranberry glass bottle h.p. with heavy gold shoulder panels above lily-of-the-valley decoration, gilded knopped stopper, Moser, ca. 1900-20, 3 1/2" h. **$650**

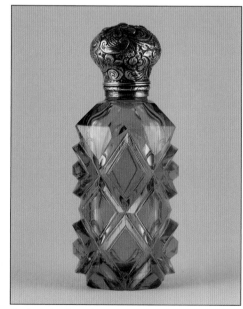

Perfume bottle and stopper, annagrun uranium glass in a cylindrical shape deeply cut around the sides with diamond panels, silver collar and fancy hinged cap with glass inner stopper, Joseph Riedel, mid-19th c., 4 1/4" h. **$450-500**

Perfume bottle and stopper, pale blue crystal bulbous shape molded as a flower blossom, fitted with a figural butterfly stopper with dauber, unsigned Irice, Czechoslovakia, 1920s, 5 3/4" h. **$2,200-3,400**

Perfume bottle and stopper, crystal flat-sided oblong ribbed shape on short feet, overlaid with ornate gilt-metal enameled filigree bands set with blue jewels, tall flat cryal shaped oblong stopper etched with a flying bird-of-paradise and ending in a dauber stub, stenciled oval "Made in Czechoslovakia" and metal tag with "Czechoslovakia," 1920s, 7 1/4" h. **$1,600-2,100**

Perfume bottle and stopper, long low clear crystal shape with flattened sides and angled shoulders, decorated around the lower half with ornate gilt-metal triple-arched filigree trimmed with green jewels, the rounded clear faceted stopper etched with a scene of seated lovers and ending in a dauber, unmarked, 1920s, 5 3/4" h. **$2,160**

Perfume bottle and stopper, dark blue faceted pyramidal shape raised on a filigree-trimmed metal base with ball feet and wrapped around the neck and shoulders with enameled and jeweled leaf and blossom mounts, tall crystal stopper molded in the shape of a stylized lady wearing a pleated gown and holding a bouquet of flowers, complete with dauber, stenciled oval "Made in Czechoslovakia," 1920s, 6" h. **$3,900**

Perfume bottle and stopper, pale yellow crystal molded as graduated overlapping flattened discs with the outer two ribbed, matching stopper with overlapping ribbed discs and ending in a dauber, unsigned, 1930s, 6" h. **$1,800-2,500**

Perfume bottle and stopper, Dubarry bottle by J. Viard and made by Depinoix, clear wide squatty round shape molded overall with a repeating wave design and multicolored patina, the upright figural frosted stopper with a kneeling nude, flea bites to stopper plug, ca. 1920s, 3 1/2" h. **$3,000-4,500**

Scent holder, Bessamin box or spice tower, silver, a tall tapering stem supporting a bulbous tower-form container set with colored stones and with a pierced band around the middle, conical cover with flag finial, Poland, 19th c., 7 1/4" h. **$1,500-2,000**

Perfume bottle and stopper, clear columnar glass bottle mounted on a flaring silver base cast with swags and floral designs, a silver collar and silver stopper cast as a sculpted bust of Bacchus, inner glass stopper, ca. 1840, 6" h. **$3,000-3,500**

Perfume bottle and stopper, flattened violin-shaped glass body in red, pink and white twisted filigrana decoration, cylindrical silver cap, Clichy factory, second half 19th c., 4 1/4" h. **$750-1,000**

Perfume bottle and stopper, flattened ovoid fancy silver-gilt body with a stippled background highlighted with delicate designs in enamels colored red, blue and white, matching ball-form cap, hallmarked, ca. 1880, 3" h. **$1,750-2,000**

Cologne bottle and stopper, Royal Flemish art glass, squatty bulbous body h.p. with flowers and butterflies, the neck and base of stopper in dark brown trimmed with heavy gold scrolls, Mt. Washington Glass Co., marked, ca. 1894, 5 3/4" h. **$6,500-8,000**

Cologne bottle and stopper, squatty bulbous cut glass, clear flashed in green and cut overall in the Marlborough patt., cut ball stopper, unsigned Dorflinger, ca. 1890-1910, 6 1/2" h. **$6,500-7,500**

Perfume bottle and stopper, clear bulbous cut glass in the Venetian patt. by Hawkes, set on a high scroll-decorated sterling silver base and with silver mounts by Gorham, ca. 1885-90, 7" h. **$1,200-1,500**

Perfume bottles and stoppers, green glass, two upright squared bottles with angled shoulders with gilt-metal neck band and flattened stoppers etched with a Cupid and Psyche scene, in a fitted filigree gilt-metal stand, one with dauber, marked in intaglio "Hoffman," 1920s, 6 1/2" h. **$1,500-3,000**

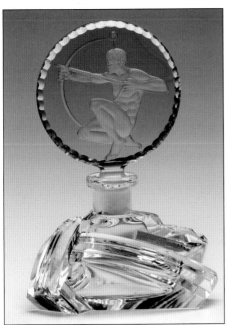

Perfume bottle and stopper, "Tula" by Dralle of Germany, designed by Hoffman of Czechoslovakia, a low clear crystal bottle with a heavily notched rockwork-like design, fitted with a large upright blue disc stopper etched with the figure of a kneeling nude male archer, with paper label, ca. 1930, 5 1/2" h. **$1,440**

Perfume bottle and stopper, "Sous la Charmille" by Brecher, a J. Viard bottle made by Depinoix, squatty bulbous clear glass tapering to a small neck and flattened blossom-form stopper, the sides enameled in shades of green and brown with leaves, ca. 1924, 2 3/4" h. **$2,520**

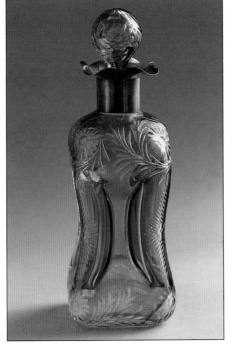

Perfume bottle and stopper, emerald green cut to clear upright bottle with pinched-in sides (also called the "Kettroff" or "glug-glug"), sterling silver collar and emerald cut to clear ball stopper, cut leafy vine design, by Stevens and Williams, silver hallmarked 1897-98, 7 1/4" h. **$2,500-3,000**

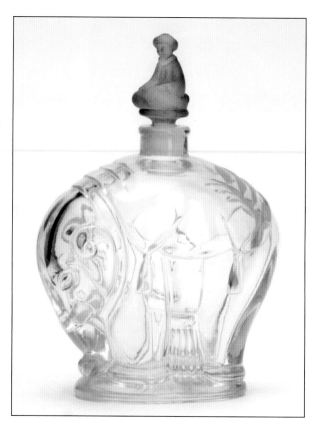

Perfume bottle and stopper, "Kismet" by Lubin, a Baccarat bottle in clear glass, figural design of an elephant with black draping down the sides, the frosted stopper in the shape of its rider, base stenciled "Baccarat," ca. 1921, 4 1/8" h. **$6,500-9,000**

Perfume bottle and stopper, footed ovoid clear glass bottle with a short neck and button stopper, enameled around the sides with dark blue and purple blossoms with slender green leaves and a butterfly to the side, signed by Gallé, ca. 1870-80, 3 3/4" h. **$1,750-2,000**

Scent bottle and stopper, Daum Nancy cameo glass, spherical white body tapering to a short neck with a clear stopper with faceted edges trimmed in gold, the body cameo-cut and enameled with a leafy vine of shaded red flowers and buds framing a black and white enameled scene of a road leading to a village, base signed with etched signature, very small old chip inside lip, small flake on corner of stopper, 3 1/4" h. **$2,185**

Perfume bottle and stopper, "Fleurs de Pommier" by Bouchon, Lalique frosted clear with blue patina, the ovoid body molded with bands of graduated arches, the high arched and pierced long stopper molded with a flowering tree, stopper engraved "R. Lalique - 939," matching number on the base, introduced in 1919, 5 1/2" h. **$10,755**

Perfume bottle and stopper, "Misti" by Piver, a Lalique clear and frosted glass container with a blue patina, squatty low round form molded overall with butterflies, blossom-form button stopper, molded "R. Lalique," ca. 1913, 2" h. **$3,000**

Perfume bottle and stopper, "Muguet," a Lalique perfume bottle in clear and frosted glass, a clear squatty bulbous bottle with a high arched frosted floral stopper, stenciled "R. Lalique," ca. 1931, 4" h. **$4,000-5,000**

Perfume bottle and stopper, deep purple Steuben glass with a tapering ovoid shape with molded columns down each corner forming side panels finely engraved with draping flower and leaf swags, pointed disc stopper, variant of No. 6604, factory signature and original paper label, ca. 1920s, 8 1/4" h. Too rare to price

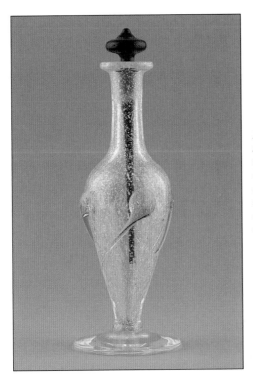

Perfume bottle and stopper, tall slender ovoid body with a very tall slender neck and pointed button stopper, colorless glass layers enclosing mica flecks, the sides applied with swirled Topaz drops, ruby stopper and dauber, Steuben Shape No. 6309, ca. 1920s, 6" h. **$2,500-3,000**

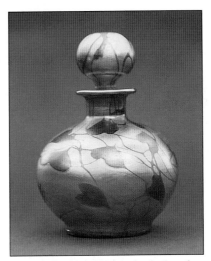

Scent bottle with cap, intaglio-carved paperweight glass, waisted cylindrical shape with deep carved scrolls surrounding large deep rose pink blossoms and green leaves, ovoid leaf and flower cast sterling silver cap opening to a glass stopper, by Tiffany Studios and Tiffany and Company, glass engraved "L.C.T. o786," ca. 1905, 5" h. **$19,120**

Perfume bottle and stopper, boule-shaped body with short flared neck and ball-shaped stopper, gold iridescent Tiffany Favrile glass with an overall green hearts and vines decoration, signed, ca. 1920s, 4 1/4" h. **$750-900**

Perfume bottle and stopper, "Diorling," clear Baccarat glass footed and ribbed ovoid bottle with a tall upright gilt-metal stopper composed of flowers on stems, signed and numbered by Baccarat, ca. 1956, 9" h. **$1,000**

Perfume bottle and stopper, "Le Roi Soliel," clear Baccarat glass round sharply tapering wave-molded bottle with a large flattened upright stopper representing the sun with the face composed of doves, designed to celebrate the liberation of France at the end of World War II, designed by Salvador Dali, missing gold metal shell-shaped case, bottle only, ca. 1945, 7" h. **$9,000-10,000**

Perfume bottle and stopper, "Fadette," a J. Viard design in clear and frosted glass, cylindrical with an overall molded floral swag design trimmed in sepia patina, figural stopper of nude lady, bottom molded "J. Viard," ca. 1924, 4" h. **$1,600-2,300**

Petroliana

Petroliana covers a broad array of gas station collectibles from signs to globes to pumps, and everything in between.

Items in this section have been organized by type of item (containers, displays, globes, signs, etc.) and have primarily been selected at the high end of the market. The focus is on the top price items, not to skew the values, but to emphasize the brands and types that are the most desirable. Some less valuable items have been included to help keep values in perspective.

As with all advertising items, factors such as brand name, intricacy of design, color, age, condition, and rarity drastically affect value.

Warning: Beware of reproduction and fantasy pieces. Virtually all categories of antiques are plagued by fakes and reproductions, and petroliana is no exception. For collectors of vintage gas and oil items, the only way to avoid reproductions is experience: Making mistakes and learning from them; talking with other collectors and dealers; finding reputable resources (including books and websites); and learning to invest wisely, buying the best examples one can afford.

Marks can be deceiving, paper labels and tags are often missing, and those that remain may be spurious. Adding to the confusion are "fantasy" pieces, globes that have to vintage counterpart, and that are often made more for visual impact than deception.

As the collector's eye sharpens, and the approach to inspecting and assessing petroliana improves, it will become easier to buy with confidence. And a knowledgeable collecting public should be the goal of all sellers, if for no other reason than the willingness to invest in quality.

For more information on petroliana, see *Warman's Gas Station Collectibles Identification and Price Guide* by Mark F. Moran.

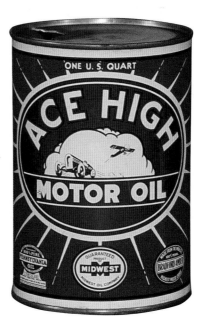

Containers

Petroliana containers are prized by many collectors. Unlike signs and globes, these were meant to be discarded after use, so they fall into the category of ephemera.

Ace High Motor Oil quart tin can, near mint. **$875+**

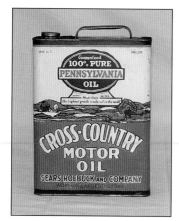

Cross-Country Motor Oil one-gallon flat tin can, sold by Sears, display side excellent, reverse poor, heavy wear.
$225+

D-X Marine Oil tin quart, fair to good condition, large dents, full.
$200+

Economy Motor Oil Wilshire Oil Co., tin quart, excellent condition-plus.
$275+

Frontier Lube Motor Oil quart tin can, excellent condition, light wear on reverse.
$250+

Mobiloil Gargoyle 1940 Close-Out three-gallon motor oil tin can, fair condition.
$150+

Navy Motor Oil 1/2-gallon tin can, good condition, no spout.
$120+

Pennzoil with airplane and owls quart tin can, near mint. **$100+**

Polarine Transmission Lubricant "B" five-pound tin can, green background, excellent condition. **$500+**

Richlube Motor Oil five-quart tin can, excellent condition, no top. **$100+**

Shell of California Motor Oil flat one-gallon embossed tin can, display side good condition, reverse very poor. **$100+**

Sinclair Pennsylvania Motor Oil (black dinosaur) tin quart can, fair to good condition, wear, no top. **$200+**

Standard Oil Co. Gas Engine Oil one-gallon tin can, good condition. **$225+**

Texaco "squatty" one-gallon motor oil tin can, good condition. **$675+**

Valvoline Motor Oil one-gallon tin can (early design), display side excellent condition, reverse fair to good. **$150+**

Zerolene Motor Oil one-quart tin, excellent condition, some wear around base. **$275+**

Globes

The globes that once decorated the tops of gasoline pumps are the holy grail for many petroliana collectors.

Early globes were a single piece of glass, often with etched or painted lettering. "Globe" is a misnomer, since none here is truly spherical, and a complete globe often has three main parts: two lenses and a body, though some came with a single lens.

The body can be made of metal, plastic, or fiberglass. A high-profile body has a standing seam around the circumference. A low-profile body has a flattened seam. A gill body has a rubber or metal gasket holding the lenses in place. A hull body accepts notched lenses, and is open where the lenses are mounted, as opposed to a glass body where the lenses rest on a low dome. Gill and hull bodies take their names from the manufacturers that created them, but as the petroliana field has grown, these names are often found with lowercase spellings.

Some collectors secure the lenses on the bodies using silicone caulk, a practice that many object to because this can contribute to paint loss and it makes the lenses difficult to examine off the bodies.

Ripple and jewel bodies are among the most desirable and hardest to find. Ripple glass bodies have an irregular textured surface, and come in clear, white, and in a range of colors. Jewel bodies have round faceted glass "jewels" set into the surface.

Globes can range in value from $50 for a common or damaged example to almost $20,000 for rarities in near-mint condition.

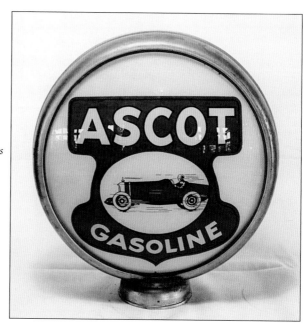

Ascot Gasoline globe with boat-tail racecar, 15" lenses in high-profile body, very good condition, very rare.
$17,000+

Ben Franklin Premium-Regular globe 13 1/2" lenses in a red ripple body with copper base. **$7,500+**

Chevron Supreme Gasoline globe 15" lenses in a high-profile fiberglass body, near mint. **$2,300+**

Crescent Gasoline globe 15" lenses in a high-profile metal body, very good condition. **$3,200+**

Flying A Kerosene globe 13 1/2" lenses in gill body, excellent condition. **$3,000+**

Hudson globe 13" lenses in red ripple body. **$3,750+**

Midland Wholesale globe 13 1/2" lenses in a white glass gill body. **$2,500+**

Mobil Kerosene globe 15" lenses in high-profile body, lenses very good condition, reverse has minor paint loss at edge. **$2,000+**

Phillips 66 globe 13 1/2" lenses, in a wide white glass body. **$900+**

Red Crown Gasoline (California) globe, 15" lenses in a high-profile metal body, near mint. **$1,700+**

Shell globe (East Coast), 15" single lens in high-profile body, lens fair condition with two small touchups on shell, paint loss on outer ring, body repainted. **$700+**

Sinclair Dino Supreme globe 13 1/2" lenses in Capco body, excellent condition. **$175+**

Skelly Fortified Gasoline globe (two stars), 13 1/2" lenses, in a wide white glass body. **$450+**

Spur Gas Gasoline globe 13 1/2" single lens in red ripple body, excellent condition. **$4,200+**

Standard Gasoline (California) globe, 15" lenses in a high-profile metal body, near mint. **$1,200+**

Texaco embossed one-piece glass globe, mint condition, probably new old stock, with copper screw base. **$1,900+**

Union 76 + Tetraethyl globe 15" single lens in high-profile body, good condition, chip at bottom of lens. **$2,300+**

Pumps

Pumps are not for everybody. They are big machines that—though relatively simple—can require significant maintenance if a collector desires to keep them in working order. That's why most serve as nonfunctioning accessories. Correct components and spare parts can be expensive, and proper restoration in manufacturer's colors can take months. As you will see here, pumps in untouched original condition are quite rare, and command some of the highest prices.

Some sellers, easily found on the Internet, stock reproduction parts for many gas pumps. Some also offer new-old-stock parts, used parts, and original-condition and restored pumps. Others carry globes, decals, signs, books, oil cans, road maps, and offer restoration, consultation, and appraisals.

Bennett 996 computing pump restored in Sinclair colors, with reproduction Dino globe, side door missing glass. **$1,000+**

Wayne 60 pump painted in Phillips 66 colors, with reproduction globe. **$2,250+**

Wayne 515F 10-gallon visible pump restored in Magnolia colors, with reproduction globe and curved pump plates. **$3,000+**

Signs

Signs are some of the most important and desired petroliana collectibles. Their color and design are eye appealing and create wonderful wall displays.

Porcelain and metal signs were intended to last for years, so they were made to endure. However, they are susceptible to scratches, chipping, rust, etc., which can dramatically lower their value. Signs in mint or near mint condition command premium prices.

Ace High Motor Oil late 1920s, single-sided tin, 20" x 13 1/2". **$2,500**

Chevron Gas Station neon sign, good condition, seven quarter-size chips touched up, original neon and can, 46" x 66". **$2,500+**

Esso double-sided porcelain metal-framed oval sign, very good condition, 26" x 38". **$650+**

Globe Gasoline double-sided tin sign, with original hangers, 42" diameter. **$2,500**

Havoline Motor Oil
single-sided porcelain
sign, near mint, dated
1941, 11" x 21 1/2".
$350+

Keynoil "A" for
Fords single-sided
tin sign, near
mint. **$1,500**

Mobiloil single-sided porcelain
framed sign, fair to good condition,
60" x 16". **$525+**

Skylark Aviation Grade Gasoline neon sign, with plane skywriting, replaced
neon and housing (or as collectors call it, the "can"), 42" x 66". **$8,000+**

Standard Gasoline 1940 Walt Disney Mickey Mouse sign, very good condition, light wear, 24" diameter. **$4,750+**

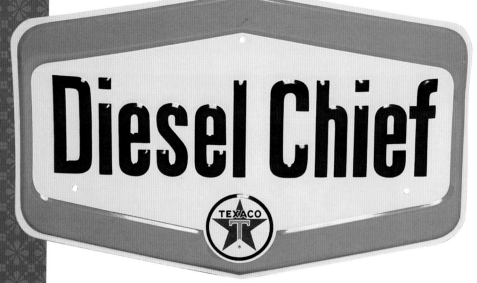

Texaco Diesel Chief single-sided tin embossed pump plate, near mint, 10" by 15". **$275+**

Washington Chief Gasoline double-sided porcelain sign with full Indian headdress profile, 72". **$20,900**

Richlube double-sided porcelain sign with racecar graphic. **$7,425**

United Motors Authorized Service double-sided porcelain die-cut sign. **$5,225**

Ford Benzol "For All Motor Cars" Authorized Distributor double-sided porcelain sign. **$4,400**

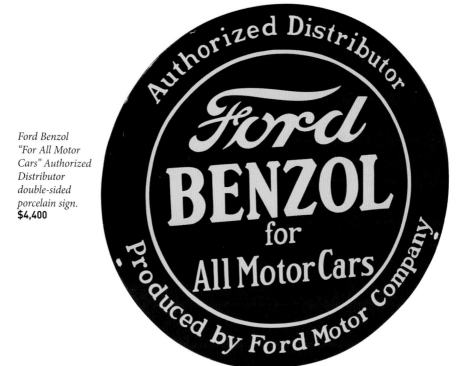

D-X 3-D identification porcelain sign, in excellent condition. **$3,300**

'Standard' (Standard Oil of New Jersey) Polarine Oil double-sided porcelain sign. **$3,190**

Mobo Auto Body Polish ("The Lustre Lasts") cardboard stand-up, circa 1925-1935. **$2,640**

The top lot of the sale was this Texaco Marine Lubricants single-sided porcelain sign. **$6,325**

Oilzum Motor Oil single-sided tin sign with logo, framed, 61" x 13". **$4,510**

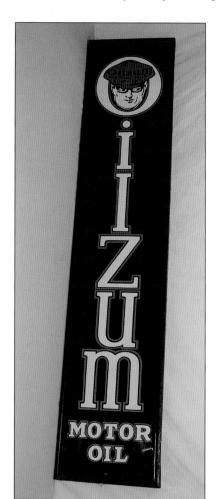

Photography

Modern photographic images date back to the 1820s with the development of chemical photography. The first permanent photograph was an image produced in 1826 by the French inventor Nicéphore Niépce. However, the picture took eight hours to expose, so he went about trying to find a new process. Working in conjunction with Louis Daguerre, they experimented with silver compounds based on a Johann Heinrich Schultz discovery in 1724 that a silver and chalk mixture darkens when exposed to light. Niépce died in 1833, but Daguerre continued the work, eventually culminating with the development of the daguerreotype in 1837.

Many advances in photographic glass plates and printing were made all through the 19th century. In 1884, American George Eastman developed the technology to replace photographic plates, leading to the technology used by film cameras today.

Eastman patented a photographic medium that used a photo-emulsion coated on paper rolls. The invention of roll film greatly sped up the process of recording multiple images.

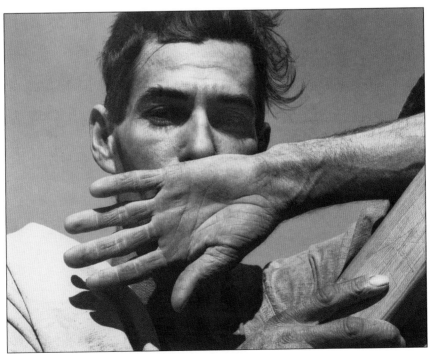

Rago Arts and Auction Center

Dorothea Lange (American, 1895-1965) Migratory Cotton Picker, Eloy, Arizona, 1940; gelatin silver print (printed later); 13" x 16" (sheet). **$9,000**

Indian soldier and wife   # 7

O.S. Goff, albumen photograph of a Crow soldier and his wife, mounted on cream card stock; titled on mount in script, "Indian soldier and wife"; portrait shows a Crow man dressed as a sergeant of the 1st U.S. Calvary; his wife, wearing a gingham dress and beaded hide moccasins, stands besides him. Lacks Goff's imprint, but taken at Fort Custer, Mont., post 1885, 9" x 7 1/4". **$1,265**

Cowan's Auctions

Tintype, quarter plate, Making Medicine, Cheyenne ledger artist, housed in a pressed paper and wood case. Making Medicine is seated wearing a military jacket with tinted gold buttons, cut hair, and he leans with his arm on a table; likely taken during his imprisonment at Fort Marion, Fla. (1875-78). **$2,300**

Cowan's Auctions

Cowan's Auctions

F.J. Haynes, President Chester A. Arthur's 1883 trip to Yellowstone, albumen image mounted on larger board. Arthur sits in the center of the scene surrounded by standing Michael V. Sheridan, Anson Stager, W.P. Clark, Dan G. Rollins and James F. Gregory; seated John S. Crosby, Phillip H. Sheridan, Arthur, Robert Lincoln, and George G. Vest, 9 1/2" x 6 1/4". **$1,035**

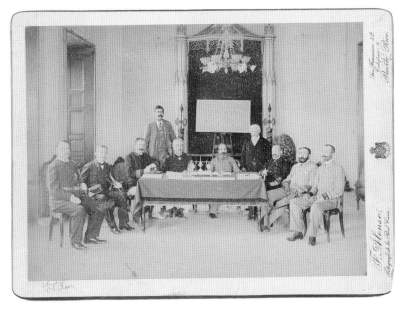

Spain signing Puerto Rico over to the United States, shows interior of what is likely the Spanish governor's palace, with five representatives of Spain/Puerto Rico on the right and five Americans on the left of a table on which is scattered treaty documents and elaborate ink stand. Seated at the table for the Americans are Gen. Nelson Miles and Rear Adm. Winfield Schley. The transfer ceremony took place Oct. 18, 1898. Imprint of F. Alonso, on 11 3/4" x 15 1/2" heavy card stock mount. **$632**

Cowan's Auctions

Wolf von dem Bussche
(German, b. 1934) Totem: The
Papago Legend of the Creation
of the Giant Cactus, Called
Saguardo, 1993; Portfolio of 12
gelatin silver prints; each signed,
dated, titled and numbered
6/44; 22" x 17 7/8" (sheet) each;
publisher: Three Plowshares,
1993. **$4,800 all**

Rago Arts and Auction Center

Rago Arts and Auction Center

August Sander (German, 1876-1964) Pastry
Cook, 1928; oversized gelatin silver print
(printed circa 1980 by Gunther Sander); with
"Aug. Sander, Lindenthal, Koln" blindstamp;
16 1/2" x 12" (sheet). **$9,000**

Rago Arts and Auction Center

F.S. Lincoln (1894-1976) Upshot of Stairway, Paris
Apartment House, Architect: Mallet-Stevens, circa 1930;
gelatin silver print (printed circa 1930); signed and titled
with studio stamp; 13 1/4" x 10 3/8" (sheet). **$3,360**

Political Items

Initially, American political campaign souvenirs were created to celebrate victories. There is a wide variety of campaign items—buttons, bandanas, tokens, pins, etc. The only limiting factor has been the promoter's imagination. The advent of television campaigning has reduced the quantity of individual items, and modern campaigns do not seem to have the variety of materials that were issued earlier.

For more information, consult *Warman's Political Collectibles* by Dr. Enoch L. Nappen, 2008.

"I Like IKE" soda can with image of an elephant holding a pro-Dwight D. Eisenhower flag, circa 1952-'56, 2 5/8" d, 4 3/4" h. **$25-$35**

John Kennedy mug, 3 1/8" h, 2 1/2" d, base, circa 1960-'63. **$20-$25**

Two campaign bottles: green Hubert Humphrey-Edmund Muskie bottle, and an amber Richard Nixon-Spiro Agnew piece, "Wheaton Glass Co.," circa 1968, 7" h, 2 1/2" x 6" at base. **$15-$25 each**

"Big stick" (an apparent reference to Theodore Roosevelt's expression "walk softly but carry a big stick") glass bottle in the shape and style of a club, and with "Patented March 19, 1907" on the bottom, 6 7/8" h, 1 1/2" d. **$35-$50**

Franklin Roosevelt matchbook welcoming the Chicago Democratic National Convention, circa 1940. **$15-$20**

"Teddy B" metal matchbox with embossed image of a bear holding a club and a Rough Rider hat. The reverse touts the "Congress Hotel," circa 1904-'08, 3/8" x 1 1/2", 2 3/4" h. **$100-$125**

Liquor bottle celebrates the 1953 Inauguration of Dwight D. Eisenhower and Richard Nixon, 11 1/2" h, 3" d. **$35-$50**

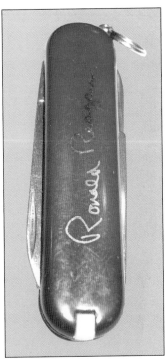

A spoon with William McKinley's image in the bowl, "Good Luck" on the front of the handle, and the reverse reading "Protection and Prosperity," circa 1896-1900; spoon with raised image of Charles Evan Hughes on handle, an eagle and "Hughes" down the handle, "Rodgers," circa 1916; similarly designed spoon, but with raised image of Woodrow Wilson and "Wilson" down the handle, "W R," circa 1916; and "Billy Possum" butter knife with raised image of a possum on the handle, circa 1908-'12. Billy Possum represented Taft. **$20-$25 each**

Penknife given as a gift by Ronald Reagan with signature across the front, "Victorinox," circa 1987-88, 3 7/8" long open. **$35-$50**

Knife sharpener with one edge reading "McKinley * Roosevelt," and the other side touting the virtues of being "Brave, Kind, Able, Honest," circa 1900, 1 5/8" x 3 3/8", 3/8" h. **$40-$60**

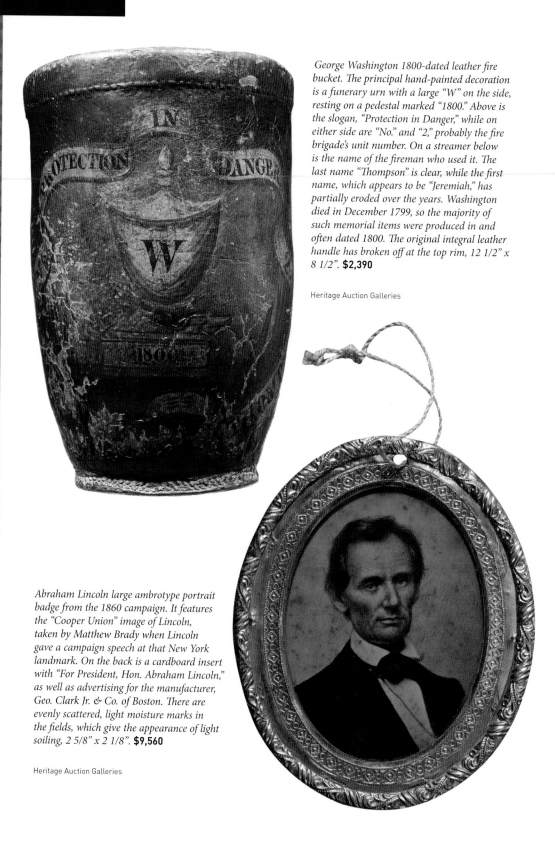

George Washington 1800-dated leather fire bucket. The principal hand-painted decoration is a funerary urn with a large "W" on the side, resting on a pedestal marked "1800." Above is the slogan, "Protection in Danger," while on either side are "No." and "2," probably the fire brigade's unit number. On a streamer below is the name of the fireman who used it. The last name "Thompson" is clear, while the first name, which appears to be "Jeremiah," has partially eroded over the years. Washington died in December 1799, so the majority of such memorial items were produced in and often dated 1800. The original integral leather handle has broken off at the top rim, 12 1/2" x 8 1/2". **$2,390**

Heritage Auction Galleries

Abraham Lincoln large ambrotype portrait badge from the 1860 campaign. It features the "Cooper Union" image of Lincoln, taken by Matthew Brady when Lincoln gave a campaign speech at that New York landmark. On the back is a cardboard insert with "For President, Hon. Abraham Lincoln," as well as advertising for the manufacturer, Geo. Clark Jr. & Co. of Boston. There are evenly scattered, light moisture marks in the fields, which give the appearance of light soiling, 2 5/8" x 2 1/8". **$9,560**

Heritage Auction Galleries

Posters

The advancement of printing techniques in the 18th century —including lithography, which was invented in 1796 by the German Alois Senefelder— allowed for cheap mass production and printing of posters. The invention of lithography was soon followed by chromolithography, which allowed for mass editions of posters illustrated in vibrant colors.

By the 1890s, chromolithography had spread throughout Europe. A number of noted artists created poster art in this period, foremost amongst them Henri de Toulouse-Lautrec and Jules Chéret. Chéret is considered to be the "father" of advertisement placards. He was a pencil artist and a scene decorator, who founded a small lithography office in Paris in 1866. He used striking characters, contrast and bright colors, and created more than 1,000 advertisements, primarily for exhibitions, theatres and products. The industry soon attracted the service of many aspiring painters who needed a source of revenue to support themselves.

Job, 1894, by Georges Meunier, Chaix, Paris, minor repaired tears at edges. Two sheets. Meunier's design in this poster is one of the best utilizing the elongated format that was current in Paris in the mid-1890s, 95" x 34 1/4". **$8,000**

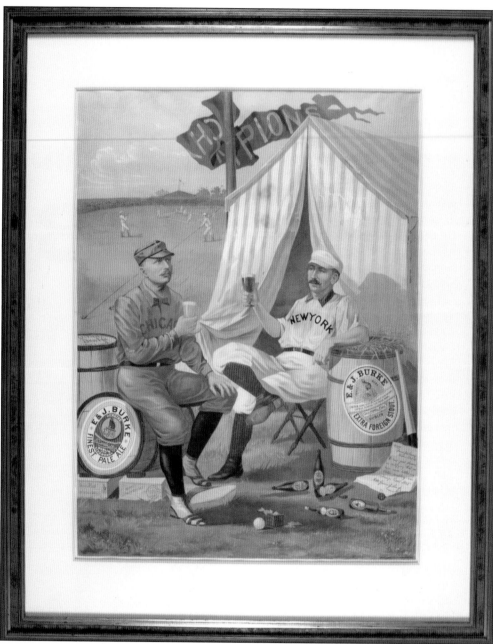

Robert Edward Auctions

Burke Ale, lithograph, featuring Cap Anson and Buck Ewing, 1889, represents the first documented paid endorsement of a product of any kind by baseball players. It is also certainly the first advertising piece featuring players in promotion of an alcoholic beverage, which is ironic, in that the use of alcohol at games in the 1880s and 1890s was such a serious problem that there was concern for the future success of the game as a pastime suitable for attendance by the entire family. The Anson-Ewing Beer poster is exceedingly rare. Only three examples are known. All of the colors are bold, flawless and vibrant; and the poster exhibits none of the tears, creases or stains so common to similar displays of this vintage. The poster (18" x 24") has been professionally cleaned for preservation purposes (no restoration) and has been mounted and framed to total dimensions of 26" x 32". **$188,000**

Swann Auction Galleries

Trinkt Zürcher Löwenbrau!, 1927, by Otto Baumberger, J. C. Muller, Zurich, repaired tear through top margin, affecting image; creases in margins. Japan, 50" x 35 1/4". **$1,300**

Sandor (Alexander Raymond Katz, 1895-1974), Chicago World's Fair, 1934, 39 1/2" x 26 1/4", Goes Litho, minor restoration at edges; expertly repaired, unobtrusive tears in margins. The Chicago World's Fair marked the first time that neon lights were used extensively, and this poster reflects the novelty, energy and brightness of the many displays. Born in Hungary, Katz was a prominent Jewish artist who worked extensively on WPA projects including murals, illustrations and stained glass. **$2,800**

Swann Auction Galleries

Swann Auction Galleries

Cunard Line, circa 1935, by Francis Bernard (1900-1979), Paul Martial, repaired tears and creases in margins and image; pinholes in corners. Bernard's contribution to the world of French graphic design was considerable. In addition to the posters he designed, he was art director of the Paul Martial studio and in charge of advertising for the Arts Menagers exhibitions as well as for the Office Technique pour l'Utilisation de l'Acier. After World War II he became the director of communication for the French State Radio and Television. During the 1930s he was a member of the Union des Artistes Moderne. During the 1930s, Bernard was the only artist within the impressive group to use photomontage. The Cunard Line was one of the largest and most prestigious companies running ships between Europe and the United States. This exceedingly rare poster combines an impeccable stylization of an ocean liner, with a sophisticated airbrush background of white smoke, a globe, with the Americas outlined in white, and a photomontage of a man waving the vessel off. A daring and modernist image, it qualifies as one of the best travel posters of the 1930s, 39 1/4" x 24 3/4". **$24,000**

Unknown designer, Chrysler, 1938, 49 1/2" x 38", minor restoration and creases along vertical and horizontal folds. Depiction of a Chrysler Imperial against a radiant cityscape. It is unusual that such a bright image, infused with pre-war optimism for such a prominent American company, should be unrecorded. **$4,200**

Sun Valley/Chicago and North Western Line, 1940, by Dwight Shepler, Midwest Offset, Chicago, restored loss in upper right corner; repaired tear through margins; abrasions in image. While the Union Pacific ran trains into Sun Valley, the Chicago and North Western Line took passengers from Chicago to Omaha, where they then boarded Union Pacific trains. An extremely rare variant of this famous poster. No other copies bearing the imprint of the Chicago and North Western Line have ever surfaced, 39 3/4" x 25". **$4,800**

Phil Von Phul (dates unknown), Stamp Out the Axis, circa 1941, 14" x 11", minor creasing in corners; light staining in image. Silk-screen on board. Between the time the United States entered World War II and 1943, when the WPA was terminated, many of the WPA artists turned their hands towards propaganda, producing some vivid and effective images. An impressive but little-known series of images emerged from the 13th Naval District in Seattle. Each of the images in this series is numbered (here it is 33), indicating that many more of these were produced than seem to have survived. Previously unrecorded. Not in the Library of Congress. **$1,500**

Swann Auction Galleries

Mobil Oil, 1952, by Blaise Bron (1918-?), horizontal folds, creases and abrasions in image. It is impossible to look at this image without seeing a resemblance to Roy Lichtenstein's early graphic work. However, this poster precedes Lichtenstein's first Pop Art creations by nearly 10 years. The influence of "hyper-real" Swiss posters from the late 1930s until 1960 on many Pop artists is a given, but no poster relates so closely to specific Pop Art as this one for the design-conscious Mobil Corp. Little biographical information exists on this artist. Another poster of his for Mobiloil appears in the 1952 International Poster Annual. Also in the late 1960s and early 1970s, he designed a few posters for fairs around Switzerland. This poster is a proto-Pop masterpiece that stands as an exceptional vanguard to the Pop movement of the 1960s, 50 1/8" x 35 1/2". **$28,800**

Movie Posters, Lobby Cards and Stills

Fighting Death (Box Office Attractions, 1914). One Sheet (27" x 41"). In the early years of the 20th century, professional daredevils were all the rage. It wasn't long before Hollywood noticed these daring young men, and signed the best of them to lucrative film contracts. One of the very best was Rodman "Daredevil" Law, a pioneering parachute performer. Law made four films between 1912 and 1914, with this marking his last silver screen appearance. The stone litho poster has missing paper along all four borders, fold wear with cross-fold separation, tears in the image area, and a tear on the right side. Professional restoration on linen. **$836**

Heritage Auction Galleries

Swann Auction Galleries

Attributed to Josef Fenneker (1895-1956), The Dance of Death, 1919, 54 1/2" x 41", restoration along vertical and horizontal folds; minor restoration in margins. Fenneker designed more than 300 movie posters. His recognizable style drew largely on German Expressionism combined with a flair for aesthetic decadence. Written by Fritz Lang, "Totentanz" is considered by the Internet Movie Database to be a "lost film (in which) a beautiful dancer's sexual allure is used by an evil cripple to entice men to their deaths. Falling in love with one of the potential victims, she is told by the cripple that he will set her free if her lover, actually a murderer himself, survives and escapes a bizarre labyrinth which runs beneath the cripple's house" (www.imdb.com). Even without a signature, this poster is clearly the work of Fenneker. Although another image by Fenneker for this film exists, this particular version is previously unrecorded. **$4,400**

Oswald the Rabbit cartoon, 1927, for Disney's fourth cartoon featuring this character, 27" x 41". **$23,000**

Hake's Americana & Collectibles

The Lady Vanishes (Gaumont, 1938). Insert (14" x 36"). British travelers Margaret Lockwood and Michael Redgrave unwittingly become entangled in espionage, kidnapping, and murder after Miss Froy (Dame May Whitty) disappears. Insert has been restored to address two corner chips, small tears in the bottom border, and fold and edge wear. There was a chip, a tape lift and a tear in the left border. There are smudges in the center, and two creases that occurred after the restoration; on linen. **$4,780**

Heritage Auction Galleries

Gunga Din (RKO, 1939). Insert (14" x 36"). The insert has been professionally restored to address fold wear with small paper losses at the center fold, a tear in the top left border and a tear at the bottom border. There were also two small chips in the top right corner and one in the top left corner. Mounted on paper. **$597**

Heritage Auction Galleries

Heritage Auction Galleries

Citizen Kane (RKO, 1941). One sheet (27" x 41") Style B. Starring Orson Welles. Unrestored poster, with brilliant colors and white paper. **$57,500**

Heritage Auction Galleries

The African Queen (United Artists, 1952). Stills (2) (8" x 10"). Adventure. Starring Humphrey Bogart and Katharine Hepburn. Directed by John Huston. Two unrestored stills with bright color. **$155**

Heritage Auction Galleries

Gone with the Wind (MGM, R-1954). Lobby card set of 8 (11" x 14"). Academy Award Winner. Starring Clark Gable and Vivien Leigh. Directed by Victor Fleming. An unrestored lobby set with bright color. **$388**

Journey to the Center of the Earth (20th Century Fox, 1959). One sheet (27" x 41"). Science Fiction. Starring Pat Boone and James Mason. Directed by Henry Levin. An unrestored poster with bright color. Folded. **$191**

Heritage Auction Galleries

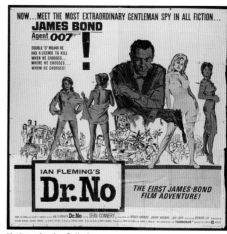

Heritage Auction Galleries

Dr. No (United Artists, 1962). Six sheet (81" x 81"). James Bond. Starring Sean Connery and Ursula Andress. Unrestored poster that displays signs of average wear and use. Folded. **$1,434**

Heritage Auction Galleries

The Man Who Shot Liberty Valance (Paramount, 1962). One sheet (27" x 41"). Western. Starring James Stewart, John Wayne, Vera Miles, Lee Marvin and Woody Strode. Directed by John Ford. An un-restored poster with bright color. Folded. **$358**

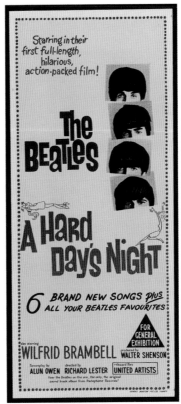

Heritage Auction Galleries

A Hard Day's Night (United Artists, 1964). Australian Day Bill (13" x 30"). Rock and Roll. Starring John Lennon, Paul McCartney, George Harrison and Ringo Starr. Directed by Richard Lester. Lightly used, unrestored poster with fresh, saturated colors. Folded, near mint. **$836**

Heritage Auction Galleries

Magnum Force (Warner Brothers, 1973). Promotional poster (20" x 28"). Warner Brothers followed up the success of Dirty Harry (1971) with this action-packed sequel, for which they released this rare portrait poster. This particular copy has some slight edge wear. Rolled, near mint. **$310**

Heritage Auction Galleries

The Empire Strikes Back (20th Century Fox, 1980). One sheet (27" x 41") Advance. Science fiction. Starring Mark Hamill, Harrison Ford and Carrie Fisher. Directed by Irvin Kershner. A restored poster with bright color. Rolled, on linen. **$505**

Ex-Lady (Warner Brothers, 1933). One sheet (27" x 41"). Before the advent of the Hollywood Production Code in 1934, the industry was turning out films dealing with adultery, incest, and pre-marital sex, and the audiences loved it! In this charming pre-Code comedy, Bette Davis plays a free-spirited, self-sufficient feminist who would rather have a career as a graphic artist then get married to lover Gene Raymond. After they do get married, they wind up having affairs with other people. This amazingly beautiful poster features one of the best poster designs of the 1930s, and is absolutely one of the greatest images of the young Davis, in her slinky pre-Code gown. **$19,120**

Records

With the advent of the more sophisticated recording materials, earlier phonograph records became collectors' items. Condition is critical. As with many types of collectibles, a grading scale has been developed.

Mint (M): Perfect condition, no flaws, scratches or scuffs in the grooves. The cardboard jacket will be crisp.

Near Mint (NM) or Mint-Minus (M-): The record will be close to perfect, with no marks in the grooves. The label will be clean, not marked, or scuffed. There will be no ring wear on the record or album cover.

Very Good Plus (VG+): Used for a record that has been played, but well taken care of. Slight scuffle or warps to the grooves is acceptable as long as it does not affect the sound. A faint ring wear discoloration is acceptable. The jacket may appear slightly worn, especially on the edges.

Very Good (VG): Used to describe a record that has some pronounced defects, as does the cover. The record will still play well. This usually is the lowest grade acceptable to a serious collector. Most records listed in price guides are of this grade.

Good (G): This category of record will be playable, but probably will have loss to the sound quality. The cover might be marked or torn.

Poor or Fair (P, F): Record is damaged, may be difficult to play. The cover will be damaged, usually marked, dirty or torn.

Note: Most records, especially popular recordings, have a value of less than $3. Picture sleeves will generally increase values, and often have an independent value.

Apple Records' promotional package, "Our First Four," 1968. This slick promotional kit was put together to be distributed to the movers and shakers of the recording industry. It included copies of the first four 45 singles by the new company: The Beatles' "Hey Jude"/"Revolution" (Apple 5722); Mary Hopkin's "Those Were the Days"/"Turn Turn Turn" (Apple 2); Jackie Lomax's "Sour Milk Tea"/"The Eagle Laughs at You" (Apple 3); and Black Dyke Mills Band's "Thingumybob"/"Yellow Submarine" (Apple 4), produced by Paul McCartney. Each 45 came in a mini-portfolio, with artist liner notes on the front, the record in a plastic sleeve on the first inside page, and a photo of the artist on the other inside page. Although the records have never been played, they are foggy after having been in their plastic sleeves for so long, and grade about VG 5. The mini-portfolios are Near Mint; the cardboard Our First Four box grades Very Good, with some wear along the edges and a repaired tear at the back tab where the box opens. **$8,365**

All photos courtesy Heritage Auction Galleries

Elvis Presley's personally owned "Loving You" rare acetate group (1957). Most of the acetates here contain alternate versions. Included: a two-sided, 10", 78 RPM acetate of "Mean Woman Blues"/"Lonesome Cowboy" (Radio Recorders 10212); a one-sided, 12", 78 RPM acetate of "Let's Have A Party" (Radio Recorders 10212, take A1X-11 and solo A-7); and a one-sided, 12", 33 1/3 RPM acetate of "Mean Woman Blues" that plays from the inside out. Both Radio Recorders discs display the original working name for "Loving You," which was "Something for the Girls!" Also included is a two-sided, 12" 33 1/3 RPM acetate with versions of several tunes that comprised the "Loving You" LP, including on Side 1: "Party" (A-2), "Party" (A1X-11), "Mean Woman Blues" (BX-7), "Lonesome Cowboy" (C-20), "Got a Lot O' Livin' To Do," and "Detour" (instrumental); and on Side 2: "Teddy Bear," "Cottontail" (instrumental), "Loving You" (farm version), "Loving You" (main title version), "Hot Dog" (Q-17), and "Got a Lot O' Livin' To Do" (R-13). Also included: a one-sided, 10" acetate of "Hot Dog" that's pretty hot, but it's not performed by Elvis. It's on a Recording United Laboratories label, with "Hill and Range" listed just below the title. Items come in a vintage hard carrying case. Certificate of authenticity from the estate of Elvis Presley at Graceland. **$9,560**

Elvis Presley and Jaye P. Morgan promotional double EP sampler (RCA 992/993, 1956). One of the rarest Elvis promotional items, this EP package was made to persuade retail stores to get into the record business. Presley and lounge singer Jaye P. Moran were paired in order to emphasize that Elvis' EP had sold 1,000 times better than Jaye P.'s had, and that record and phonograph player sales were on the rise — a not-so-subtle campaign to encourage retailers to place bigger orders with red-hot RCA. The cover is a double-gatefold pocket sleeve, with Presley printed on the front and Morgan on the back. Promotional info appears on the inside. **$9,560**

Tony Sheridan and The Beatles (billed as The Beat Brothers), "My Bonnie"/"The Saints" rare promo pink label 45 (Decca 31382, 1962). Before The Fab Four's worldwide breakthrough in 1964, the Fab Four (of whom George Harrison was still a teen) backed Tony Sheridan on these recordings. Condition: MT 9. Letter of authentication and grade certification by Perry Cox. **$8,962**

Beatles "Yesterday and Today" Butcher Cover sealed First State mono LP (Capitol T2553, 1966). To many, the original cover of the Beatles' U.S. release "Yesterday and Today," is the holy grail of Beatles collectibles. The rarity was pulled from record store shelves in the U.S. almost immediately after the album's release in 1966, ordered to be destroyed, replaced by the more subdued "Trunk Cover" version. **$26,290**

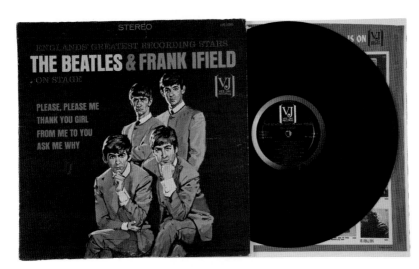

The Beatles, "The Beatles and Frank Ifield On Stage," rare stereo LP (Vee-Jay 1085, 1964). Vee-Jay Records was attempting to make the most out of its Beatles archives by repackaging The Fab Four's tunes, including this unlikely pairing of the group's Vee-Jay recordings with those of British Pop singer Frank Ifield. This album was released with two different cover variations, and this is the rarer one. **$5,975**

Elvis Presley, Sun Records group of five 78 RPM records (1954-55). These historic Elvis Sun singles are all in 78 rpm format. They are: "That's All Right"/"Blue Moon of Kentucky" (Sun 209, 1954) in GD-VG 4; "Good Rockin' Tonight"/"I Don't Care If the Sun Don't Shine" (Sun 210, 1954) in VG 5; "Milkcow Blues Boogie"/"You're a Heartbreaker" (Sun 215, 1955) in VG-EX 6; "I'm Left, You're Right, She's Gone"/"Baby Let's Play House" (Sun 217, 1955) in VG-EX 6; and "Mystery Train"/"I Forgot to Remember To Forget" (Sun 223, 1955) in VG 5. **$2,629**

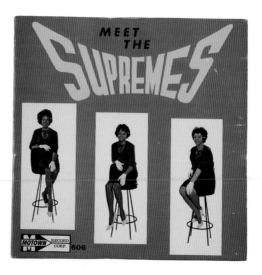

The Supremes, "Meet the Supremes," mono LP (Motown 606, 1963). The teenage trio was still relatively obscure to most of the country outside of Detroit, and the group's two singles released in 1962 barely cracked Billboard's Hot 100. "Where Did Our Love Go" was still months away when this first album was released in 1963. Condition: EX 7/VG 5. **$298**

Fats Domino, group of six LPs (Imperial, 1956-64). This inductee of The Rock and Roll Hall of Fame's first class is represented by a maroon label version of "Rock and Rollin' With Fats Domino" (Imperial 9004, 1956) in EX 7/EX 7; "This Is Fats Domino!" (Imperial 9028, 1957) in NM 8/MT 9; "Fats Domino Swings" (Imperial 9062, 1959) in EX 7/MT 9; "Let the Four Winds Blow" (Imperial 9153, 1961) in NM 8/MT 9; "What A Party!" (Imperial 9164, 1961) in EX 7/MT 9; and "Fats On Fire" (ABC-Paramount 479 white label promo, 1964) in EX 7/NM 8. **$131**

Billie Holiday, early acetates (Audiodisc, 1936-38). This five-acetate collection includes some of Lady Day's earliest hits on the Brunswick label from the mid- to late-1930s: "It's Like Reaching For the Moon"/"Guess Who," "Nice Work If You Can Get It"/"Things Are Looking Up," "My Last Affair"/"You Showed My the Way," "I'll Never Be the Same"/"I Found a New Baby," and "You're Too Lovely to Last"/"Why Do I Always Depend On You." The recordings play from the inside out. **$418**

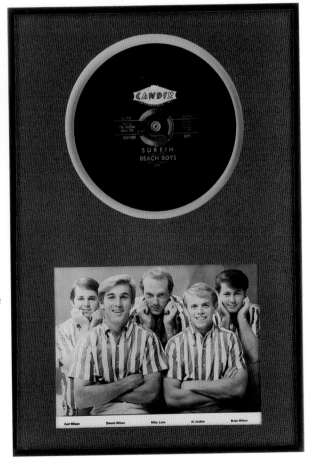

Danny & The Juniors, "At the Hop," record and signature display (ABC Paramount 9871, 1957). The single was one of the great early rock 'n' roll hits: "At the Hop" commanded the No. 1 spot on Billboard's Top 100 for seven weeks in early 1958, holding off other singles by the likes of Elvis Presley, Buddy Holly, Ricky Nelson and Fats Domino. The 14 1/2" x 32 1/2" framed display has a NM 8 copy of the single, signatures of group members Danny Rapp, David White and Joe Terranova from the backs of endorsed checks for a Alan Freed appearance, and sheet music for the hit. **$310**

The Beach Boys, "Surfin'," rare promo 45 display (Candix 301, 1961). Before The Beach Boys signed with Capitol Records in 1962, the group had a minor hit with "Surfin'," first released on the "X" label (X-301), then on the Candix label in 1961 (first as Candix 301, then as Candix 331, the most common pressing). The first Candix pressing (301) is much rarer than the second, and promo copies are even rarer. The promo copy of "Surfin" on Candix 301 offered here has been framed (12.25" x 18.25") with a black and white 8 1/2" x 6 1/2" publicity photo of the group from the mid-1960s. The disc appears about EX 7. **$358**

Silver

Silver has been known since ancient times and has long been valued as a precious metal, used to make ornaments, jewelry, tableware and utensils, and coins.

Pure silver is too soft to be fashioned into strong, durable, and serviceable utensils. Therefore, a way was found to give silver the required degree of hardness by adding alloys of copper and nickel. Silversmithing in America goes back to the early 17th century in Boston and New York and the early 18th century in Philadelphia. Boston artisans were influenced by the English styles; New Yorkers by the Dutch.

Some of the following photographs are from *Warman's Sterling Silver Flatware, 2nd Edition,* by Phil Dreis, unless otherwise noted.

Skinner Inc.

Creamer, silver repousse, Andrew Ellicott Warner, 1786-1870, Baltimore, the sides chased and embossed with chinoiserie motifs including pagodas, boat scenes and dense scrolled foliage, a shield-shaped cartouche below spout, angled ribbed handle with grape cluster terminals, marked "A.E.WARNER" in serrated rectangle, and 11 and an underlined 8, 5 3/4" h, approx. 13 troy oz. **$2,251**

Skinner Inc.

Tea service, three pieces, coin silver, Peter Chitry, New York, early 19th century, comprising a teapot, covered sugar bowl and creamer, oval lobed bodies with fruit-form finials, shaped serpent spout, an anthemion leaf and grapevine borders on stepped oval bases, marked "P. Chitry" on bases, 7 1/4" to 9 1/2" h, approx. 55 troy oz.; together with a later plated, similarly formed, unmarked teapot and a plated rectangular tray with engraved scrolled floral and foliate design marked "Wm. Rogers 4090," teapot 9 3/4", tray 14" x 22 1/2", handles are hollow, the bases all have several small dents around them, wear to the plated pieces, the tray has surface wear. **$1,896 all**

Porringer, American, probably Massachusetts, second quarter 18th century, round bowl with domed center, pierced keyhole-pattern handle with "A+B to D+A & M+W" engraved on the back of handle (an inscription on a tag attached to the handle reads: "Andrew Bowditch of Salem Mass. to Daniel Appleton and Mary Williams Boston"), 1 1/2" h, 4 1/4" d, 6 3/4" l, approx. 4 troy oz., several soft dents to bulbous area of bowl, rim a little out of round. **$651**

Skinner Inc.

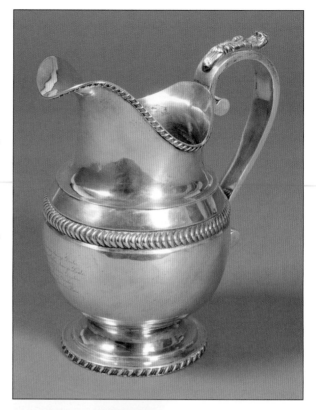

Pitcher, classical, coin silver, presentation, John B. Jones, Boston, 1782-1854, the circa-1830 pitcher with double scroll cast handle, rectangular in section with applied leaf on top, bands of gadrooning on rim, middle and base, marked "J.B. Jones" on base, the side engraved with the names of five generations of males by the name of Dexter residing in or around Boston, 9 3/4" h, approx. 31 troy oz., subtle dents and several pinhead size pits on bulbous area. **$1,185**

Skinner Inc.

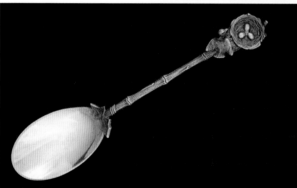

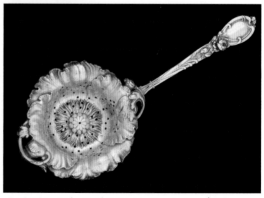

Bird's Nest by Gorham, ice cream spoon, 5 7/8". **$1,295**

Fuchsia by Whiting, sugar sifter, 8 1/4". **$1,295**

La Parisienne by Reed & Barton, tea strainer. **$495**

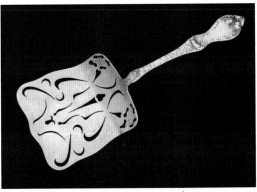

Les Cinq Fleurs by Reed & Barton, pierced asparagus server. **$495**

Cattails by Durgin, sauce ladle, 5 1/2". **$695**

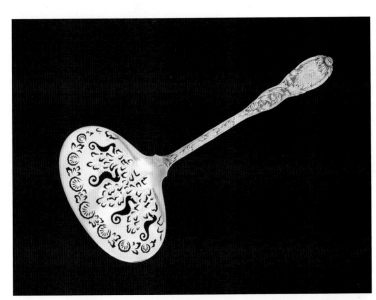

Chrysanthemum by Tiffany & Co., fish server, pierced with seahorses, French style. **$17,500**

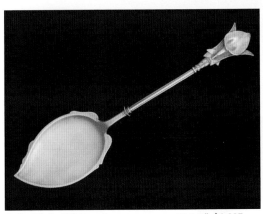

Calla Lily by Whiting, ice cream server, 10 1/2". **$1,295**

Lily by Whiting, cucumber server. **$495**

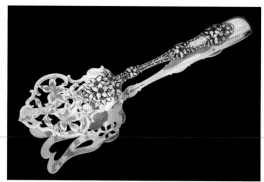

Old Orange Blossom by Alvin, asparagus tongs, 9 1/2".
$4,950

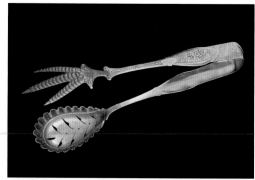

Montezuma by George W. Shiebler & Co., ice tongs, 9 1/2". **$695**

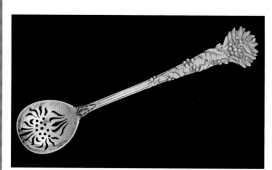

Holly by Tiffany & Co., pierced olive spoon. **$650**

Lady's by Gorham, sauce ladle with bucket bowl, 6 1/2".
$795

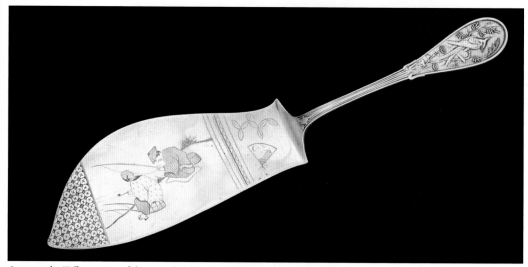

Japanese by Tiffany & Co., fish server, bright cut with fishermen, 12". **$6,900**

Space Collectibles
A Star is Born

— Noah Fleisher, Heritage Auction Galleries

Human conquest of the cosmos has the ability to inspire humans like little else and, in the brief time we've been slipping these surly bonds, we've done remarkably well, all things considered. In the cosmic sense this span but a blink of blink. We've walked on the moon, sent craft to mars to explore the surface, sent satellites hurtling headlong into the unknown of the Milky Way beyond our system and we've taken pictures of the beginning of time. These are but baby steps for which future generations will be grateful because they will enjoy the fruits of this early labor.

Noah Fleisher

Little wonder then that the pieces, parts, ephemera and personal memorabilia associated with America's space program – the men and women who, in large part, made science fiction a reality – have made collectors of all sorts sit up and take notice.

"The supply of the really important items is certainly finite," said Howard Weinberger, Senior Space Consultant for Heritage Auction Galleries in Dallas, and CEO of Asset Alternatives. "The old saying is that if you collected all the personal items from the six missions that landed on the moon, all of it would fit in a small suitcase."

Weinberger is talking about the cream of the crop, the things that the Apollo astronauts took special pains with to make sure they were on the lunar surface and spent time in the vacuum of space. The rest of the field – from souvenir patches, parts and models, autographs and well beyond – has as much room for variance of budget as a collector could wish and a plethora of material that – like the very subject it covers – can sometimes seem infinite.

Unlike so many categories of collecting, the market for space memorabilia is still being established. The subject has long been popular, but the ability to get the very best of The Right Stuff was not there until recently, as many of the astronauts themselves – or their families, if they've passed on – have realized the value, both historic and financial, of their accomplishments. The more that the remaining original astronauts release key pieces of their extra-terrestrial lives, the more established the market will become.

One of the most important things space collecting has going for it is its appeal, said Weinberger. The steady increase in prices at auction in the three years he's been working with Heritage shows just how broad this appeal is.

"I think it's a function of the fact that people are now aware that these items can be bought," said Weinberger, who is among the few with the connections to bring the choicest pieces to auction. "The genre is unique because the demographic, in my opinion, is among the top three to five potential demographics for collecting."

Meaning there's almost no soul on this planet who doesn't know about, and isn't at least peripherally fascinated by, space travel.

"Show a baseball card, a comic book or a regional American quilt to a woman in Asia," Weinberger said, "and it won't translate. If you go back to 1969, to Apollo 11 and the first moon landing, you have the entire planet watching. Everybody remembers where they were when Neil Armstrong walked on the moon, or when Allan Sheppard went up with Mercury."

The broad scope of potential buyers is indeed as varied as the material, as a few minutes with the following pages will show. As the field sorts itself out, it is tough to break down into categories. The astronauts, and all the workers at NASA – from the men who walked on the moon to the guys who swept up at the end of the day – were all aware from the beginning of the historic nature of their pursuit – and it potential value.

This prospective worth, then, necessitates at least an attempt at breaking the hobby into categories. According to Weinberger, this is not something that should be done by item type, but rather by mission type and purpose.

"There's not a lot of the very best stuff, so there is a hierarchy of sorts that has evolved," he said. "The highest rung is for items that actually landed on the moon and went on the surface. Then it's something that landed on the moon but didn't leave the capsule. After that it's memorabilia that flew to the moon but only stayed in orbit. From there it's about things that flew in space, things that were strictly in earth orbit, and things that didn't fly in space but are of a personal nature belonging to the astronauts, or having their autographs."

Within these several categories, however, again there can be a striking difference in price depending on the name and the program it's associated with.

Whatever level a collector is looking at to get into the market for space memorabilia, the most important thing is authenticity, especially at the high end. In fact, Weinberger said, if it comes from an astronaut's personal collection, a signature and/or a letter of authentication is of paramount importance.

"No matter what it is, even if it's purchased personally from an astronaut, it has to be certified," he said. "The most desirable certification is having the signature on the item itself. If it has that, and a letter as well, then so much the better."

The most important thing to get started is not a broad general knowledge of what's out there, but to simply have a passion for it no matter how much cash you can put in. You can buy autographs, first-day covers or specially minted Robbins medals that flew on every Apollo mission. You can spend a few hundred or a few hundred thousand dollars; either way, it's an accessible market.

"You can start with something basic," Weinberger said. "The overall amount of memorabilia related to space is endless."

It's a good thing, then, that the enthusiasm of collectors, especially for something as inspiring as space travel, seems to be equally as endless.

All photos courtesy Heritage Auction Galleries

U.S. Flag carried on the moon by Neil Armstrong, affixed to a 12" x 14" wooden shield plaque, flag is 6" x 3 3/4" and an Apollo 11 patch, covered in clear plastic. The 5" x 3" metallic plaque affixed certifies that "This flag was carried on the moon by/ astronaut Neil Armstrong/ on July 20, 1969/ and presented to/ Joe D. Garino Jr./ by/ The Apollo 11 Astronauts." As Armstrong set foot on the lunar surface, he carried this flag. Accompanied by a signed certificate of authentication from Garino verifying its provenance.
$56,763

Front and verso of a 3" x 5" buff-colored lightweight card, one
horizontal fold affecting some text. The astronauts of the Apollo
8 mission were so inspired by their view of the earth from moon
orbit the previous Christmas Eve that they read the biblical
account of the creation story from Genesis. Noted atheist
Madalyn Murray O'Hair brought suit against NASA over this
Bible reading, asking the courts to ban any further such activity.

   Though the courts eventually rejected the suit, NASA was
quite nervous about further religious activities throughout the
rest of the Apollo program. Buzz Aldrin, a Christian and an
elder at the Webster, Texas, Presbyterian Church, wished to
express his personal faith and give thanks to God by the taking
of Holy Communion on the moon. His church furnished
him with the wine and wafer, which he stowed secretly in his
kit. He described the activity in his book Return to Earth
(Bantam Books, 1973): "During the first idle moment in
the LM before eating our snack, I reached into my personal
preference kit and pulled out two small packages which had
been specially prepared at my request. One contained a
small amount of wine, the other a small wafer. With them
and a small chalice from the kit, I took communion on the
moon, reading to myself from a small card I carried on
which I had written the portion of the Book of John used in
the traditional communion ceremony."
From the personal collection of Dr. Buzz Aldrin and also
accompanied by a signed letter of authenticity from him.
$179,250

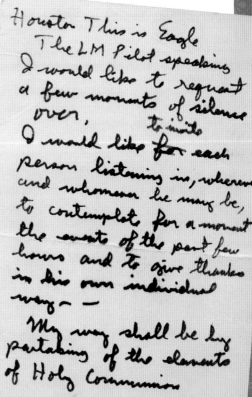

Mercury 7 Type M astronaut's test gloves
worn by John Glenn and Wally Schirra.
Two 11" x 4" aluminized nylon gloves
manufactured by the B.F. Goodrich Co. for
NASA during the agency's testing of the
Mercury astronauts' spacesuits. Both gloves
include an internal cloth Project Mercury
label. One glove has the name "Glenn" and
one "Shirra" (sic) written in black marker
inside the aluminum fittings. **$7,170 both**

Apollo 10 Command Module Pilot John Young's flown space suit patches (four) directly from his personal collection, certified and signed on the display frame. A 10" x 17" framed display containing all four pressure suit patches from the May 18-26, 1969, Apollo 10 mission, a dress rehearsal for the first manned lunar landing. On the paper backing of the frame, Young has written: "I certify that these 4 patches were on my Apollo 10 Pressure Suit when I went to the MOON. John Young." **$31,070**

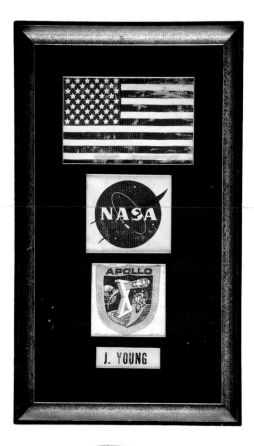

NEIL A. ARMSTRONG

Neil Armstrong color space suit photo signed but not inscribed, the "smiling" pose. An 8" x 10" NASA lithographed print showing the Apollo 11 Commander, helmet off, in front of a large image of the moon. He has signed boldly in blue felt-tip on his white spacesuit beneath the American flag patch. **$8,365**

Buzz Aldrin's 1923-S Peace silver dollar flown on the moon mission aboard Apollo 11. This was part of his Personal Preference Kit (PPK). Accompanied by a signed letter of authenticity from him. **$31,070**

Apollo 11 signed and flown commemorative cover with notation. Neil Armstrong, Michael Collins and Buzz Aldrin have all signed in blue felt-tip this NASA Manned Spacecraft Center Stamp Club Official Commemorative Cover of the First Manned Lunar Exploration with a colorful cachet of two astronauts on the lunar surface. From the personal collection of Dr. Buzz Aldrin and accompanied by a signed letter of authenticity from him. **$26,290**

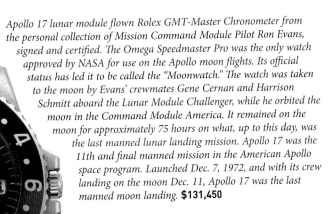

Apollo 17 lunar module flown Rolex GMT-Master Chronometer from the personal collection of Mission Command Module Pilot Ron Evans, signed and certified. The Omega Speedmaster Pro was the only watch approved by NASA for use on the Apollo moon flights. Its official status has led it to be called the "Moonwatch." The watch was taken to the moon by Evans' crewmates Gene Cernan and Harrison Schmitt aboard the Lunar Module Challenger, while he orbited the moon in the Command Module America. It remained on the moon for approximately 75 hours on what, up to this day, was the last manned lunar landing mission. Apollo 17 was the 11th and final manned mission in the American Apollo space program. Launched Dec. 7, 1972, and with its crew landing on the moon Dec. 11, Apollo 17 was the last manned moon landing. **$131,450**

Apollo 8 flown unopened two-ounce bottle of Coronet brandy from the personal collection of Mission Command Module Pilot James Lovell, packed among the astronaut's Christmas food rations. Apollo 8 launched Dec. 21, 1968, as the first manned mission from the John F. Kennedy Space Center in Florida. Apollo 8 traveled to the moon, orbiting 10 times over the course of 20 hours, during which the crew made a Christmas Eve television broadcast. At the time, the broadcast was the most watched TV program of all time. **$17,925**

Russian Soyuz flown Sokol KV-2 pressurized spacesuit, including helmet, avionics, gloves, boots, and slip-ons, as made by Zvedza for Soyuz cosmonauts. This model was first used on Soyuz T-2 in 1980 and is still in use today during launch and descent. **$31,070**

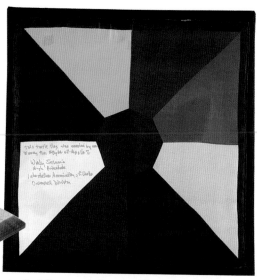

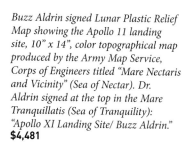

Apollo 7 flown turtle flag signed by Wally Schirra, the Imperial Potentate of the Interstellar Association of Turtles. Membership in this group has been sought by other astronauts since the Apollo years. Signed by Wally Schirra. **$3,585**

Apollo 8 flown rotational controller handle signed by and from the personal collection of Mission Command Module Pilot James Lovell. A milled aluminum handle, approximately 4 1/2" tall with a black "trigger" and indented finger grips, custom mounted. Includes a signed letter of authenticity from Lovell on his letterhead. **$21,510**

Buzz Aldrin signed Lunar Plastic Relief Map showing the Apollo 11 landing site, 10" x 14", color topographical map produced by the Army Map Service, Corps of Engineers titled "Mare Nectaris and Vicinity" (Sea of Nectar). Dr. Aldrin signed at the top in the Mare Tranquillatis (Sea of Tranquility): "Apollo XI Landing Site/ Buzz Aldrin." **$4,481**

Sports

People have been saving sports-related equipment since the inception of sports. Some was passed down from generation to generation for reuse; the rest was stored in dark spaces in closets, attics, and basements.

Two key trends brought collectors' attention to sports collectibles. First, decorators began using old sports items, especially in restaurant décor. Second, collectors began to discover the thrill of owning the "real" thing.

Sports collectibles are more accessible than ever before because of online auctions and several auction houses that dedicate themselves to that segment of the hobby. Provenance is extremely important when investing in high-ticket sports collectibles. Being able to know the history of the object may greatly enhance the value, with a premium paid for items secured from the player or directly from their estate.

Robert Edward Auctions

New York Giants Hall-of-Fame pitcher Christy Mathewson game-used baseball in which he struck out a record 16 batters against St. Louis, Oct. 3, 1904. **$44,062**

Robert Edward Auctions

Lou Gehrig's 1938 New York Yankees road jersey worn during his last full season in baseball. Gehrig, nicknamed "The Iron Horse" for his durability, played 2,130 consecutive games during his 17-year career with the Yankees. Gehrig was elected into the Baseball Hall of Fame in 1939. **$329,000**

Robert Edward Auctions

Unions vs. Excelsiors 1859 Trophy Ball, one of the earliest Trophy Balls ever seen. Both New York clubs were charter members of the The National Association of Base Ball Players and two of the best teams of the era. **$23,500**

Robert Edward Auctions

Base Ball Polka sheet music, 1867. **$12,925**

1934 Lou Gehrig game-used tour of Japan jersey

It was not Moe Berg-inspired intelligence gathering that led to this buried treasure, but rather a simple telephone call from the son of a serious ex-girlfriend of the legendary Yankees first baseman. Despite their fractured romance, this ex-girlfriend remained close with Lou and the Gehrig family, a bond that survived past her former love's tragic 1941 death and until Lou's mother herself passed away in the 1950s. For over half a century this uniform, resided in the family home of Gehrig's ex-girlfriend, its residents largely unaware of the historic and monetary value stored in the attic. Though Gehrig had twice barnstormed the United States with Babe Ruth in the late 1920s, and participated in the original 1931 Japanese Tour, there is little question but that the 1934 Baseball Tour of Japan was his most important exhibition. The same could be said of the 1934 tour's relevance to baseball history, as Major League Baseball continues to reap talent from Japan and the region. While Gehrig's 17-year Hall-of-Fame career with the New York Yankees will always make us think of him first in pinstripes, the grey flannel of the presented uniform could effectively be argued to have even greater relevance as a representation of history's most consequential road team. **$507,875**

Heritage Auction
Galleries

Heritage Auction Galleries

Denton True "Cy" Young game-used Boston Red Sox uniform, 1908. Young pitched in the Major Leagues for 22 years, winning 511 games. This jersey was displayed in The Cy Young Museum in Young's hometown of Newcomerstown, Ohio, for 25 years. **$657,250**

Heritage Auction Galleries

Lou Gehrig's 1928 New York Yankees World Championship wristwatch. The Hamilton-made championship watches were presented only to players and staff members of the Yankees. Only a handful of the watches have surfaced over the years, making them extremely rare finds. **$155,350**

Heritage Auction Galleries

1937 Robert T. "Bobby" Jones August Green Jacket

This jacket is arguably the most important Bobby Jones artifact that exists, which puts it quite solidly in the running for the most important collectible from the history of golf as well. While Jones joined Babe Ruth, Jack Dempsey and Bill Tilden as the leading icon of his respective field during the Golden Age of Sport, his most enduring contribution to the game is the Masters Tournament, contested on the Augusta, Georgia grounds he personally transformed from untamed woodlands during the Great Depression. The fabled Green Jacket serves as the tangible symbol of golf's greatest achievement, awarded to the victor of the Masters. As closely guarded as it is coveted, the Green Jacket today is restricted to the grounds of Augusta with winners strongly urged against taking the garments "off campus," and absolutely forbidden from selling them. Super Bowl rings, World Series trophies and Championship belts may routinely enter the hobby, but the Green Jacket remains the most elusive of prey for collectors. **$310,700**

Heritage Auction
Galleries

Miracle on Ice Olmpic Gold Medal

This 1980 U.S. Hockey "Miracle on Ice" Olympic Gold Medal was presented to Mark Wells, a member of one of the most famous sports team of alltime. Coached by Herb Brooks and made immortal by the words of TV sportscaster Al Michaels – "Do you believe in miracles?" – the 1980 U.S. hockey team stunned the sports world by beating the Soviet hockey juggernaut and then Finland in the gold-medal game of the 1980 Olympics. Wells, who suffers from a rare genetic disease that affected his spinal cord, sold the medal to a private collector years before it was sold at auction to help pay medical expenses. **$310,700**

The Magnificent Yankee: Mickey Mantle

During his 18-year Major League career, Mickey Mantle led the New York Yankees to seven World Series titles while being named American League MVP three times. In 1956 Mantle won the Triple Crown, by leading the league in home runs, runs batted in, and batting average. In 1961 he and Yankee teammate Roger Maris produced one of the most memorable home run races in the history of baseball. Maris hit 61 homers that year, breaking Babe Ruth's home run record set in 1927. Mantle hit 54 home runs in an injury-shortened season.

By the time he retired after the 1968 season, Mantle had hit 536 home runs and was selected to the American League All-Star team 16 times. Inducted into the Baseball Hall of Fame in 1974, Mantle died in 1995. But he remains one of the most popular baseball players of all time. His baseball cards, associated memorabilia, and signed items are highly collectible.

For more information on Mickey Mantle, see *Mickey Mantle: Memories and Memorabilia* by Larry Canale.

Heritage Auction Galleries

Mickey Mantle signed photograph, 18" x 10". **$448**

IT IS TIME, SAYS
YANKEE BRASS, FOR
MICKEY MANTLE
TO ASSUME THE ROLE
OF INSPIRATIONAL
LEADER...TO BE THE
TAKE-CHARGE GUY...
AND, AMONG OTHER
THINGS, TO LEAD THE
YANKS IN THEIR
CHARGE FROM THE
DUGOUT TO THEIR
POSITIONS IN THE
FIELD... EVEN AS
JOE DIMAG IN
DAYS OF YORE

Robert Edward Auctions

Mickey Mantle artwork, artist Willard Mullin original pen-and-ink on coquille board, early 1950s, 14.5" x 19.75", signed by artist. **$3,525**

Heritage Auction Galleries

1948 Mickey Mantle High School Junior Yearbook, Bengal Tales, leather bound, 8.5" x 11". **$823**

Heritage Auction Galleries

Advertising counter display for Haggar Slacks, cardboard, 14" x 18.75". **$3,819**

Heritage Auction Galleries

Photograph, New York Yankees 1984 Old Timer's Day, signed by Joe Dimaggio, Mickey Mantle, and Roger Maris. **$1,880**

Heritage Auction Galleries

Mickey Mantle signed high school basketball photograph. **$537**

Mickey Mantle original painting, 1962, signed by artist LeRoy Neiman, framed, 42" x 42". **$119,500**

Heritage Auction Galleries

Robert Edward Auctions

Mickey Mantle World Series Display, 40" x 52.5", framed, features 16 World Series ticket stubs from games in which Mantle hit a record 18 home runs. Also features cut signatures of the 15 pitchers who gave up the home runs to Mantle. **$6,463**

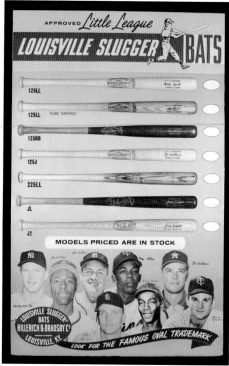

Robert Edward Auctions

Retail poster showcasing the Hillerich & Bradsby line of Louisville Slugger Little League bats for the 1967 season, exceedingly rare, 22.5" x 35.5", features endorsements from eight of the game's top stars: Mickey Mantle, Roger Maris, Hank Aaron, Al Kaline, Eddie Mathews, Ernie Banks, Tony Oliva and Harmon Killebrew. **$7,050**

Photograph, 1949 Independence (Kansas) Yankees, signed, Mickey Mantle (first row, far right), 8" x 10", black and white. **$4,182**

Heritage Auction Galleries

1952 Topps Mickey Mantle card. **$250,000**

Ron Lewis print featuring 11 members of the 500 Home Run Club, signed by (from left) Ted Williams, Frank Robinson, Harmon Killebrew, Reggie Jackson, Mickey Mantle, Willie Mays, Hank Aaron, Mike Schmidt, Ernie Banks, Eddie Mathews, and Willie McCovey. **$1,400**

Heritage Auction Galleries

Toys

Future of the Market: Antique Toys

— By Catherine Saunders-Watson

One of the biggest events in the world of toys was the sale of the 59-year collection amassed by K-B Toys' co-founder Donald Kaufman.

The Kaufman collection's magnitude, depth and maturity positioned it above all others. It contained no duplicates, many one-offs, and every known color variation. Liquidating this fine collection required five auctions and generated more than $12.1 million in total sales. The 10,000-piece collection has a new home all over the globe.

Catherine Saunders-Watson

This breathtaking assemblage of several thousand toys – even Kaufman himself doesn't know how many there are – was extraordinary in its breadth and quality.

I feel quite comfortable in going on record with these predictions, based on the Kaufman results. These are five categories I like for investment purposes:

Hubley's Royal Circus series – My no. 1 pick for American cast iron is Hubley's series of Royal Circus vans, which depict old-fashioned, wheeled cages used for transporting circus animals. This charming series of toys is a perennial favorite with collectors. En masse, the toys display beautifully in any collection, and I believe their values are going to hold strong in the marketplace, especially for those examples exhibiting fine, original paint. Kaufman owned the most elusive of the Royal Circus vans – a Monkey Cage, complete with figures of impish monkeys and an ingeniously designed mesh interior housing that revolves as the toy is pulled along. Estimated at $30,000-$40,000, it sold for a staggering $97,750.

Marklin tin – The premier brand in European tin toys and trains is Marklin. I see no turning back for this brand. There will always be buyers worldwide for this German maker's beautifully crafted designs. It's not unusual for Marklin toys to top the prices realized in major toy sales, and that's precisely what happened at the Kaufman sale. A rare, hand-painted circa-1909 "Fidelitas" clown-car caravan measuring 37 1/2" long lured not only collectors of European clockwork toys but also collectors of clown toys. (Anytime you have crossover interest from two or more categories, that's like having back-up insurance on your investment.). Estimated at $30,000-$40,000, the Fidelitas handily exceeded expectations to reach top-lot status at $103,500. The buyer was a private collector from Europe.

Early European tin cars – The fascination many of us have for full-size classic cars was grounded in childhood play. Some collectors reclaim their youth by chasing examples of the very toys they actually played with, but serious investment-oriented collectors know the money is in early German, French and Spanish autos. Seven of the top 10 lots sold in Kaufman Part I fell into this category. An extraordinary production by the little-known Barcelona firm Hispania proved to be the connoisseurs' choice. Believed to be the largest of all manufactured toy limousines at 22 1/2" in length, the circa-1907 luxury car was as finely detailed as its full-size counterpart of a century ago. The toy was purchased for $80,500 – probably 80,000 times its original price!

Here are some other prices achieved by European tin cars in the sale: circa 1906-1909 Marklin two-seat open roadster, $57,500; circa-1914 Marklin roadster with spare tire on toolbox trunk, $57,500; circa-1912 Bing luxury taxi, $46,000; and Fischer Father Christmas in open car, $39,100. Other brands we favor for investment are Carette and Gunthermann.

Racers – In more than 20 years of writing about toys, I've never seen a dip in the market for antique tin racers such as the Gordon Bennet cars in the Kaufman sale. With the rule usually being "the larger the racer, the higher the price," this auction made a strong statement when a possibly unique 6 3/4" example zoomed past its $6,000-$7,500 estimate to cross the finish line at $25,300.

Figural biscuit tins – Here's a wild-card category. Unless you've spent time in the U.K., you may not know what biscuit tins are, but they left quite a few people slack-jawed in the auction room at Bertoia's when they hammered incredible prices. In latter 19th- and early 20th-century Europe, biscuits – or cookies, as we call them in the United States – were packaged in novelty tins that had a second life after the contents were consumed. Quite often the tins were crafted as toys, and with bakeries in ferocious competition for market share, the tins were sometimes nicer than toys available in retail shops. The most desirable biscuit tins are those depicting vehicles, including cars, delivery vans, airplanes, motorcycles, racers and boats. They can run well into the thousands of dollars.

Kaufman's collection held some beauties. An Alfa-Romeo biscuit tin for the Italian company Biscotti Delser was especially rare in that it was outfitted with a clockwork motor. Estimated at $10,000-$12,000, it produced a sweet payday for when it sold for $25,300.

Caution: Sometimes tin toys are represented as biscuit tins when in actuality they are standard manufactured toys of lesser value. I've never seen a case of intentional deceit; it's just that these tins require a particular expertise in order to be properly identified. When buying biscuit tins, it pays to work with a specialty dealer.

Since I've now brought up the subject, I'd like to emphasize that any investor with an inclination to sink their money into old toys should not spend a cent till they've tapped into the toy network and know who the reputable dealers are. Trust is everything when you're buying antique toys.

Nowadays, auctions are the dominant source for investment-grade toys. There are several outstanding auction houses that specialize in toys. When you buy from toy auctioneers of this caliber, you know your purchases have been vetted and described by people who really know the toy field.

There's an added bonus to buying at auction that you don't read about very

Bertoia Auctions

Sally Kaufman (center) holding Donald Kaufman's first toy purchase, an Arcade International Harvester truck, which was presented to her as a gift from Bertoia's and members of the toy community. Left to right: Rich Bertoia, Jeanne Bertoia, Sally Kaufman, Lauren Bertoia-Costanza, Michael Bertoia.

often, if at all: preview scrutiny. At any auction preview, the toys are carefully examined by dealers and collectors who've been at it for many years. If something isn't "right," if it looks like there's a touch of repaint or a replaced part, you may be sure it will be pointed out by someone at the preview and duly noted on the catalog addendum. This can only help in your quest to purchase authentic, original toys, and it's why I recommend buying from auction houses that specialize in toys.

Bertoia Auctions

Arcade "White" moving van, Lammerts advertising, Kaufman collection. **$29,900**

There's another avenue one can take in purchasing toys for investment, and I touched on it earlier. These are the nostalgia toys you may remember from childhood. Because so many of these later toys were mass-produced – even overproduced – during an era in which the collecting phenomenon had already become well entrenched, it takes skill and exceptional market expertise to buy wisely. In this category I would say proceed with caution, as the market is much more fickle than that of antique toys, whose numbers and availability are already well established – there are no more factory finds with the potential of flooding the market when it comes to the antiques, but I wouldn't count out that possibility vis a vis newer toys.

The toys to which I refer when I say "nostalgia" toys are: Star Wars, Star Trek, Transformers, G.I. Joe and other action figures, Barbies and Superheroes. Be sure that if you buy these types of toys for investment, you choose only items you really love because then it won't hurt quite as badly if their values drop.

Personally, my recommendation for boomer-era investment toys would be tin robots of the 1950s and 1960s, preferably mint/boxed; Nightmare Before Christmas rarities, early (Gold and Silver Age) Superhero comics acquired only from experienced, reputable dealers and auction houses, and monster collectibles, which are hotter than ever. Kids loved to be creeped out, and those Saturday matinees with Wolfman and Frankenstein seem to have made a lasting impression on our generation of collectors.

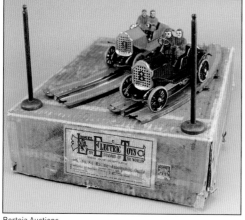

Bertoia Auctions

Boxed Lionel No. 84 racecars, tin autos with composition drivers, Kaufman collection. **$12,650**

Bertoia Auctions

American National fire pumper pedal car, Kaufman collection. **$10,350**

Bertoia Auctions

American National 1925 Packard pedal car, Kaufman collection. **$5,750**

Bertoia Auctions

Kenton City Telephone truck, Kaufman collection. **$7,475**

Bertoia Auctions

Buddy L pile driver on treads, Kaufman collection. **$8,625**

Bertoia Auctions

Steelcraft Dugan Bros. delivery truck, Kaufman collection. **$6,900**

Bertoia Auctions

Buddy L fire engine with box, Kaufman collection. **$8,050**

Tinplate clockwork Hans Eberl Kaufmann's delivery van, Kaufman collection. **$11,500**

Bertoia Auctions

Cowboy Toys

Pinback button display, thin cardboard holds full complement of cello buttons, each 1 1/2" diameter with image in center of smiling boy wearing coonskin cap. Only five of the 48 buttons have correct spelling of "Davy" name; 11" x 17". **$354**

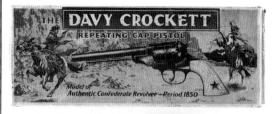

Toy cap pistol, metal gun is 10 1/2" long with "Davy Crockett" name in low relief on frame and star design incised on plastic grips, attached to thin cardboard box is marked "Outlaw Apache," with Davy Crockett label pasted on lid over original text; made in England by BCM, 1 1/4" x 11" wide, circa 1950s. **$575**

Alarm clock, painted metal case with brass luster frame around the glass cover over the clock face, image of Davy in seated position holding a guitar as one squirrel lays against his leg and another rests on his raised arm. This squirrel has a separate head that moves as seconds tick. Unique figural clock hands are a rifle and tomahawk. Circa 1955, 2" x 7 1/2" x 5" tall. **$488**

Windup toy, celluloid Mickey figure depicted in cowboy attire including neckerchief and pair of guns tucked in his belt, with string lasso in one hand and reins in the other while seated atop a painted wood horse; missing a paper hat; built-in key makes clockwork move figure forward in a galloping motion; 3" x 7" x 7" tall, Japan, circa 1930s. **$575**

Dexterity Puzzles

Dexterity puzzle, box is cardboard with clear thin plastic lid, Popeye characters around sides include Popeye, Olive Oyl, Wimpy, Swee' Pea, and the Jeep; inside has small die-cut thin paper figures of Popeye, Olive Oyl, and clown with small piece of foil on one side of feet along with star design playing surface with numbers for scoring. Underside has text instructions including "Slap And Rub Firmly Across Top Of Box With Fingertips Or Coat Sleeve Repeatedly. Then Comics Will Dance, Hop And Skip. You Will Be Amazed To See Them Come To Life! Fingers Must Be Absolutely Dry"; copyright King Features Syndicate Inc., circa 1930s, 4 7/8" diameter x 1 1/2" deep. **$382**

Group of three dexterity puzzles with textured paper-covered cardboard frame and glass cover over the playing surface, circa 1934 by Marks Bros. Co., titles are "Mickey Mouse The Entertainer," "Mickey Mouse In His Garden," and "Mickey Mouse The Farmer" with each measuring 4" x 6" x 3/4" deep. **$224**

Early dexterity puzzle depicting automobile and driver, 2 1/2" with glass cover over embossed cardboard showing driver in hat, goggles, and heavy coat at the wheel of his auto headed down a road with great dust cloud behind; inside puzzle are five white balls to get into small recesses on the radiator front; mirror on underside. **$111**

World War II-era dexterity puzzle has metal frame with glass cover over cardboard insert showing "Atomic Bomb" dropping from the sky headed toward the country of Japan with the designation for the cities Tokyo, Hiroshima, and Nagasaki; the latter two have small cut-outs in the cardboard next to the name, and this is where a pair of celluloid pellets with interior bb are to be positioned. A rather gruesome game given the consequences, but emblematic of the era; 3 1/4" x 4 3/8" x 7/8" deep. **$118**

Pinbacks

Pinback badge, premium, depicting classic enamel image of Superman shown waist up breaking chest chains with his name in text at bottom coming out of circular border with enamel stars surrounded by brass luster burst design; 1949 Fo-Lee Gum Corp., Philadelphia. 3" x 4 1/4" high; quality leather wallet made by Pioneer has embossed design on front. **$8,475**

Pinback button, 1" celluloid pinback button with intense cream glow-in-the-dark background to show at its center the black silhouetted Shadow in hat and cape with his gun leveled, 1939. **$455**

Popeye

Figural string holder depicting Popeye's pet, painted plaster with recessed back to hold string ball and hole in mouth for string. Has hanging loop at top for display, dated 1955 with incised text at top "American Cartoon" and his name incised on underside, 7" x 7 3/4". **$2,656**

Tin toy car, circa late 1950s, thin cardboard box is 3 1/2" x 8 1/4" wide x 3 3/4" deep with art images on all five sides of lid showing Olive Oyl driving convertible; Number J-4050 with lid text including "Sculptured Figure With Hair"; tin car is 8 1/2" long with smiling Olive Oyl, sporting long ponytail, behind the wheel. **$1,043**

Toy cap gun set, 1961 King Features Syndicate Inc., made by Halco, Pittsburgh, Pennsylvania, die-cut thin cardboard has choice graphics of Popeye dressed as cowboy holding two pistols with horse looking at him, 8" x 12", inside is a pair of 4 3/4" tall thin leather holsters with Popeye image on each and shiny cast metal "Pal" guns made by Kilgore in each pocket. Set also has leather belt wrapped in place at bottom. Reverse side has text: "After The Holster Set Has Been Removed From The Card, The Picture Makes A Fine Wall Plaque For A Child's Bedroom Or Playroom." Die-cut hole at top of display card is unpunched. **$253**

Brass folk art figure produced by fan of Jeep, Popeye's orchid-eating, truth-telling pet who can see the future Jeep. Figure was probably created shortly after Aug. 9, 1936, after Jeep left his 4th dimensional world to join Popeye and us in our three-dimensional world; figure stands 4"tall and is solid brass nearly 3/8" thick. **$230**

Toy celluloid figure of Popeye with pipe in mouth; when wound, head goes up and down and figure waddles about; 5 3/4" tall, circa 1930s, made in Japan for Australian market. Thin cardboard box is 1 1/2" x 2 1/4" x 6", box's front and back panels show Popeye throwing a punch with his hat in mid air, side panels show him looking at loop, and end panels show him hatless, throwing a punch with stars in the air; complete with key. **$612**

Left: *Large and small varieties of mid-1930s Rosebud Art Company pipe toss games. One is 4 1/4" x 9 1/8" boxed variety, the other is 5" x 10 7/8" variety. Each contains die-cut thin cardboard target figure of Popeye with wood block to stand on and three die-cut thin cardboard rings. One figure is 8 1/4" tall, the other is 10" tall. Smaller box has directions printed on inside of lid with wood block glued in place, the other has no instructions and wood block is loose.* **Right:** *Ring toss game comes in 10 1/2" x 16" x 1 1/2" deep cardboard box by Rosebud Art Company New York, ©1919-1929-1933 King Features Syndicate Inc., has two attached wooden blocks to hold 10 1/4" tall Olive Oyl figure and 10 1/8" tall Popeye figure, complete with roped rings with wood attachment.* **$208**

Wristwatch, chrome accent case with dial images of Popeye, Olive Oyl, Swee'Pea, and Wimpy. One of two varieties. This one has Popeye's name in two words and standard hands whereas other version has no name and different hands. Leather band is a replacement; circa 1948, 1 3/4" diameter. **$172**

Candy boxes, pair, each 2 1/2" by 3 3/4" by 1" deep, from a 1950s numbered set by Super Novelty Candy Co. Inc. Fronts feature single character image as a perforated card panel, backs have comic panel cartoon with story that continues from box to box. Boxes are No. 12 Oscar and No. 15 Popeye. Additional character images on side panels. **$140**

Premium Rings

Premium ring depicting Clarabell the Clown character from "Howdy Doody" network television show; on Clarabell's head is mounted a small brass hat fully 1/4" tall; ring base, as on the Howdy version, shows two images of Clarabell with his elaborate collar, and the brass loop to hold a battery has the same maker's name "Brownie Mfg. Co." along with "Pat. No. 2,516,180."; circa 1950, rare. **$4,174**

Premium ring, 1934 pulp magazine ring depicting metallic skull image with numeral 5 on forehead with metallic base, the insignia of Jimmy Christopher, fictional undercover ace whose adventures fighting spies and foreign agents took place from 1934 until the beginning of World War II; ring was used for distribution in the United States. **$10,925**

Rare prototype Sky King premium ring, circa 1950, never produced but created by Armstrong for the Robbins Co. to present to the executives of the radio show's sponsor, Peter Pan peanut butter; ring has perfectly formed adjustable bands, base design is same as the 1949 Sky King Electronic Television Picture Ring with image of Sky King's horse "Yellow Fury" and airplane "Flying Arrow"; base joins to a black metal frame that holds a large diameter (15/16" x 2") heavy aluminum tube with slightly recessed center area and features a knurled pattern around the circumference at the eyepiece end, both intended to facilitate rotating the tube with one hand while the other holds the ring towards light to view the interior; interior displays a kaleidoscopic effect with die-cut portrait illustration of Sky King; only one known to exist. **$16,100**

Vehicles & Trains

Vindex Packard Club Sedan, circa 1929, formerly in the collections of Dick Ford and Donald Kaufman. **$8,625**

Bing 1 gauge train set with "Express" electric locomotive and tender, Speisewagon dining car, Wagons-Lits sleeping car. **$12,650**

This early 20th century Marklin steam-powered, horse-drawn fire pumper features a hand-painted body with copper-finished upright boiler and two finely painted figures. Thirteen inches from hitch to platform. **$17,250**

Circa-1909 Marklin "Priscilla" steamboat, 19 inches long, formerly in the Bill Bertoia collection. **$63,250**

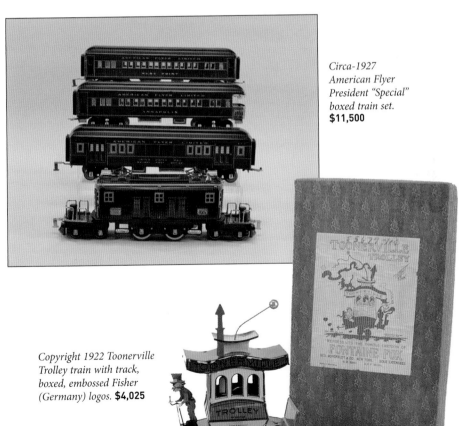

Circa-1927 American Flyer President "Special" boxed train set. **$11,500**

Copyright 1922 Toonerville Trolley train with track, boxed, embossed Fisher (Germany) logos. **$4,025**

Windups

Windup toy depicting comic strip character Henry tin litho with celluloid figures and wind-up key in left side. Made in Japan and distributed by George Borgfeldt Corp., New York; original thin cardboard box has lid graphics of Henry smiling and waving while seated in back of three-wheel vehicle being driven by young black boy. Lid top shows him with pyramids and palm trees in the background; front and back panel shows him going past mountain range and waving hanky; circa 1930s; toy is 5" long. **$3,162**

Windup Boob McNutt toy made by Ferdinand Strauss Corp., New York. No. 41, tin litho wind-up toy depicts Boob standing full figure with note on his back, "I'm Boob McNutt R. L. Goldberg." When wound, Boob's separate upper torso moves back and forth, arms swing, and toy moves about, 8 3/4", accompanied by thin cardboard box that has nice graphics on front and back showing Boob dancing, signed at lower right by cartoonist R. L. Goldberg. Side panels each feature a different daily comic strip with Boob; 2 3/4" x 4" x 9" tall, toy has repairs, 1924. **$670**

Wind up toy clown made in Germany, circa 1900s; 6" tall tin litho figure with built-in key on side and wheels next to feet pushing 4" diameter double hoop. Maker unknown. **$747**

Windup Mickey Mouse toy with wire metal tail and built-in key. Underside of one foot has copyright label. Figure's legs move back and forth rapidly as Mickey "rambles about." Made in Japan, distributed by Borgfeldt, 4" x 5" x 7", 1930s. **$659**

Windup toy marked "Donald Duck Walt Disney Japan" on back and inspection sticker on Donald's stomach. Mickey, Minnie, Donald, and Pluto characters on umbrella above Donald's head; includes original box, distributed by George Borgfeldt, Japanese, pre-war, 11" tall. **$950**

Stock German tin three-wheel car, working clockwork, pre-war, circa 1912. Complete with original female driver, 5" long. **$860**

Toy robot, battery operated with robot face remote control, original wrench and hands, includes very colorful original box, 8 3/4". **$850**

Windup tin litho Chein Disney Roller Coaster, includes original box and two original tin litho roller coaster cars; depictions of Disney characters around base include The Three Little Pigs, Mickey Mouse, Mad Hatter, Pinocchio, Donald Duck, and others; 19 1/2" long. **$475**

Fischer Father Christmas in auto, circa 1912, one of very few known. **$25,875**

J. & E. Stevens "Fowler" cast-iron mechanical bank, circa 1892. **$17,250**

Rare 26-inch chalkware Father Christmas figure. **$10,925**

Mechanical "Peek-a-Boo" Cat in pot, pictured in 1893 Ives catalog. **$8,050**

Vintage Clothing

The history of fashion is a mirror to the future. Nearly every style has already been done in some form and is reproduced with variations today. The popularity and demand for vintage pieces is growing because clothing and accessories are great collectibles that are also a good investment.

Many factors come into play when assessing value. When shopping vintage, keep the following in mind:

Popularity: How well known the designer is affects the price.

Condition: Collectors tend to want the original design condition with no modifications or repairs.

Relevance: The piece should be a meaningful representation of a designer's work.

When you're hot you're hot: As a trend develops, it is shown in fashion magazines, and the original vintage pieces go up in value (and plummet when it goes out of favor).

Location: Prices fluctuate from one geographic region to another.

Value: The appeal of vintage items has greatly increased over the last few years. Our rule of thumb is to buy quality.

Late 1950s candy-striped bathing suit ensemble, all pieces of nylon, the bra-top with shaped bustline pieced in chevron stripes with contrasting red and white striped trim, halter neck tie, center back closure; the short bolero jacket with a spread collar and lapels, short cuffed sleeves with a slight puff at shoulders, patch pockets at waist, worn open; the short flared skirt-style bottoms of 14 gored panels pieced in chevron stripes, 2" w. waistband, center back zipper and single button closure, trunks underneath of white nylon tricot, bottoms labeled "I. Magnin and Co.," excellent condition, trunks stained, late 1950s. **$350**

Lovely 1950s Christian Dior cocktail dress, salmon-colored duchess satin, the bodice with horizontal accordian pleating and a halter neck with a self-fabric strap around the neck, a 5 1/2" w. waistband above the 33" l. sunburst pleated skirt, self-fabric-covered buttons down the center back stopping 18" from the hemline and revealing an inverted pleat running the length of the skirt, labeled "Christian Dior Original - Made in U.S.A. - Christian Dior - New York Inc.," excellent condition, four buttons missing, later strapless bra sewn into the bodice. **$3,500**

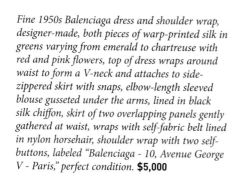

Fine 1950s Balenciaga dress and shoulder wrap, designer-made, both pieces of warp-printed silk in greens varying from emerald to chartreuse with red and pink flowers, top of dress wraps around waist to form a V-neck and attaches to side-zippered skirt with snaps, elbow-length sleeved blouse gusseted under the arms, lined in black silk chiffon, skirt of two overlapping panels gently gathered at waist, wraps with self-fabric belt lined in nylon horsehair, shoulder wrap with two self-buttons, labeled "Balenciaga - 10, Avenue George V - Paris," perfect condition. **$5,000**

Lovely 1950s Duchess satin formal with shrug, sweetheart strapless neckline and sequins and beading overall, self-fabric beaded belt, bodice boned at every seam, grosgrain inner waist belt, side zipper closure, hem faced with stiff tulle, fair condition, some discoloration, tearing in parts and some beads and sequins missing. **$1,800**

Labeled 1950s Schiaparelli robe, pale pink nylon with gathered neckline and loosely gathered sleeves, pink velvet ribbon and lace-trimmed yoke, ribbon belt, snap closure on bodice, hook and eye closure at waist, labeled "Schiaparelli - New York," perfect condition. **$150**

Late 1950s Dior wool skirt suit, both pieces of grey wool, the short slim-fitting jacked with a small collar and lapel, oversized buttons and bound buttonholes down the center front, decorative flaps high on the waist suggesting pockets, long sleeves, back buttoned waistbelt and side vents, lined with grey silk; the straight skirt with tiny tucks under 1" w. waistband, center back zipper and hook closure, lined with grey silk, jacket labeled "Christian Dior-New York - Marsal Park Avenue," good condition, some wear to lining, two tiny wear holes on front, late 1950s/ early 1960s. **$475**

Labeled 1950s embroidered sun dress composed of eight panels of white bark cloth ground with light blue flower embroidery with green stems and leaves, flower appliquéd straps over ivory muslin, tight bodice and full skirt, center back zipper, labeled "Tina Leser Original," excellent condition. **$500**

1950s varsity jacket, green boiled wool with cream-colored leather sleeves and pocket edging, acryllic knit collar, cuffs and waist, lined with green lustrous fabric, center front snap closure, labeled "Timberline by Bill Bros. - Milwaukee - Size 44," good condition, some discoloration to sleeves, tearing to lining (shown with 1970s varsity jacket at right). **$150**

1950s blue gabardine two-piece suit with subtle slubs of red and darker blue, the jacket with a narrow collar and lapels, single patch breast pocket, two oversized patch pockets at hips, single-breasted with two-button closure at center front, decorative buttons on cuffs, unlined; the trousers feature narrow belt loops, no waistband with pleats running the length of the leg, on-seam slit pockets at hips, back welt pockets, tapered legs with cuffs at hem, zippered fly, jacket labeled "M-H Clothes of Distinction," very good condition, some age darkening to seams and around pockets and jacket cuffs. **$500**

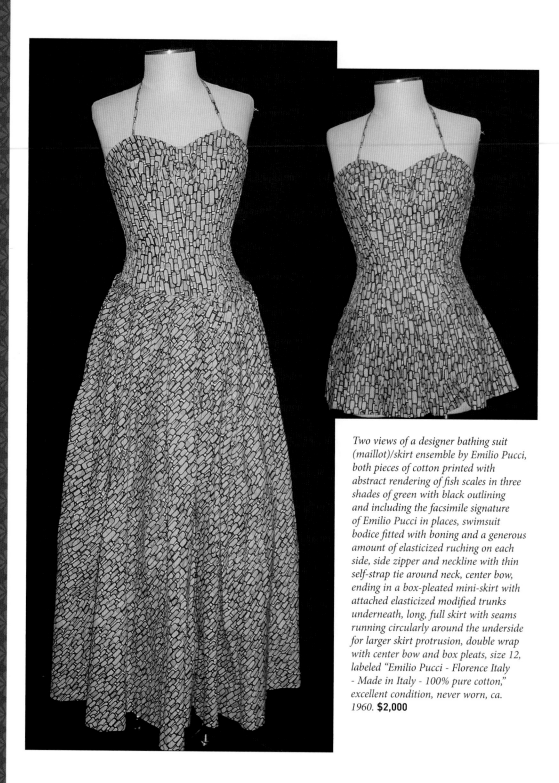

Two views of a designer bathing suit (maillot)/skirt ensemble by Emilio Pucci, both pieces of cotton printed with abstract rendering of fish scales in three shades of green with black outlining and including the facsimile signature of Emilio Pucci in places, swimsuit bodice fitted with boning and a generous amount of elasticized ruching on each side, side zipper and neckline with thin self-strap tie around neck, center bow, ending in a box-pleated mini-skirt with attached elasticized modified trunks underneath, long, full skirt with seams running circularly around the underside for larger skirt protrusion, double wrap with center bow and box pleats, size 12, labeled "Emilio Pucci - Florence Italy - Made in Italy - 100% pure cotton," excellent condition, never worn, ca. 1960. **$2,000**

Fine Pauline trigere coat and dress ensemble, both pieces of brocaded fabric with a black ground decorated overall with gold spheres; the dress features a wide scoop neck, long sleeves tapering to snap cuffs, tucks high on bustline achieving a smock-style effect continuing to the full bodice and skirt with an 18" l. straight-cut bottom tier, center back zipper, lined with sheet black organdy, accompanying belt of same fabric with fabric-covered buckle and hidden hook closure faced with black cotton faille; the swing-style coat with a 2 3/4" w. stand-up collar structured underneath with wire for support and overlap hidden hooks and eyes and single oversized wrapped button closure, raglan bracelet-length sleeves, a 2" w. padded band at upper thigh level continuing to 18" l. straight-cut bottom tier, lined with black knit jersey, labeled "Pauline Trigere," excellent condition. **$1,200**

Blue chiffon cocktail dress, ca. 1960, dusty blue sleeveless design with minutely tucked chiffon bodice, self-fabric piping at rounded neckline and armscyes, 4" w. mauve satin insertion at high waistline with side bow finish and trailing ends, purple acetate full skirt with tucked chiffon overlay, bodice lined with fine blue net, center back zipper, labeled "R and K Originals," excellent condition, some fading to satin insertion and bow, ca. 1960. **$275**

1960s apricot "baby doll"-style dress, acetate sleeveless dress with apricot-colored chiffon overlay, the bodice featuring strips of embroidered chiffon around the square neckline and empire waistline, bishop sleeves made from sturdier organdy with insertions of the same embroidered chiffon running vertically, band of the same lace over acetate just above the elbows, lower length of sleeves faced with stiff tulle for fullness and tapering to elastic cuffs, skirt of dress tucked under the waistband for fullness, center back zipper with a white grosgrain ribbon bow, mid- to late 1960s, good condition, minor tears to chiffon. **$175**

Designer peasant-style dress by Geoffrey Beene, silk with an orange ground with stylized flowers in shades of yellow, green, pink and black, low scoop neckline and unlined bodice, five pairs of orange grommets and self-fabric cording to lace-up, empire waistline, gently gathered long skirt lined in ivory-colored organza and ending in a doubled flounced tier, fitted armhole and sleeve also ending in a double flounced cuff, low scoop back, center back zipper with hook and eye closure, labeled by Geoffrey Beene, late 1960s, perfect condition. **$1,500-1,800**

1960s Hattie Carnegie shantung silk dress with a beige ground with red, pink and yellow flowers and green leaves, wide scoop neck with a tucked bustline, elbow-length sleeves, rounded waistline and straight skirt, center back zipper, labeled "Hattie Carnegie Blue Room," excellent condition, some alteration work. **$500**

1960s Pepsi-Cola dress, shift-style, yellow cotton sleeveless design with Pepsi-Cola slogans and a large bottle printed design, round neckline, darts at bustline, center back zipper, labeled "Regatta by Mill Fabrics Corporation - Penney's - 18," mint condition with original tags. **$350**

Late 1960s wild floral print dress, very thin jersey material in a wild and colorful floral print, bateau neckline, three-quarters length slim-fitting sleeves, skirt falls to lower knee, self-fabric cord tie belt, labeled "42," late 1960s, excellent condition. **$350**

1960s suede and tweed jacket and skirt ensemble, the loose-bodied jacket of light brown suede with a stand-up collar and open placket faced with light brown and white flat tweed fabric, kimono-style short sleeves with turn-back cuffs also faced with same tweed, two patch hand-warmer pockets at center front trimmed with tweed, lined with beige crepe; the pencil skirt of same tweed falls to mid-calf with 1 1/2" w. suede waistband, tweed-wrapped button and tab closure, center back seam edges with same suede, kick slit near hem with suede detail, jacket labeled "Created by Royal Suedes of New York," late 1960s, excellent condition, some age wear to suede. **$200**

1960s Betsey Johnson mini-dress, pink cotton with small bow and ribbon print, shirred and elastic long sleeves, princess seaming front and back, white buttons down center front, labeled "DESIGNED by Betsey Johnson for Paraphernalia," excellent condition, mid-1960s. **$400-$500**

Two 1960s men's plaid jackets.
Left: Red, yellow and ivory plaid in an open weave, possibly silk-cotton blend, beige satin monogrammed lining, two flap pockets, single chest slit pocket, two inside slit pockets with plaid fabric edging, back vent, single button closure center front, labeled "Mark Chrisman - Pompano Beach - Boca Raton - Naples, Florida - Dry Clean Only," excellent condition. **$125**

Right: Blue, yellow, white and brown plaid patchwork madras-style in a cotton blend, deep back vent, white satin lining, two flap pockets, two inside slit pockets and two-button front closure, excellent condition. **$125**

Two 1960s men's shirts.
Left: Green and yellow "shirt-jac" (combined shirt and jacket), cotton blend, spread collar, chest patch pocket, center front button closure, excellent condition. **$42**

Right: Gray iridescent silk, small vertical tucks down center front, chest patch monogrammed pocket, cuffed shirt sleeves, center front button closure, tucks at back near shoulder yoke, straight hem, labeled "Custom Care by Alfred of New York – Imported Pure Silk," excellent condition. **$65**

Early 1960s labeled rayon "shirt jac," black rayon with insertions of white, red and grey stripes down the center front, spread collar, long sleeves with banded buttoned cuffs, 2" w. self-fabric waistband, white plastic buttons down center front, labeled "Clubman - L - Shirt Jac," early 1960s, mint condition. **$150**

1970s Hungarian embroidered blouse, finely textured unbleached gauze featuring floral yarn embroidery at the center front and smocking and overstitching around the neckline, short puff sleeves and waist, light blue cord drawstring at V-neckline, labeled "Hand Embroidery Made in Hungary - Karavan N.Y.," excellent condition, tiny pinhole at front, slight age yellowing over left shoulder. **$175-$200**

Yellow dress by Ronald Amey, wool knit, mock-turtle neckline, raglan-type long full sleeves with openings at the shoulders and tapering at the cuffs with carved Lucite and gold-rimmed buttons and loop closures, bodice gathered from shoulder yoke and at elastic-covered waistline, attached 3" w. self-fabric covered belt with button and loop closure, skirt lined with yellow china silk, rolled hemline, center back zipper closure, labeled "Ronald Amey New York," and a fabric care label, excellent condition, minor pilling mainly at neckline. **$400**

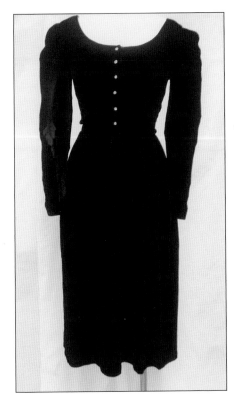

1970s midnight blue silk velvet long dress, wide scoop neck, slightly padded shoulders, long sleeves gathered at shoulders and tapering to wrists with functioning prong-set rhinestone buttons up the cuff, same buttons down center front of bodice, empire waist with gathered mid-calf skirt, lingerie straps at shoulder, neckline lined with blue acetate, excellent condition, lining around neck shows some wear. **$200**

1970s plaid halter dress and shawl, twilled polyester, halter bodice with hook and eye closure at upper neck gathered for fullness, darts at bustline, bias-cut wide skirt, zipper down center back, with matching shawl, labeled "Lillie Rubin," late 1970s, excellent condition, the set. **$125**

Two views of a 1970s brocade gown by Mary Norton, bands of light green, orange and pale yellow with silver lame thread running throughout, bodice features a wide V-neckline with attached light green organdy swatch that drapes around neck and falls down the back, trimmed with gold-flecked lace, bodice tucked at center for fullness around the bustline with self-fabric bows at center seam, kimono-style three-quarter-length sleeves with underarm gussets, high waistline and tucks underneath creating a full skirt, center back zipper, lined with orange satin, labeled "Mary Norton - Coral Way - Miami, Florida - Bay Harbor Islands-Miami Beach - Main St.-Blowing Rock, N.C.," good condition, some tears along seams, discoloration to lining under armscyes, early 1970s. **$250**

1970s orange hot pants, crushed rayon velvet with patch pockets and self-belt loops, snap button and fly closure, measures 8 1/2" from waistband to cuffs, labeled "Velpanne - Ameritex," mint condition. **$50-$55**

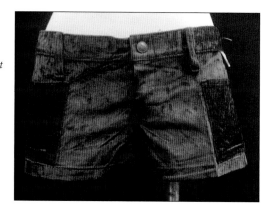

Two pairs of 1970s decorated denim jeans.
Left: Blue denim with home-made patchwork embellishments on lower flares, five-pocket styling, perhaps a 'marriage' of two different pairs, excellent condition, intentional fraying of threads and patches, front button missing . **$250**

Right: Blue denim trimmed with stripes of colorful grosgrain ribbon diagonally stitched, excellent condition. **$75-$125**

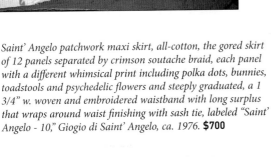

Saint' Angelo patchwork maxi skirt, all-cotton, the gored skirt of 12 panels separated by crimson soutache braid, each panel with a different whimsical print including polka dots, bunnies, toadstools and psychedelic flowers and steeply graduated, a 1 3/4" w. woven and embroidered waistband with long surplus that wraps around waist finishing with sash tie, labeled "Saint' Angelo - 10," Giogio di Saint' Angelo, ca. 1976. **$700**

Two knitted wool ponchos from the 1970s.
Left: White, brown and orange acrylic yarn in a banded design, excellent condition. **$35**

Right: Green and yellow wool yarn, with a yellow drawstring and pom-pons, yellow yarn fringe, excellent condition. **$85**

1970s jacket, pants and shirt ensemble, formal yellow shirt of polyester-cotton blend with tucks and lace on center pront, narrow lace edging at cuffs, labeled "After Six," excellent condition, **$55**; patterned textured polyester clip-on bow tie, 1960s, excellent condition, **$13**; plaid trousers of 100% wool with slight flare at bottom, tab buttoned pocket at right hip, two-inch wide waistband and two-inch wide self-fabric belt loops, top-lined, center front zipper closure and top hooks, excellent condition, **$100-125**; brown jacket of polyester twill with satin collar, padding at shoulder, hand-stitched lining, two deep vents at back, center front button closure, excellent condition, jacket. **$150**

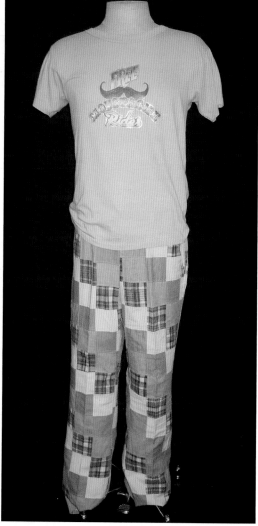

Tee shirt and pants outfit, circa 1970, shirt of peach-colored cotton and polyester blend with iron-on patch reading "Free Moustache Rides," good condition, some fabric wear and fading, ca. 1970, **$55**; cotton pants (possible blend) in a madras patchwork design in shades of beige, pink, brown and red, two-inch waistband angle set welt pockets in front and straight welt pockets in back, labeled "A JAYMAR SLACK" and fabric care label, ca. 1970, excellent condition. **$175**

Western

John Wayne

John Wayne's epic five-decade film career included more than 175 films. Although Wayne starred in just about every movie genre imaginable from war to romantic comedies, he is best remembered for his work in westerns. Wayne, who was born in Iowa but moved with his family to California when he was a boy, came to define the strong, tough, independent cowboy of Hollywood's Old West. He was nominated three times for the Academy Award, winning the Oscar for Best Actor in 1969 for True Grit.

Born Marion Robert Morrison in 1907, Wayne died June 11, 1979. He was 72. In the fall of 2011, Wayne's family offered an expansive collection of never-before-released personal and professional items from the movie star's personal archives. The auction was handled by Heritage Auction Galleries, Dallas.

Oil painting by John Decker, 1945, rendered on board, depicting Wayne in cowboy garb, signed in the lower left corner "John Decker 45" in its original, elaborate wooden frame, 32" x 28". **$71,700**

John Wayne, with Anthony Quinn, at the Golden Globe Awards.

JOHN WAYNE
BEST
MOTION PICTURE ACTOR
DRAMA
1969

"TRUE GRIT"

HOLLYWOOD FOREIGN
PRESS ASSOCIATION

#3136

Golden Globe award for "True Grit," Paramount, 1969, gold-colored metal on a white marble base, 9" x 3" x 3", front placard reads, "John Wayne / Best / Motion Picture Actor / Drama / 1969 / "True Grit" / Hollywood Foreign / Press Association / #3136." **$143,400**

Western saddle and stand, 1960s, made for Wayne for both his professional and private use; rendered in high quality brown leather, hand-stitched detailing on seat, with a "JW" monogram embossed on back of cantle, conchos with leather tassels on front and back, rope affixed to right side, decorative rope belt affixed to front, either fender stamped "Colorado Saddlery / Denver"; appearing to be well-used; included with its custom dark-stained wooden display stand. **$71,700**

Cowboy hat from "Big Jake," "The Cowboys," and "The Train Robbers," made of tan felt, colorful embroidery on leather hatband, inside handwritten annotations in black felt tip ink reading "J. Wayne #2" and "Chuck Roberson 2" [Wayne's longtime stunt double]; worn by Wayne as he portrayed Jacob McCandles, Wil Andersen, and Lane in the three different films; also worn by Roberson in "Big Jake" as the two men frequently shared the same costume pieces. **$119,500**

Cavalry hat worn by Wayne in "The Horse Soldiers" (United Artists, 1959), "Circus World" (Paramount, 1964), "The Undefeated" (20th Century Fox, 1969), and "Rio Lobo" (National General Pictures, 1970), made of black felt, brown cord 'acorn' hatband with further black ribbon detail, black velvet cavalry insignia on crown, inside has piece of tape with a handwritten annotation in pencil reading "John Wayne #1"; worn as Wayne portrayed Col. John Marlowe, Matt Masters, Col. John Henry Thomas, and Col. Cord McNally in the four different films. **$35,850**

Stetson cowboy hat from "The Man Who Shot Liberty Valance," Paramount, 1962, made of tan felt, thin brown leather cord hatband, inside stamped with the Stetson logo and "John Wayne"; worn as Wayne portrayed Tom Doniphon in the film directed by John Ford and co-starring James Stewart. **$41,825**

Cowboy hat from "Rooster Cogburn," Universal, 1975, made of black felt, elaborate braided brown leather and twine hatband, leather twine chin strap, inside stamped "Nudie's / Rodeo Tailors / North Hollywood / California," worn as Wayne portrayed the title character in the film that co-starred Katharine Hepburn. **$77,675**

Andy Warhol limited edition signed print from the "Cowboys and Indians" Series, 1986, 36" x 36", titled "John Wayne," numbered and signed in pencil in the lower right hand corner "221/250 Andy Warhol." **$77,670**

Eye patch from "True Grit," Paramount Pictures, 1969, made of black leather with fine wire mesh covering a cut-out hole; makeup residue still evident on inside patch; one of many worn by Wayne throughout the film as he portrayed the iconic character, "Rooster Cogburn." **$47,800**

Beret from "The Green Berets," Warner Bros./Seven Arts, 1968, traditional design, made of green wool, striped military patch on front with added silver-colored metal eagle pin; worn as Wayne portrayed "Colonel Mike Kirby" in the film that he starred in and directed. **$179,250**

Coat and cap from publicity stills for "The Quiet Man," Republic, 1952. A classic overcoat made of brown and rust-colored plaid hound's-tooth wool, four-button front closure, with a buttoned fabric band on each sleeve, label in inside pocket reads "John Wayne / 3/11/47"; together with a black, green, and brown plaid wool cap; both pieces worn by Wayne in publicity photographs though not seen in the final version of the film; coat also seems to be the same one used in a brief scene from the 1953 Warner Bros. film, "Trouble Along the Way." **$31,070**

John Wayne's last driver's license, 1977, issued by the State of California on "May 12, 1977," with an expiration date of 1981. **$89,625**

Ronald Reagan handwritten letter, circa 1977, penned in black felt-tip ink on personalized stationery, dated May 15, reading in part, "We didn't know of a sure way that an extra letter might reach you. But as you can see we found a way. Don't tip the messenger he was happy to do it. ...We can handle the gasoline shortage, the anti-nuclear freaks & even the crazy way the admin. is dealing with the Russians - we can't take much more of you being out of action. ...Duke you are not only in our thoughts - you are in our prayers every day. And those prayers are born of our love & affection for you," signed in the lower right corner "Nancy" [in her hand] "& Ron" [in his hand]; with original transmittal envelope without a stamp or postmark since it was hand-delivered. **$21,510**

World War II Collectibles

In the 65 years since the end of World War II, veterans, collectors, and history buffs have eagerly bought, sold and traded the "spoils of war." Actually, souvenir collecting began as soon as troops set foot on foreign soil. Soldiers from every nation involved in the greatest armed conflict mankind has known eagerly sought items that would remind them of their time in the service, validate their presence during the making of history, and potentially generate income when they returned home. Such items might also be bartered with fellow soldiers for highly prized or scarce goods. Helmets, medals, Lugers, field gear, daggers, and other pieces of war material filled parcels, which were mailed home or stuffed into the duffel bags of soldiers who gathered them.

As soon as hostilities ended in 1945, the populations of the defeated nations quickly realized that they could make money by selling souvenirs to their former enemies. This was particularly true in Germany and Japan, which hosted large contingents of occupying U.S. soldiers and troops from other Allied nations. The flow of war material increased. Values became well established. For instance, a Luger was worth several packs of cigarettes, a helmet, just one. A Japanese sword was worth two boxes of K-rations, and an Arisaka bayonet was worth a chocolate Hershey bar.

Over the years, these values have remained proportionally consistent. Today, that "two-pack" Luger might be worth $4,000 and that one-pack helmet, $1,000. The Japanese sword might fetch $1,200 and the Arisaka bayonet $85. Though values have increased dramatically, demand has not slackened. In fact, World War II collecting is the largest segment of the militaria hobby.

AAF P-51 Ace's identified group that included the flyer's A-2 jacket, flight gear, documents, and gun camera. **$9,975**

www.advanceguardmilitaria.com

The A-2 flight jacket was one of the most popular leather jackets during the war. **$495-$1,238**

www.advanceguardmilitaria.com

A-2 jacket with painted squadron insignia. **$1,238-$2,145**

www.advanceguardmilitaria.com

P1941 jacket worn by both Navy and USMC troops. **$58-$83**

Charles D. Pautler

John F. Graf collection

Model 1941 field jacket with original insignia. **$400**

Charles D. Pautler

The Model 1943 field jacket, first issued in 1943, widely distributed and remained in service through the Korean War. **$66-$132**

Australian-made Ike jacket with insignia for a 5th Air Force aerial gunner. **$245**

9th Air Force senior pilot's Ike jacket with bullion insignia. **$400**

www.advanceguardmilitaria.com

82nd Airborne Division PFC's Ike jacket. **$490**

Camp Ripley Museum

German Luftwaffe officer's visor cap. **$900**

Hermann Historica OHG

Waffen SS visor cap for a medical officer. **$3,000**

Camp Ripley Museum

German political leader's cap. **$1,200**

Manion's International
Auction House

German Afrika korps artillery officer field cap. **$1,380**

*German SS
Model 1934 black
kratzchen hat.*
$7,937

Manion's International Auction House

German army Model 35 double decal helmet. **$1,450**

Charles D. Pautler

German Waffen SS Model 42 single decal helmet. **$3,500**

Japanese Type 90 naval landing force steel helmet. **$1,200**

Peter Suciu

www.advanceguardmilitaria.com

Japanese Army officer's pith helmet with colonel's insignia sewn on side. **$375**

Peter Suciu

Japanese Type 90 naval landing force steel helmet. **$1,200**

U.S. Army officer's visor cap. **$195**

Charles D. Pautler

www.advanceguardmilitaria.com

U.S. Navy officer's khaki cap. **$295**

Charles D. Pautler

U.S. Army Air Force's officer's khaki summer visor cap formed into "crusher" shape. **$275**

U.S. Army enlisted visor cap. **$65**

John F. Graf collection

Hermann Historica OHG

*German Knight's Cross of the
War Merit Cross.* **$11,000**

Hermann Historica OHG

*German Tank Badge for
the Legion Condor, II Type.*
$3,000

Hermann Historica OHG

*German Proficiency Badge of
the SS in bronze.* **$6,500**

*German Cross in
gold, made by C.F.
Zimmermann.* **$2,500**

Hermann Historica OHG

Manion's International Auction House

*German SS 25-Year Long Service
Gilt Swastika Medal.* **$2,296**

Hermann Historica OHG

U-Boat badge with diamonds. **$25,000**

Mohawk Arms Inc. Militaria Auctions

Japan Order of the Rising Sun, 5th Class. **$250**

Soviet Union Gold Medal of the Hero of Socialist Labor. **$1,000**

www.advanceguardmilitaria.com

Colin R. Bruce II

Soviet Union Order of Honor, Type II. **$45**

Soviet Union Order of Suvorov, II Class, Type II. **$2,800**

Colin R. Bruce II

Soviet Union
Honorable Railroad
Worker, Type II. **$100**

Colin R. Bruce II

Distinguished
Service Medal,
U.S. Navy. **$400**

Colin R. Bruce II

www.advanceguardmilitaria.com

U.S. Army Purple Heart
with Oak Leaf cluster
signifying an additional
receipt of the award. **$100**

Charles D. Pautler

U.S. Victory Medal. **$15**

Index

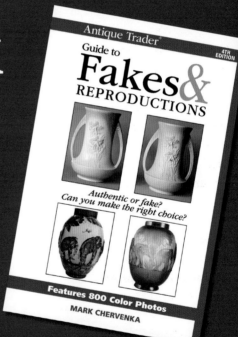

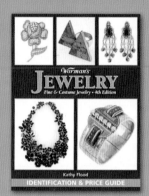
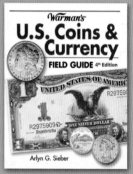
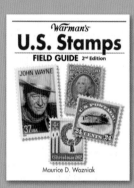

HERITAGE

CONSIGN NOW TO OUR UPCOMING AUCTIONS
THE GOLD STANDARD OF THE AUCTION INDUSTRY!

From rare coins to comic books, from fine art to first editions, if you're a collector, Heritage can turn your collection into cash!

1. Ivan Konstantinovich Aivazovsky
   Pushkin at the Waters Edge, 1886
   SOLD for $1,613,250
   October 2007 | HA.com/676*33219

2. Apollo 17 Lunar Module Flown Rolex GMT-Master Chronometer from Mission Command Module Pilot Ron Evans
   SOLD for $131,450
   October 2009 | HA.com/6033*41170

3. Fancy Light Brownish-Pink Diamond, Diamond, Platinum Ring
   SOLD for $358,500
   May 2011 | HA.com/5067*58455

4. Detective Comics #27 (DC, 1939)
   CGC VF 8.0
   Off-white to white pages
   SOLD for $1,075,500
   February 2010 | HA.com/7017*91126

5. Legendary 1907 Rolled Edge Eagle $10 Satin PR67 NGC
   SOLD for $2,185,000
   January 2011 | HA.com/1151*5238

6. Major Roger Alden's Copy of *The Federalist*, by Alexander Hamilton, James Madison, and John Jay
   SOLD for $262,900
   June 2008 | HA.com/683*57044

7. American Handcarved Cigar Store Indian
   SOLD for $203,150
   May 2010 | HA.com/6035*47323

8. 1927 Lou Gehrig Game Worn New York Yankees Jersey
   SOLD for $717,000
   November 2010 | HA.com/7028*81216

9. 'Terms of Surrender' letters signed by Confederate General Robert E. Lee
   SOLD for $537,750
   December 2007 | HA.com/674*72102

10. 40cm Matte Bleu de Malte Alligator Birkin Bag with Palladium Hardware
    SOLD for $71,700
    May 2011 | HA.com/5073*56090

11. Fine Cased and Shell Carved Ivory-Gripped Texas or Holster Model No. 5 Paterson Revolver, with 9-inch Barrel and Attached Loading Lever
    SOLD for $977,500
    September 2011 | HA.com/6073*33005

12. Jessie Willcox Smith
    A Child's Garden of Verses,
    book illustration, 1905
    SOLD for $310,700
    February 2010 | HA.com/5034*87361

For information on any of our 33 Collectibles categories, visit us at **HA.com**
or call **800-872-6467** to speak to one of our knowledgeable Consignment Directors.

Annual Sales Exceed $750 Million | 600,000+ Online Bidder-Members

HERITAGE HA.com
AUCTIONS

3500 Maple Avenue | Dallas, Texas 75219 | 800-872-6467 | HA.com

DALLAS | NEW YORK | BEVERLY HILLS | SAN FRANCISCO | PARIS | GENEVA

TX & NY Auctioneer license: Samuel Foose 11727 & 0952360. Heritage Auction Galleries CA Bond #RSB2004175; CA Auctioneer Bond: Carolyn Mani #RSB2005661
Buyer's Premium 12 - 25%, see HA.com for details.   22886

12/12

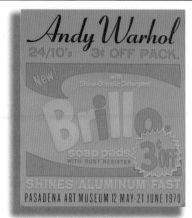
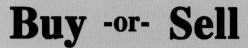
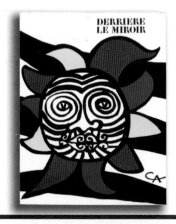